DATA WAREHOUSING
Concepts, Technologies, Implementations, and Management

HARRY SINGH, PhD.

To join a Prentice Hall PTR
Internet mailing list point to:
http://www.prenhall.com/mail_lists/

PRENTICE HALL PTR
Upper Saddle River, New Jersey 07458

Library of Congress Cataloging-in-Publication Data

Singh, Harry
    Data warehousing: concepts, technologies, implementations, and management /
  Harry Singh.
       p.   cm.
    Includes bibliographical references and index.
    ISBN 0-13-591793-X
    1. Data warehousing. I. Title.
QA76.9.D37S56 1997
005.74—dc21   97-13761
                                                CIP

Editorial Production: bookworks
Acquisitions Editor: Michael Meehan
Manufacturing Buyer: Alexis R. Heydt
Cover Designer: Kiwi Design
Cover Design Director: Jayne Conte
Marketing Manager: Stephen Solomon

 © 1998 by Prentice Hall PTR
Prentice-Hall, Inc.
A Simon & Schuster Company
Upper Saddle River, NJ 07458

Prentice Hall Books are widely used by corporate and government agencies for training, marketing, and resale.

The publisher offers discounts on this book when ordered in bulk quantities. For more information contact:

  Corporate Sales Department
  Phone: 800-382-3419
  FAX: 201-236-7141
  E-mail: corpsales@prenhall.com

or write:

  Corporate Sales Department
  Prentice Hall PTR
  1 Lake Street
  Upper Saddle River, NJ 07458

Printed in the United States of America

10 9 8 7 6 5 4 3 2 1

ISBN 0-13-591793-X

Prentice-Hall International (UK) Limited, *London*
Prentice-Hall of Australia Pty. Limited, *Sydney*
Prentice-Hall Canada Inc., *Toronto*
Prentice-Hall Hispanoamericana, S.A., *Mexico*
Prentice-Hall of India Private Limited, *New Delhi*
Prentice-Hall of Japan, *Tokyo*
Simon & Schuster Asia Pte. Ltd., *Singapore*
Editora Prentice-Hall do Brasil, Ltda., *Rio de Janeiro*

Dedication

To my children, Sarita, Sushila, Sanjay, and Samita, for their love,
to my many friends, especially Dr. Prakash Ahuja, for their inspiration,
and to my parents, for their high ethics and convictions during my informative years.

Trademarks

CONTENTS

CHAPTER 5   DATA WAREHOUSE TECHNOLOGIES   *86*

PREFACE

"Even if you're on the right track, you'll get run over if you just sit there"
Will Rogers

INTRODUCTION

Data Warehouse is a concept that provides business solutions to organizations. This concept involves integration of various technologies and their implementations. The 1990s have brought a growing data glut problem to the worlds of science, business, and government. Our capabilities for collecting and storing data of all kinds have far outpaced our abilities to analyze, summarize, and extract "knowledge" from this data.

Traditional methods of data analysis, based mainly on the human dealing directly with the data, simply do not scale to handling voluminous data sets. While database technology has provided us with the basic tools for the efficient storage and lookup of large data sets, the issue of how to help humans understand and analyze large bodies of data remains a difficult and unsolved problem. To deal with the data glut, a new generation of intelligent tools for automated data extraction and knowledge discovery is needed. This need has been recognized by researchers in different areas, including machine learning, statistics, intelligent databases, expert systems, neural computing, and data visualization.

To compete in the information age, companies must prepare now to handle the deluge of information on which critical decisions must be based. Massive amounts of data can now be collected and processed in a very short time. But once it's been collected, the data must be analyzed to determine its significance. Failure to implement systems and methods to handle the analysis of this data will place those who don't at a serious disadvantage. As more and more data becomes available, the process of locating and extracting useful information will become more complex. Data warehousing is part of that solution.

Growing interest in data warehousing, coupled with the realization that the specialists in these areas were not always aware of the state of the art in other areas, led me to write this book.

THE PURPOSES SERVED

Data warehouses come in all shapes and sizes. Some are small and trivial. Some are diverse and complex. Some span a single database, while others span the heterogeneous mix of the entire enterprise. But whatever they may look like and whatever their complexity, data warehouses hold the promise to transform data into knowledge and help businesses compete. This book is about sharing knowledge from concepts to systematically building and implementing a data warehouse in an architected environment.

Throughout most of this book, the emphasis is on technologies and options. It is the purpose of this book neither to underrate them, nor to overrate them; neither to glorify them, nor to abhor them, but rather to help us *understand* them. This book undertakes to investigate these technologies in a comprehensive and evenhanded way. It tries to show that data warehousing is not just a "thing," but a set of concepts that stem from a number of technological constraints.

The success of the many individuals and corporations in building alliances for data warehousing solutions, has motivated me to present an updated view of the state-of-the-art. This book is composed of carefully selected topics to provide a uniform treatment of certain key issues, including concepts, techniques, and implementations.

The data warehouse is a method of storing historical and integrated data for use in *decision-support* systems. This book describes how to use a data warehouse once it has been constructed and addresses the issues and techniques essential for successful migration to a data warehouse, the core of *decision-support* information processing. The book also explains why a split between operational and informational data is necessary and how to do it. The book analyzes and discusses such key topics as construction of metadata, partitioning of data, granularity of data, migration, and more.

This book describes techniques necessary to use technologies to face the challenge of the 90s and beyond. The introductory chapters give a broad coverage of the areas of knowledge discovery and data warehouse fundamentals. The remaining chapters focus on particular methods and options. I believe this collection gives a broad overview of the state of the art and equips the reader in building, implementing, and successfully using data warehouses.

This text is intended as a self-administered course for a wide variety of computer professionals, database administrators, technical staff, and who need an in-depth understanding of implementing and using data warehouses. The primary focus is on actual development of a data warehouse. It is well suited for the following audiences:

- Database administrators for the data warehouse
- Application developers
- Users
- Technical support groups

- Systems architects and managers
- Systems analysts
- Data model and database designers

The book covers the very basic concepts and leads the reader step-by-step through to the implementation and usage of a data warehouse. This book will become a practical reference guide, a cookbook for data warehousing. The reader should be able to take away the following knowledge from this book:

- Basic data warehousing concepts.
- Differing methods in building a data warehouse solution.
- Type of data warehouse suitable for the environment and the corporate strategy.
- Metadata, repositories, dictionaries, and their relationships.
- Data warehouse modeling and building considerations.
- On-Line Analytical Processing and multidimensional analysis options.
- Data warehouse management and usage.
- Exploration of *decision-support* technologies of the near future.

ORGANIZATION OF THE BOOK

Broadly speaking, this book is organized into four major sections: Basics, Implementation Cycle, Decision-Support Technologies, and Building and Management.

Basics

Part I (Chapters 1-3) lays the foundation for data warehouse concepts, at a very high level, starting with a discussion of the components and the environments, leading to various types of data warehouse solutions suited for a particular environment.

Technologies

Part II (Chapters 4-7) describes the implementation development cycle, architecture, data models, and the data sources needed to start building a successful data warehouse.

Decision-Support Technologies

Part III (Chapters 8-10) focuses on exploiting technologies, including object-oriented tools, neural computing, parallel databases, and *decision-support* systems that may form the basis of tomorrow's requirements. It also explores the analysis options and techniques.

Building and Management

Part IV (Chapters 11-12) builds upon the implementation development processes discussed in previous chapters that are required for an effective data warehouse, describes the processes for populating and managing the warehouse, and finally provides the know-how to access and use it, with emphasis on analysis tools for *decision support* and reporting.

The book is concluded with a summary of a checklist of critical success factors for implementations, avoiding common pitfalls, and strategies, followed by comprehensive glossary of terms, a bibliography for further references, and an index.

The book is organized in a modular manner. If a reader has prior knowledge of certain subjects, the reader will not need to start from the beginning. For example, if the reader is already knowledgeable in basic warehousing concepts and the development cycle, the reader can directly proceed to the following chapters.

Those readers will benefit the most from this book who have some understanding or experience with systems in general and some knowledge of relational database technology for technical discussions. Those who lack this technical training will also benefit by gaining a strong understanding of what a data warehouse is, its development cycle, its components, how to use it for business results.

ACKNOWLEDGMENTS

This book started as an in-house initiative to define the role of a mainframe in the data warehouse environment. It soon grew into a project to cover repository enterprise options and solutions among diverse operating systems and hardware platforms.

Many thanks to the technical reviewers used by Lisa Garboski of bookworks and Beth Sturla of Prentice Hall. Their insight, comments, criticism, and suggestions added greatly to the final result.

Special thanks to Clive Boustred, a friend in the database and object worlds, who not only contributed to the content but also reviewed the complete manuscript and made significant contributions to the accuracy and readability of the text.

Harry Singh

1

OVERVIEW

INTRODUCTION

The tide has shifted from **getting data** in to **getting data out** of a database. The future technology development efforts are concentrated on helping users wring every bit of information out of their data stores.

At a recent conference, a business executive met a leading management prophet and asked: "Oh Prophet, how will I ensure success for my company?" The Prophet replied: *"Information."* The executive asked: "Oh Prophet, what should I fear most?" The Prophet replied, *"Data."*

Data is everywhere. How can we turn that data into information? Studies indicate that the amount of data in a given organization doubles every five years. Most organizations do not suffer from a lack of data, but rather from an overabundance of redundant and inconsistent data that is difficult to manage effectively, is increasingly difficult to access, and is difficult to use for decision-making purposes.

To compete in the information age, companies must prepare now to handle the deluge of information on which critical decisions must be based. Massive amounts of data can now be collected and processed in a very short time. But once it's been collected, the data must be analyzed to determine its significance. Failure to implement systems and methods to handle the analysis of this data will place those who don't at a serious disadvantage.

By successfully combining an improved understanding of their markets and reengineering their information systems, companies can meet the challenges of competing in a global economy and delivering better products faster without increasing their costs. In order to remain competitive, companies must leverage their data assets to gain a better understanding of their business. In addition, information technology departments have to make the most cost-effective use of their resources.

Waiting is not an option. As the available time for making critical business decisions grows shorter, those who don't have the means to proactively analyze business information will not be able to compete. As more and more data becomes available, the process of locating and extracting useful information is becoming more complex.

Data warehousing is not a new concept. It was presented as a solution originally by IBM as the *"information warehouse"* and has had numerous rebirths in recent times. IBM's concept met with skepticism because accessing non-relational data stores (such as IMS or VSAM) was too complex and degraded operational system performance. Data warehousing reminds us of an old mainframe concept from the mid-1970s: Take data out of production databases, clean it up a bit, and load the data into an end-user database.

The latest wave has been evangelized by Bill Inmon, who has promoted the subject through numerous publications and presentations. Mr. Inmon describes the data warehouse as subject oriented, integrated, time-variant, and non-volatile.

A data warehouse, simply stated, is the physical separation of an organization's operational data systems from its *decision-support* systems. It includes a repository of information that is built using data from far-flung, and often departmentally isolated, systems of enterprise-wide computing so that the data can be modeled and analyzed by business managers.

Data in the warehouse is organized by subject, rather than application, so that the warehouse contains only the information necessary for *decision-support* processing. The data is collected over time and used for comparisons, trends, and forecasting. The data is not updated in real time but is refreshed from operational systems on a regular basis, when the data transfer will not adversely affect the performance of operational systems.

In addition, the warehouse repository is created to be read from, not written to or altered. Endusers of the data warehouse are not data entry personnel entering transactions. Instead, the users are business managers making decisions based on the existing data.

GUIDE TO THE READER

Any data processing professional who has browsed through the trade press could not have missed the computing industry's love fest with data warehousing. This book is in response to the current trends in the client/server and Intranet applications of data warehouse solutions.

Essentially every enterprise is beginning to implement some type of a "data warehousing" solution—may it be for a full-fledged comprehensive data warehouse, virtual data warehouse, or simple departmental data mart. But, the options and potential are limitless. Since the book is targeted for a wide variety of audiences in the industry, practically every enterprise in the Western hemisphere (large or small) will benefit from such a book, in addition to individuals. Most large enterprises have workstations, databases, and legacy data running either on departmental or central enterprise servers.

Description

The author leads the reader, step by step, from the very basic concepts through the most advanced technologies available. This book is not a beginner's introduction to computers or database technologies. This book will serve you better as a reference and a guide to facilitate learning and building successful data warehouses.

This book addresses the issues and techniques essential for successful migration to a data warehouse, the core of *decision-support* processing. Throughout the book, you will find step-by-step comparisons, wherever possible, between operational and informational systems. The author

- Lays the foundation for data warehouse concepts with a discussion of the components and the environments, leading to various types of data warehouse solutions suited for a particular environment.

- Describes the implementation development cycle, architecture, data models, and the data sources needed to start building a successful data warehouse.

- Describes techniques necessary to use technologies to face the challenge of the new paradigms—how to store data to meet an organization's *decision-support* needs and provide users with a common, simple, transparent access to information regardless of where it resides.

- Analyzes and discusses such key topics as granularity of data, partitioning data, metadata, the time basis for *Decision-Support* System (DSS) data, system of record, migration, and more.

- Provides detailed discussions and analysis of major issues including why a split between operational and informational databases is necessary and how to accomplish it, the lack of data creditability, integration of DSS data, and how the relational technology fits with DSS needs.

- Focuses on exploiting technologies, including object-oriented tools, neural computing, parallel databases, and *decision-support* systems that may form the basis of tomorrow's requirements. It also explores the analysis options and techniques.

- Builds upon the implementation development processes discussed in previous chapters that are required for an effective data warehouse, describes the processes for populating and managing the warehouse, and finally provides the know-how to access and use it, with emphasis on analysis tools for decision support and reporting.

The reader should be able to take away the following knowledge from this book:

- What a Data Warehouse Is
- Benefits of a Data Warehouse
- Data Warehouse Architecture
- Data Mining
- Types of Data Warehouses
- Data Mart Warehouses
- Multidimensional versus Relational Databases
- Operational versus Extract Pumps
- Data Access Protocols
- Data Migration and Transformation
- Front-End Tools
- Metadata in Operational Environment
- Metadata in Data Warehouse
- Data Warehouse Modeling
- Data Warehousing for the MPP (Massively Parallel Processing) and SMP (Symmetric Multiprocessing) Environments
- Building a Practical Data Warehouse
- Managing the Growing Data Warehouse

In addition, the author focuses on a myriad aspects of data warehouse development and on the issues to consider when building a warehouse. You'll learn why current skills may need to be enhanced for data warehousing and you'll be introduced to new and adapted techniques needed to independently develop source data, warehouse data, and metadata models. The book is concluded with comprehensive bibliography, glossary, and index.

The Audience

This book is intended as a learning guide for those who are seasoned database users/programmers/administrators or simply decision makers who are delving into the world of data warehousing. This text is for you if you are a user of corporate data, an educator, a network administrator, a database professional, a decision maker, a marketing analyst, MIS (Management Information Systems) or business manager, or simply a supporter of new technologies.

PREREQUISITES

As previously mentioned, this book is not a beginner's introduction to computers. It assumes that you know the fundamentals of computing, some knowledge of database technologies, and an understanding of the *decision-support* requirements.

You know what an architecture is and that you have read the debates about massively parallel or the symmetric multiprocessor processors. Therefore, one of the first steps in learning about data warehousing is to grasp its idiosyncrasies.

WAREHOUSING IN BRIEF

During the past few years, we have seen a drift of power and influence away from the database technologies to the tools technologies. In the late eighties, it was quite common to hear large user organizations talk of strategic Database Management Systems (DBMSs), implying that a common data manager was to be implemented throughout the organization. Today the situation is quite different and many users have resigned themselves to the fact that they not only have to use different DBMSs, but they also need to use different generations of DBMSs. Indeed, it is a well-quoted statistic that the average organization uses 2.5 DBMSs.

This diversity of data managers is a natural outcome of the quite different capabilities of different types of DBMSs, and we should expect to see this diversity increase as new technologies appear. Clearly, there is a need to isolate the business from differences in database technology, so that a unified view of the organization's data can be presented to business users. This notion of presenting a unified view has given importance to data warehousing. The business need to isolate users from technology differences has made the creation of data warehousing strategies a matter of prime importance.

The ultimate goal of data warehousing is the creation of a single logical view of data which may reside in many disparate physical databases. This provides developers and business users with a single working model of the enterprise's data, something which is absent in virtually every organization. Access to this data improves customer service and quality by helping the company assess emerging business activity. For example, by combining historical sales activity with current trends, the data warehouse helps the company derive future forecasts. This data, in turn, is used by decision makers in the company's manufacturing process to increase or decrease production of various components.

The Role of Middleware

The middleware refers to the client/server architecture and data communications. Middleware is the software which provides general access to data on different databases and on different platforms. Connectivity through middleware enables heterogeneous databases to be connected together to provide a single view. Middleware may be provided by other kinds of tools, such as enduser query tools. Data extraction tools are specialized middleware of a kind. Any such technology which claims to enable the building and implementation of a data warehouse must satisfy a number of criteria:

- It should incorporate controls and management tools to manage an enterprise-wide view of data.
- It must provide a single database, operating system, and network-independent interface to the user and developer.
- It should provide an easy-to-use API (Application Programming Interface) which can be embedded into applications.
- It should support a wide variety of data managers and operating environments.

All these requirements point very firmly to middleware as a prime candidate for data warehousing technology. More generically, middleware occupies the key role of isolating applications from infrastructure for client/server. Physical databases are part of such infrastructure. From this perspective, the data warehouse sits within the middleware layer, acting as a single, consistent interface to the database infrastructure.

The Technologies

Most corporate data warehouses consist of three main types of technology components:

- Mainframe production data held in hierarchical and network DBMSs. It is estimated that a large percentage of corporate data is held in these types of DBMSs.
- Departmental data held in proprietary file systems (e.g., VSAM, RMS) and (RDBMS) Relational Database Management Systems (e.g., Informix, Oracle).
- Private data held on workstations and private servers.

For some organizations, there is a fourth technology, and that is parallel database technology. For massive databases which are used for *decision-support* purposes, parallel technologies enable queries to be run which would otherwise be impossible. The data warehouse itself is enabled through middleware technologies, and alliances between middleware technology providers and hardware suppliers have created a new stratum for data warehouse technologies.

The Dangers of Data Warehousing

Data warehousing should not be viewed as a purely top-down activity. It is not an opportunity to create a standardized enterprise-wide approach to data storage and retrieval. At its best, data warehousing integrates many disparate activities and data sources. At its worst, it is an attempt to restrict the enterprise by artificially created constraints.

The late eighties represented an era of almost unprecedented enterprise-wide folly. Corporate data models came and went as enterprises learned that it was not possible to create a stable snapshot of the data an organization needed to use. It is to be hoped that data warehousing does not become another religion.

If there is a single key to survival in the 1990s and beyond, it is being able to analyze, plan, and react to changing business conditions in a much more rapid fashion. To do this, top managers, analysts, and knowledge workers in our enterprises need more and better information.

Information technology itself has made possible revolutions in the way that organizations today operate throughout the world. But the sad truth is that in many organizations, in spite of the availability of more and more powerful computers on everyone's desks and communication networks that span the globe, large numbers of executives and decision makers cannot get their hands on critical information that already exists in the organization.

Every day, organizations, large and small, create billions of bytes of data about all aspects of their business, millions of individual facts about their customers, products, operations, and people. But for the most part, this data is locked up in a myriad computer systems and is exceedingly difficult to get at.

Experts have estimated that only a small fraction of the data that is captured, processed, and stored in the enterprise is actually available to executives and decision makers. While technologies for the manipulation and presentation of data have literally exploded, it is only recently that those involved in developing strategies for large enterprises have concluded that large segments of enterprise are "data poor."

Data Warehousing—Providing Data Access to the Enterprise

Recently, a set of significant new concepts and tools have evolved into a new technology that makes it possible to attack the problem of providing all the key people within the enterprise with access to whatever level of information is needed for the enterprise to survive and prosper in an increasingly competitive world.

The term that has come to characterize this new technology is "data warehousing." Data warehousing has grown out of the repeated attempts on the part of various researchers and organizations to provide their organizations with a flexible, effective, and efficient means of getting at the sets of data that have come to represent one of the organization's most critical and valuable assets.

Data warehousing is a field that has grown out of integration of a number of different technologies and experiences over the last two decades. These experiences have allowed the industry to identify the key problems that have to be solved.

An Architectural Perspective

A data warehouse is an architecture, not an infrastructure. The first step in developing a data warehouse is to define the warehouse in terms of architecture and infrastructure. Architecture is the set of rules or structures that provide a framework for the overall design of a system or product while infrastructure refers to the platforms, databases, gateways, networks, front-end tools, and other components required to make the architecture function.

The development of a data warehouse, whose primary component is a read-only database, is used for *decision support*. Data is extracted from source systems, databases, and files. It is integrated and transformed before being loaded into the data warehouse. A separate read-only database holds the *decision-support* data, and users access the data warehouse through a front-end tool or application.

The infrastructure must train all involved in *decision-support* technology, train developers and database administrators in relational databases, develop or buy data transformation and integration tools, develop database administration skills, and review communications hardware and software, job-scheduling software, front-end software, and metadata navigation tools.

Thirty or so years ago, MIS provided overnight or weekend access to that data through tools that filtered and aggregated the detail records. Batch response was often inadequate, however, not because strategic decisions cannot wait a day or a week, but because it might require many iterations to isolate the appropriate level of data for a given query. Today, the strategic analysis is conversational in nature and ironically the answers generate new questions.

About 20 years ago, some of the strategic data was made available interactively. This solved some of the turnaround problems, but growing data and user volumes introduced capacity problems. MIS was often forced to revert to batch turnaround for the tough queries. When a choice had to be made between tactical operational processing and strategic analysis of history, the tactical needs always won. Endusers were unhappy with the lead time required to develop a strategic reporting application and enhance it as requirements changed. They needed to react quickly as the business changed. In some cases, they changed the business.

Then PCs began to proliferate in some organizations. Users were no longer limited to dumb terminals linked to untouchable mainframes. With the advent of desktop computing, users began to build their own applications with PC-based databases and spreadsheets. They would extract or double-enter selected information from the mainframe historical data and analyze it with quick and dirty homegrown applications. The "glass house" bottleneck was circumvented, but control, capacity, and integrity issues often got out of hand.

The current hype and excitement derive from the hope that comprehensive, flexible, efficient, and cost-effective solutions that do not excessively compromise any objectives are now available. From the technology side, data warehouses are exploiting cheaper processing power in the form of UNIX-based symmetric multiprocessors, massively parallel processors, personal computers, and mainframes.

Larger and faster storage devices permit retention and analysis of extensive history. Database management systems feature improved performance and capacity and have recently addressed specific warehousing needs such as parallel processing and replication. Data warehouses have also been used by organizations as initial stepping stones from mainframe environments into client/server computing and can also be used within a program of legacy asset management.

Organizationally, other forces are at work. Reengineering and downsizing typically cut layers of middle management that historically have distilled data and passed it upward. More users are cross-trained and able to analyze their own information. The distribution of computing power and expertise generated by the desktop PC has made many users comfortable with database manipulation. These users want "hands-on" access to historical data to analyze trends, exceptions, and root causes.

The old model of MIS returning with standardized reports weeks after receiving user requests is no longer acceptable to most organizations.

SUMMARY

The efficient management of information is one of the most critical challenges facing companies today. Without knowing it, the foundations of many organizations are being weakened by their own robust core systems, which gather massive amounts of data across various divisions and departments. Instead of building and reinforcing business operations, this data, which is dispersed and often duplicated across the organization, is eroding the very infrastructure it was collected to support.

The success of every business activity—from resource management to customer service—is dependent upon how an organization utilizes its critical data. Yet, many companies have still not invested in the blueprints for building the data warehouse necessary to integrate information across all products and services. Meanwhile, their competitors are finding ways to collect, translate, analyze, and use such information in unlimited ways.

An organization that is not using information technology to understand and serve its customers better will be outperformed, outsold, outsmarted, and probably out of business before the end of the next decade.

2

DATA WAREHOUSE CONCEPTS

WHAT IS DATA WAREHOUSING?

The good news is that top brass believes in the benefits of a data warehouse. The bad news is that unless Information Technology (IT) departments boost their credibility, the implementations will be scattered and form a chain of islands in a crowded ocean.

Data warehousing is the process of integrating enterprise-wide corporate data into a single repository from which end users can easily run queries, make reports, and perform analysis. A data warehouse is a *decision-support* environment that leverages data stored in different sources, organizing it and delivering it to decision makers across the enterprise, regardless of their platform or technical skill level. In a nutshell, *data warehousing is the data management and analysis technology.*

There are plenty of people to tell you what a warehouse should do, and many who would like to tell you which products you need to do it right. There are even people who will tell you how to design a data warehouse. But, where is the definition of what it is actually all about?

Is it a warehouse or is it a database? We must get a good understanding of exactly what the difference is between a data warehouse and a database.

A data warehouse is supposed to be a place where data gets stored so that applications can access and share it easily. But a database product does that already. DB2, Informix, Oracle, Sybase, and the countless legions of DBMS providers have been selling us their wares for years based on this simple functional definition. So then, what makes a warehouse so different?

The first criterion that almost everyone seems to agree upon for a definition is that a warehouse holds read-only data. Actually, that is also the first rule of data warehousing. The theory behind it is that "normal" databases hold operational type data and that many of the *decision-support* type applications associated with the warehouse put too much strain on the databases that run them. But then, is a data warehouse nothing more than a nice name for a replicated, operational system? (Since we all know that data replication is bad, we call it a warehouse?)

Defining a data warehouse as simply a read-only database at least makes some sense. Unfortunately, this rather limited view of what the warehouse is all about still falls short of including all of the other features and characteristics that different people seem to be associating with it.

For example, if you make a copy of some operational system's data and attach some sort of query tool, multidimensional database, or neural network to it, does that turn this read-only database into a warehouse? There must be more to it than that!

Even if we were to accept the read-only rule as part of how one defines a data warehouse, we cannot simply leave it at that. If you had only one data mining or executive information system to run, then you would not be building a warehouse at all; you would simply be building a database of a sort—something we have been doing for years.

We need to establish the next criterion for our definition of a warehouse. In general, our database is not a data warehouse unless we also

- Collect information from a lot of different disparate sources and use it as the place where this disparity can be reconciled, and
- Place the data into a warehouse because we intend to allow several different applications to make use of the same information.

These criteria bring the term data warehouse much closer to our understanding of the warehouse term—a place where we store many different things for convenience's sake. By broadening our definition to include the reconciliation of a lot of different sources of data and making that reconciled information available to a number of varied applications, we begin to approach the robustness and value-added which most people associate with the term data warehouse.

A Competitive Tool

Business decision makers need answers for a host of questions that directly impact their ability to be competitive in today's fast changing markets. They need clear and meaningful answers to any hard, complex question of data, and they need it quickly.

Raw data necessary for sound business analysis is stored in a variety of locations and formats: hierarchical databases, flat files, COBOL data sets, to name a few. Additionally, factual detail is often captured, stored, and managed by systems that were designed to automate day-to-day operations.

A data warehouse is a competitive tool that gives every enduser the ability to access quality enterprise-wide data. By filing the data into a central point of storage, a data warehouse provides an integrated representation of the multiple sources of information dispatched across the enterprise. It ensures the consistency of management rules and conventions applied to the data. A data warehouse is therefore a reflection of corporate, rather than simply individual, needs.

A data warehouse leverages the investments most companies have already made in legacy systems, allowing business users to effectively make the transition from traditional corporate data access to informational access.

The data warehouse is a new way to look at enterprise computing at the strategic or architectural level. The term data warehouse is currently being used to describe a number of different facilities. Some companies use all of the components of data warehousing listed below in combination, while others just use one of the following.

Data Mart

This is a subset of the enterprise-wide data warehouse. Typically, it performs the role of a departmental, regional, or functional data warehouse. As part of the iterative data warehouse process, the organization may build a series of data marts over time and eventually link them via an enterprise-wide logical data warehouse.

Logical Data Warehouse

This contains all the metadata, business rules, and processing logic required to scrub, organize, package, and preprocess the data. In addition, it contains the information required to find and access the actual data, wherever it resides.

Giant Physical Database in the Sky

This is an actual, physical database into which all the data for the data warehouse is gathered, along with the metadata and the processing logic used to scrub, organize, package, and preprocess the data for enduser access.

Definition

W.H. Inmon (1993), in his landmark work *Building the Data Warehouse*, offers the following definition of a data warehouse: "A data warehouse is a subject-oriented, integrated, time-variant, non-volatile collection of data in support of management's decision making process."

Subject-oriented means the data warehouse focuses on the high-level entities of the business; in higher education's case, subjects such as students, courses, accounts, and employees. This is in contrast to operational systems, which deal with processes such as student registration or rolling up financial accounts.

Integrated means the data is stored in a consistent format (i.e., naming conventions, domain constraints, physical attributes, and measurements). For example, production systems may have several unique coding schemes for ethnicity. In the data warehouse, there is only one coding scheme.

Time-variant means the data associates with a point in time (i.e., semester, fiscal year, and pay period).

Lastly, *non-volatile* means the data doesn't change once it gets into the warehouse.

The Scope

Data warehouses can provide a central repository for large amounts of diverse and valuable information. They provide an excellent source for the information needed to build data marts which contain the summaries and tables used to support On-Line Analytical Processing (OLAP). But having the information alone is not enough.

The ability to use the information to make insightful decisions depends on having appropriate tools to extract specific data, convert it into business information, and monitor changes. The problem is no longer a lack of data, rather it is how to search through the tremendous amounts of data for useful information.

The solution lies in the use of intelligent software agents which can automate the tedious task of extracting the detail information and can then present it in business terms. The most useful agents deliver not only summary information but also the ability to drill down, drill through, develop forecasts, and export the information to other *decision-support* tools. By using tools to collect, organize, and extract the most current and useful information, massive amounts of data can be converted from information to insight.

Regardless of the scope or definition, data warehouse is only a concept. In a data warehouse, the data is gathered from various sources into a single integrated, subject-oriented database. Users can then query and analyze the information in the data warehouse to drive informed business decisions in ways that were not possible before.

Practical Implications

Building a production data warehouse is not just another systems integration exercise. The methodologies and design principles needed are very different from those used in the development of traditional on-line transaction processing applications.

As enterprises battle for survival in the 1990s, they face the daunting task of refurbishing their information architectures in a way that leverages, without disrupting, their On-Line Transaction Processing (OLTP) systems. Many have turned to the data warehouse, an architecture that collects valuable corporate data from OLTP systems and prepares it to respond to user queries.

Usually built on a Relational Database Management System (RDBMS), a warehouse is designed to free mission-critical on-line analytical processing (OLAP) systems from these resource-consuming queries. These equally mission-critical data warehouses contain data that has been extracted, cleansed, and transformed from legacy and OLTP systems. They comprise, in short, an on-line collection of business-related information that has been optimized to support decision making. The data warehouse positions the enterprise to satisfy four interrelated demands on corporations to

- Prepare their systems and their users for constant evolution.
- Improve the productivity and revenue contribution of every employee.
- Maximize profits by performing core business processes better than their competitors and by eliminating as many resource-draining practices as possible.
- Apply science to information.

Perhaps the single most important ongoing occurrence to affect data warehousing has been the information explosion. Organizations realize that, given the fundamental relationship between knowledge and power, utilization of this information is key to their competitive positioning. In the increasingly competitive late-1990s to early-2000s, OLTP and data warehousing will provide compelling business solutions with quick return on investment.

Why a Data Warehouse?

In today's competitive business environment, understanding and managing information are crucial for companies to make timely decisions and respond to changing business conditions. Data processing applications have proliferated across a wide variety of operating systems over the last two decades, complicating the task of locating and integrating data for *decision support*. Further, as decision-making authority becomes distributed through all levels of an organization, more and more people need access to the information necessary for making business decisions. As a result, to manage and use business information competitively, many organizations today are building data warehouses.

A data warehouse supports business analysis and decision making by creating an integrated database of consistent, subject-oriented, historical information. It integrates data from multiple, incompatible systems into one consolidated database. By transforming data into meaningful information, a data warehouse allows business managers to perform more substantive, accurate, and consistent analysis.

Significant cost benefits, time savings, and productivity gains are associated with using a data warehouse for information processing. First, data can easily be accessed and analyzed without time-consuming manipulation and processing. Decisions can be made more quickly and with confidence that the data is both timely and accurate. Integrated information can be kept in categories that are meaningful to profitable operation.

Trends can be analyzed and predicted with the availability of historical data. And the data warehouse assures that everyone is using the same data at the same level of extraction, which eliminates conflicting analytical results and arguments over the source and quality of data used for analysis. In short, the data warehouse enables information processing to be done in a credible, efficient manner.

BENEFITS OF A DATA WAREHOUSE

Data warehousing improves the productivity of corporate decision makers through consolidation, conversion, transformation, and integration of operational data and provides a consistent view of the enterprise. Examples of tangible benefits of a data warehouse initiative are

- Improved product inventory turns.
- Decreased costs of product introduction with improved selection of target markets.
- Determination of the effectiveness of marketing programs, allowing elimination of weaker programs and enhancement of stronger ones.

For the remainder of the decade, data warehouse strategies will play a critical role in migrating *decision-support* systems to the desktop while maintaining ties to corporate data sources. Examples of high value-added data warehousing applications include sales/inventories, business intelligence, customer service, asset/liability management, and business process reengineering.

The bottom line is that data warehouses are an increasingly critical component of the systems that support the ever-increasing tempo of business competition.

Data warehousing, the creation of an enterprise-wide data store, is the first step toward managing the volumes of data. The data warehouse is becoming an integral part of many information delivery systems because it provides a single, central location where a reconciled version of data extracted from a wide variety of operational systems is stored. Over the last few years, improvements in price, performance, scalability, and robustness of open computing systems have made data warehousing a central component of IT strategies.

The data warehousing marketplace is expected to increase by leaps and bounds. Not only is the size of the industry increasing at a very rapid rate, the quantities of information that organizations wish to access for decision-making purposes are also increasing. The data warehouse implementations range from a few gigabytes to hundreds of gigabytes and even terabytes.

NEED FOR A DATA WAREHOUSE

The data warehouse concept sprang from the growing competitive need to quickly analyze business information. Existing operational systems cannot meet this need because

- They lack on-line historical data.
- The data required for analysis resides in different operational systems.
- The query performance is extremely poor which in turn impacts performance of operational systems.
- The operational DBMS designs are inadequate for *decision support*.

As a result, information stored in operational systems is inaccessible to business decision makers. A data warehouse eliminates these problems by storing the current and historical data from disparate operational systems that business decision makers need in a single, consolidated system. This makes data readily accessible to the people who need it without interrupting on-line operational workloads.

Once the concept of a data warehouse has been adopted, a specialized RDBMS must be chosen. Conventional RDBMSs are tuned for On-Line Transaction Processing (OLTP) and fall short of the mark when used as a data warehouse because

- They cannot provide adequate query performance.
- They do not include the necessary features to easily process business questions.
- They do not load and index data efficiently.
- They cannot provide adequate support for the large data stores required.

Transaction processing RDBMSs automate business operations and must be efficient at updating individual records thousands of times per second. In comparison, data warehouse RDBMSs are designed to manage a business and require the capability to efficiently support the analysis of hundreds of gigabytes and billions of records of data.

The data warehouse is becoming an extremely valuable asset of the enterprise. To realize the full potential of the investment, the data warehouse must be readily available to the decision-making majority. Users must be able to share live reports that include not only text but also the calculations and assumptions supporting the analyses. The recipient must be able to drill, pivot, or add to the original report, continuing the analysis process in a collaborative manner.

This liberal sharing of live reports presents a significant security challenge. A user will seldom know the level of security of each recipient. Multilevel security prevents the inadvertent distribution of information to unauthorized users. A user cannot access, drill, or add to an analysis without appropriate security. The security issue will escalate as the data warehouse is made available to more users, unless some of the following requirements are met:

- Security must be set for each user and workgroup.
- Security must be tied to the database.
- Security must be tied to business dimensions.
- Security must be easily maintained.

A three-tier client/server architecture is essential to meet security requirements when a large number of users are provided access to the data warehouse, particularly when users have the capability to share and collaborate freely. Security must be maintained individually and set by level along key database dimensions. If a report is distributed to a user that does not have authorization to view the data, the user will be unable to display the report. Furthermore a user will be precluded from drilling to any level of detail, if the user is not authorized.

Almost every enterprise in every industry has discovered the benefits of data warehousing, such as:

Telecommunications	Utilities
Banking	Universities
Manufacturing	Insurance
Health Care	Consumer Goods

The most common application areas are

Risk management	Asset management
Financial analysis	Inventory analysis
Marketing programs	Customer relationship management
Product profit trends	Statistical analysis
Procurement analysis	Claims analysis
Customer database integration	

Analysis Is Increasing in Complexity

Raw data is worthless without the analysis and interpretation required to convert it to practical information. The sheer volume of available data already taxes available analysis solutions, and the problem is compounded by complex data interrelationships. A two-dimensional view can no longer produce a "true" picture of any given business issue.

Enterprise data today is multidimensional—it is interrelated and usually hierarchical. Sales information, budget information, and forecast data are interdependent, and solving business problems requires analyzing many, or all, of these interrelationships. For example, a forecast of new product sales in multiple regions is not complete without also taking into account each region's past purchasing patterns and new product adoption rates. All necessary information to make such decisions must be simultaneously available to the forecaster in order to present a true multidimensional perspective.

A Spreadsheet Provides a Limited View

Multidimensional data may reside in spreadsheets, relational databases, or legacy data managers. The data-access and analysis tools must be able to take enterprise data from a variety of sources and give workgroups the accessibility, power, and flexibility they need to view it in every conceivable way. Only multidimensional analysis can give you a clear picture of the business at any given time.

Outside Influences

Today, companies are being forced to do the same amount of work (or more) with fewer people. As companies right-size, their structures must change to reflect reallocated resources. As a result, all organizational changes affect enterprise analysis and reporting functions, which in turn, demand flexible new methods to manage changing business dimensions, such as,

- Increased competition and global economic pressures require organizations to find new competitive points of difference. Those who can quickly pinpoint market positions and trends can more quickly take appropriate action and gain competitive advantage.
- Maintaining a competitive edge and improving customer satisfaction has become the battle cry of the `90s. To evaluate processes and establish performance benchmarks, organizations must devise new methods for collecting, analyzing, and tracking process metrics. Metrics must not only provide information about *what* results occurred—they must also offer clues as to *why*. Managers must be able to view interrelated data from multiple perspectives to accurately interpret its meaning.

Leveraging Existing Technology Investments

Database and spreadsheet applications shoulder much of the computing burden in most organizations. The cost of change is high, and with the technology and training investment already made, maximizing the value of these tools is essential. New systems will be considered only if they can be justified in terms of economy and productivity.

STRUCTURE OF A DATA WAREHOUSE

Data warehouses have a distinct structure. There are different levels of summarization and detail that describe the data warehouse. Figure 2.1 shows that the different components of the data warehouse are

- Current data
- Older data
- Summarized data
- Metadata

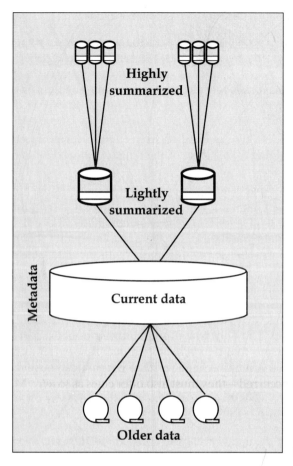

FIGURE 2.1   Data Warehouse Structure.

Current Data

Far and away the major concern is the *current data*. Such data

- Reflects the most recent happenings, which are always of great interest.
- Is voluminous because it is stored at the lowest level of granularity.
- Is almost always stored on disk storage, which is fast to access, but expensive and complex to manage.

Older Data

Older data is data that is infrequently accessed and is stored at a level of detail consistent with current detailed data. While not mandatory that it be stored on an alternate storage medium, because of the anticipated large volume of data coupled with the infrequent access of the data, the storage medium for older data is usually removable storage such as an automatic tape library.

Summarized Data

The *summarized data* is of two flavors, according the processing need and storage. These are

- *Lightly summarized data* is data that is distilled from the low level of detail found at the current detailed level. This level of the data warehouse is almost always stored on disk storage.
- *Highly summarized data* is compact and easily accessible. Sometimes the highly summarized data is found in the data warehouse environment and in other cases the highly summarized data is found outside the immediate walls of the technology that houses the data warehouse. (In any case, the highly summarized data is part of the data warehouse regardless of where the data is physically housed.)

Note that not every summarization ever done gets stored in the data warehouse. There will be many occasions where analysis will be done and one type or the other of summary will be produced. The only type of summarization that is permanently stored in the data warehouse is that data which is frequently used. In other words, if you produce a summarized result that has a very low probability of ever being used again, then that summarization is not stored in the data warehouse.

Metadata

The most important component of the data warehouse is *metadata*. *Metadata* is data about data. In many ways metadata sits in a different dimension than other data warehouse data, because metadata contains no data directly taken from the operational environment. But you may want to understand when that was created, what system it came from, and what different tools have accessed it to move it from where it was originally to where it is now. If you need to change it or access it in some other way, who's in charge of it, who owns it, who's the steward for it? So it's data about data: It's all the things that surround the actual content of the data to give a person an understanding of how it was created and how it is maintained.

Metadata plays a more special role in the data warehouse environment than it ever did in the classical operational environment. Metadata is used as

- A directory to help in locating the contents of the data warehouse.
- A guide to the mapping of data as the data is transformed from the operational environment to the data warehouse environment.
- A guide to the algorithms used for summarization between the current data and the summarized data, and so forth.

Metadata contains information about (at least)

- Structure of the data,
- Algorithms used for summarization, and
- Mapping from the operational environment to the data warehouse.

Before warehouse data can be accessed efficiently, it is necessary to understand what data is available in the warehouse, and where that data is located. Metadata provides you with a catalog of data in the data warehouse and the pointers to this data. In addition to helping you locate the data you desire, the metadata may contain

- Data extraction/transformation history.
- Data usage statistics.
- Data warehouse table sizes.
- Column aliases.
- Data summarization/modeling algorithms.

In a well-designed architecture, metadata maps the entities with which you are familiar (dimensions, attributes, and metrics) to tables and columns within the data warehouse. Specifically, this metadata includes

- Attribute hierarchies.
- Attributes to dimensions.
- Physical mapping of attributes, metrics.
- Performance metrics.
- Distinct elements per attribute.

In a typical implementation, the data warehouse application is coupled to the warehouse via the metadata, allowing changes to the data warehouse to be immediately reflected in the enduser data-access application. For example, if a corporation restructures to eliminate a layer of management, as soon as the data corresponding to the new organizational hierarchy is added to the warehouse, the application should "reconfigure" itself using the metadata to reflect the new hierarchy.

DATA WAREHOUSE FUNCTIONS

Figure 2.2 depicts the flow of data from the original source to the user, and includes management and implementation capabilities. For example, there are access mechanisms required to retrieve data from heterogeneous operational databases. That data is then transformed and delivered to the "data warehouse store" based on a

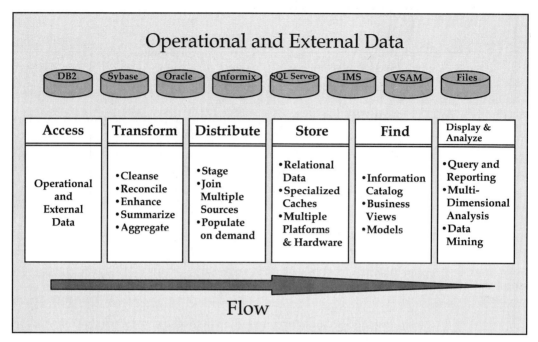

FIGURE 2.2   Data Warehouse Functions.

selected model (or mapping definition). The information that describes the model and definition of the source data elements is called "metadata."

The metadata is the means by which the enduser finds and understands the data in the warehouse. The data transformation and movement processes are executed whenever an update to the warehouse data is desired. And, there should be capability to manage and automate the processes required to execute these functions. Open interfaces, defined by an architecture, would enable easier integration of the products that implement those functions, particularly in a multivendor environment. Having quality consulting services can help assure a successful and cost-effective implementation.

Many implementations provide one or more of the above described data warehouse functions. However, it can take a significant amount of work and specialized programming to provide the interoperability needed between products from multiple vendors to enable them to perform the required data warehouse processes.

Data Flow within the Data Warehouse

There is a normal and predictable flow of data within the data warehouse. Figure 2.3 shows that flow.

Most data enters the data warehouse from the operational environment. As data enters the data warehouse from the operational environment, it is transformed, as

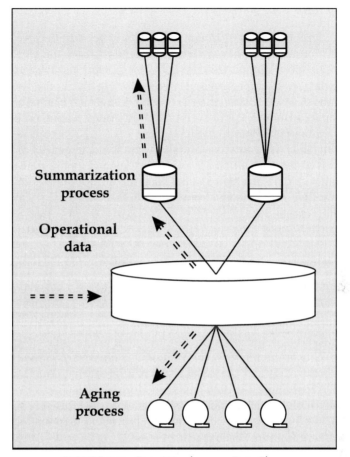

FIGURE 2.3   Data Warehouse—Data Flow.

was described earlier. Upon entering the data warehouse, data goes into the current level of detail. It resides there and is used there until one of three events occurs:

- It is purged,
- It is summarized, and/or
- It is archived.

The aging process inside a data warehouse moves current data to older data, based on the age of data. The summarization process uses the detail of data to calculate the lightly summarized data and the highly summarized data.

There are a few exceptions to the flow. However, in general, for the vast majority of the data found inside a data warehouse, the data flow is as depicted.

Usage

The different levels of data within the data warehouse receive different levels of usage. As a rule, the higher the level of summarization, the more the data is used.

The more summarized the data, the quicker and the more efficient it is to get to the data. If an enterprise finds that it is doing much processing at the detailed levels of the data warehouse, then a correspondingly large amount of machine resources are being consumed. It is in everyone's best interests to do processing at as high a level of summarization as possible.

In many ways getting to detailed data is like a security blanket, even when other levels of summarization are available. Good response time can be achieved when dealing with data at a high level of summarization, while poor response time results from dealing with data at a low level of detail.

Building Considerations

You should consider the following in building and administering the data warehouse.

Indexing

Data at the higher levels of summarization can be freely indexed, while data at the lower levels of detail is so voluminous that it can be indexed sparingly. By the same token, data at the higher levels of detail can be restructured relatively easily, while the volume of data at the lower levels is so great that data cannot be easily restructured. Accordingly, the data model and formal design work done, that lays the foundation for the data warehouse, applies almost exclusively to the current level of detail. In other words, the data modeling activities do not apply to the levels of summarization, in almost each case.

Partitioning

Another structural consideration is that of the partitioning of data warehouse data. Figure 2.4 shows that current-level detail is almost always partitioned. Partitioning can be done in two ways: at the DBMS level and/or at the application level. In DBMS partitioning, the DBMS is aware of the partitions and manages them accordingly. In the case of application partitioning, only the application programmer is aware of the partitions, and responsibility for the management of the partitions is left up to the programmer.

Under DBMS partitioning, much infrastructure work is done automatically. But there is a tremendous degree of inflexibility associated with the automatic management of the partitions. In the case of application partitioning of data warehouse data, much work falls to the programmer, but the end result is much flexibility in the management of data in the data warehouse.

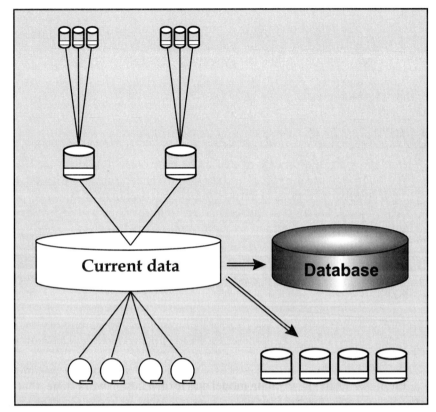

FIGURE 2.4   Data Warehouse Partitioning.

Other Considerations

While the data warehouse components work in the fashion described for almost all data, there are a few worthwhile exceptions that need to be discussed. Public data is summary data that has been calculated outside the boundaries of the data warehouse but is used throughout the corporation.

Public summary data is stored and managed in the data warehouse, even though its calculation is well outside the data warehouse scope.

Another consideration is that of permanent detail data. Permanent detail data results in the need of a corporation to store data at a detailed level permanently for ethical or legal reasons. If a corporation is exposing its workers to hazardous substances, there is a need for permanent detail data. If a corporation produces a product that involves public safety, such as building airplane parts, there is a need for permanent detail data.

In summary, a data warehouse is a subject-oriented, integrated, time-variant, non-volatile collection of data in support of management's decision needs. Each of the salient aspects of a data warehouse carries its own implications. Metadata is also an important part of the data warehouse environment. Each of the levels of detail carry their own considerations.

DATA MINING

Data mining is the process of extracting previously unknown but significant information from large databases and using it to make crucial business decisions. Every day, ongoing operations generate tremendous amounts of sales transactions, inventory systems, billing procedures, and customer service activities. For example, it is data that, when transformed into information, can be used to capitalize on emerging opportunities, extend market presence, and serve as input for strategic decision making—all for the sake of gaining competitive advantage. The challenge is getting it into the hands of people with established knowledge about the business so they can better understand the marketplace and their customer base.

Data mining leverages that data asset by transforming it into information, and information into reliable decisions. The potential is tremendous. Data mining has major implications across the enterprise—for productivity, profitability, customer satisfaction, and overall competitiveness.

Data mining analysis tends to be bottom-up, and the best techniques have been developed with an orientation toward large volumes of data. This is important in the context of the data warehouse, where a typical enterprise usually wishes to use as much of the collected data as possible to arrive at reliable conclusions and decisions.

Data mining is about discovering facts—some seemingly extraneous at first—but when viewed in a broader context and applied with human intellect and supportive technology, they turn out to hold profound meaning and knowledge. Knowledge is power—the power to compete and win. It drives decisions. It drives progress.

Competitiveness increasingly depends on the quality of decision making, so it is no wonder that enterprises often try to improve the quality of decisions by learning from past transactions and decisions. To support this process, operational data generated by business transactions is consolidated in a data warehouse, which is often a relational database system (RDBMS). Users of the data warehouse should know what questions to ask in order to identify patterns and gather needed information. Data mining facilitates further exploration by discovering the implicit patterns in the data. Hence, data mining significantly augments the value of the data warehouse.

Data mining is relevant to many different types of businesses. Data mining has been applied in industries such as merchandising, health care, insurance, and finance. For example, retail stores obtain profiles of customers and their buying patterns, and supermarkets analyze their sales and the effect of advertising on sales. Such "target marketing" is becoming increasingly important.

Data Mining Process

Collecting the data to mine is a difficult process by itself. While operational data is often collected for business processes, once the immediate use of the data has passed, the data is often archived. Such data can now be exploited for data mining; however, a suitable system infrastructure requires high Input/Output (I/O) bandwidth for fast loading and parallelism to reduce the time for initial loads or updates.

The data extraction process, as shown in Figure 2.5, extracts useful subsets of data for mining. Sampling may limit the size of the extracted data, and selection predicates may be applied to focus on applicable subsets of data. Aggregation may be done if summary statistics are useful.

There are two stages in the process of data mining to be used when searching for information:

- Initial searches should be carried out on summary information to develop a bird's eye view of the information.
- Focus on the detailed data in order to provide a clearer view.

The concept of data mining provides organizations with the ability to analyze and monitor trends and variations within their business that provide information to aid the decision-making process.

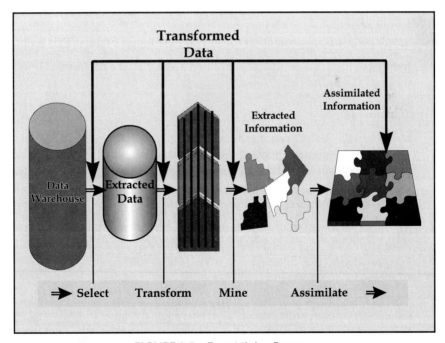

FIGURE 2.5 Data Mining Process.

The driving force that makes data mining acceptable to endusers is train of thought processing, where the response from a query will stimulate the next line of inquiry. To provide this type of investigation requires quick responses, making performance a key issue for data mining systems.

Operational (or transaction) data is often not in the most suitable form for mining. The data needs to be cleansed, with incorrect fields being corrected or otherwise marked. This cleansing process can be quite sophisticated, with a lot of business knowledge being encoded in the cleansing rules. Fields that are not necessary for the analyses may be omitted in order to reduce storage requirements and speed access for analysis. Some degree of normalization may be performed to reduce the amount of redundant data. Conversely, some denormalization may be performed to speed up data access. Additional fields may be added using "overlays." For example, demographic overlays are commonly used in marketing research.

The Enabling Components

Middleware

The emergence of middleware is the single most significant development that enables data mining. Without this software connecting heterogeneous data sources, the resulting information would not provide a complete picture and could not reap the same reward.

Network

The advances in networking are a key factor in providing increased bandwidth across heterogeneous protocols and therefore the necessary performance to provide train of thought processing.

Data Source

Many of the DBMS vendors now provide parallel support to enable rapid query against large volumes of data. This enables gigabytes of data to be queried in seconds where previously it would have taken minutes.

Operating System

Multiple processor architectures enable high-performance computers to provide the train of thought response times required for successful data mining analysis.

Related Technologies and Rules

To make data mining feasible, the appropriate data has to be collected and stored in a data warehouse, and adequate system resources have to be available to make the data mining process feasible.

Many *statistical analysis systems* such as SAS and SPSS have been used to detect unusual patterns and explain patterns using linear statistical models. Such systems have their place and will continue to be used. Data mining techniques will not replace such analyses but, in fact, may spur more directed analyses based on the results of data mining.

Ad hoc querying and report generation are commonly used by many businesses to provide input to their decision making. At a basic level, report generation tools are used. Applications utilizing the ad hoc querying capabilities of relational database systems are ubiquitous. Data mining helps focus the use of these systems and techniques so that relevant information is obtained faster and efficiently.

Multidimensional spreadsheets and databases are becoming popular for data analyses that require summary views of the data along multiple dimensions. Data mining technologies perform automatic analysis that can help enhance the value of the data exploration ("drill-down," "drill-up" summarization along various dimensions) supported by multidimensional tools.

Neural networks have been applied successfully in a few applications that involve classification. However, they suffer because the resulting network is viewed as a black box, and no explanation of the results is provided. The lack of such explanations inhibits confidence, acceptance, and application of results. Also, neural networks suffer from long learning times, which become intolerable when large volumes of data need to be processed.

The enabling power of data mining is even more clearly seen with respect to data visualization, which can make it possible to gain a deeper, intuitive understanding of the data. Data mining can enable you to focus attention on important patterns and trends and explore those patterns and trends in depth using visualization techniques. Data mining and data visualization work especially well together. Data visualization by itself runs the danger of being overwhelmed by the sheer volume of the data in commercial databases.

Data mining, when complemented by the techniques described above, adds significant value beyond the use of the traditional techniques.

The techniques needed to generate these results automatically require significant I/O bandwidth and computational power, and the data sets are large and need to be scanned fast. So for acceptable response time, the operations need to be parallelized, and the hardware and software must support these kinds of processing. The data mining techniques themselves require significant I/O bandwidth, large main memories, a lot of computational power, and scalable parallelism. The SMP servers seem to meet all these requirements.

Data Mining Platforms

Data mining technologies are characterized by intensive computations on large volumes of data. Significant processing power is critical, and parallelism is a key to enabling significant data mining. The systems should scale so that, as the demands for analysis grow, the system can be upgraded to provide the necessary analysis in a timely and cost-effective fashion.

Clearly, a balanced system architecture that supports I/O, computation, and scaling in a cost-effective fashion is desirable. Systems used for updating operational data can be distinct from those used for the data warehouse, so the current enterprise investment in database and transaction platforms need not be wasted.

The requirements placed on a system for data mining are a superset of those for the data warehouse. Large main memories are necessary for good performance. Good memory management in the multiprocessor system is needed to ensure that thrashing at any level of the memory hierarchy does not result in inadequate performance.

The larger the volume of data that can be processed by data mining, the greater the confidence in the results. Hence, the highest capacity and performance systems are of interest in this area.

There are two broad, alternative parallel architectures available now:

1.   Massively Parallel Processing (MPP) systems. Examples are Teradata from AT&T and SR4300 from Hitachi.
2.   Symmetric Multiprocessing (SMP) systems. Examples are servers from HP and Sequent.

Until now, doubts about their ability to meet the demand of data warehousing and mining have kept SMP systems from widespread use for these purposes. Today, however, the high-performance, symmetric multiprocessing servers meet all these requirements. Unlike MPP systems, these servers are also excellent choices for general-purpose use, thus helping to amortize the investment in system capacity.

The parallel loading capabilities of the Oracle7 RDBMS make it possible to populate and refresh the repository in a timely fashion. The parallel query option enables quick retrieval of data from the warehouse for mining. The parallel query option can also be used for the complex queries that would be suggested by the data mining analysis.

Data Mining Tools

Data mining has been around for some years but has only recently come of age because of a variety of tools and technological trends:

• Improved hardware cost/performance ratio.
• Improved performance in parallel technology.
• More flexible and intuitive query software.
• Greatly advanced middleware connectivity.

Example

To visualize where data mining techniques can be used most effectively here is an example. Fashions change frequently in the retail trade and timely analysis of information can be used to predict the latest trends on a store-by-store basis. This analysis can be used to reduce stock levels, reduce capital outlay, and ensure stock is placed where it can provide greatest results. The resulting increase in efficiency and profit margin provides competitive advantage. An increase of 1% profit margin can make the difference between success and failure in the highly competitive retail trade.

Data mining tools provide access to the data warehouse and enable query, analysis, and presentation of data. The data warehouse provides one logical view of an organization's data which may bring together many distributed, heterogeneous data sources. Once the data warehouse is functional, then the process of data mining can take place.

Data Mining Tool Characteristics

The data that is to be mined is often lodged deep within very large company archives (often terabytes of data). To provide coherent information from this unstructured data requires sophisticated tools. To get the desired results from the data requires manipulation and synchronizing into a format usable by the tool.

The mining tools still currently require creative analysis to detect trends, although some have an element of intelligence to detect patterns. Many of the tools are integrated as part of a total data warehouse solution, although some of the more popular tools are independent. Because of the emergent nature of the market for data mining tools, there is no standard set of features to look for in any particular product.

OPERATIONAL WAREHOUSE

There are two fundamental types of data within any enterprise as shown in Figure 2.6. The first and most widely understood is termed *operational data*. Operational data is the data that directly supports the business functions and for which the majority of applications have been written since business programming became a practice. The second type of data is *informational data*. This is the data that supports the decision-making process of an organization, and as a specific form of data, it is not as well understood as operational data. Many organizations have not as yet made the distinction between the two data forms.

The driving force behind the evolution to the data warehouse is the need to gain informational access as opposed to operational access to corporate data. Operational access means access to the current state of specific instances of data. Informational access, by contrast, implies access to large volumes of data for higher-level assessment, planning, and strategic *decision-support* activities.

Differentiating operational data from informational data dictates a fundamentally different design criteria for the operational database versus the data warehouse database. In brief, data is stored in its elemental form, there is no redundant storage of data, and any required data that does not represent an elemental data element is derived from an amalgamation of elementary-data elements. Data can be both extracted from and stored in the database. In general, the *database is optimized for the update process, not the extraction process*.

The data warehouse is not built to support the functional process of the enterprise. It is built to facilitate the *use of information*. The source of data for the data

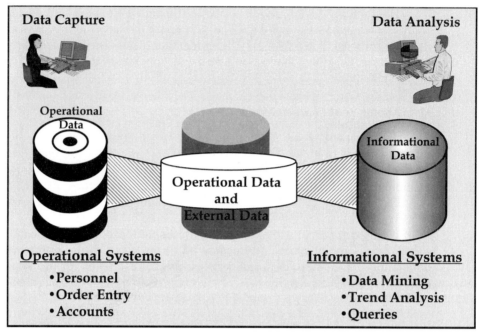

Data Capture

Data Analysis

Operational
Data

Operational Data
and
External Data

Informational
Data

Operational Systems

- **Personnel**
- **Order Entry**
- **Accounts**

Informational Systems

- **Data Mining**
- **Trend Analysis**
- **Queries**

FIGURE 2.6   Data to Information.

warehouse is the operational database, which is optimized for the extraction process. In fact, the data warehouse can only be updated by the operational database; it is a read-only resource.

The data warehouse is ideal as a centrally maintained, distributed resource. The user community can help design it and is then free to use it to build its own applications for access. The first step in data warehousing is to simply create a specialized, replicated database that is optimized for the "what-if" informational needs. The only additional technology needed for this step is a method to perform the extraction of data from the operational database into the data warehouse including the appropriate machinations for aggregation. Although it is certainly possible to develop this interface, there are a number of commercially available solutions from the major database vendors.

Operational versus Informational Systems

The need for better quality information that can be easily accessed and analyzed is the driving force behind data warehouse development for most companies. This need is driven by the fundamental differences in operational and informational processing:

OPERATIONAL SYSTEMS	INFORMATIONAL SYSTEMS
Supports day-to-day decisions	Supports long-term, strategic decisions
Transaction driven	Analysis driven
Data constantly changes	Data rarely changes
Repetitive processing	Heuristic processing
Holds current data	Holds historical data
Stores detailed data	Stores summarized and detailed data
Application oriented	Subject oriented
Predictable pattern of usage	Unpredictable pattern of usage
Serves clerical, transactional community	Serves managerial community

In addition, the data warehouse overcomes the problems that can arise when using the operational environment for *decision-support* analysis, such as the following.

Lack of Integration

Operational systems are typically dispersed throughout an organization and have been independently developed or purchased over time without regard to or integration with one another. Operational systems have often been built on diverse types of databases and are run in heterogeneous mainframe and client/server hardware environments, making them incompatible and difficult to integrate for *decision support*.

Lack of History

The operational environment provides no historical perspective for use in decision making. Because of space limitations and to maintain performance levels, most transactional systems do not keep records very long.

Lack of Credibility

The data is constantly changing, making it difficult to assess the accuracy or timeliness of the data, or to perform analysis that can be traced or repeated.

Performance Considerations

To process hundreds or thousands of transactions per second, operational systems store data in formats designed to optimize transaction performance rather than to support business analysis. Conducting analysis and transaction processing on the same system substantially degrades the performance of the operational system, jeopardizing the execution of routine business transactions that are critical to organizations.

Difficulty in Gaining Enterprise-Wide Perspective

Organizations often maintain separate operational systems for each specific business function, such as inventory management, purchasing, and point-of-sale transac-

tions. This makes cross-functional analysis
databases difficult.

The data warehouse addresses these
model, map, filter, integrate, condense, and
rate database of meaningful information t
upon. It empowers users with direct access t
improving productivity. It can also be used
cal information for legal or ethical purposes
ment or regulatory agencies. In these ca
historical, non-volatile information is essent

SUMMARY

With access to more precise and accurate info
ter business decisions, implement the right n
people. The bottom line is that segmentatio
more cost-effective initiatives and save consid

Operational systems are application se
views of business entities such as a customer. ... information
concerning a customer's savings, loans, and deposit accounts is often stored in separate applications. In contrast to this, a data warehouse provides a universal view of the customer. The enduser has access to integrated and analytical information rather than raw data.

In this section, we have briefly examined the concepts inherent in a data warehouse application and operation. In the succeeding chapters, we will detail the architectures, technologies, and implementation techniques.

3

TYPES OF DATA WAREHOUSE SOLUTIONS

INTRODUCTION

Businesses today recognize that collecting data is one thing, and transforming data into information, the kind of information people need to analyze business processes and make decisions, is another.

Enterprises of all sizes and in different industries are finding that they can realize a business advantage by implementing a data warehouse. Seeking to maximize the usefulness and value of their corporate data while controlling the resources they expend collecting and manipulating it, many companies are building data warehouses.

It is generally accepted that data warehousing provides an excellent approach for transforming data into useful and reliable information to support the business decision-making process. A data warehouse provides the base for the powerful analytical and decision-making techniques that are so important in today's competitive environment, such as data mining and multidimensional data analysis, as well as the more traditional query and reporting. Making use of these analytical techniques along with data warehousing can result in more informed decision-making capability and lead to a significant business advantage.

A data warehouse is a subject-oriented store of information created specifically for understanding, analyzing, and solving real business problems. It can contain data that is of interest to all the organizations in an enterprise, or to a department or workgroup.

A properly implemented data warehouse can give its users access to the information they need to understand their business, to make decisions, and to solve problems. For example, many firms now require their customer service personnel to make customer-support decisions on the spot. Empowered to solve unique customer problems, these employees need access to specific, explicit kinds of customer information to do their job efficiently and effectively.

For the past few years, data warehousing has been accepted as a means for companies to empower decision makers and achieve competitive advantage in the challenging business environment. In a traditional *decision-support* environment, production and ad hoc worlds coexist in a mainframe environment. With the emergence of word processing and spreadsheet tools, endusers are becoming increasingly self-sufficient. They have become accustomed to manipulating data themselves and no longer want to wait for IT to get the data they need.

The mix of traditional and desktop processing has generated the need to reexamine the data warehouse environments better suited for a particular enterprise. This phenomenon has aroused a number of additional issues such as,

- Creation of a single, static database (DBMS).
- The need for a central, single metadata source that links sources, targets, and queries.
- The need to separate the informational data from the operational data.
- The need for access to operational data.
- Do we distribute islands of data physically closer to the enduser?

In this chapter, we will address some of these issues so that you can get a better idea what options are available and are better suited for your environment. There are numerous types of data warehouses that can be implemented, and we will discuss the most commonly employed.

HOW TO CHOOSE A DATA WAREHOUSE

Organizations run their business systems with operational applications. These are transaction- or batch-oriented applications such as order entry, point of sale, inventory, accounting, and payroll. They tend to create or collect data and to access small amounts of data for inquiry and update. The operational data is organized and optimized for this type of use. Because they are running the day-to-day business systems, operational applications create and use data that is volatile (it changes frequently), real time (contains only current values of data), and is specifically related to a particular application or set of applications. It is typically not in a format or structure that is easily understood or easily accessed by endusers for informational purposes.

The Data-to-Information Transformation

Most organizations need two different data environments: one optimized for operational applications and the other for informational applications. Figure 3.1 depicts the two environments. The data used for these two types of applications is fundamentally different. If the same data environment is used to support both, the performance, capability, and benefit of both will be compromised. For example, operational applications and databases are typically optimized for fast response time and typically cannot tolerate the impact when accessed by informational applications.

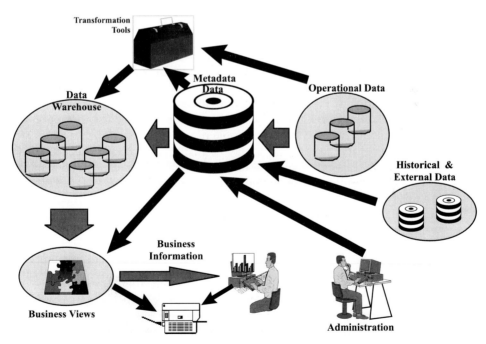

FIGURE 3.1   Data-to-Information Transformation.

The original data for both types of applications is the same and may have been generated internally or extracted from external sources. In either case, data to support the informational applications typically needs to be transformed. The extent of the data transformation required depends on the quality and organization of the source data.

The following is a description of the different configurations of data that can be defined to satisfy the requirements of a particular data warehouse implementation.

Real-Time Data

This is sometimes called operational data because it is typically used only by operational applications. It contains all the individual, detailed data records, where each update overlays the previous entry (the history of changes is not preserved). Real-time data may exist redundantly in multiple locations that may or may not be synchronized with each other. It may also be inconsistent in representation, meaning, or both.

For example, in international banking, endusers may need to analyze data from several branch offices. The data needs to reflect a common currency and a common exchange rate at a specific point in time. However, if operational systems are well modeled and integrated, real-time data could be accessed by informational applications. Otherwise, the data may need to be reconciled.

Reconciled Data

Reconciled data contains detailed records from the real-time level which has been cleansed, adjusted, or enhanced so that the data can be used by informational applications. That is, inconsistencies such as those mentioned in the section on real-time data have been fixed. There will also be problems with data types, incomplete records, and so forth. It may also be that the real-time data is not in a data store whose technology is suitable for informational processing.

For example, relational technology is more suitable for informational processing, because of its capability of multiple record processing, rather than "record-at-a-time" processing. The problem may be further complicated because the real-time data is stored in a heterogeneous database environment comprised of multiple types of databases and database technologies from multiple vendors. It may be advisable in this situation to provide data extraction and transformation processes to move and combine the disparate data into a single database technology to satisfy the needs of the informational applications.

Derived Data

Reconciled data is suitable for informational applications but may not be practical or advisable in all situations. Manipulation of large volumes of data in elemental form may require a tremendous amount of processor resources. Endusers seldom want record-by-record reports; rather they typically need only summaries of the large volumes of data. To satisfy this requirement, an efficient approach is to provide a separate database with the detailed records already summarized. This would significantly reduce resource requirements and increase application response time. This is particularly important with the move to a client/server environment.

Derived data, then, has been summarized, averaged, or aggregated from multiple sources of the real-time or reconciled data for improved processing capability.

Changed Data

A changed data store contains a record of all the changes (adds, deletes, updates) to selected real-time data. The data is kept as a continuum and reflects the history of changes. This data is timestamped to document when the change was made. Since all changes are included, any level of point-in-time analysis can be achieved. For example, a bank might wish to know trends for customer deposits by specific branch locations, which might impact staffing or cash pickup.

Having the history of information by point in time would allow such analysis. Keeping the history of changed data will present additional issues for data management. The data will need to be archived in such a way as to make retrieval easy when it is desired. There will also be considerations for the media used to store these potentially large volumes of data in a cost-effective way.

Metadata

The term "metadata" is used for descriptive information about other data elements or data types, such as files, reports, workflow processes, and so forth. Metadata becomes very important to endusers as they attempt to access data and develop their own information applications. They need to understand what data is available for them to access, exactly what that data represents, how current it is, and so on.

As a data warehouse is built, there is a requirement both to capture the data and to make the metadata available. Metadata is usually found in data dictionaries, database catalogs, programs, and copy libraries and is typically used only by professional programmers. Now there is a requirement to transform the metadata definitions into business terms for endusers. And, a mechanism is needed to make it easy for endusers to search for and use this metadata.

Metadata is everything your tools—be they data warehouse tools or other IS mainstays like an application development environment or a system management platform—know about your data and about your computing environment. If two tools cannot share the same metadata, then you are never going to get them to work together very well. Metadata represents both the system information as well as the user information. Metadata may maintain systems information such as,

- How it was derived.
- What legacy environment this initially resided in.
- What alterations it went through.

On the other hand, the metadata may be more user oriented:

- What a particular field, such as *territory*, means in a particular database.
- How its meaning has changed historically.
- What business criteria are to use this information.

Depending on the nature of the operational systems and the kinds and numbers of endusers that will access the data warehouse, these different types of data can be combined to create a solution that is cost-effective. There are two basic types of metadata involved in data warehousing:

- Business metadata is used to help endusers understand what data is in the warehouse, in business terms they can understand.
- Technical metadata, such as data elements and transformation mappings, is used to build and maintain the data warehouse processes.

The metadata store is built and maintained by the data warehouse administrators. Metadata management is key to the processes involved in data warehousing and to the support of the enduser requirement to access the data.

The Data-to-Information Process

There are a number of different functions involved in creating a data warehousing environment. The basic functions represent a process that will be ongoing in building and maintaining the data warehouse as it grows and changes. Because it is an ongoing process, there are extended capabilities required to minimize the impact on the operations and technical resources.

In general, data is extracted from internal operational data and from data available in sources external to the enterprise. That data is transformed and placed in the data warehouse data stores based on the selected business subject area structure. Business views of the data are developed as part of the structure and made available to the users for easy access to the data for their business purposes. Definitions for the data elements, transformation processes, and business views are stored as metadata.

TYPES OF DATA WAREHOUSES

A majority of the enterprises prefer to build and implement a single centralized data warehouse environment. The justification for such a schema has many reasons.

- A single repository makes sense if the volume of data can be managed easily.
- The data is integrated across the enterprise and only that view is used at the headquarters.

- On the other hand, it may be impractical to integrate and access the data at a single site if it is dispersed over multiple locations.

Business Factors

Fundamentally, one single solution does not fit all warehouse scenarios. We realize that not all of the potential data warehouse types are included, but the data warehouses discussed in this chapter cover a majority of the prevalent situations. The type of data warehouse depends on a number of business factors, such as the following:

Business Objectives

Many enterprises know that they need a data warehouse but are not certain about their priorities or options. The priorities impact the warehouse model as to its size, location, frequency of use, and maintenance. For many companies, a properly scoped and executed legacy data administration effort can prove extremely cost-effective in building a data warehouse.

Location of the Current Data

One of the major challenges in delivering data to the user is understanding where the data is and what we know about it. It is extremely important that we understand where the data is and what its characteristics and attributes are so we can select the proper tools. Complicating the issue is the fact that many legacy applications have redefined the old historical data to conserve space and maximize performance for archiving and backup.

Need to Move the Data

When the new warehouse project is initiated, in most cases it is assumed that the data must be moved. First of all, it is simpler to leave the data at its original location unless it is absolutely necessary to move it. However, you may wish to investigate whether the data can stay where it is, considering the available query, report writer, and the gateway technology tools that can operate on it. These technologies may allow you to bypass some data replication and movement. The data movement or the use of such technologies can only be decided by considering a combination of

- Quality of the existing data
- The size of the usable data
- Data design
- Performance impact of a direct query
- Performance impact on the current production systems
- Availability and ease of use of the tool

Movement of Data

There are a myriad tools available to move any type of data to any place. But the lack of understanding of the attributes of the data make it very difficult to use any such tools effectively. For most enterprises, understanding their existing data poses a larger challenge than moving it.

Location to Which the Data Needs to Be Moved

This is a significant issue in the design of a data warehouse. Before designing to move data, you must consider if the data store is host-based or LAN-based. This is the time you must decide which data store is to be used.

Decision-Support Requirements

While the term "data warehouse" may not be a household word, most companies are deeply entrenched in supporting Executive Information Systems (EISs) and *decision-support* system (DSS) activities.

Data Preparation

Once the data is moved, you need to consider a number of factors to refresh the data. Just replacing the existing data in a field with new information will not reflect the historical change in data over time. Therefore, you must choose to replace the data or look for ways to update it based on incremental changes. You must also choose how to coordinate master files with transaction files and a host of other considerations.

Query and Reporting Requirements

One of the most important data warehouse implementation decisions is to determine what query tools are needed, deployable, and available. For a poorly built data warehouse, a range of tools will need to be deployed to address the different needs of information workers, advanced warehouse users, application developers, executive users, and other endusers.

Integration of the Data Model

Many enterprises design data models as part of the data warehouse effort. If you choose that approach, you must integrate the results into your development process and the enduser tool facilities.

Management and Administration

Once the data warehouse is built, you must put mechanisms and policies in place for managing and maintaining the warehouse.

Implementation Alternatives

Based on the above criteria, users can exercise a lot of flexibility in choosing the technology and the type of a warehouse to implement. There are a large variety of implementation alternatives for a LAN-based local warehouse that supports a specific functional department or workgroup, sometimes referred to as a "data mart," to a comprehensive implementation for an enterprise-wide data warehouse. This range of available solutions is depicted in Figure 3.2. Two of the fundamental data warehouse types are

- *Host-Based Warehouses*: Usually IT controlled and on traditional systems.
- *LAN-Based Warehouses*: Usually managed either centrally or from the workgroup environment.

These can be further refined based on the location of the source data and operation data for access. These are

- Operational data warehouses
- LAN-based workgroup data warehouses
- Multistage data warehouses
- Stationary data warehouses
- Distributed data warehouses
- Virtual warehouses

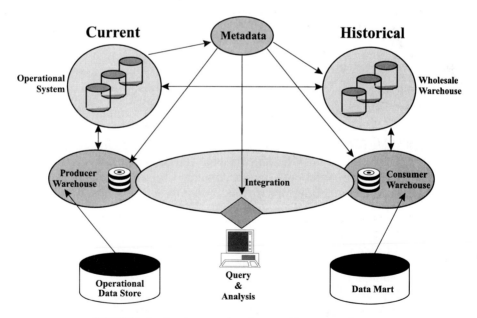

FIGURE 3.2 Implementation Range of Data Warehouses.

HOST-BASED DATA WAREHOUSES

There are at least two types of host-based data warehouses that can be implemented:

- Host-based mainframe data warehouses that reside on high-volume databases supported by robust and reliable high-capacity systems, such as IBM System/390, UNISYS, and Data General Sequent Systems; and databases such as Sybase, Oracle, Informix, and DB2.
- Host-based LAN data warehouses, where data delivery can be managed either centrally or from the workgroup environment. The size of the data warehouse or the database depends on the platform.

Data extraction and transformation tools allow the automated extraction and cleansing of data from production systems. Invariably, it is not feasible to allow direct access by query tools to these types of systems for the following reasons.

1. A heavy load of complex warehousing queries would probably have too much of a detrimental impact upon the mission-critical Transaction Processing (TP)-oriented applications.
2. These TP systems have been optimized in their database design for transaction throughput. In almost all cases, a database is designed either for optimal query or transaction processing. A complex business query requires the joining of many normalized tables, and as a result performance will generally be poor and the query construct highly complex.
3. There is no guarantee that data in two or more production systems will be consistent.

Host-Based (MVS) Data Warehouses

Those data warehouses that reside on high-volume databases on MVS are the host-based type of data warehouses. Often the DBMS is DB2 with a large variety of original sources for legacy data, including VSAM, DB2, flat files, and Information Management System. For many Fortune 100 companies, this is usually the first foray into the data warehouse implementation, as shown in Figure 3.3.

Before embarking on designing, building, and implementing such a warehouse, some additional considerations must be given because

1. Such databases usually have very high volumes of data storage.
2. Such warehouses may require support for both MVS and client-based report and query facilities.
3. These warehouses have very complex source systems.

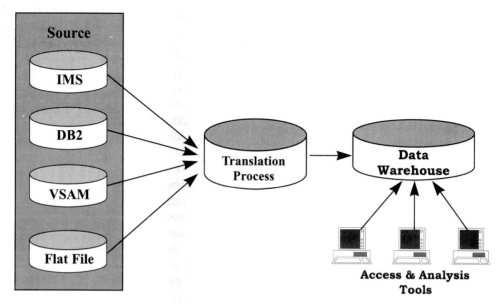

FIGURE 3.3   Host-Based (MVS) Data Warehouse.

4.   Such systems require continuous maintenance since these must also be used for mission-critical purposes.

In order to make such data warehouse building successful, the following steps are usually followed:

- *Unload phase* involves selecting and scrubbing the operational data,
- *Transform phase* for translating it into an appropriate form and defining the rules for accessing and storing it.
- *Load phase* for moving the data directly into DB2 tables or a special file for moving it to another database or non-MVS Warehouse.

An integrated metadata repository is central to any data warehouse environment. Such a facility is needed for documenting data sources, data translation rules, and user access to the warehouse. It provides a dynamic link between the multiple data source databases and the DB2 or the eventual data warehouse.

A *metadata repository* is essential to design, build, and maintain data warehouse processes. It should be capable of providing information as to what data exists in both the operational system and data warehouse, where the data is located, the mapping of the operational data to the warehouse fields, and enduser access mechanisms.

Query, reporting, and maintenance are another indispensable part of such a data warehouse. In today's environment, a Windows-based query and reporting mechanism is extremely useful. However, an MVS-based query and reporting tool for DB2, VSAM data, and sequential files is very desirable.

Host-Based (UNIX) Data Warehouses

Oracle and Informix RDBMSs provide the facilities for such data warehouses. Both of these databases can extract data from MVS-based databases as well as a larger number of other UNIX-based databases.

These types of warehouses follow the same steps as the host-based-MVS data warehouses. In addition, the data from other networked servers can also be accessed since file attribute consistency is prevalent across internetworks.

HOST-BASED SINGLE-STAGE (LAN) DATA WAREHOUSES

With a LAN-based warehouse (Figure 3.4), data delivery can be managed either centrally or from the workgroup environment so business groups can meet and manage their own information needs without burdening centralized IT resources, enjoying the autonomy of their own data mart without compromising overall data integrity and security in the enterprise.

Even though LAN-based data warehouses are common, seem easier to access, and provide numerous cost benefits, they do present a series of challenges:

- LAN-based warehousing solutions are normally limited by both DBMS and hardware scalability factors.
- Many LAN-based enterprises have not implemented adequate job scheduling, recovery management, organized maintenance, and performance monitoring procedures to support robust warehousing solutions.
- Often these warehouses are dependent on other platforms for source data. Building an environment that has data integrity, recoverability, and security takes very diligent design and careful planning and implementation. Otherwise, synchronization of changes and loads from sources to server could cause innumerable problems.

A LAN-based warehouse supports data from many sources, requiring minimal initial investment and technical know-how. A LAN-based warehouse can also work with replication tools for populating and updating the data warehouse. This type of warehouse can contain business views, histories, aggregations, versioning, and heterogeneous source support, such as,

- DB2 family
- IMS, VSAM, flat file (MVS and VM)
- Oracle, Sybase, Informix, Redbrick, Ingress, IDMS, and others

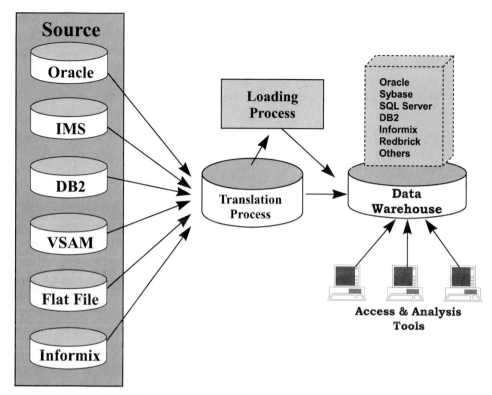

FIGURE 3.4 LAN-Based Single-Stage (LAN) Warehouse.

A LAN-based warehouse is normally driven by a single metadata store and supports existing DSS applications, enabling business users to locate data in their data warehouse. The LAN-based warehouse can provide business users with a complete data-to-information solution. The LAN-based warehouse can also share metadata with the ability to catalog business information and make it available to anyone who needs it.

The industry offers a variety of client/server database query, analysis, and reporting tools that make the job of gathering, analyzing, and presenting information easier than ever. In fact, any data analysis tool, including those designed for Windows, OS/2, or DOS, can be used with a LAN-based warehouse using the ODBC or DB2 for OS/2 SQL.

Such a warehouse can be designed for the workgroup environment using a common "data repository," sometimes called "data mart." And, as the needs of the workgroup grow, a LAN-based warehouse can grow or integrate with a larger, more centralized warehouse.

As a metadata-driven system, a LAN-based warehouse enables you to understand your data, a crucial ingredient when you're building a data warehouse. Metadata, which is information about your data, allows you to see how data is related and what it truly means within your business. For example, a product price may be stored in many different places throughout your computer systems and mean something different on each particular system.

With this type of a warehouse, you enter metadata into the system to define your data sources, which are then mapped through to the data warehouse. This enables you to track where your *decision-support* data comes from and understand what it means at the source. This also enables executive users to find the business view of the metadata to better understand the aggregations, histories, data derivations, data sources, and descriptions for the data in the warehouse.

LAN-BASED WORKGROUP DATA WAREHOUSES

A LAN-based workgroup warehouse is an integrated architecture for building and maintaining a data warehouse in a LAN environment. In this warehouse, you extract data from a variety of sources and provide multiple LAN-based warehouses. Frequently chosen warehouse databases include DB2 family, Oracle, SYBASE, and Informix. Other databases that can also be included, though infrequently, are IMS, VSAM, flat file, MVS, and VM. Figure 3.5 depicts a typical configuration.

Designed for the workgroup environment, a LAN-based workgroup warehouse is ideal for any business organization that wishes to build a data warehouse,

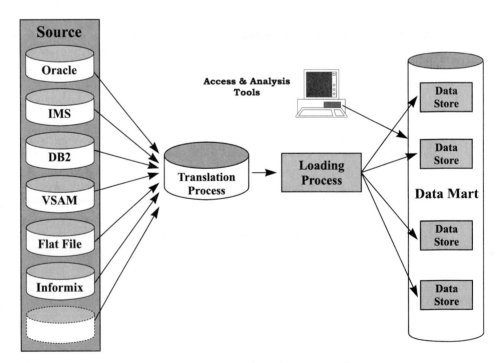

FIGURE 3.5   LAN-Based Workgroup Warehouse.

often called a data mart. This type of a data warehouse usually requires minimal initial investment and technical training. Its low startup cost and ease of use allow a workgroup to quickly build and easily manage its own custom data mart. And, as the needs of the workgroup grow, a LAN-based workgroup warehouse can grow or integrate with a larger, more centralized warehouse.

With a LAN-based workgroup warehouse, data delivery can be managed either centrally or from the workgroup environment, so business groups can meet and manage their own information needs without burdening centralized IT resources, enjoying the autonomy of their own data mart without compromising overall data integrity and security in the enterprise.

Data Delivery

With a LAN-based workgroup warehouse, users need minimal technical knowledge to create and maintain a store of information that's customized for use at the department, business unit, or workgroup level. A LAN-based workgroup warehouse ensures the delivery of data from corporate resources by providing transparent access to the data in the warehouse.

A carefully selected tool set for data warehouse definitions lets users control exactly how data is transformed into meaningful business information, and automatically extract, transfer, transform, and refresh the data warehouse. For example, decision makers can use such tools to aggregate data from multiple sources to provide a single view of the data they need, or they can create derivations directly. A LAN-based workgroup warehouse, if needed, could be constructed to allow business users to access the source data directly. Users can also maintain multiple editions of any data set, so business users can view trends in their business needed to make decisions.

Metadata for the Business User

As a metadata-driven system, the LAN-based workgroup warehouse enables you to understand your data, a crucial ingredient when you're building a data warehouse. Metadata allows you to see how data is related and what it truly means within your business. For example, a product price may be stored in many different places throughout your computer systems and mean something different on each particular system.

With a LAN-based workgroup warehouse, you enter metadata into the system to define your data sources, which are then mapped through business views to the data warehouse. This enables you to track where your *decision-support* data comes from and understand what it means at the source.

Administrative Tool

In general, a LAN-based workgroup warehouse itself will not be visible to business users, as it's primarily an administrative tool. The LAN-based workgroup warehouse can be used as a generalized information catalog to provide graphical representations of the metadata. The LAN-based workgroup warehouse enables business users to find metadata to better understand the aggregations, histories, data derivations, data sources, and descriptions for the data in the warehouse. Other tools enable business users to access warehouse data through a browse, search, and "drill-down" interface.

For flexibility of configuration, a LAN-based workgroup warehouse can reside on the same server as the data warehouse or it can be remote from the warehouse, and it can manage several different data warehouses. Different functional components of a LAN-based workgroup warehouse reside on separate servers to maximize performance, scalability, and flexibility.

Associated Common Issues

- Lack of understanding how to distribute data and supporting intentional data redundancy for performance reasons.

- Many organizations may not have adequate job scheduling, recovery management, and performance monitoring to support robust warehousing solutions.

- Although providing positive cost benefits, LAN-based warehousing solutions can be limited by both hardware and DBMS limitations.

- For many large enterprises, similar skills in database design, maintenance, and recovery are not present in every workgroup environment.

MULTISTAGE DATA WAREHOUSES

This configuration is well suited to environments where endusers in different capacities require access to both summarized data for up-to-the-minute tactical decisions as well as summarized, cumulative data for long-term strategic decisions. Both the Operation Data Store (ODS) and the data warehouse may reside on host-based or LAN-based databases, depending on volume and usage requirements. These include DB2, Oracle, Informix, IMS, flat files, and Sybase. In general, the operation data store serves as the source for the data warehouse.

Typically, the ODS stores only the most up-to-date records. The data warehouse stores the historical evolution of the records. At first, the records in both databases will be very similar.

For example, the record for a new customer will look the same. As changes to the customer record occur, the ODS will be refreshed to reflect only the most current information, whereas the data warehouse will contain both the historical information and the new information. Thus the volume requirements of the data warehouse will exceed the volume requirements of the ODS over time. It is not common to reach a ratio of 4 to 1 in practice.

Tactical decisions are based largely on data in the ODS. Long-term strategic decisions require the historical trend analysis that is only available from the data warehouse. Figure 3.6 depicts a typical multistage data warehouse.

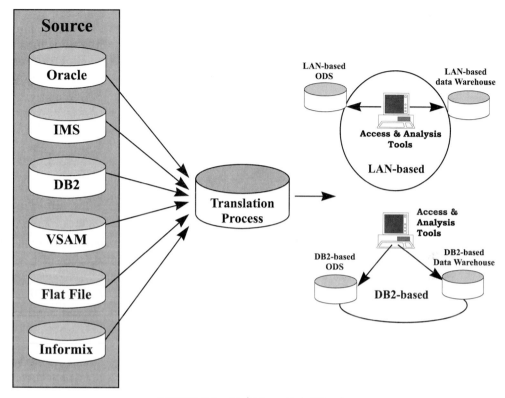

FIGURE 3.6   Multistage Data Warehouse.

Multistage warehouses are the ultimate in enterprise solutions. But they also are not without problems which the enterprise must address. Some of these:

- Must maintain data once loaded.
- May cause more frequent updates to the ODS.
- Have highly complex source systems.
- Require support for both MVS and client-based report writers.
- Require the ODS to offer more rapid response time.
- Need constant synchronization of changes and loads from sources to server.
- Require highly skilled personnel in many technologies simultaneously.
- Have LAN-based operating system limitations.
- Have limitations of hardware scalability.
- Have very high volume of storage and activity.

STATIONARY DATA WAREHOUSES

In this type of a data warehouse, the data is not moved from the sources, as shown in Figure 3.7. Instead, the users are given direct access to the data. For many organizations, infrequent access, volume issues, or corporate necessities dictate such an approach.

This schema does generate a number of problems for the users, such as,

- Identifying the location of the data for the users.
- Providing users the ability to query different DBMSs as if they were all a single DBMS with a single API.
- Impacting performance since the users will be competing with the production data stores.

Such a warehouse will require highly specialized and sophisticated "middleware," possibly with a single interface to the user. This may also necessitate a facility to display the extracted data for the user, prior to report generation. An integrated metadata repository becomes an absolute necessity under this environment.

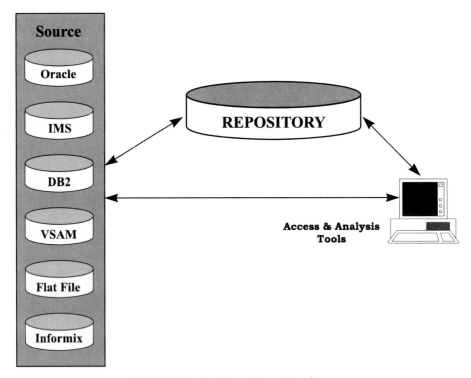

FIGURE 3.7 Stationary Data Warehouse.

DISTRIBUTED DATA WAREHOUSES

The concept of a distributed data warehouse suggests that there are at least two types of distributed data warehouses and their variations for the enterprise: local warehouses which are distributed throughout the enterprise and a global warehouse (Figure 3.8).

The possibility of a local distributed data warehouse is enticing and corrupting if there is a need for some degree of local control. However, the technology, economics, and politics favor a single centralized data warehouse. Still, there are situations when a distributed warehouse is the only viable alternative.

It makes business sense to build distributed data warehouses when there are diverse businesses under the same enterprise umbrella. This approach may be necessitated if a local warehouse already existed, prior to joining the enterprise. Local data warehouses have the following common characteristics:

- Activity occurs at the local level.
- Majority of the operational processing is done at the local site.
- Local site is autonomous.
- Each local data warehouse has its own unique structure and content of data.
- The data is unique and of prime importance to that locality only.
- Majority of the data is local and not replicated.
- Any intersection of data between local data warehouses is coincidental.
- Local site serves different geographic regions.

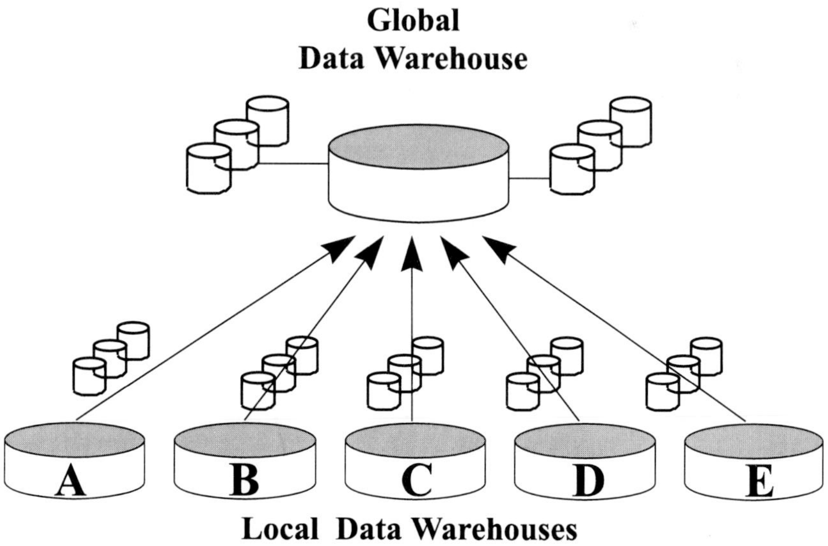

FIGURE 3.8   Distributed Data Warehouse.

- Local warehouse serves different technical communities.
- The scope of the local data warehouse is limited to the local site.
- Local warehouse also contains historical data and is integrated only within the local site.

The primary motivation in implementing distributed data warehouses is that integration of the entire enterprise data does not make sense. It is reasonable to assume that an enterprise will have at least some natural intersections of data from one local site to another. If there is an intersection, then it is usually contained in a global warehouse. On the other hand, the scope of a global warehouse goes beyond local boundaries. It can contain data that is common across the enterprise and the data is integrated. Figure 3.8 demonstrates a conceptual view of such a global warehouse with local autonomous distributed warehouses.

VIRTUAL DATA WAREHOUSE

The data warehouse is a great idea, but it is complex to build and requires work and investment. A data warehouse is expensive and requires a new discipline, new technology, and a shift of control. Why don't we get all the benefits of a data warehouse without going through this transformation with new technology? Just use a cheap, fast, and easy approach by eliminating the transformation steps of repositories for metadata and another database. This approach is getting popular and is termed the "virtual data warehouse" (Figure 3.9).

Virtual as well as physical data warehouses are enabled via the repository. The real key to the technology is the creation of a virtual view of databases, allowing the creation of a "virtual warehouse" as opposed to a physical warehouse. In a virtual warehouse, you have a logical description of all the databases and their structures, and individuals who want to get at information in those databases don't have to know anything about them. To accomplish this, there is a need to define four kinds of information:

- A data dictionary containing the definitions of the various databases, what their structure is, and what information is in the databases.
- A description of the relationship among the data elements. For example, you might have customer information in four places—one place is the master record and others are subsidiary records. There are also one-to-many relationships.
- The description of the way the user will interface with the system—what the menus are or what various screens look like, how information is presented, how to put an error in, or how to tell a user they need to wait while information is validated.
- The algorithms and business rules that define what to do and how to do it.

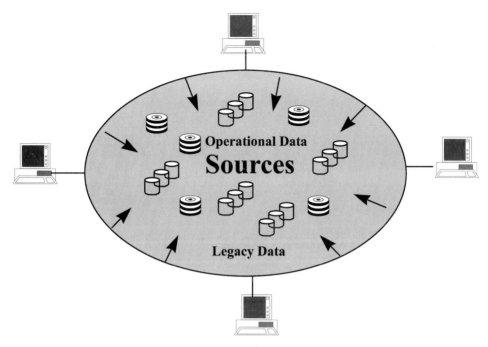

FIGURE 3.9 Virtual Data Warehouse.

This approach creates a single "virtual database," as shown in Figure 3.9, from all your data resources. The data resources can be local or remote. In this type of a warehouse, the data is not moved from the sources. Instead the users are given direct access to the data. The direct access to the data is sometimes through simple SQL queries or with complex queries via data-access middleware.

With this approach, it is possible to access remote data sources including IMS, Oracle, VSAM, Sybase, DB2, and other major RDBMSs. Some middleware employ Open Database Connectivity (ODBC) interface protocol whereas others use simple Call Level Interface (CLI). The following table identifies some of the commonly available database resources and platforms.

As many businesses move to client/server computing, they're finding it difficult to access databases across their complex, multivendor networks. Virtual data warehouse schema lets a client application access data distributed across multiple data sources through a single Structured Query Language (SQL) statement and a single interface. All data sources are accessed as though they are local—users and their applications don't even need to know the physical location of the data.

This essentially enables users to develop a virtual, enterprise-wide relational database. Middleware-access software can provide a single database image of all your data—for relational and non-relational, local and remote—as though the data is local. It can access and generate tables located across multiple data sources with a

TABLE 3.1   Virtual Data Warehouse Sources

DATABASE	OPERATING SYSTEM PLATFORM
Oracle	Non-UNIX and UNIX platforms, MVS, VM, Intel, Solaris, MPP, others
Sybase	DOS, OS/2, Windows, Windows NT, Intel, Netware
Informix	UNIX platforms
VSAM	MVS
Microsoft SQL Server	DOS and Windows
IMS	MVS
DB2	MVS, UNIX, OS/400, VM, VSE, OS/2, Solaris
Redbrick	UNIX, MPP, RISC, Intel, UNISYS OPUS, AIX

single SQL statement. Also, users can access data without knowing its physical location. This process can be optimized so your work gets done in a hurry.

There is a great benefit in starting with a virtual warehouse, since many organizations do not want to replicate information in the physical data warehouse. Some organizations decide to provide both, by creating a data warehouse containing summary-level data, or snapshots taken over time, with access to legacy data for transaction detail.

A virtual data warehouse is easy and fast, but it is not without its problems. Since the queries must compete with the production data transactions, performance can be considerably degraded. Since there is no metadata or no summary data or individual DSS integration or history, all queries must be repeated, causing additional burden on the system. Above all, there is no cleansing or refreshing process involved, causing the queries to be very complex.

CONCLUSIONS

Historically, the implementation of a data warehouse has been limited to the resource constraints and priorities of the IT organization. The task of implementing a data warehouse can be a very big effort, taking a significant amount of time. And, depending on the implementation alternative chosen, this could dramatically impact the time it takes to see a payback, or return on investment. There are pros and cons to any implementation technique and it all comes down to a management decision based on the capabilities of the products and resources that are available.

The selection of a right implementation schema can provide added flexibility for the enterprise, the functional departments, or the workgroups to implement their own data warehouse (or data mart), or take an active part in a central data warehouse implementation, with minimal impact on IT resources. This can take some of the pressure off of IT, and at the same time get user support implemented faster.

In LAN-based data warehouses, departments and workgroups can now assume more of the responsibilities in implementing their systems while at the same time developing a closer working relationship with IT.

There are many approaches to any systems implementation, and data warehousing is no exception. Some of these data warehouse implementation alternatives are:

Stand-Alone Data Mart

This approach enables a department or workgroup to implement a data mart with minimal, or no, impact on the IT organization. It may require some technical skills, but those resources could be managed by the department or workgroup. In this case, the data to populate the data mart is primarily provided by sources other than the IT organization. For example, the department could have its own test or production facility from which it gathers data for input to the data mart. This approach would also apply to those smaller organizations that might not have the support of an IT organization.

Dependent Data Mart

This approach is similar to the stand-alone data mart, except that connectivity to the data sources that are managed by the IT organization is required. These data sources could include the operational data and external data, as well as the global data warehouse. The workgroup decides what data they want to access, the frequency of access, and may even provide the tools and skills necessary to extract the data.

Global Warehouse

The global data warehouse implies that the primary impact and implementation responsibility belong to IT. They would be responsible for an overall architecture to support the enterprise, using host- or LAN-based schemas.

The requirements and implementation priority would be based on the needs of the enterprise as a whole. This global warehouse could be physically centralized or logically centralized and physically distributed over multiple platforms. And, the design could include support for any number of data marts. But, those data marts would not be the same as the stand-alone or dependent data marts previously described. They are data marts designed specifically to be part of the global data warehouse and are populated from it. All of the standard systems implementation alternatives are still available. It is just that now there is more flexibility in choosing which to use. For example, typically top-down means that the global data warehouse is planned and designed before any implementation activities are begun.

Individual departments or workgroups may feel they need to implement a data mart themselves to satisfy an immediate need. Although it would be beneficial to have an overall plan in place, these types of implementations could happen with or without such an overall plan.

Starting with a small confinable project, you could create a manageable solution and realize a quicker return on investment. Product planners, for example, may need to access historical data on product sales, summarized by region. The branch offices may have this data in their operational systems, but the product planners are unable to access it or may find they can access it but it is not in a structure they can work with. In this example, the product planners could create a data mart to satisfy their specific need. A virtual warehouse may also satisfy this type of implementation.

While individual departments or workgroups could implement, manage, and run their host- or LAN-based, stand-alone, or dependent data marts, they could also choose to be integrated into the larger global or enterprise data warehouse at a later time. With the warehouses originally implemented outside any global data warehouse plan, this would be a more difficult approach. However, it could provide benefits to the overall enterprise with economies of scale and common goals while extending the reach and range available to the departments or workgroups.

With either approach, starting small is advised. Starting small may mean targeting a single subject area or business area. For example, a department store chain may have executives, store managers, and buyers who all need access to inventory data. The executives may want to see summaries of inventory across the entire chain, while store managers only want to track inventory in their region, and buyers may need to see both.

4

DATA WAREHOUSE ARCHITECTURE

INTRODUCTION

An architecture is a set of rules or structures providing framework for the overall design of a system or product. There are architectures for specific products, networking architectures, client/server architectures, data architectures, and many others.

Because the fundamentals of a data warehouse architecture are much more important than the specific (and aggressively marketed) tools that will implement the architecture, details of infrastructure will not be addressed here. Many tools currently in vogue will have a short life span. The fundamental need for any warehouse is that it be flexible enough to accommodate the changing data and data analysis needs of the organization. We cannot hope to support the business requirements for evolving data analysis unless the warehouse architecture addresses the key issues related to each of the three major components of the warehouse.

1. *Warehouse Population*—Downloading, from the operational systems, historical events, and related information are needed to isolate and aggregate those events. Volumes are likely to be high, so performance and cost are important considerations for both the warehouse and operational feeds.
2. *Warehouse Administration*—Maintaining the metadata that provides the necessary derivation, exception recognition, integrity, security, controls, and so forth. Simplistically, metadata is a warehouse repository that defines the rules and content of the warehouse and maps this data to the query user on one end and the operational sources of data on the other.
3. *Decision-Support Engine*—Supplying a flexible, responsive, interactive, and easy-to-use method of constructing and executing warehouse queries. Periodic strategic reports should be incorporated into the architecture of the DSS engine.

What Is Today's Data Warehouse?

Aberdeen Group defines a data warehouse as an enterprise-scale database derived from one or more other internal databases and intended for enduser *decision-support* use. A data warehousing solution provides the hardware and software necessary to carry out all aspects of data warehousing: periodic download from heterogeneous corporate databases, *decision-support* data management, enduser data access and analysis support, design, installation, and administration of a data warehouse.

The precise definition of what constitutes a data warehouse is in flux. Simply, a data warehouse has two main components: an information store of historical events (the data warehouse) and the tools to accomplish strategic analysis of that information (a *Decision-Support* System, or DSS). By any definition, however, a comprehensive data warehouse is much more than archived events equipped with a general-purpose front-end query tool.

Strategies for a Data Architecture

Figure 4.1 illustrates various components of a data architecture that must be considered before any data warehouse can be implemented. A data architecture provides this framework by identifying and understanding how the data will move throughout the system and be utilized within the enterprise.

The warehouse's architecture must be cost-effective, adaptable, and easily implemented. Proven and reliable technology should be employed—technology that

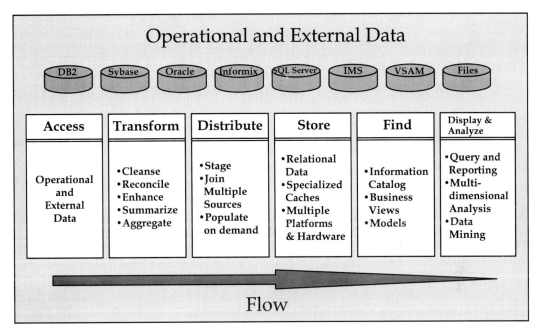

FIGURE 4.1   Data Warehouse Components.

not only supports the current technical infrastructure of the organization but is also flexible for future growth.

Implementing the right technical foundation is critical to the success of a data warehouse. As companies spread out into multiple buildings across cities, states, and even countries, their corporate communications infrastructure must be able to adequately support data collection, distribution, replication, and access. By capitalizing on and enhancing existing networks, companies can realize optimal benefits with minimal investment in new technologies and equipment.

Storage capacity is another critical component. Large amounts of data are often a requirement for the data warehouse. Relational Database Management Systems (RDBMSs) can be an effective way to store large amounts of data. Use of these databases can offer unsurpassed business analysis and management capabilities. Issues to consider for selecting the right storage media and method include data load times, synchronization, recovery, summarization levels, method of data security implementation, data distribution, data access and query speed, and ease of maintenance.

In large organizations, mainframes and parallel processors can ease the burdens of loading, retrieval, translation, and distribution of vast amounts of data. However, some organizations may choose to implement a client/server environment, which can provide convenience and strength at the desktop for accessing, manipulating, and presenting data, and in some instances can be robust enough to house the entire warehouse.

Another consideration in storage is the distribution of data throughout the organization. Data must be put into the hands of the people who are responsible for the achievement of business objectives and strategies—the process managers. It does not make sense to build large centralized corporate warehouses when you are in a distributed business environment. The reverse is also true. Careful attention should be paid to the needs of the organization before designing the data warehouse network.

Information Access

Access to the information is the key technical component. For organizations that are "drowning in data and dying for information," a well-designed data warehouse can give the right people access to the right information at the right time. Tools, typically graphical user interface tools that enable access to the warehouse, should facilitate the retrieval, analysis, and transfer of information to the process managers in the organization.

When properly architected, the data warehouse and its access tools allow users to retrieve information quickly and easily. Access must also be supported by an infrastructure that builds a bridge between the questions process managers ask and the answers within the data warehouse. The data model structure and the user interface must be aligned with strategies to make this a reality.

The primary goal of the architecture is to define a structure that helps customers build effective data warehouse implementations—implementations that give users and applications easy access to data. The architecture identifies and defines the components, interfaces, and protocols that establish this structure. We will discuss these components and structures in the following sections.

WHY A DATA WAREHOUSE ARCHITECTURE?

The data warehouse architecture in Figure 4.2 depicts a framework for understanding data warehousing and how the components of data warehousing fit together. Only the most sophisticated organizations will be able to put together such an architecture the first time out. The data warehouse architecture provides a useful way of determining if the organization is moving toward a reasonable data warehousing framework.

The data warehouse architecture is designed to address a number of problems that users currently face. Before explaining the architecture, it may be helpful to review these problems.

Data/Information Access

In many enterprises, data abounds and is scattered. In many companies, information is hard to decipher. For example, a spreadsheet user needing to get data from a network file server and combine it with data from a local relational database could be extremely difficult.

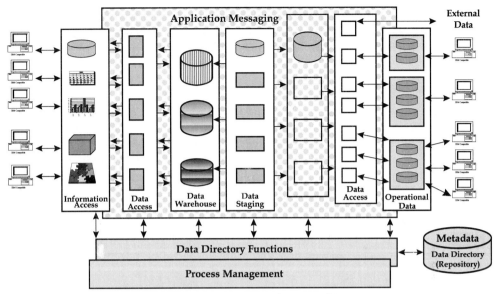

FIGURE 4.2   Data Warehouse Architecture.

Information is a strategic weapon in today's fast-paced global business environment. Companies are realizing that the key to successful competition and growth lies in their abilities to quickly obtain the right information for spotting trends, forecasting market changes, and analyzing performance. And in an effort to better manage the sheer volume of data available, they have invested heavily in information systems and technologies at both the corporate information system level and on individuals' desktops.

Through this proliferation of computers, the users have become technologically literate. Yet, many are not able to penetrate the tangled maze of data sources that exist, let alone extract meaningful information from them. Workgroups also lack effective means to share information easily and fully utilize each individual's strengths. What transcends is an environment of people working as individual islands in a sea of data, each with their own views and analyses.

Unless the users can easily access data, analyze it, and turn it into useful information, their companies will be at a strategic disadvantage. What's needed today is an analysis system that speeds and simplifies access to the data contained in corporate information systems. It must allow users to analyze complex, interrelated data sets and share this information with each other. Finally, it must convert raw data to useful information while maintaining a shareable, updated copy of core enterprise data.

Traditional data-access and analysis tools are no longer adequate for handling the growing complexity of business information needs—a fundamental change in process is required. Today's solution requires an analysis system which can consolidate data from individual spreadsheets, relational databases, and legacy systems for easy access and multidimensional analysis, while maintaining an organization's investment in its existing information systems.

Data Access Factors

Access to data is complicated by a number of factors. The data is scattered, proprietary to its owner, stored in different formats, and created with different access capabilities, rendering it drastically incompatible.

Data on one system has no consistency with data on another in definition, format, or timeliness, making it hard to compare or integrate. In many enterprises, the same data exists in different applications. This leads to even more problems because the question of which system has the "real" data for a piece of business information cannot easily be answered.

Two sets of problems are most often articulated: problems faced by endusers looking for usable information, and problems faced by organizations supporting the data stores and applications.

The users need accurate, up-to-date information to perform their business function. In many organizations getting this information is confusing and time-consuming, and the data may not even be available. When the data is available, it does not easily yield usable information.

The data warehouse architecture is designed to address such problems that customers currently face. In addition, the problems related to data may include:

No Single View of Data

Often, we find it difficult to know what data is available, where it is, and how to get it. Some data is accessible only to the operating departments that use the data. Some data is duplicated or subsetted for specific application needs.

Different User Tools

Different data stores are accessed by different tools. The enduser, who must access data from several sources, must learn several tools. Some of these tools may be supported and maintained by local departments, others by the support organization, posing problems of support and maintenance.

Lack of Consistency

After endusers are allowed access to the data, they must understand what the data means. Are the definitions used to describe it available? Are they identical from one data store to another? They often find that it is in differing, perhaps incompatible formats, making it difficult to combine or compare.

Lack of Useful Historical Capability

The users want or need to aggregate the data. They may also need to keep historical data, a record of the events that caused changes to the data, and other information useful for the support of decision making. Most operational application systems do not actually keep or manage historical information. Those systems generally archive data onto various external media for backup/recovery purposes, which further compounds the problem of accessing historical information.

Conflict between Application Types

Both informational and operational applications may need to access the same data. Because these two types of applications usually have different data designs, different data requirements, and different approaches to accessing data, concurrent use of a shared database is often a problem.

Problems in Administering Data

Data administration problems arise from the multiplicity and complexity of the data, from the corresponding multiplicity and complexity of support tools, and from the lack of an overall structure and administrative control point.

Proliferation of Complex Extract Applications

Because operational data is kept in different types of data stores and endusers increasingly want access to that data, they have to deal with an increasing number of differing applications and interfaces. Most existing informational applications are based upon data which is extracted periodically from operational databases, enhanced in some way, and then totally reloaded into informational data stores.

Data Configurations

The problems must be put in the context of the multiple data configurations that are used to solve real-world problems. Multiple configurations arise for various reasons. For example, there may be a need for data to support both operational applications and large numbers of ad hoc queries. Or it may be necessary to keep historical data for such things as trend analysis, and so forth.

There are a number of typical data configurations that can be used, each with different characteristics. Four are commonly employed.

Single Copy Configuration

Only *one copy* of data (Figure 4.3) is used for both operational and informational applications. Data is originally recorded in the real-time data store. This is sometimes also called the operational data. It contains all the individual, detailed records, where each update overlays the previous entry (history of changes is not preserved).

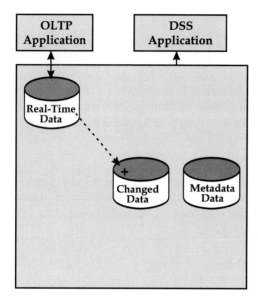

FIGURE 4.3 Single Copy Data Configuration.

In some organizations, all of this data may all reside in a single data store type (e.g., a relational) database. If such is the case, set-oriented processing is greatly enhanced, since relational database management systems have comprehensive set-oriented, non-navigational Application Programming Interfaces (APIs), a catalog of descriptive data, indexing, and an appropriate search engine, thus allowing for efficient processing of a substantial volume of informational requests.

Other organizations may have a more heterogeneous environment. In that case, it may contain different types of data:

- The real-time data may reside on a mixture of non-relational and relational data managers. In its current condition (without undergoing a "cleansing" operation), the data may not be suitable for use by informational requests.

- The changed data store contains the record of all the changes (adds, deletes, updates) to selected real-time data. These changes are detected and materialized by either the applications making the changes or by the underlying database or file managers. The data is kept as a continuum and reflects the history of changes to the appropriate real-time data. This data is timestamped with at least the date-time when the change occurred in real life (i.e., the date-time of the transaction making the change). Since all changes are included, any level of point in time subsetting can be achieved.

- *Metadata*, as used in this text, is descriptive data about an item, where the item can be any type of data (files, reports, work-flow processes, and so forth). The description of such a file (including the description of its records and fields) is the metadata. For informational applications, a subset of the metadata is of interest to endusers: useful when they search for the data, and (once the data is located) useful in understanding its meaning. It should be noted that once they locate this data, endusers are also interested in what available reports/queries exist for this data. The identification of these items is considered part of the metadata as well.

In general, metadata mimics the homogeneity or heterogeneity of the data it describes. Although such things as information models and definition repositories can make the definitions more homogeneous, the present situation is one of heterogeneity. A basic assumption here is that data—and its metadata—will continue to be heterogeneous.

Reconciled Data Configuration

In this configuration (Figure 4.4), a new level is present—the reconciled data. Reconciled data contains detailed records from the real-time level which has been reconciled (cleaned, adjusted, enhanced) so that the data can be used by informational applications. There are at least three different situations when this level becomes necessary.

- The real-time data is residing in heterogeneous data stores; multiple value-added copies of the same data exist; the data is not clean (problems with data types, incomplete records, and so forth).

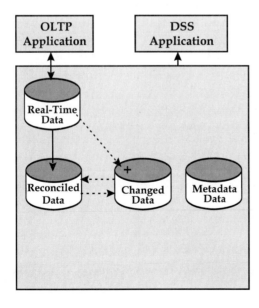

FIGURE 4.4 Reconciled Data Configuration.

As a result, multiple enduser tools may be needed (a single tool may not support all the different data store types in use). If one copy of the data is selected, other users may choose different copies, creating possibly different answers to the same question. Finally, if data needs to be cleansed/reconciled from different sources, the user may not be capable of doing so.

- The real-time data is in a data store whose technology is not suitable for set-oriented processing.

- The real-time data is in a data store whose technology is suitable for set operations, but is being used for non-set-oriented transactions.

In order to meet these needs, one places the real-time data in a *separate data store* whose technology is suitable for set-oriented processing. This is a "clean" (reconciled) set of data representing the real-time data. As in the case of the real-time data, this level contains individual, detailed records. The data store can be materialized via periodic extracts from the real-time store and reloads into the reconciled data store. Reconciliation/cleansing happens in between these two actions via generalized tools or user-written applications. The reconciled level is usually stored in relational data stores and the data may be normalized.

Derived Data Configuration

This configuration provides a derived data level (Figure 4.5) of data store. Derived data has its origin in detailed, actual records and can contain derivations of the detailed records (such as summarizations or joins) or semantic subsets of the detailed

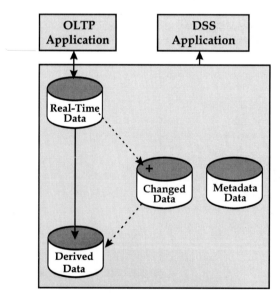

FIGURE 4.5   Derived Data Configuration.

records (based on a variety of criteria, including time). Each set can represent a particular point in time, and the sets can be kept to record history.

The derived data can be used to construct an exact point-in-time copy without quiescing the real-time data updating. It should be noted that point-in-time derived data may also be achieved by other means, such as timestamping the real-time data. However, these other means may not support reconstruction of data as it existed at any point in time.

This configuration is typically used when the data needs of informational applications are fairly well known and the performance needs are high (i.e., the derived data is placed on servers as close to endusers as possible, for example on LAN servers). Reconciliation/cleansing in this configuration is either not needed (the real-time data is "clean"), or if it is needed, it is done via generalized tools or user-written applications before applying it to the derived data.

Hybrid Data Configuration

This configuration introduces the notion of deriving data from the reconciled level (instead of directly from the real-time level). Since both the reconciled and derived levels (Figure 4.6) typically reside on relational data stores, this task is significantly simpler than creating derived data directly from heterogeneous real-time data.

With data existing in multiple configurations, heterogeneity and complexity increase, and the users have an even more difficult time understanding where the data they want is located, and what form it is in.

One of the goals of the data warehouse architecture is to support these various data configurations and to make it easier for users and administrators to perform their tasks in this complex environment.

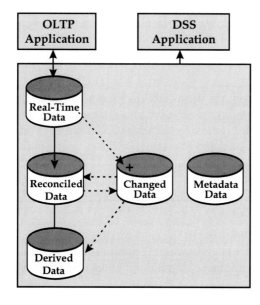

FIGURE 4.6 Hybrid Data Configuration.

ARCHITECTURAL COMPONENTS

Each data warehouse is different, but all are characterized by a handful of key components:

- A data model to define the warehouse contents
- A carefully designed warehouse database, whether hierarchical, relational, or multidimensional
- Numerous utilities for data scrubbing, copy management, data transport, data replication, and cross-platform communication
- A warehouse server optimized for fast reporting and query processing
- A front-end *Decision-Support* System (DSS) for reporting and trend analysis

Before addressing how these features should be provided via an appropriately designed and developed data delivery architecture, it is useful to provide a high-level overview of the various data delivery components. The architecture and its components are graphically depicted in Figure 4.1.

The foundation of any *decision-support* architecture is the data warehouse (Figure 4.2). This is a *relational database*, separate from all operational databases, which is optimized for *decision support*. It is non-volatile, subject oriented, with a schema tuned for OLAP rather than OLTP. It is populated from existing operational systems, which may be based on relational, hierarchical, or sequential database technology.

The client is a set of client tools which allow the enduser to analyze the contents of the data warehouse via graphical, tabular, geographic, and syntactic reports. The ideal client supports both ad hoc analytical functionality, such as drill-down, multidimensional pivoting, and data surfing, as well as executive-level reporting via custom newspapers, dynamic sideshows, intelligent agents, and exception alerts.

Data Warehouse

The data warehouse is the foundation of any *decision-support* application, and its proper design is critical for effective *decision-support* data delivery and performance. *Decision-support* queries, due to their broad scope and analytical intensity, typically require data models to be optimized to improve query performance. In addition to impacting query performance, the data model affects data storage requirements and data loading performance.

Metadata

Metadata is to the data warehouse what the card catalog is to the traditional library. It serves to identify the contents and location of data in the warehouse. In our architecture, we expand the traditional data cataloging function of metadata to include definitions of data from a *decision-support* perspective. Since metadata provides *de-*

cision-support-oriented pointers to warehouse data, metadata is a bridge between the data warehouse and the *decision-support* application. In addition to providing a logical linkage between data and application, metadata can

- pinpoint access to information across the entire data warehouse, and
- enable development of applications which "automatically" update themselves to reflect data warehouse content changes.

There are a three major types of metadata environments:

- *Metadata for the data warehouse* contains descriptive source-system information, transformation information, along with other information essential to making the transition from legacy data to data warehouse information. Other metadata such as scheduling, monitoring, metrics, and profiling information may also be kept in the data warehouse. This metadata can serve dual purposes: during data architecture phase as well as the analysis phase.
- Metadata for the operational data store.
- Metadata for the legacy application.

Operational Data

Corporations have a variety of On-Line Transaction Processing (OLTP) systems such as financial, order entry, work scheduling, and point-of-sale systems which create operational data. This data is part of the corporate infrastructure and is detailed, non-redundant, and updatable and reflects current period values. In contrast, data required by *decision-support* analysts is often summarized, has a lengthy time horizon, is redundant to the support of varying data views, and is non-updatable. In order to provide data to *decision-support* analysts, relevant operational data is extracted from OLTP systems, cleansed, encoded, and summarized. After being transformed into a format suitable for *decision support*, the data is uploaded into the data warehouse.

Operational Databases

The source of the operational data is generally from interactive on-lines and the operational database is designed with great care. The data warehouse is not built to support the functional process of the enterprise. It is built to facilitate the use of information. The source of data for the data warehouse is the operational database, which is optimized for the extraction process. In fact, the data warehouse can only be updated by the operational database; it is a read-only resource.

Unlike the operational database, the normal-form rules do not apply and any denormalization in the design that will facilitate the information-gathering process is acceptable. Therefore, fields containing summarized and other forms of derived data are perfectly acceptable. "Most access of the warehouse is at the higher levels of summarization. These levels contain less data than the lower levels do and are indexed on many fields. The lower levels of data are indexed on only a few fields" (Inmon and Kelley, 1993, p. 38). Furthermore, the design is iterative in nature.

Since a warehouse does not support a suite of update applications, it is not dependent on a predefined data structure. Because the warehouse assumes the predominance of ad hoc usage, design changes can be made as the need becomes apparent. Therefore, there is minimal impact resulting from design-change requests because only the interface between the two databases is affected.

A DATA WAREHOUSE ARCHITECTURAL MODEL

A data warehouse architecture is a way of representing the overall structure of data, communication, processing, and presentation that exists for enduser computing within the enterprise. Each data warehouse is different, but all are characterized by common key components. At its most basic level, a data warehouse works by separating the regular data processing requirements of production applications from the ad hoc data processing exercise carried out by users.

Production applications, such as payroll, accounts payable, product purchasing, and inventory control, are designed for On-Line Transaction Processing (OLTP). Such applications gather detailed data from day-to-day operations. On the other hand, data warehouse applications are designed to support the users' ad hoc data requirements, an activity recently dubbed On-Line Analytical Processing (OLAP). These include applications such as forecasting, profiling, summary reporting, and trend analysis.

Production databases are updated continuously either by hand or via OLTP applications. In contrast, a warehouse database is updated from operational systems on a periodic basis, usually during off-hours. As OLTP data accumulates in production databases, it is periodically extracted, filtered, and then loaded into a dedicated warehouse server that is accessible to users. As the warehouse is populated, it must be restructured: tables denormalized, data cleansed of errors and redundancies, and new fields and keys added to reflect the needs of users for sorting, combining, and summarizing data.

Once the data warehouse architecture is in place, there are two primary methods for populating the warehouse with data:

- Bulk downloads, in which the entire database is refreshed on a periodic basis.
- Change-based replication, in which only the differences are copied or replicated between OLTP and OLAP servers.

To improve query performance, warehouse databases often include summarized and predefined views in the database. Additional information, such as stock averages, credit information, and other summaries from external sources may also be included in the warehouse.

Therefore, the data warehouse architectural model is made up of a number of interconnected parts (shown in Figure 4.2):

- Operational Database/External Database Layer
- Information-Access Layer
- Data-Access Layer
- Data Directory (Metadata) Layer
- Process Management Layer
- Application Messaging Layer
- Data Warehouse Layer
- Data Staging Layer

Information-Access Layer

The information-access layer of the data warehouse architecture is the layer that the enduser deals with directly. In particular, it represents the tools that the enduser normally uses day to day, for example, Excel, Lotus 1-2-3, Focus, Access, SAS. This layer also includes the hardware and software involved in displaying and printing reports, spreadsheets, graphs, and charts for analysis and presentation. Over the past two decades, the information-access layer has expanded enormously, especially as endusers have moved to the desktop.

Today, more and more sophisticated tools exist on the desktop for manipulating, analyzing, and presenting data; however, there are significant problems in making the raw data contained in operational systems available easily and seamlessly to enduser tools. One of the keys to this is to find a common data language that can be used throughout the enterprise.

Data-Access Layer

The data-access layer of the data warehouse architecture is involved with allowing the information-access layer to talk to the operational layer. In the network world today, the common data language that has emerged is Structured Query Language (SQL). Originally, SQL was developed by IBM as a query language, but over the last 20 years it has become the de facto standard for data interchange.

One of the key breakthroughs of the last few years has been the development of a series of data-access "filters" such as EDA/SQL that make it possible to use SQL to access nearly all DBMSs and data file systems, relational or non-relational. These filters make it possible for state-of-art information access tools to access data stored on database management systems that are 20 years old.

The data-access layer not only spans different DBMSs and file systems on the same hardware; it also spans manufacturers and network protocols as well. One of the keys to a data warehousing strategy is to provide endusers with "universal data access." Universal data access means that, theoretically at least, endusers, regardless of location or information-access tool, should be able to access any or all of the data in the enterprise that is necessary for them to do their job.

The data-access layer then is responsible for interfacing between information-access tools and operational databases. In some cases, this is all that certain endusers need. However, in general, organizations are developing a much more sophisticated scheme to support data warehousing.

Data Directory (Metadata) Layer

In order to provide for universal data access, it is absolutely necessary to maintain some form of data directory or repository of metadata information. Metadata is the data about data within the enterprise. Record descriptions in a COBOL program are metadata. So are DIMENSION statements in a FORTRAN program, or SQL CREATE statements.

In order to have a fully functional warehouse, it is necessary to have a variety of metadata available: data about the enduser views of data and data about the operational databases. Ideally, endusers should be able to access data from the data warehouse (or from the operational databases) without having to know where that data resides or the form in which it is stored.

Process Management Layer

The process management layer is involved in scheduling the various tasks that must be accomplished to build and maintain the data warehouse and data directory information. The process management layer can be thought of as the scheduler or the high-level job control for the many processes (procedures) that must occur to keep the data warehouse up to date.

Application Messaging Layer

The application messaging layer has to do with transporting information around the enterprise computing network. Application messaging is also referred to as "middleware," but it can involve more that just networking protocols. Application messaging, for example, can be used to isolate applications, operational or informational, from the exact data format on either end. Application messaging can also be used to collect transactions or messages and deliver them to a certain location at a certain time. Application messaging is the transport system underlying the data warehouse.

Operational Data/External Data

Operational systems process data to support critical operational needs. In order to do that, operational databases have been historically created to provide an efficient processing structure for a relatively small number of well-defined business transactions. Because of the limited focus of operational systems, the databases designed to support operational systems are difficult to use to access the data for other management or informational purposes. This difficulty in accessing operational data is amplified by the fact that many operational systems are often 10 to 15 years old. The age of some of these systems means that the data-access technology available to obtain operational data is itself dated.

Clearly, the goal of data warehousing is to free the information that is locked up in the operational databases and to mix it with information from other, often external, sources of data. Increasingly, large organizations are acquiring additional data from outside the databases. This information includes demographic, econometric, competitive, and purchasing trends. The so-called "information superhighway" is providing access to more data resources every day.

Data Warehouse (Physical) Layer

The (core) data warehouse is where the actual data used primarily for informational uses occurs. In some cases, one can think of the data warehouse simply as a logical or virtual view of data. In many instances, the data warehouse may not actually involve storing data.

In a physical data warehouse, in some instances, many copies of operational and or external data, are actually stored in a form that is easy to access and is highly flexible. Increasingly, data warehouses are stored on client/server platforms, but they are often stored on mainframes as well.

Data Staging Layer

The final component of the data warehouse architecture is data staging. Data staging is also called copy management or replication management, but in fact, it includes all of the processes necessary to select, edit, summarize, combine, and load data warehouse and information-access data from operational and/or external databases.

Data staging often involves complex programming, but increasingly data warehousing tools are being created that help in this process. Data staging may also involve data quality analysis programs and filters that identify patterns and data structures within existing operational data.

IMPLEMENTATION OPTIONS

There are a number of different options that may be considered in moving to data warehousing. These include

- Rehosting mainframe applications
- Two-tier architecture using mainframe as a server
- Three-tier data warehouse architecture
- Four-tier data warehouse architecture

Rehosting Mainframe Applications

This means taking existing applications and moving them to microprocessor-based servers. The servers may run under UNIX, Windows NT, or OS/2. Tools, such as DB2, IMS, and MicroFocus COBOL, can run without major changes on the new host processor. The operating environment may be DOS, Windows, OS/2, or UNIX.

Porting legacy code to low-cost servers is a proven, low-risk approach to reducing the cost of computing. This is specifically attractive for data warehousing environments because the existing legacy data and databases can be ported to lower-cost platforms.

In the one-tier architecture, the data warehouse, DSS engine, and DSS client all reside on the same hardware platform. This configuration is ideal for the isolated salesperson who needs *decision-support* capabilities against a small database of customer information. You can place all components of the DSS architecture on a laptop and function effectively, even without reliable dial-up or LAN access.

A sophisticated partitioning and distribution strategy is necessary to create the individual data sets for each user. For example, users are limited in practice to analyzing a data set of no more than 500 megabytes in volume, due primarily to storage constraints. Performance will always be inferior to that which can be achieved with a multitiered strategy.

For this reason, the one-tier topology cannot be considered a robust choice for enterprise-wide data access, and other alternatives need to be considered.

Two-Tier Architecture Using Mainframe Server

This simpler architecture focuses the performance, integrity, and administration of the warehouse in the more traditional "glass house." This option incorporates a front-end client component and a back-end server component that utilizes existing host computers as database servers.

The function of the front-end applications is to hide the complexity of the existing mainframe systems. This approach is attractive because it utilizes existing legacy systems as database servers and requires minimal investment in additional hardware and software. However, two-tier architecture is not scalable and cannot support large numbers of on-line endusers without additional software modifications.

The two-tier model requires SQL to be hidden beneath the Graphical User Interface (GUI), or executed as stored procedures in the RDBMS. An Application Programming Interface (API) is required for communications between the PC client and database server.

This approach does encourage the development of large front-end systems, where the majority of the new processing is done on the desktop workstations. In order to support adequate response time for increased numbers of users, the processing and data-access capabilities of the host computers must be increased or they may be replaced with less-expensive multiprocessors.

The two-tier topology runs into significant performance problems associated with PC and network limitations. When large numbers of users access and query the database at the same time, serious performance degradations occur. Moving large amounts of data over the network for PC-based analysis causes congestion on the network, not to mention the need for substantial PC capacity.

In the two-tier topology, the data warehouse resides on a dedicated RDBMS server, while the DSS engine and DSS client reside on the client hardware. This approach offers much more scalability and performance than the one-tier model, at the cost of a dedicated server. In cases where a local area network is available, this is generally preferable to the single-tier model.

Three-Tier Data Warehouse Architecture

The three-tier architecture differs from the two-tier architecture by strictly enforcing a logical separation of the graphical user interface, business logic, and data. The logic can be run on the same server as the data warehouse or physically on another server, as shown in Figure 4.7. This topology enables complex yet efficient business analyses on a high-performance *decision-support* server—separating the user presentation and the data.

The typical data warehouse architecture consists of three tiers. At the base is a relational or object-oriented DBMS and a specially designed database (the warehouse). In the middle tier are the programs, gateways, and networks that feed the data warehouse from operational data and other sources. The top tier consists of the reports and query tools that actually deliver the value to your business people.

The three-tier architecture recognizes the existence of three distinct layers of software—presentation, core application logic, and data—and places each of these layers on its own processor. The advantage of this approach is the ability it provides to offload processor-intensive tasks from the client workstation, thus allowing organizations to utilize "thin clients" (that is, clients with lesser amounts of memory and

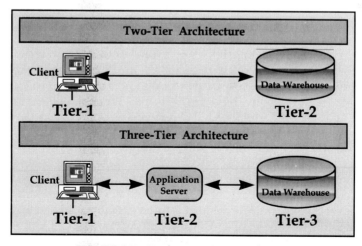

FIGURE 4.7   Implementation Topologies.

processor power). This advantage in scalability must be weighed against the greater cost and complexity of the solution.

Putting the data closer to the enduser can simplify security, improve response time, and reduce the load on the central warehouse processor. Costs are imposed as the warehouse is maintained and data must be replicated to the local servers. With this topology, users are not required to know where or how the data is stored, or the complexities of databases to use the applications and it also simplifies SQL generation and optimizes performance.

Some data may be easily partitioned to a single location and other data may have to be replicated to all local servers. For example, invoices and customers may belong to a regional office, but the products do not. Some users will require access to "all" data, so the central site must either furnish an "all-locations" location or provide access to the central warehouse. It may also be expedient to reduce the volume on local servers by limiting the amount of event history stored at the local level.

The DSS engine will be more complex because it must determine, for each request, whether the data is local or central. If central access is required, it may make sense to deliver data to the local server and then to the enduser. Delivering "next level" detail to the user means that drill-down does not require an expensive research of the central warehouse.

The other disadvantage is that three-tier architectures necessitate some local data administration. Data design at the local level may be controlled, recovered, and optimized in very different ways compared to the central warehouse. In general, the data will be "read-only" but the local system could add local data and applications.

The three-tier architecture is widely used for data warehousing today. Source data on host computers resides at tier-3. Data and business rules that are shared across the enterprise, such as target databases for data warehouses, are stored on high-speed database servers at tier-2. Graphically oriented enduser interfaces run on LAN-based PCs or workstations at tier-1.

Four-Tier Data Warehouse Architecture

It may be advantageous to deliver some data to the desktop, either by replicating from the local warehouse or targeting the query to a desktop database instead of, or in addition to, the screen. "What if" processing can be accomplished without polluting the data in the local or central warehouses. Endusers are usually made responsible for their own desktop data recovery.

It is important to note that there is no single "correct" data warehousing architecture. For some enterprises, the two-tier approach is an attractive solution because it minimizes the cost and complexity of building a data warehouse. For other organizations that require greater performance and scalability, the three-tier architecture may be more appropriate. In this architecture, data extracted from legacy systems is cleansed, transformed, and stored in high-speed database servers, which are used as the target database for front-end data access.

Organizations that have more modest requirements may choose to build small data marts, which utilize a LAN-based architecture.

DECISION-SUPPORT ARCHITECTURE

In this section, we detail key enduser requirements for *decision-support* applications, the components of a robust *decision-support* architecture which addresses these enduser requirements, and the functional characteristics of each architectural component. This is an architecture that requires little or no application maintenance, is extensible as new data sources are added, provides excellent query performance, supports complex filtering criteria, allows flexible ad hoc navigation and analysis, and is robust enough to support mission-critical data delivery applications. This architecture leverages investments in existing SQL-based relational databases in order to provide On-Line Analytical Processing (OLAP) capabilities. The result is a metadata-driven, scalable OLAP environment suitable for enterprise-wide *decision support* against very large databases.

Decision-Support Definitions

Before discussing the *decision-support* architecture in detail, there are several terms which require definition.

- *Facts* are variables or measures, normally stored as numeric fields, which are the focus of the *decision-support* investigation. Examples of facts include sales, revenues, marketing expenses, and so forth.
- *Metrics* are analytical measures calculated from facts at runtime. Many metrics may be derived from a few facts. Attributes represent conceptual (normally character-based) metric qualifiers which can be used for filtering and analysis of information. For example, attributes of the metric sales might include city, state, store, day, month, year, product line, vendor, color, and event. These attributes are represented by physical columns in the database.
- *Dimensions* are logical groupings of attributes with a common atomic key relationship. Three of the most common dimensions to be found in the data warehouse are product, location, and time. The attributes city, state, and store are all associated with the location dimension, while day, month, and year are all attributes of the time dimension.

The Data Warehouse

The proper design of the data warehouse calls for a holistic engineering methodology. Assuming that the choice of server platform hardware and RDBMS software has already been made, the architect is still faced with the task of designing a schema which balances the conflicting requirements of (1) analytical functionality, (2) query performance, and (3) database maintainability. In truth, the choices of hardware, software, and schema are actually intertwined

There are two primary types of tables to be stored within the data warehouse: fact tables and dimension tables. *Fact tables* contain multiple fact columns, related by a common multidimensional key. In other words, the primary key of the fact table will generally consist of attributes from more than one dimension. Dimension tables contain multiple attribute columns (normally character-based information), related to the same atomic attribute (i.e., in the same dimension). The primary attribute keys are almost always numeric integers, since these yield superior indices for query performance.

Analytical richness is normally achieved by incorporating additional facts and attributes into the data warehouse, or by storing facts at a more atomic level. For example, a data warehouse which contains sales for every item, in every store, on every day offers greater richness than one containing sales by region, month, and department. The richness of the data warehouse can also be enhanced by adding additional attributes to the dimension tables, thus providing new access paths to the data along with additional consolidation hierarchies.

Increasing the atomicity and dimensionality of the data warehouse creates a number of maintenance and performance challenges. There are three general techniques for reengineering the data warehouse to improve performance: *summarization, denormalization,* and *partitioning.*

Summarization

Summarization is achieved by creating partially redundant fact tables within the data warehouse. These tables contain the same facts as the atomic-level tables, but with all data aggregated to a higher-level primary key. Dramatic performance improvements result from the ability of the DSS engine to repath queries to more aggregate fact tables at runtime, thus avoiding multiple aggregate and sort operations.

One of the most powerful performance optimization techniques is the use of multiple, summarized primary data tables. Data is typically loaded into the data warehouse from operational systems at an atomic level of detail. Most *decision-support* queries however, require aggregate-level, consolidated information and not atomic detail. If processed against the atomic level, these queries require the retrieval of many records to yield aggregate information, and require that the data be mathematically summarized at query runtime, further impeding query performance.

To improve query performance, data can be presummarized and stored along frequently accessed consolidation hierarchies. It is impossible to presummarize atomic detail if the consolidation hierarchy is not known. Fortunately, these consolidation hierarchies are often identical to the attribute hierarchies within a dimension. In fact, for best query performance, primary data tables should exist at each attribute intersection across all attribute hierarchies.

At first glance, the addition of summary tables may appear to dramatically increase data storage requirements. However, since summary tables get progressively smaller as one approaches the most aggregate level of the attribute hierarchy, only a 20–100 percent increase in data storage is typically required to physically store all attribute-hierarchy-defined consolidation paths. This modest increase in disk storage typically yields a two-to-tenfold increase in query performance over non-consolidated data warehouse designs.

Denormalization

Denormalization, in this context, refers to the replacement of an attribute column with multiple fact columns on the fact table. This results in the juxtaposition of information within a fact table so that the overall number of records is reduced by increasing the number of columns per record. Denormalization simplifies the primary key of the fact table at the cost of a sophisticated fact column encoding scheme. Performance is improved by grouping a number of related records together so that they can be retrieved with less disk I/O, decreasing the index size and decreasing the number of records which must be scanned in order to locate the appropriate information.

Denormalization improves performance by either reducing the number of joins required during query execution, or reducing the number of rows to be retrieved from the primary data table.

There are three principal denormalization techniques:

1. Include Descriptors in Primary Data Tables: Rather than placing ID descriptors in a separate descriptor table, descriptors may be placed in the primary data table in order to eliminate a join.

2. Include Child Records in Parent Record: By adding columns to the primary data table, child records can be added to the parent record, thereby allowing all child records to be retrieved with every parent record retrieval. This technique improves performance by eliminating a join and removing child record criteria from the WHERE clause. However, query flexibility is impaired since child record attributes are added to columns of the parent record and can no longer be used as filtering criteria. This technique works best when there are a fixed and relatively small number of child records.

3. Include Most Recent Child Record in Parent Record: In some systems, the most recent child record is used much more frequently than other child records. In these cases, adding the most recent child record to the parent record can improve performance.

Partitioning

Partitioning refers to the segmentation of a fact table into smaller fragments for easier management and/or better performance. Partitioning may be conservative or non-conservative. Conservative partitioning schemes simply disperse 100 percent of the records between a number of different fragments. Non-conservative schemes resemble extract routines, in that they actually create redundant fragments which constitute a subset of the contents of the original fact table. When these fragments are distributed, we have a powerful data marting scheme. Partitioning improves performance by allowing queries to be redirected to a fact table fragment which is much smaller than the corresponding master table.

A final technique used to improve query performance is data partitioning. In a partitioned data model, multiple tables are created to store atomic-level data. Partitioning of large atomic data tables into multiple smaller tables provides the following advantages:

1.   Query response time is improved.
2.   Incremental data backup and recovery are accelerated.
3.   Time required to load into indexed tables is decreased.

Disadvantages of partitioning include:

1.   Joins and unions are required to retrieve related data from multiple tables.
2.   More intelligent query generation is required to determine which tables contain user-requested data.
3.   Additional metadata is required to describe the partitioned warehouse.

Naming Conventions

All column names referring to the same attribute or metric should be consistent throughout the warehouse. While perhaps obvious, name consistency is extremely important for understanding data. Consistency is absolutely required when using query generators which dynamically determine join columns based on column name.

DSS Engine

The DSS engine is the heart of the DSS architecture. It transforms data requests into SQL queries to be sent to the data warehouse and formats query results for presentation. To support these functions, the DSS engine includes a dynamic SQL query generator, a multidimensional data analysis engine, a mathematical equation processor, and a cross-tabulation engine.

The role of the DSS engine is to decouple the DSS client from the data warehouse. At the heart of the DSS engine is a dynamic SQL query generator which analyzes filters, reports, and metadata at runtime to create a query execution plan (many SQL statements may be required) optimized for the current data warehouse. The DSS engine plays an essential role in the construction of filters, since this activity normally requires users to navigate a complex web of multi-attribute hierarchies while selecting specific attribute elements. Since there are innumerable ways to combine two related attributes within a given dimension, it is important to provide a flexible, metadata-driven criteria selection tool which can be quickly reconfigured. This, in turn, requires a powerful and flexible DSS engine.

The DSS engine should support OLAP (On-line Analytical Processing) requests, such as, "Show me this year's versus last year's market share comparisons," which may require an entire sequence of queries to be performed in order to extract the proper results from the data warehouse. Also, certain attribute relationships may require the generation of correlated subqueries in place of simple joins to ensure that the proper information is returned.

Another key role performed by the DSS engine is the transparent support of performance-optimized data warehouse structures, such as summarized, denormalized, or partitioned fact tables. This requires that additional layers of processing be performed by the DSS engine in order to transform the performance optimized structures back into normal views for final extraction by the DSS client. Properly implemented, these structures result in performance drastically superior to that which might be obtained via conventional normalized schemas.

The Data Access Engine (DAE) provides linkage between the client and the data warehouse. In essence, the DAE is a transmission mechanism between the multidimensional DSS client, which has been optimized for enduser clarity and analytical sophistication, and the relational data warehouse, which has been optimized for data storage and maintenance. Whenever an enduser requests an analysis, the DSS engine performs an intricate set of transformations, converting a multidimensional request ("Display sales by vendor and color in Chicago last month") into a relational query valid for a particular data warehouse schema, then converting a relational result set back into a multidimensional report.

The key to application maintainability and performance is to perform this intricate set of transforms at runtime, dynamically generating an execution plan which is optimized for a given reporting request and database schema. In order to do this, the DSS engine reads a metadata map of the data warehouse. This metadata serves as a sort of card catalog, providing the DSS engine with an index of attributes, dimensions, metrics, hierarchies, tables, and columns within the data warehouse.

The DSS Client

The primary role of the DSS client is to provide the enduser with a powerful, intuitive, graphical tool for creating new analyses and navigating the data warehouse. This requires the establishment of a multidimensional analytical framework which closely matches the business attributes with which the user is familiar. The DSS client must then provide the user with tools to create and manipulate the fundamental *decision-support* objects: *filters, templates, reports,* and *agents.*

The template determines the facts and metrics to be viewed, along with their granularity, multidimensional orientation, and formatting. Reports may possess hundreds of properties. They may be grids, graphs, maps, text, animations, synthesized speech, spreadsheets, electronic newsletters, or compound application documents. An example of a simple report would be "Weekly Sales by Store," formatted as a plain table.

The filter performs the qualification function, narrowing the amount of information to be viewed so that it is intelligible. Users may wish to construct filters using certain attribute elements, metrics, dates, date ranges, and/or wildcard formulas. Sophisticated filters will probably require the use of set theory operators such as union, intersection, and not. A typical filter might be: "Display information concerning sales of red and yellow towels in the New England area, except for Boston and Hartford, which occurred during the month of December." Certain filters are best constructed by combining other filters together.

The report is created by combining a template with a filter. The filter selects a certain location in the *n*-dimensional state space of the data warehouse. The template is the viewing instrument (information probe) for assessing the terrain.

Once a report has been created, there are a number of operations which can be supported for interactive *decision support* against the data warehouse. The most well known is drill-down, where the user selects a subset of the information in the current analysis and views its constituent elements. Another feature users desire is multidimensional pivot, which in this case is nothing more than the ad hoc redefinition of a template property at runtime. The template/filter duality make possible a third mode of ad hoc analysis, which we call data surfing. This effect is achieved by allowing the user to drop a new filter or report onto an existing report. The result is a new window into the data warehouse which has been horizontally shifted. For example, instead of viewing the "Profit & Loss" template for California, we now view it for Florida.

By combining libraries of filters and templates with drill-down, pivoting, and data surfing, the user can engage in a stream-of-consciousness navigation of the enterprise. Each of the following steps results in a different view of the data:

1. Display the Profitability Report for all stores nationwide.
2. Focus on high-volume stores.
3. In California.
4. During major fall promotional campaigns.
5. Subtract the new stores.
6. Zoom in on the advertised items.
7. Switch to Inventory.
8. Switch to Sales.
9. Return to Profitability.
10. Sort by Profits.
11. Drill down on our most profitable three stores.
12. Break down items by Department.
13. Drill down on the most profitable Departments to view Profits by Class and Store.

An agent is essentially a collection of reports, scheduled to execute with some periodicity. This approach elegantly leverages the filter and template object model, allowing users to create their own *decision-support* applications without custom programming. Agents can be used to gather frequently used information for an executive, or to generate alerts notifying users when something has gone awry. The range of functionality of an agent is limited only by the library of templates which can be embedded within it. Likewise, the intelligence of the agent is directly related to the sophistication of its filters.

For maximum benefit, it is important to allow for the sharing of filters, templates, reports, and agents over the network. This creates significant workgroup leverage by allowing changes to propagate throughout an organization instantly. For example, one user can create a filter to track items which are on sale. Another can create a filter to catalog all test markets. A third can create a filter which selects out days when it rained last year. The fourth can then combine the filters created by associates to perform an analysis of the items on sale in all test markets during the days when it did not rain last year. Without object sharing, this might take hours. With shared objects, it takes seconds.

Certain *decision-support* systems are impossible to construct or maintain without the proper shared object model.

In summary, the *decision-support* architecture contains three holistically related components: the data warehouse, DSS client, and the DSS engine. The capabilities of the DSS engine determine the structures which can be supported in the data warehouse, as well as the features available in the DSS client. For maximum performance, maintainability, and feature set, it is essential that the primary DSS objects (filters, templates, reports, agents) be propagated throughout the architecture and shared across the network.

SUMMARY AND CONCLUSIONS

Data warehousing is a technology of potentially enormous worth to an enterprise. It is, however, fragile. If IT has too much input, the business user will be deterred. If the facilities are not linked to business requirements, the system will fall into disuse. If dollar returns are not measured, the system cannot be justified except as a luxury. If executives delegate its use, the potential cultural gain is lost. If, however, the system is well justified, carefully implemented, and driven by business intelligence, data warehousing is a tool that can give leaders leverage on the pressing challenges they confront.

Over time, the specification of the interfaces and protocols of the data warehouse architecture will evolve to expand the scope of support in the following areas:

- Type of accessible stores
  - Files
  - Traditional databases
  - Relational databases
  - Object databases

- Type of data supported
  - Formatted
  - Non-formatted (image, audio, video)
  - Compound (collections of data of differing types)
  - Complex (highly structured data with many relationships)

- Type of access interface (view of data)
  - Traditional APIs
  - Relational APIs (SQL)
  - Object APIs
  - Other APIs

The evolution of the data warehouse architecture will in turn expand the scope of the types of applications that can be served by the data warehouse framework.

5

DATA WAREHOUSE TECHNOLOGIES

INTRODUCTION

One of the challenges of information processing in the 1990s is how to process larger and larger databases, containing increasingly complex data, without sacrificing response time. A data warehousing system provides users with business intelligence for decision making. Data warehousing is a new generation of data access, manipulation, and presentation technologies that allow users to answer business questions using internal and external data.

We can think of a data warehousing system as providing business intelligence tools that process and transform warehouse data into business information. At present, a majority of the warehouse data is acquired (and integrated) from multiple internal operational systems and external information providers. In the future, warehouse databases will often contain data from other sources. For example, as use of the Internet and the World Wide Web increases, Web servers are proving to be a valuable source of data for warehousing systems.

According to a recent survey, a large percentage of the data warehouses have fewer than 50 users. Building a data warehouse is a time-consuming and expensive task. The promise of data warehousing is information access for the decision-making majority, not just a handful of users. If data warehousing only meets the needs of a small user community, this initiative will not fulfill that promise, just as *decision-support* systems failed in the past to achieve broad enterprise acceptance. A scalable architecture goes well beyond performance issues. Maintenance, security, and flexibility are equally important.

The client/server architecture gives organizations the opportunity to deploy specialized servers which are optimized for handling specific data management problems.

Lotus Notes is a specialized client/server data server that manages enterprise-wide document storage and flow. Other types of servers are frequently used to manage complex data like images or simple data like electronic mail. One of the major concerns for any enterprise is how to ensure that data remains integrated and accessible to a wide variety of servers.

Until recently, organizations have tried to target Relational Database Management Systems (RDBMSs) for the complete spectrum of database applications. It is becoming increasingly apparent that there are major categories of database applications which are not suitably serviced by relational database systems.

The Internet is a model of how *unstructured* text and image information can be accessed and collaboration can occur. The enterprise must adopt a similar model to providing *structured* data access and collaborative information sharing. The promise of data warehousing is fulfilled only when information is used by the decision-making majority.

DEFINING THE TECHNICAL ARCHITECTURE

Once the requirements have been defined, a technical architecture that is economical, flexible, and able to be incrementally implemented must be developed. This architecture should be designed using proven technology that supports the organization's current and future technical strategy. The architecture must include the following characteristics.

The Right Technology

Deploying the correct technology to do the right job will be critical to the success. Here are some examples.

- *Mainframes and Massively Parallel Processors*. Large organizations may need to use the mainframe for retrieving, translating, loading, and distributing large quantities of data. Parallel processors may also be needed for storage and retrieval of data.

- *Client*/Server *Environments*. This technology offers power at the desktop for data access, formatting, and presentation tools. Data that should be distributed can be on this platform. If the size of the data requirements is appropriate, the entire data warehouse can reside in this environment.

- *Relational Database Management Systems (RDBMSs)*. Today, RDBMSs are the most efficient and effective means of storing and retrieving vast amounts of data. Designed appropriately, the database can offer unsurpassed power for organizations to analyze and manage their business. Critical RDBMS issues relate to data load times, synchronization, recovery, summarization levels, method of data security implementation, data distribution, data access and query speed, and ease of maintenance.

- *Communications.* Many companies are large, diverse, and dispersed. Existing networks should be used, with enhancements made only where necessary to deliver optimal results.

The Information Highway (Data Collection, Translation, Loading, and Distribution)

The design and implementation of the information highway will determine whether the effort succeeds or fails. Critical issues are synchronization, mapping, timing, data transfer, and level of maintenance effort. A design approach which is sensible, flexible, and economical will provide a maintenance-free approach to addressing these issues.

Access to Information

Most organizations are *drowning in data and dying for information.* The infrastructure defined by the architecture must accomplish this objective in an economical, achievable, and realistic manner. The access tools should support quick and easy retrieval and transfer of information to the clients and their applications—empowering their self-sufficiency. The information repository and the access tools should be designed to eliminate the need for authorized clients to understand the complex data model, translate the data, and work through an extensive learning curve.

Enterprise Data Model

Wise institutions look at information about their users across the enterprise. Unfortunately, many organizations do not follow this model. For example, some organizations still provide access to customer information residing in disparate mainframe applications by using inflexible and costly mainframe-based reporting tools. The enterprise data model should reengineer the data collected from the legacy application so that all customer relationships, products, services, and profitability can be viewed consistently and accurately.

   The correct design of the data model will ensure success and provide a competitive advantage for years to come.

The Data Model: A Blueprint for Success

The enterprise data model provides the architectural framework for constructing future systems and databases. A picture of the interrelationships among the organization's data, the model is based on the entities of the business and their interactions, rather than on the organization's dynamic processes or functions. Consolidation and integration of information across legacy applications must be supported by the model, providing the blueprint for the development of the data warehouse components. When complete, the data model provides the criteria to evaluate the completeness and consistency of a design that will allow the migration of legacy information to one common data structure.

   Developing a data model involves analyzing and defining the entities identified during the definition process. After the enterprise model is built, the model must be validated and data must be mapped from legacy applications to the model, with more validation to follow.

A well-designed data model will provide the following functions:

- Answer the business users' questions and support the key business processes.
- Recognize the similarities and differences in data stored in legacy systems and extract only pertinent data from these systems.
- Control the collection and loading processes of the legacy systems.
- Map the key business processes back to customer needs.

Map the Data

The data mapping process is a means of validating, defining, and expanding the enterprise data model. This bottom-up process maps and defines every data element (attribute) from all sources of data from legacy applications and external sources. Issues that should be addressed during data mapping include, but are not limited to:

- *Integration of data across applications*: Most organizations have redundant data elements that are called the same thing but are defined differently, or that have different names but have the same meaning. These data elements are researched and adjusted.
- *Resolution of idiosyncrasies of legacy applications*: Mapping of data with various record types, clauses, and default values presents challenges for data collection and loading. The rules for the data transformation process are loaded in the Repository Manager. Application and business experts must participate in identification and design sessions and provide the necessary background to complete this process.
- *Synchronization of loading and determination of frequency*: Data warehouse synchronization is a key to success. The Repository Manager must provide the capability, with supporting interfaces, to not only document but also control the collection and loading process and its frequency.

Validate Data Mapping

After the data mapping exercises, there is another validation process required to ensure that information is going to the proper place in the data model. During this phase, the analysis sessions are reassembled to review each entity and attribute of the data model to confirm its value. This is a critical step in assuring user acceptance. Any modifications that are needed should be made to the model following this validation session.

Implement the Data Warehouse

The data warehouse is the physical collection of information from existing legacy systems that consolidates historical information and translates information into a uniform format that makes the data available for information sharing, reporting, trending analysis, and *decision support*. The warehouse contains pertinent data modeled for the "knowledge worker." Since all business functions performed by the organization should be supported by the warehouse, data is integrated across all lines of business, products, and services.

It's important to implement the warehouse in an incremental fashion. By getting the first phase up and running quickly, users tend to be more supportive and positive about the new system. If implementation takes too long, users often become frustrated and impatient.

Data Directory (Metadata Repository)

The data directory should to be used as a resource tool for gathering information about the data available in the data warehouse. The data directory is organized much like other databases within the warehouse.

The information presented within the data directory, for any table, is broken down in one of two ways. You can either look at the table at a detailed level or you can view the fields within the table. If you are unfamiliar with a particular table, then review the detailed level first.

In order to have a fully functional warehouse, it is necessary to have a variety of metadata available: data about the enduser views of data, and data about the operational databases. Ideally, endusers should be able to access data from the data warehouse (or from the operational databases) without having to know where that data resides or the form in which it is stored.

Develop the Repository Manager

The Repository Manager is the cornerstone of any technical architecture. Coupled with the user-access interface, it is an intuitive tool. Repository Manager components include the following:

- *Data Dictionary*—The data dictionary contains data definitions, descriptions, update frequency, ownership, and last date of update—all information that is gathered and maintained by the user concerning the data, its sources, contents, and images.
- *Report Dictionary*—The report dictionary contains descriptions of all reports, including data elements, how and where the data elements are used, sort fields, selection fields, and calculated fields.
- *Loading and Mapping Rules*—These are the data transformation and migration rules for extracting, loading, summarizing, and calculating data.
- *Entity Definition and Relationships*—This component contains the entity libraries, which include all joins, keys, and cross-reference tables. This information is used to build dynamic views.
- *Security Table*—The security table protects data views, entities, and attributes so they can be accessed only by authorized users. All authorization levels should be maintained.

Build the User-Access Interface

The goal of the user-access interface is to eliminate, or significantly reduce, support, synchronization, training, and learning curves. The user-access interface is usually built with a graphical user interface such as SQL Windows®, PowerBuilder®, Visual Basic, or a graphical tool that has ODBC interfaces connecting it to relational databases.

Data analysis and reporting tools should be integrated with the user interface. The interface uses the road maps stored in the repository that link individual users to the data that supports them. These interfaces and tools are structured in a way that minimize training and support requirements and hide the complexities of the infrastructure and data model behind the interface.

DSS TOPOLOGIES

Decision-support systems have evolved over the last two decades from inflexible mainframe systems, to isolated PC tools, to client/server data dippers, and now, high-performance and extensible enterprise *decision-support* applications.

Requirements

As *decision-support* systems become more critical to corporate success, the users are beginning to work as partners on design, deployment, and management. They can move from simply tapping data and making lists to performing complex analyses producing competitively useful information. The most successful systems have one thing in common—three-tier, client/server architecture. Before we can discuss three-tier, let us examine other such architectures which are still being deployed in some circles.

One-Tier Stand-Alone

PCs, or PC-like devices connected to a central server, can be used for full-functioned OLAP analyses in a one-tier mode. The client and server may be on the same processor.

Two-Tier Architecture

The two-tier architecture involved a client and a server. The client interfaces with the user and plays the role of a requester, whereas, the server has all the data and the software to run the queries.

In summary, non-technical users now demand access to the "raw" corporate data. Creating open data warehouses is the first step. An open data warehouse can be built using one or more RDBMSs. However, non-technical users cannot write SQL code and SQL has limited analytic capabilities.

The current crop of development tools and applications isolate non-technical users from SQL code generation in one way or another. Generally, the SQL code is written by developers and embedded under the graphical user interface or executed as stored procedures. But the resulting two-tier model lacks the ability to provide the business analysis required by decision makers, the horsepower to work with large amounts of data and users, as well as the flexibility to work in a heterogeneous software and hardware environment.

Three-Tier Architecture

Three-tiered architecture addresses performance, reliability, and resource management by moving complex application logic to a *decision-support* server independent of databases and PCs. The server provides efficient data access, accelerated response, scheduled background processing, and serving of preprocessed reports. Because this architecture ensures a strict separation of the GUI, business logic, and DBMS tiers, developers are provided with a wide range of front ends and data warehousing options.

Maintenance is simplified because the complex application logic is centralized on the server rather than spread over hundreds of PCs in the network. In the three-tiered model, the client is dedicated to presentation logic and services and has an API for invoking the applications in a middle layer. The database server is dedicated to data services and file services (which you could optimize without the risk of using stored procedures). The middle layer is an application server on which the business logic executes, and from which data logic invokes data services.

Considerations for Three-Tier Client/Server

Many MIS managers are facing software problems these days, as legacy systems reach the end of their life cycles. Just when client/server systems are needed to offload some mainframe functions, they too are stretched to the limit. One possible solution is to move from two-tiered client/server to a three-tiered architecture.

Client/server applications are now abundant. The learning curve has been completed. But people are trying to do more with it than it is capable of. Three-tiered architecture is the next logical progression. Three-tiered systems place applications on a separate server, which either contains the entire application or, more frequently, shares the application with other servers, clients, or the mainframe.

With the mainframe, we had one system doing everything. With client/server, we chain sawed the functions into two parts. But neither architecture provided the flexibility to separate the application in a way that would optimize performance as a three-tiered architecture does.

Developing Three-Tiered Systems

People who create their own systems are in a distinct minority. Most companies look to packaged products. Few firms have the expertise to develop three-tiered systems, even though new tools make this process much easier. Prepackaged tools normally require the company to reengineer around the package, and not everyone is willing or able to do that.

Companies that plan to develop their own three-tiered systems have to consider carefully the three logical aspects of their systems: data, application, and user interface.

The fact that data should be kept separate from applications means that data consistency is especially important in order to ensure that the same data can flow through all systems. One way to provide that consistency is to build a data warehouse.

The application, on the other hand, should vary, depending on the user for which it's intended. To maximize a three-tiered architecture, each function should spend the necessary time to define its own business rules, which are incorporated into the application server.

The GUI front end should be developed separately from the application logic. The trick is to be able to change the logic completely while keeping the front end basically intact, besides altering a menu item or two.

Servers

The *Decision-Support* Systems (DSSs) are the applications that make use of the data warehouse. You need a mix of LAN servers, large multiprocessing servers, and even massively parallel machines to make your data warehouse efficient. There are three things you should know about choosing a server, right upfront:

- *First*, there is no right answer. Although the warehousing concept has been around for many years, the idea has only recently caught hold of everyone's imagination, perhaps because database and hardware technology has finally matured to the point where data warehouses can be built on a broad scale. You're helping to write the rules as you go along.

- *Second*, choosing the right server has as much, or more, to do with creating a useful environment as it does with finding raw CPU (Central Processing Unit) power. When you choose a server, you need scalable parallel-processing technology that supports comprehensive data-warehousing solutions.

   Whether you go the one-stop-shop route or assemble the solution yourself, the package should include *decision-support* tools, enduser data-access and analysis support, and hardware and software that can periodically download data from heterogeneous corporate databases.

- *Third*, combined performance is the key. You must test out the exact combination of server, operating system, database, and tools. Substituting one UNIX for another, or using a small pilot system to predict the performance of a larger production system is a pointless exercise.

On the one hand, Symmetric Multiprocessing (SMP) offers scalable shared-memory UNIX systems that range from 2 to 64 processors, although most of the midrange systems use 4 to 8 processors. On the other hand, more specialized multiprocessor capabilities can be designed primarily for databases of a few hundred gigabytes and larger.

Servers in the latter camp are often referred to as massively parallel or "shared nothing" systems. Processors in this category number up to more than 500, and each processor, or node, has its own memory (hence the "shared nothing" designation).

Data warehouse and *decision-support* capacity planning require a different mindset than does OLTP capacity planning, in which you can mathematically estimate the size and type of queries that will go against the database and know precisely the number of users tapping the database.

Because transactions are simple and straightforward, users expect a fast response time. But *decision support* is a whole new ball game. Once you start giving people access to data that they can use in unprecedented ways, they will be more creative than you thought. One query leads to another, making it difficult to determine ahead of time all of the kinds of queries, data types, and indexing you'll need in the warehouse. The number of users and the complexity of queries multiply like rabbits.

Data warehouse *capacity planning*, is achieved "somewhere between blind faith and prayer." Because underestimating size and usage is the rule, some experts advise to double the initial estimates of CPU power, memory, and storage.

Even with initial estimates, it's critical to choose scalable systems to support inevitable but hard-to-quantify future growth. The initial data warehouse may include only 60 to 100 GB of data, which is rather small for a massively parallel system that can handle more than a terabyte. Despite the many vagaries of data warehousing and the relative youth of the field, most agree on a few general rules of thumb when it comes to server capacity.

- *Small databases, with simple queries.* Look to LAN servers for data marts when the database is under 5 GB. Simple queries on small departmental or divisional databases don't necessarily benefit from parallel scalable RDBMSs anyway.
- *Medium to large databases, with more complex queries.* Response time is faster on SMP systems than it is on uniprocessors, and they tend to be more cost-effective than "shared-nothing" systems. Large amounts of memory reduce outside seek time during queries, speeding performance when querying large databases.
- *Huge databases, very complex queries.* When your database grows beyond the level of use that can be handled by a single SMP system, you'll have to step up to *clusters* or MPP machines. Conventional wisdom suggests that SMP machines begin to max out with databases at the 500-GB level.

Multitier Security

Data security is a concern as an organization begins any large-scale deployment of a data warehousing application. A data warehouse is often aggregated and organized in a manner to facilitate access and analysis. In the wrong hands, this data could turn into a liability that could compromise the organization.

Security can be implemented on any tier to enforce data-access privileges. It is practically impossible for any unauthorized user to access sensitive corporate information.

Distributed Relational Data Marts

Many software technologies can be used to create distributed relational data marts, thereby creating an open and easy-to-manage data delivery mechanism. Agents can be instructed to create the data marts on the data warehouse server, the OLAP server, or on any other server. The network administrators can significantly reduce data transfer time and cost and greatly decrease the technical obstacles for large-scale deployment. Organizations can, thus

- Reduce network bottlenecks.
- Substitute lower-cost batch cycles for interactive cycles.
- Utilize lower-cost hardware for processing interactive information requests.
- Support remote sites.

Decision-Support Modeling

Decision-support data, most often loaded in a data warehouse, represents broad views of summarized information. The hard part of *decision support* is mapping your legacy data—the data actually in your operational systems—to that *decision-support* structure. This is difficult because the underlying metadata for those operational systems is often lacking, sending you on an archeological dig to find out what these things mean.

The *decision-support* applications are also denormalized, in that they are summarized. The detail is then summarized to a predefined level and then made available to users in *decision-support* applications.

Transaction Oriented

Transaction-oriented, high-performance applications present a different set of challenges. While the structures of the *decision-support* model and the transaction-oriented model are similar, a higher level of performance is demanded from the transaction-oriented model, and therefore the level of detail is greater.

Clever application of the science of data modeling is most crucial in the transaction environment. Data is most often denormalized to accommodate the high volume. Experimenting with the denormalization can dictate the right level. Denormalization is important when you are dealing with high-volume transactions, or where speed is the primary factor in putting together your database. The transaction-oriented applications are usually more denormalized, eliminating posting data to numerous tables.

Deployment Strategies: Different Challenges, Different Approaches

The art and science of data modeling are applied differently depending on the ultimate use of the data *decision support* or transaction. But is modeling different in the centralized and distributed deployment environments, or in the client/server and the mainframe environments?

From a logical perspective, modeling does not differ for a centralized versus distributed environment. The database, whether it is centralized or distributed, has to be viewed first in its entirety. It is only after the logical data model has been conceptualized and documented as a whole that proper distribution decisions can be made.

The logical data model is a planning tool. Although the modeler may know initially that the data will be distributed, that should not affect the initial blueprint, nor should it impact the understanding and definition of the business rules.

Designing in a Centralized vs. Distributed Environment

During the physical implementation, consistency must be ensured across various processors. Obviously, in a centralized environment consistency is easily accomplished. The problem in the distributed environment is not maintaining the model, but in maintaining the data and in ensuring its integrity, particularly when data is replicated across processors.

Two-phase commit supports the client/server environment by streamlining data updates in remote locations.

MULTIDIMENSIONAL DATABASES

Multidimensional technology can be attractive since it provides the DSS analyst with a multidimensional conceptual view of data. However, it is important to separate the requirement to view data multidimensionally from the requirement to physically store data multidimensionally. Data can be stored relationally (or in any other format) and still be viewed multidimensionally.

In short, multidimensional database technology is not necessary for *decision support* and, in fact, faces significant hurdles before its adoption as a viable alternative to relational database technology. There are many major limitations of multidimensional databases that must be overcome before this technology can be considered in lieu of relational technology, such as:

Database Management Tools

As with other database engines, multidimensional databases need to provide adequate management tools. These include the ability to

- Ensure database integrity through backup and restore capabilities.
- Tune databases for optimum performance.
- Provide user security at multiple levels.
- Limit resource usage based on user privileges.

On the other hand, all major relational engines provide a full suite of data, performance, and security management utilities.

Support for Drill-Down to Atomic-Level Detail

Because transaction detail is never stored in multidimensional databases, it is awkward to access row-level detail when using multidimensional technology since an entirely different API is required. Atomic-level transactions are often stored in relational formats, enabling relational-based *decision-support* systems to provide a seamless row-level drill-down capability.

Incremental Database Refresh

A multidimensional database should allow updates to any subset of the database without restricting access to unaffected parts, or rebuilding the database from scratch. With multidimensional databases, often the entire "data cube" must be reloaded when data is modified and all data is inaccessible during the data loading process. Relational databases provide incremental data update and insert capabilities and do not restrict use of existing data as new data is loaded.

Multiple Array Support

Multidimensional databases do not support the creation of multiple, related multidimensional arrays within a single database structure. Relational architectures typically permit defining up to 256 tables in a single database.

Database Joins

Multidimensional databases do not support the logical joining of multiple multidimensional arrays. The inability to join multidimensional databases with each other, or with relational databases, limits query flexibility by eliminating the possibility of using characteristics tables to dynamically segment data.

Subset Selection

As with relational databases, a multidimensional database should provide for data subsetting, limiting the amount of data for analysis.

Local Data Support

In addition to client/server support, a multidimensional database should seamlessly support local storage and data manipulation, enabling users to select subsets of data for local, unattached processing. Since there are numerous local RDBMSs which support the SQL standard for data access, data subsets can easily be downloaded into a variety of engines for local, unattached processing.

SQL Interface

Multidimensional databases do not support industry-standard SQL interfaces for data access. Rather, they each have their own proprietary data-access APIs. As long as the SQL standard is not supported, proprietary, engine-specific data-access and analysis tools must be utilized.

The previously mentioned multidimensional technology limitations and the requirement to incorporate a proprietary database technology into the corporate data processing environment should be weighed by those considering multidimensional databases. Historically, the users of multidimensional technology have based their decisions on the need for improved DSS query performance and on the requirement for a multidimensional conceptual data view.

With recent, dramatic improvements in indexing techniques, superior support for handling of sparse data, and the advent of symmetric multiprocessor hardware support, relational technologies have effectively closed the performance gap that once existed. Coupled with newer architectures that provide data consolidation and a multidimensional conceptual view, industry-standard relational architectures provide a full complement of multidimensional database features without resorting to the use of proprietary database engines.

Performance scalability, the ability to support a multitude of data access paths, the ability to leverage standard data-access tools, and support for multidimensional data views make relational databases the preferred choice for enterprise-wide DSS implementations.

Performance and Analytical Problems

To address some of the performance and analytical problems associated with the first-generation query tool approach, a series of vendors have developed a separate technology optimized for queries and analysis. A Multidimensional Database (MDD) is a specialized engine that stores data in proprietary array formats that correspond to the business dimensions understood by users. By abandoning industry-standard SQL and developing proprietary Application Programming Interfaces (APIs), the MDDs can go beyond the limitations of SQL and perform more analytical functionality in the server itself.

Because the MDD storage techniques and access methods are fundamentally different than relational technology, it is very difficult for users to effectively integrate the two. Users must replicate data from the relational data warehouse into the proprietary multidimensional format, resulting in enormous overhead and maintenance costs.

Scalability

MDDs deliver impressive query performance by effectively precalculating or pre-consolidating the transactional data. Any question that can be answered from a previous calculation, instead of calculated on the fly, results in higher query performance. This technique is absolutely critical to performance when the data volume reaches any significant size.

To fully preconsolidate incoming data, MDDs typically require an enormous amount of overhead, both in processing time and in storage cost. An input file of 200 MB can easily expand to 5 GB of required storage in an MDD. A file of this size often takes days to load and consolidate. Users are relatively immature compared to the relational users in taking advantage of key performance techniques, such as multithreading, multi-user concurrency, and parallelization. For these reasons, MDDs fundamentally do not scale and are not viable as a platform for the underlying data warehouse.

To combat the scalability issues, many enterprises are experimenting with the data mart approach. In this scenario, a scalable, parallel relational database is used for the primary (large) data warehouse, and subsets or summarized data from the warehouse are extracted and replicated to the proprietary MDDs.

Problems with Replication and Drill-Through

Unfortunately, the data mart approach almost always fails. The replication and synchronization efforts of loading data from the relational database into the proprietary format require enormous efforts and are often unreliable. The drill-through functionality is not automatic and usually requires creating an astronomical number of views (one for every possible query) on the relational server and tedious programming effort on the multidimensional server.

RELATIONAL OLAP

The Relational OLAP (ROLAP) approach begins with the premise that data does not need to be stored multidimensionally to be viewed multidimensionally. A scalable, parallel, relational database provides the storage and high-speed access to the underlying data. A middle analysis tier provides the multidimensional conceptual view of the data and the extended analytical functionality that are not available in the underlying relational server. The presentation tier delivers the results to users.

ROLAP systems provide the benefits of full analytical functionality while maintaining the openness, scalability, and performance of the leading relational database systems. To achieve these benefits, ROLAP designs require a database design technique known as "dimensional modeling," as exemplified by the star schema, as well as a more robust set of metadata to organize the system.

More Robust Metadata

ROLAP systems go beyond putting simple business labels on existing relational tables and columns. ROLAP systems classify and group the underlying relational structures according to a logical, multidimensional model. Hierarchies are defined so that relationships and drill paths can be derived.

ROLAP technology insulates users from the underlying relational model, going one step beyond query tools which simply hide SQL but not the need for users to understand relational concepts. Users, and even application designers, see only the logical, multidimensional model.

A defining characteristic of ROLAP systems is automatic, sophisticated SQL generation that is always performed dynamically and transparently, at query execution time to users and applications. This enables system designers to later change how data is precalculated, without having to change any of the *decision-support* applications.

The Batch vs. Dynamic Trade-Off

In any OLAP system there is a trade-off between how much work to do to set up the system versus how much work to do to perform an ad hoc query. If we always knew exactly what every query was to be, and in what sequence queries would be run, we could specifically optimize the calculation process to derive one result from another in the shortest amount of time. Unfortunately, with a data warehouse we do not have that luxury.

Traditional query tool strategies generally load all of the raw data into a data warehouse and let the query tool ask any question desired. In this situation, almost all of the work in formulating the query results is done at query execution time. The consequence is unacceptable performance when using large data warehouses.

MDDs, on the other hand, take the approach of exhaustively precalculating the results of every query. This results in fast query response, but inordinate delays and scalability problems when trying to load the system.

ROLAP systems enable the system designer to balance this trade-off anywhere in the middle. In fact, with a ROLAP system, this is a tuning issue that can be tweaked after the initial deployment of the data warehouse, since all of the batch processing and query processing characteristics are driven from the metadata. ROLAP systems are fundamentally neutral as to how much to precalculate and how much to dynamically consolidate "on the fly" at query execution time. This enables the ROLAP system to scale to larger data warehouses with higher performance than any of the previous techniques.

Advances in Relational Technology for OLAP

With the increasing demand for data warehousing on relational platforms, the leading database vendors are adding significant functionality that dramatically improves response time for OLAP-style queries, further differentiating the ROLAP solution from its alternatives.

Parallelization

One of the key problems with data warehouses is the sheer volume of data. Parallelization techniques are critical to break down complex actions into smaller parts, each of which can be executed in parallel. The net result is faster execution. The different database vendors have achieved significantly different results and completeness of their parallelization efforts. Therefore, not all parts of most database products have yet been optimized for parallel execution.

The best performance unequivocally results from an internal, or "core" parallelism of the major operations, including both query operations and loading operations. The query processor in the leading parallel database implementation supports hashed partition operators that completely parallelize sorts, joins, and aggregate functions, which are the most important operations in OLAP-style queries.

Just as importantly are the loading, backup, and restore operations, often overlooked in database selection benchmarks. Full parallelization of each of these operations becomes absolutely critical for data warehouses of any significant size.

Data Partitioning

Effective data partitioning is another prong in the attack on large data volumes. Partitioning enables the database to automatically distribute portions of a table or tables into more than one piece, which enhances the ability of the database to parallelize operations and eases maintenance on the large data sets.

Partitioning also enables the database to distribute data over multiple physical storage devices, which can be operating at full speed in parallel. The leading parallel database implementations support a variety of partitioning options, including range-based partitioning, hash-based partitioning, and round-robin partitioning, which are critical in data warehouses.

DSS Indexes

There are several specialized indexes that enhance relational database performance for *decision-support* applications. The most important type for OLAP-style queries is the multitable index, a generalization of the star join index. A multitable index includes columns from more than one table in the same index, effectively precomputing the joins between the tables. Because joins are the slower operations in query processing, this index can dramatically improve query response time.

Another important new index is the bitmap index. Instead of using a traditional tree to represent the index, bitmaps represent the presence of a given value for a field such as a "0" or "1" for true or false. Bitmaps efficiently index low-cardinality data. That is, the data that has few possibilities for the actual value. Examples of low-cardinality fields include "sex" which can only be male or female, or purchase type, which might be cash, check, or charge. Bitmaps are much smaller than a traditional index on such data and can be evaluated concurrently much more quickly than reading the data directly or via an alternative index.

As with any new index technology that is fundamental to the core database query processing and optimization, it is important that the index be built into the core database environment, with a shared storage manager, query cost model, and point of administration.

Analytical Extensibility

With the advent of object-relational techniques, it is now possible for organizations and third parties to natively extend the core analytical capabilities of the database server itself. Organizations can add user-defined aggregate functions and user-defined analysis functions to the database using a well-defined object programming model. Once these functions are defined, they behave just like a built-in function, with the full parallelization and performance characteristics of the core database.

Integrated Relational OLAP

Relational OLAP technology, while an impressive solution for the most complex *decision-support* requirements, is nonetheless limited by its non-integrated, disparate tier architecture. The problem is that the data is physically separated from the analytical processing. For many queries this is not a major problem; however, it limits the scope of the analysis that is possible.

In a traditional ROLAP system, the analysis engine formulates optimized SQL statements that it sends to the RDBMS server. It then takes the data back from the server, reintegrates it, and performs further analysis and computations before delivering the finished results to the user. This usually means that data travels over the network twice: once to the analysis server and again to the client application.

The next logical step in the evolution of OLAP technology is the integration of the ROLAP engine with the scalable, parallel RDBMS itself—integrated relational OLAP.

Internal Parallelism

By merging ROLAP technology into the parallel architecture of the RDBMS, all major analysis functions can also be executed in parallel, such as user-defined aggregation functions, comparative analysis, bucket analysis, multidimensional pivoting and presentation, and statistical profiling. Answering questions that require looking at more data than is returned to the client application, such as multipass queries, for example, "Display sales by store for all stores in the top 10% of my stores in the Western region," are better answered within the database server than on a separate application tier, which would otherwise require dramatically more network traffic.

Integrated Optimizers

Both ROLAP systems and the relational databases themselves include sophisticated cost-based optimization algorithms. The database generally decides how to execute the specific SQL statements, including which indexes to access, the methods used to perform joins, and the degree of parallelization to employ. The integrated relational OLAP system can employ database statistics, knowledge of indexes, knowledge of aggregation and partition strategy, and so on, into an integrated optimization process that significantly improves access strategy and overall performance.

Improved Parallel Loading

The gating factor for many data warehouse implementations is the amount of time required to perform the periodic load to update the warehouse, including the corresponding derived calculations, such as precalculated aggregates. For traditional MDD systems, the "load window" effectively limits the scalability of the overall database to small, departmental applications.

Internal Data Mining

Data mining employs automated agent technology to scan the mammoth quantities of data housed in the warehouse in search of trends and patterns that might have been difficult for the human analyst to find on his own. Data mining software generally requires scanning the warehouse at a very detailed level. Historically, the data mining software is physically separate from the database, and as such, it has had trouble analyzing the volumes of data demanded in today's data warehouse in reasonable amounts of time. With extensible database technology, for the first time mining technology can be embedded in the database itself where it belongs, opening new doors for automated analysis.

The OLAP Client/Server

The integration of OLAP and relational technology is the natural progression in the evolution of solutions to complex *decision-support* problems.

With the extensions to the relational technology, the very nature of the DBMS itself is changing. The DBMS is no longer limited to what can be expressed using the SQL language. Client tools can ask for data using a natural, object-oriented, multidimensional language instead of the underlying relational concepts. The object-oriented interface is a full-feature language that includes all of the analytical functionality needed but was not previously available in SQL.

INTRANET SYSTEMS

Corporations recognize that information placed in the hands of decision makers is a powerful tool. To meet decision makers' nearly insatiable appetite for information, data is being extracted from operational systems and placed in data warehouses.

Delivery of data warehouse information to decision makers throughout the enterprise and around the world has been an expensive challenge. Once data has been extracted and organized for user access, analytic software must be loaded on each user's PC, users must be trained, and ongoing user support staffs must be recruited. User requirements and even the users themselves change constantly, resulting in a significant support burden. The World Wide Web offers a solution. In addition to simplifying the deployment of data warehouse access, an intranet can introduce a new level of collaborative interactive analysis and information sharing among decision makers.

Most intranets currently manage unstructured content—text, image, and audio data types—as "static" HTML documents. A data warehouse stores structured content—raw alphanumeric data. With the right tools and the right architecture, a data warehouse can be made accessible over an enterprise intranet, forming the basis for a comprehensive enterprise information infrastructure. There are three important advantages of such an infrastructure:

- Intranet economics
- Information integration
- User collaboration

Intranet Economics

The cost of client/server computing is high when communications, support, and other hidden costs are considered. In fact, an often-cited Gartner Group study suggests that client/server computing is more costly than mainframe computing. Certainly the personal computer has become bloated with processing power, memory, software, and user-managed files of considerable proportions. The result is a "fat" client architecture.

Intranets are changing the economics of supporting a large population of knowledge workers. An intranet is a "thin" client architecture. Not only does an intranet reduce communications costs, but some speculate that the personal computer may be replaced with a low-cost intranet device. Whether corporations will indeed replace existing PCs is debatable; at a minimum an intranet will increase the life expectancy of the latest round of PC upgrades.

The thin client model requires server distribution of applications software. This is where Sun's Java plays a role. Java allows software to be served to an intranet browser in code fragments or applets. The only portion of the application software that needs to be installed on the client is a browser such as Netscape Navigator. And application software is acquired only when needed for a specific application. One possibility is metering that tracks the number of users that download an applet or some other measure of usage.

Another possibility is the use of a tiered pricing model tied to server size. The result is likely to be another round of competitive pricing battles. The economics of an intranet are lower communications costs, less expensive thin client hardware, and, in some cases, reduced application software licensing costs.

Information Integration

One of the most valuable assets of the enterprise is the operational data used in managing day-to-day business activities. This numeric data provides frequent measures of performance. By developing a data warehouse, corporations are organizing the data in a way that makes it useful to decision makers. When a data warehouse is put on an intranet, users can toggle between structured data analysis (producing reports in columns and rows) and unstructured browsing. One software application can be used to view data both ways. The marketing manager of a retailer can display on his or her screen both an advertising image and a report on the sales of those products featured in the ad.

User Collaboration

An intranet is as much about communicating at an interactive level as it is about making structured and unstructured content easily accessible. Few people would disagree with the view that decision making improves with timely, accurate, and complete information. An intranet influences how the ideas and experience of a workgroup are exchanged as part of knowledge sharing. The experience and new ideas of users form the basis of rapid-fire questions. This is the analysis and problem resolution process. Unstructured and structured content searches provide answers to questions, but answering one question inevitably leads to more questions. The quality of questions and the completeness of the answers are the basis for the best decisions.

The key benefits of an intranet are information-enriched communications and collaborative problem resolution. An intranet facilitates these capabilities on both a workgroup and an enterprise scale that is not possible under the communication constraints of a regular LAN-based application.

Types of Information on an Intranet

Today, most users can communicate via a corporate e-mail system. While an e-mail system allows text files to be exchanged, it does not facilitate true collaboration. Lotus Notes is one step closer to a collaborative method of exchanging valuable information, but the focus is still textual file sharing. True collaboration requires interactive sharing of information in such a way that the recipient can continue an analysis or branch off in an entirely new direction without assistance. For example, if I receive a report from another intranet user, I should immediately be able to drill down or drill up on any report dimension, pivot and rotate the results, add additional calculations as part of my analysis, and then pass my work to others in the organization. This requires dynamic report creation based on data stored in a warehouse.

True collaboration for business decision making requires a higher level of interactive analysis and knowledge sharing than exists today in most text-oriented groupware products. Users need to dynamically explore the data warehouse and freely build on each other's analysis of a business issue, jumping to structured content searches at any point in the analysis process.

Requirements for Putting a Data Warehouse on an Intranet

Data warehouses employ relational database management systems that use SQL to retrieve rows and columns of numeric data, while unstructured content is managed as Hyper Text Markup Language (HTML) documents. The challenge in putting a data warehouse on an intranet is in properly enabling SQL data warehouse access from HTML browsers. Four application software services can be provided:

- Analytic layer
- File management

- Security
- Agents

Analytic Layer

Putting structured data content on the intranet requires a server-resident analytic layer to generate SQL on the fly, perform computations, and format reports based on user requests. In essence, a specialized structured content Web server is required to support data warehouse access from an HTML browser client-initiated request. Often, this Web server will be the same hardware platform used to manage all or a portion of the structured content database.

The Web server for structured content must be configured to support the higher processing loads of a robust analytic layer. The analytic layer will typically make heavy demands on a relational database layer and the number of queries and results communicated between these layers will be large. Therefore, there should be a high-speed network connection between these layers or they should reside on the same machine. This processing capability could be supplied, for example, by a Symmetrical Multiprocessor (SMP) configuration with enough memory to minimize virtual memory I/O operations. Due to the variability in the sizes of the data sets being analyzed, these sizing parameters should be determined empirically via benchmarking.

The analytic layer shares some capabilities with spreadsheet software. The power of a spreadsheet is derived from a user's ability to author custom calculations based on facts stored in cells in a spreadsheet. For example, facts (numeric data) are stored in two dimensions: letters A, B, C, D, and so on, and numbers 1, 2, 3, 4, and so on. Combining the two dimensions, A1, provides a unique address. This unique address can be used to create a formula for a required calculation, A1–B1. The number of calculated rows and columns in a spreadsheet application often far outnumbers the number of stored facts.

A spreadsheet provides two additional powerful capabilities. First, users can replicate formulas for calculations down a column or across a row easily. Second, the calculation logic is automatically updated if new rows or columns of data are inserted into a spreadsheet.

A data warehouse has multiple dimensions—product, market, customer, outlet, vendor, period, and so on—as opposed to a two-dimensional spreadsheet. The combination of values for each of the multiple data warehouse dimensions provides a unique address. The analytic layer on the structured content Web server allows users to apply calculations based on database dimensions to create more useful reports. Furthermore, once authored, calculations can be shared with other users much as calculation formulas are replicated within a spreadsheet. And, the calculation logic is maintained as the data warehouse is updated each day, week, or month.

Like a spreadsheet, reports that users request from a data warehouse often contain more calculated rows and columns than raw data. Without a robust analytic layer in front of a data warehouse, the user is limited to a simple listing of stored data elements. The analytic layer is key to addressing business questions that users must answer.

File Management

Collaboration requires interactive analysis and knowledge sharing. A report requested by one user is valuable when it is shared with other users to gain their insight and ideas. The recipients should be able to continue the analysis initiated by the original author. In this way, the analysis process becomes an interactive exchange. Many users can pursue different analysis paths from a common starting point.

To meet the challenge of providing interactive analysis of a data warehouse, users must have access and be able to change their copy of the logic used to create the report. Users must be able to access public files and manage their personal files over an intranet connection. A sophisticated server-based file management system is required to support user collaboration and maintain security at this level.

Security

The liberal sharing of information and collaboration among users on an intranet immediately raises data security issues. A data warehouse contains highly confidential performance data for the entire enterprise. Only a few users have security authorization to view data anywhere in a warehouse. Most users must be provided access to only a relevant portion of a warehouse. Data must be secured, but if too tightly controlled the value of the warehouse will never be fully realized.

The security issues are indeed complex. To illustrate the point, a sales vice-president has authorization to view financial data at a national, regional, and sales territory level. At the territory level, the financial data would include all salary data for sales representatives. If the sales vice-president creates a report and decides to share it, the regional managers should have access to only territory information for their region and be blocked from accessing territory information for other regions. In other words, if a user is not authorized to receive and access a report, then that user must not be able to view the report or drill into areas where the user does not have authorization.

Again, there is a subtle capability that is being described. Reports that are created from data stored in the warehouse should not simply be shared as text files. All reports should include the underlying logic, giving the recipient the ability to immediately analyze and modify the report, as well as the logic and assumptions supporting the analyses. Before a recipient can view the report or build upon the analysis, the authorization level for that user is verified. For effective collaboration, reports must be shared throughout the workgroup and enterprise. If the recipients are not authorized, their access to report logic should be denied.

Encryption of data can provide a higher level of security than is generally available for business applications. For example, utilizing the Netscape Secure Socket Layer (SSL) and a commerce server, data passing between the client and server can be encrypted. This enables business users to run important applications over unsecured communication lines without worrying about an intruder tapping into the network and viewing the transmitted information.

Agents

One of the common complaints about e-mail and even voice mail is that a mail box fills up faster than a user has time to isolate and address the really important issues. Agents are intended to work on behalf of users to isolate important information sought by a user. An agent can be triggered by some predefined event or at a specified time interval. The agent sends an alert to notify specific users on a "need-to-know basis." Agents must have the ability to run continually as background processes on an intranet logic server because each user is almost always disconnected, a result of the stateless nature of Web servers. This provides a means of automating the routine analysis process. And, when users sign on to the network, the agents must be smart enough to notify users of conditions that occurred while they were disconnected.

Because data warehouses tend to grow exponentially, it is critical that agents proactively monitor and manage activities, alerting decision makers only when specific conditions exist. It is unrealistic to believe that decision makers could be productive by aimlessly data surfing through potentially hundreds of gigabytes of data looking for valuable insight. The decision maker should be free to concentrate on the immediate and critical issues while the system ensures that developing conditions will not go undetected.

Structured/Unstructured Content Server

The Common Gateway Interface (CGI) facility of Web server software provides a method to execute server-resident software. Building secure applications for an intranet requires a well thought out security strategy, as well as the appropriate application architecture. Most Web applications provide all users with the same access permissions to the reachable files on the server. It is certainly possible to send a DBMS query from a Web browser and enforce any DBMS security just as if the query came from a traditional LAN-based client application. The maintenance of security for each report application and user creates a significant burden. This approach is best suited to simple requests such as a query to determine a user's current credit card balance.

Business users require a system that maps them to their server account by verifying user names and passwords. When server applications are run, they will have access to their files secured by user, group, and permission levels. The same issue exists with database security. Users must be mapped to the appropriate database user or group in the relational database in order to control the data that a user can access. And, because the number of users may be large, the administration of the security system should be centralized at the server and minimized to the extent possible.

A second issue with the CGI interface is that it does not offer a continuous connection to the database. As a result, it is impossible to support an application requiring multiple interactive queries—a data warehousing requirement. One approach to solving this problem is to employ a message-based protocol between the client browser and the server-resident analytic layer using the CGI.

By mapping a user to a server account and starting a UNIX process that executes as that user, a continuous connection is maintained between the logic layer and database during iterative queries over the lifetime of that process. This facilitates the execution of efficient SQL query strategies and computational routines to meet the user requirements for structured content analysis. For example, an HTML form can request that the user enter their UNIX user name and password and database user name and password. Using Netscape's SSL facilities, the passwords are then encrypted before being transmitted over the network.

This information is then passed as parameters or through environment variables, to a CGI program, which could be a C, C++, or Perl program. That software then verifies the UNIX user name and password via operating system security features and starts a process that executes as that user. This process could then connect to the Relational Database Management System (RDBMS) using its API and the supplied user name and password. Once this connection to the RDBMS is established, many queries and result sets can be processed. A final output report can be generated, converted to an HTML document, and sent back to the client browser for display to the user.

Rethinking the Enterprise Information Infrastructure

The network computer era allows users to evolve into "knowledge sharers" and emphasizes the powerful advantage of collaborative problem resolution. Knowledge sharing requires the free flow of all types of information among users, not just text file transfer, but an interactive data analysis capability that encourages the exchange of experiences and ideas.

An intranet should be the basis for rethinking the enterprise information infrastructure. By putting a data warehouse on an intranet and deploying structured content Web servers, organizations gain economic and rapid application deployment benefits. More important in the long term is that users will collaborate more freely on an intranet, hopefully resulting in thorough analysis of business issues, free flow exchange of experience and ideas, and faster competitive response.

Today's corporations want to have superior knowledge. An intranet is where knowledge is placed in the hands of decision makers. An intranet is far more than a place to manage e-mail and text file management; it is the infrastructure for a comprehensive *decision-support* system.

SUMMARY

The data warehouse should not be seen as just a product, or a collection of products, or an individual technology, or a simple solution to a standard end-user information access problem. Data warehousing is properly an architected solution in which individual items such as extraction of data from production applications, delivery of data to the place it is needed, consolidation of data into a usable structure, and browsing capabilities are handled in the method most conducive to the characteristics of a specific environment.

A three-tiered taxonomy presents major classes of data warehousing architectures: from a relatively simple reporting system intended primarily for enduser computing, to a moderately complex environment encompassing data from multiple applications, and to highly complex uses of distributed servers, relational data mixed with text and image documents, and complicated On-Line Analytical Processing (OLAP) client engines.

Data warehousing is not a new phenomenon. All large organizations already have data warehouses, but they are just not managing them. Over the next few years, the growth of data warehousing is going to be enormous with new products and technologies coming out frequently.

In order to get the most out of this period, it is going to be important that data warehouse planners and developers have a clear idea of what they are looking for and then choose strategies and methods that will provide them with performance today and flexibility for tomorrow.

In short, the data warehouse concept has received much attention recently by both the database industry and the database research community in general. Data warehouses will provide a means for querying huge amounts of amassed data that was accumulated in the past but never utilized for anything useful. Until recently, it was impossible to provide a system that could allow for efficient means for processing the vast amount of data that companies had collected for the purpose of analytics.

Data warehouses will provide corporate users with a means to perform such tasks as data mining to find valuable tidbits of information in their vast seas of data. With this technology, decision makers in companies may now have a vehicle to process the possibly terabytes of data that are the byproduct of the automation era of the past decade and a half in a meaningful way. The need for this technology is evident in the demand by companies to deploy data warehouses for information discovery purposes.

6

METADATA

INTRODUCTION

Metadata is the term that is used to describe the definition of the data that is stored in the data warehouse. Metadata is an important aspect of the data warehouse environment. Metadata has been a part of the information processing schema for a long time. However, in the world of data warehousing, metadata has taken a new level of importance. It is with metadata that the most effective use of warehouse data analysis is achieved.

Without metadata, it is not possible for a user to interact with the data in the data warehouse since the user has no means of knowing how the tables are structured, what the precise definitions of the data are, where the data originated, or how aged the data is. The value of metadata stems from its ability to be used as a standard description for a wide variety of data structures.

112

In this chapter, we will explore the components, factors, structures, and the repository that make metadata an essential tool for successful data warehousing applications.

WHAT IS METADATA

Metadata is often defined as data about data, or, only a little less vaguely, as the information required to make scientific data useful. Indeed, the term means different things to different people and defies precise definition. We will use it in only a general sense, taking refuge behind an operational shift to defining context instead.

For successful communication it is essential that both parties share a common set of assumptions (here referred to as a context) according to which the messages that pass are to be interpreted. In natural language such contexts are generally largely implicit and are elucidated by question and answer only when apparent inconsistencies indicate that there may be a problem in interpretation. However, computers typically require that all relevant assumptions be explicit.

At the center of traditional approaches to database design is a schema. A schema describes the conceptual or logical data structures of all the objects or entities with which the database is concerned, together with all the relationships between them known to the database. In such a well-defined context, the difference between metadata and data disappears—metadata is simply data. However, when the context is extended or modified, new information, metadata, is needed to provide unambiguous interpretation and a new schema. Thus, according to this perspective, the distinction between metadata and data is merely one of use, and the focus shifts to another formidable task, that of defining context. Metadata becomes the additional data that must be invoked to implement the change in context. The prefix "meta" does not attach to the data itself but derives from the circumstance of change.

Here a context is simply a set of assumptions, with a unique name or identifier. An approach to building such sets, including the categories of assumptions that are needed, is discussed below under "templates." Subject to certain significant caveats, such contexts can then be combined or manipulated using the operations of set algebra such as union and intersection. Note, however, that each party involved in a communication must first declare by name or establish by enumeration an *Initial Context* for themselves. These initial contexts must then be reconciled (to a first approximation by set union) into a *Unified Context* within which messages can be unambiguously interpreted. To achieve this unification, metadata (or, if you prefer, data) must be exchanged or otherwise invoked.

IMPORTANCE OF METADATA

Before warehouse data can be accessed efficiently, it is necessary to understand what data is available in the warehouse, and where that data is located. Metadata provides a catalog of data in the data warehouse and the pointers to this data. In addition to helping locate the data, the metadata may contain

- Data extraction/transformation history
- Column aliases
- Data warehouse table sizes
- Data summarization/modeling algorithms
- Data usage statistics

While much has been written about metadata, there has been little discussion of the impact of metadata on data warehouse architectures. In a well-designed architecture, metadata maps the entities, such as dimensions, attributes, and metrics, to tables and columns within the data warehouse. Specifically, this metadata includes

- Dimension, attribute, metric definitions.
- Attribute hierarchies—a mapping of parent/child relationships amongst attributes.
- Attribute to dimension mapping—indicates the dimension to which each attribute belongs.
- Metric to attribute mapping—indicates which attributes logically qualify each metric.
- Physical mapping of attributes, metrics—a mapping of attributes and metrics to the tables and columns in the data warehouse.
- Performance metrics—details of the performance characteristics of tables in the warehouse. Performance metadata includes the number of rows in each table and the indexes existing on each table. While most RDBMSs have query optimizers, this information is required for optimized query construction, rather than the tactics of how to optimize the performance of a given SQL query.
- Distinct elements per attribute—often, DSS analysts need knowledge of available elements within an attribute in order to formulate their queries. By presenting analysts with available elements, they do not need to guess whether elements exist in the warehouse, the spelling of those elements, and so on. Metadata provides a list of distinct elements for each attribute, or a pointer to such a list.

In well-designed data warehouse architectures, the application is coupled to the warehouse via the metadata, allowing changes to the data warehouse to be immediately reflected in the enduser data access application. For example, if a corporation restructures to eliminate a layer of management, as soon as the data corresponding to the new organizational hierarchy is added to the warehouse, the data warehouse application should "reconfigure" itself using the metadata to reflect the new hierarchy.

By using metadata to describe warehouse content and structure and by integrating this metadata with a powerful data warehouse, application construction and maintenance can be simplified dramatically.

THE ROLE OF METADATA

The previous sections have made many mentions of metadata, because this is a key component of any data warehouse or OLAP application. It is used to describe many aspects of the applications, including hierarchical relationships, stored formulae, whether calculations have to be performed before or after consolidation, currency conversion information, time series information, item descriptions and notes for reporting, security and access controls, data update status, formatting information, data sources, availability of precalculated summary tables, and data storage parameters. In the absence of this information, the actual data is not intelligible and it would not be wise to attempt to view or update it.

Because Multidimensional Databases (MDDs) are intended specifically for OLAP applications, they handle metadata intrinsically (and largely automatically) within the database. RDBMSs are more general-purpose technologies, and such application-specific information is normally built as part of the application development. Thus, relational OLAPs have to implement this themselves and even though the metadata is usually stored within the RDBMS, only applications which "understand" the metadata can make any business sense of the stored base and summary tables. This usually means that the relational OLAP client software or client API must be used, and direct connections from other applications to the database on the server are unable to take advantage of the multidimensional intelligence. Therefore, the connection is only possible with substantial custom programming, if at all. Conversely, MDDs are able to implement their APIs directly from the database engine, so a variety of other client or server applications can connect without losing the effects of the metadata.

Operational Environments

The role of metadata in the data warehouse environment is very different than that in the operational environment. In the operational environment, metadata is relegated to the same level of importance as documentation and is optional, whereas, the role of metadata in the data warehouse environment is mandatory.

The operational systems are primarily used by computer-literate professionals who are able to browse through the systems. On the other hand, the DSS analysis community does not have a high degree of computer literacy. Therefore, this set of users needs assistance to use the data warehouse effectively. Metadata serves this purpose quite well.

Metadata becomes of prime importance for managing the mapping between the operational environment and the data warehouse environment. As we have learned, data undergoes a significant transformation as it passes from the operational to the data warehouse environment. This process goes through conversion, filtering, summarization, and structural changes. Metadata in a data warehouse is an ideal place to keep track of such transformations. The importance of keeping a careful record of the transformation is evidenced by the events that occur when data warehouse data needs to be tracked to its source.

The data warehouse represents data spanning over large time periods. It is absolutely normal for a data warehouse to change during that span. Metadata helps keep track of the changing structure of the data in the warehouse. Therefore, it is not uncommon to find many structures of data over time in data warehouse environments. On the other hand, only one correct definition of the data structure is usually found in the operational environment.

External and Unstructured Data Environments

Metadata is an important component of the data warehouse as compared to the operational environment. However, metadata takes on entirely different dimensions in the face of storing and managing external and unstructured data. It is through metadata that external data is registered, accessed, and controlled in the data warehouse environment, as depicted in Figure 6.1.

Metadata eliminates the need for the user to look into the source documents for either the unstructured or external data sources. Typical contents of metadata for external data are

- Document identification
- Source of the document
- Description of the document
- Classification of the document
- Date of entry into the warehouse

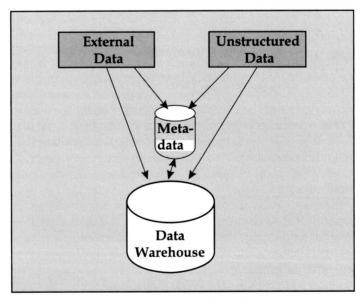

FIGURE 6.1   Role of Metadata.

- Document length
- References for location of the external and/or unstructured data

One of the primary advantages of the metadata is the ability to create a tailored notification file. This eliminates the need for storing such data in the actual data warehouse, if it is not convenient or cost-effective.

COMPONENTS OF METADATA

There are several components of stored data:

- The data characteristics:
  - Data format
  - When the data was acquired and compiled
  - Who compiled it
  - Method of compilation and accuracy
  - Scale of compilation
  - Positional and attribute accuracy
  - Projections and coordinate system
  - Interpretation of data items
  - Where the data is available
- The precalculated results
- The indexing structured required to access these quickly
- The metadata to describe and manage the physical data structures

The metadata is usually stored in a number of dimensions and other tables. For maximum efficiency, it is often held in specialized formats that are custom-built for a particular relational OLAP or analysis. For best performance, the metadata may be compiled into a binary form that maps multidimensional structures to relational tables. There are no (agreed upon) industry standards for metadata storage, so all relational OLAP tools have their own imposed schemas for data tables and metadata.

In order to answer any particular query, the data warehouse application will have to use the metadata to determine which are the nearest stored results and in which tables they are held, query all the relevant base and summary tables, combine the resulting information using temporary tables in the database or in its own memory, perform the remaining multidimensional calculations, and then provide the results to the users. The viewing tool must be able to take full advantage of all the multidimensional mapping (i.e., records to dimensions) and application data that is held in the metadata. This will not be possible if the stored data is viewed directly without going through the relational OLAP application's metadata.

APPLICATIONS OF METADATA

The potential applications are many, but five are of prime importance:

- Managing the data extract.
- Warehouse data discovery by using metadata to describe the data warehouse structure and contents to find and access data in the warehouse.
- Making the data available to the data warehouse based on data extract scheduling.
- Data synchronization by tracking the imported data and capturing the rules for obtaining synchronized views of the data.
- Measuring and reporting on the quality of data imported into the warehouse based on specific uses.

THE METADATA REPOSITORY

Existing database management systems are dominated by commercial applications. These tend to have schemas that are relatively static, though the contents may be updated frequently. Priorities are transactional integrity and efficiency of routine use, though as the tools (such as SQL queries) have become available, exploratory queries from management have become more prominent.

Applications, on the other hand, are generally adding not only more data but also new types of data. Deletions tend to occur only en masse when entire data sets are discarded as obsolete or not worth maintaining. Success is measured by the discovery of new relations within the data and by the new questions they stimulate, not by transactional efficiency.

The flexibility to deal with rapidly evolving schemas and for handling exploratory queries effectively must be our fundamental priorities. In addition, the same networks are encouraging individual initiative, challenging the very notion of a centralized authority able to impose standards across *any* realistic domain of participants. Thus new concepts are required, which redefine the functional relationships of users, contributors, designers, and operators of our information systems.

Supporting and managing data for a data warehouse require a variety of metadata, such as the suppliers of data, views of the data, and processes used to extract, validate, load, and archive the data. The value of metadata stems from its ability to be used as a standard description for a wide variety of data structures.

The descriptions and structures must be stored in a repository. The repository is used to store information about data lineage (i.e., to look at any field in a data warehouse schema, where did that field come from? Which operational data source? And what transformations did it go through? And lastly, the repository that will be used to store the transformation packages.) The benefit of this metadata repository is that it provides a standard way of entering and representing metadata that results in better integration between the different stages of data warehousing.

There are a variety of tools available that help in designing the metadata repository as well as the metadata model. Some of the key attributes of these tools are

- Intuitive interface
- Transparent access to data
- Support for a catalog of information (metadata)
- Multiple query and analysis methods
- Multiple presentation styles for information.

The data warehouse can only be of benefit if the data in it is converted into information, and in turn used to create knowledge for key decision makers. It is of little value having the most advanced data warehouse in the industry if the information generated and the support for maintenance and development of the data warehouse are not properly channeled. This is dependent on a number of factors.

Technology Issues

To engineer a data warehouse metadata repository requires the combination of several technologies into a single cohesive structure. It has elements from each of the following:

- *Hardware*—The server, be it MPP/SMP or a high-end server.
- *Database(s)*—Traditional RDBMS or post RDBMS, optimized for query or not.
- *Middleware*—Glues the databases together to form a single view of the repository data.
- *Enduser tools*—Integration of mining, DSS tools, using AI, expert systems, neural nets, or standard analysis techniques.
- *Warehouse management tools*—Organize and reorganize the data, form new views, build/remove summary tables, and so on.
- *Services*—Provided to help in the construction of a planned implementation of the warehouse from pilot to enterprise coverage.

Decision-Support Tools

A data warehouse would become another data dump without the provision of tools to investigate the data. The selection of the right tool is paramount to obtaining the best possible information from the warehouse. It must be remembered that in most cases we are looking for small previously unknown patterns in the data, relationships that have, so far, gone undiscovered.

Use the wrong tool and they will remain undiscovered. The warehouse must support every conceivable type of query and investigation that can be imagined, if the *decision-support* function is to perform effectively. Existing tools such as spreadsheets and preferred query and reporting tools should also be supported if the user desires.

Middleware

Effective selection of technologies should be driven by the existing infrastructure. The technology enabling this progression is provided in the middleware layer. Components providing such architecture should be selected to provide flexibility for any strategic change of direction or any ill-suited products that will undoubtedly occur. Strategic design for the warehouse should aim for a central repository for metadata. This will simplify management and improve efficiency for user access and support alike.

Database

As we discussed in previous sections, there is some contention between the emerging databases aiming specifically at the warehousing market and the more established RDBMSs. The new breed of databases which combine high performance, query optimization, and multiple dimensions are ideally suited to data warehouse applications. On the other hand, the established database vendors, who are heavily dependent on supporting transactional processing, are providing parallel options for their databases to provide the rapid response times required in a warehouse solution.

Traditional databases are quite easily adaptable to provide query, rather than transactional, optimization. The emerging databases appear to be making significant inroads into the warehousing market.

Parallel Hardware

It is *not* a prerequisite that a data warehouse have a large all-powerful computer. Modest systems which are well managed could provide the means for a small data mart. It is only when the volumes of data to be processed get into large figures, say, over 500 Gb and you require quick response from your query tool, that large MPP-/SMP-based systems become cost-effective. Support for low-cost storage is essential, considering the massive volumes achieved with early warehouse projects. This size is likely to increase further still as the thirst for more information increases. The MPP platforms of today can provide the commercial user with a scalable, cost-effective solution which is an ideal companion to a scalable pilot, data-warehousing solution. The ability for MPP systems to scale from only a few processors to hundreds if not thousands of processors allows a gradual incremental growth that can be combined with the gradual growth of the data warehouse

A MODEL FOR METADATA

The metadata reference model is a logical analysis of the structure of the external interface of autonomous modules (i.e., databases) loosely linked within a complete information system. The relevant communications within that system are between users and databases, and between databases themselves. For an important subset of

applications, the ultimate objective is to effect one-way transfer of information between users now and users decades in the future.

The environment for such communication is presumed to be similar to that
provided by the Internet, a rapidly evolving, open association of autonomous units,
with a minimal set of operating rules, and no central authority capable of imposing
uniform standards except by common agreement. Technologies, such as Gopher,
and the World Wide Web, with user interfaces such as Mosaic and Netscape, provide
navigational markers and flexible access tools, but useful user-oriented higher-level
data structures for full-service information systems have still to be evolved. The
emergence of knowledge-based software agents which navigate the network and perform chores on behalf of users only accentuates the need for clear external interfaces
to logical units in the information system.

A Metadata Reference Model

A metadata reference model is an analysis of the uses of metadata (in the general
sense of the word) in a number of different areas of data management activity, each
with its own characteristic requirements:

- Query, browse, retrieval
- Ingest, quality assurance, reprocessing
- Machine-to-machine transfer
- Storage, archival

The logical structure of the external interface is quite distinct from any implementation of particular databases, focusing instead on the information that has to pass
across the interface for the enterprise to be successful. Each module or database appears as a structured data expression that has the following properties:

- Self-describing to users and machines
- Can be entered and manipulated at different levels
- Presents different views according to level
- Is persistent
- Is dynamically extensible
- Is portable to different implementations while preserving its external interface
- Contains an extensible set of methods and utilities for manipulating and trans-
  forming data
- Has a look and feel that can be tailored to user discipline and data stream structure

It is assumed that individual structured data expressions are normally built
around particular data holdings, often centered on an established data stream, with
ancillary information from elsewhere added as required. The lowest level, an atomic expression, is conceived as structurally simple (e.g., a few relational tables with

SQL access), though it may contain very large volumes of data. Higher levels would build more complex structures. The term "level" is used here to specify entry points and degree of complexity of constituent subexpressions, but the number of such levels varies between databases. Users typically match the level to their prior familiarity with the subject matter, so some approximate naming convention for levels is desirable.

The central issue is how to define, structure, and describe the range of contexts within which a particular database must function. This range can be built to any particular level on the characteristics of individual data streams, drawing on a set of default conventions and rule-based knowledge which are identified by discipline, subdiscipline, and specialty, expanded from the top down.

These databases can be complemented within the association by issue-oriented high-level modules, which provide structured learning paths for the user through key documents and published literature down to selected derived products and original data sets. Such high-level modules act essentially as multiple indices over the population of databases. This structured data expression should be able to exchange information in any of the basic modes, such as,

- Tables and data structures
- Graphs and diagrams
- Images
- Equations and mathematical models
- Algorithms and implementable procedures
- Electronic documents and other formats combining several modes

Not all these may be economically feasible at first, but full implementation will require them all.

Services

Though it is supposed that each database retains design autonomy over its internal implementation and contents, for the association of many databases to function there need to be certain system-wide services which are centrally administered. Besides standard network connectivity, transport, and communication protocols, special attention needs to be paid to a process for assembling inputs on at least the following issues.

User Authorization and Authentication

Even if the contents of the database are available for full and open exchange, it is still necessary to restrict the ability to modify those contents, and to account for the use of resources. Since many users are other computers known only by a network address, there has to be some centrally coordinated register of authorized users in various categories, and some technique for authenticating stated identities.

Globally Unique Names and Their Disciplinary Aliases

Discrete names for discrete entities form the glue that holds a computer network together. When a variable or data structure is generated by reprocessing for which no external name exists, the variable or structure can be described and be assigned a global name with an appropriate disciplinary alias, so that it is easier to use.

Model Description Languages—Particularly for Structured Data Objects

A structured data expression must include methods to describe itself, both to another computer and to a user. Such descriptions must be in one of a few model description languages, and the initial negotiations between communicating partners should include the selection of a suitable one. This negotiation protocol is the key to graceful evolution.

Templates to Help Define Context

A central concept in the reference model is the articulation of a set of hierarchically structured templates, named for example by a tag—each of which defines a set of default assumptions and can be used individually or by set union to construct approximations to initial contexts. The assumptions in disciplinary templates should include coverage of the following categories:

- Public names for variables
- Logical and associative relationships between variables
- Descriptions of standard measurement and analysis procedures, including suggestions for relevant metadata
- Descriptions of standard theoretical models
- Units, levels of precision

Each of the above must be expressed in an appropriate format, rule base, or language. The primary information is semantic, but much value for database management would come from structuring relations in the template according to the following classes:

- Fundamental—logically based, can be hardwired into database manipulations.
- Proximity—physically/intellectually based associations, things most likely to be retrieved together, crucial for implementation efficiency.
- Transformation—associated with implementable algorithms that are themselves entries in the database, for example, Celsius <-> Fahrenheit or internal <-> external formats.
- Derivative—value-added products that become new entries in the database and deflect queries from the original.
- Guide—explanations and cross-references driven by science content, intended to inform a user.

Likewise, each instrument system or data stream has its own set of obvious metadata. This includes log books, calibrations, and other information that is necessary to reflect the original purpose of the measurements or analysis.

In special cases, ad hoc formats can be developed for more systematic sets of default templates for data streams similar to those that would aid communication. Approximations to initial contexts for a dialogue between a user and database can be provided by the default assumptions. Each set of default assumptions would then be modified, if necessary, before merger into a single unified context.

Such templates would take much of the pain (for users at least) out of establishing effective communication and should stimulate the development of interactive forms and software agents to assist the two-way flow of information between users and the database.

Query, Browse, and Retrieval

This interface is driven by a user's need to answer questions efficiently. Specific queries could be managed by an appropriate user-based software agent working to a more detailed user profile.

Ingest, Quality Assurance, and Reprocessing

This interface is driven by the need to acquire a high-quality data set with a precisely defined data dictionary and to ensure the logical integrity of the database. The information that needs to be acquired falls into following categories, relating to

- Scientific content,
- Logical structure, and
- Patterns of use.

Linkages that need to be defined are expressed by

- Internal representation of the data dictionary—external representation.
- Internal names—external names.
- Assumptions about context—explicit representation.
- Variables—attributes.
- Assumed mathematical and logical equivalencies—tests for database integrity.
- Assumed transformation algorithms and utilities.
- Content quality control—action in case of exceptions, such as permissible ranges of attributes, tolerances in transformations, missing data, and attaching quality control flags.
- Built-in attributes, such as sticky notes attached to blocks of data.
- Proximity relationships—efficient internal representations. Proximity relationships are criteria indicating relative probability that data items will need to

be accessed together. They provide information fundamental to efficient database design, such hardwired relationships and pointer structure.

- Dimensionality of data source, in the areas of space and time, scientific associations between variables, and relevance blocks for metadata.
- Known and projected reprocessing algorithms—implications for the database.
- Linkage definitions—a decision model for database design and operations.

This aspect of the database requires semantic and logical attributes which can be translated smoothly into an internal representation (subschema) and are efficiently accessed and manipulated with available hardware and software.

Machine-Machine Transfer

This interface is driven by the need to transfer all or part of the information in the structured data object to another operating system on a different hardware configuration, while preserving the integrity of the data and metadata and all the logical relationships among them. Such a capability is also fundamental to transferring an existing database to a more efficient implementation within the same environment.

Machine-to-machine transfer between different operating environments places many demands on the completeness and robustness of the descriptions of data structure.

Storage and Archive

This interface is driven by need for efficient implementation of search and retrieval. This requires a balance between

- Storage system and media costs
- Access and processing costs
- User time and satisfaction while seeking and retrieving information
- Scientist and knowledge engineer time importing information
- Extensibility and evolutionary potential of the system

External/Unstructured Data and the Model

The normal role of the data model is to shape the environment. But external and unstructured data are not amenable to any extent since there is very little relationship between the data model and the external data.

Required Information

A decision model is an analysis of the choices that have to be made at the design stage and at the operation stage, and how they impact the overall goal. It provides a framework for assessing the utility of information being sought both through interactive forms and through statistical analysis of database use, for the purposes of ensuring the logical integrity of the database and increasing its overall efficiency. A decision model requires

- Specification of design assumptions and anticipated changes.
- Logical data dictionary and proximity information. This information has to be garnered systematically from various sources, including a careful review of scientists' insights of fundamental logical relations that can be relied on for database structure, and proximity relations indicating which variables are most likely to be retrieved together.
- Expected frequency of accesses for various inputs.
- Analysis tools for estimating resource requirements.
- Performance evaluation criteria and tools.

A central requirement for this aspect is a decision model which shows, for each major database architecture, how such information would actually be used in selecting a design. It may be necessary to formalize such decision models, using heuristic rules for a variety of local data models.

The use of interactive forms to capture the metadata necessary for efficient database implementation, and the collection of appropriate statistics on performance both depend on a good analysis of what the implementation choices are. Given appropriate models and the right input information, examining a variety of scenarios should indicate which designs are more likely to be robust.

A greater choice of local data models may also be needed. Requirements for easy evolution and modification of the schema seem to imply greater flexibility than is available from existing relational or tree-structured data models. Such flexibility would seem to be provided by an object-oriented functional representation.

SUMMARY

All disciplines face a computer-enabled explosion of data, or the widespread use of networks and distributed servers that greatly facilitate the availability of data, *and* the opportunities for misinterpreting it. What we typically regard as the data is but a small part of the information that has to be assembled, interrelated, and communicated. This additional information (metadata) is central to our objectives, yet we have few tools to assist in describing effectively what all these bits mean.

A test of the adequacy of our present information systems is to imagine what our successors will think 20 years from now as they examine our records and try to determine whether the apparent changes between now and then are real, or are merely undetected artifacts of the way we took the measurements or analyzed the data. This requires standards of documentation and quality assurance that far exceed what we are presently able to achieve routinely and are sufficient for fail-safe unambiguous communication about scientifically crucial details without benefit of the interactive questioning.

In the conventional transaction processing environment, the need for data about data is generally satisfied by a data dictionary or a repository. In the data warehouse environment, the need for data about data is greater because it is vital that the users understand what the data represents. On the other hand, in the transaction processing environment, it is sufficient to describe the data structures and the data definitions. The degree to which the data is available to the user contributes significantly to the initial success of the data warehouse.

In this chapter, we discussed the role of metadata and some aspects about metadata repository and modeling.

7

DATA WAREHOUSE MODELING: KEY TO DECISION SUPPORT

INTRODUCTION

Before starting to design a data warehouse, it is imperative for the organization to clearly understand the anticipated key problems and technical obstacles. The data warehouse model is the central component of the data warehouse building environment. It is also the primary tool for strategic planning, communicating data requirements throughout the organization, implementing integrated systems, and organizing data in the data warehouse.

The data warehouse model represents the integrated information requirements of the enterprise. It is designed to support the analysis and *decision-support* requirements of the entire business organization.

Each data model should address a specific functional area of the enterprise data architecture. The flexible design of each data model allows you to focus on specific requirements immediately rather than perform time-consuming repetitive functional analysis.

A number of components constitute the data warehouse model. These components are developed and maintained within an environment that provides the tools for rapid development of models as well as physical design and data administration.

Why Data Modeling?

As markets become increasingly competitive, the ability to react quickly and decisively to market trends is more critical than ever. In today's corporate environment, the volume and complexity of information available to organizations can be overwhelming. Companies who are able to organize and analyze this barrage of data most effectively will find themselves at a tremendous competitive advantage. For this reason, data warehouse modeling is emerging as a key planning tool of corporate strategy.

Data warehousing is the process of integrating enterprise-wide corporate data into a single repository from which endusers can run reports and perform ad hoc data analysis. Because of the enormous quantities of information available to companies, data warehouses often grow to be very large. As a result, one of the most significant challenges of implementing a data warehouse model is ensuring high performance.

Organizations have an insatiable appetite for data but usually lack the neural connections to process it. The volume of data is irrelevant if it is not organized so that it adds value. To an organization, this value means turning data into usable information. Modeling for warehousing is one approach to making sense of this mountain of data. It will help to remember some of the following salient characteristics:

- Modeling is not tied to any physical representation of data.
- Modeling is not inseparable from multidimensional databases.
- Modeling does not involve squeezing information into cubes.

In contrast to On-Line Transaction Processing (OLTP) systems, which are designed around entities, functional decomposition, state transition analysis, and interrelationships, the data warehouse model is based on dimensions, hierarchies, facts, and sparsity.

What Is a "Data Model"?

A data model is a graphic representation of the data within a specific area of interest. That area of interest may be as broad as all the integrated data requirements of a complete enterprise (enterprise data model) or as focused as a single business area or application (subject area data models). Frequently a data model represents a business functional area (marketing, sales, customer, financials, manufacturing) or a business area that is to be analyzed or automated (problem tracking, reporting). A good data model depicts or describes the following:

- Entities (tables).
- Attributes (columns).
- Complete definitions of entities and attributes.
- The relationships among data, represented as relationship lines.
- Data cardinality, which describes the real or implied business rules that govern the data relationships.
- Primary, secondary, and alternate keys.
- Large-format, clear graphics.

The goal of the data model is to clearly convey the meaning of data, the relationships among the data, and the attributes of the data and record the precise definitions of data. A data model is the standard and accepted way of analyzing data and designing and implementing databases.

The data model for a business organization tends not to change greatly over time unless the business organization changes the fundamental way that it does business. The way that data is used, the processes, can vary greatly even between organizations functioning in the same industry. However, the data required by organizations within the same industry tends to be very similar. This is why we can assume that data models have basic stability within the organization while process models are relatively unstable. This commonality of functional data is the basic tenant that allows "cookbook" data models for an industry to be applied by organizations operating in that industry.

Normally, most data models are developed using CASE tools. Such CASE tools provide the supporting software for development of the model including the graphics, data dictionary, links to other tools, and supporting utilities.

What Is the Enterprise Data Model?

The enterprise data model for each industry-specific data environment represents all the integrated primary data requirements of a typical organization operating within that industry. The data is leveled for presentation so that the entities represent each business subject area, business functional area, and the dominant relationships between key data are represented. Such a model is generally supported by a data dictionary (metadata).

What Is the Data Warehouse Model?

The data warehouse model for each industry-specific data environment describes the target data structures and their data relationships in support of the enterprise-wide information requirements of a typical organization operating within that industry. Each industry-specific data warehouse model is derived directly from the same-industry enterprise data model. The enterprise data model's logical data structures are the foundation for the development of corresponding data warehouse data structures. The data warehouse data structures are consistent with how data is typically structured to provide enterprise-wide information. The data warehouse model for each industry has the following characteristics:

- Summarized data for *decision support* and analysis.
- Multiple levels of summarization.
- Data that is rarely updated.
- Integrated data from multiple sources.
- Design driven by evolving information needs.
- Oriented by business area, function, or subject.
- Provides integrated information across the entire enterprise.
- Granularity of data for analysis over extended periods of time.
- Constructed iteratively by subject area.
- Provides clean, reliable data to business area "data marts" or *decision support*.

The data warehouse is surrounded by any number of functional *decision-support* systems or "data marts" serving the associated functional areas. As data moves from the data warehouse to local *decision-support* system or "data mart" systems, control of the data is turned over to local administrators. The data warehouse remains a consistent source of data over time for the organization regardless of how data is processed locally.

The focus of the data warehouse model is centralized, integrated, dependable data that can be used by the organization as a whole and provide data to local data marts or *decision-support* systems.

DATA MODELING CONCEPTS AND TERMS

Data modeling is a technique developed to structure data around natural business concepts and to provide a foundation for sophisticated data analysis. The data warehouse is conceptually the center of the *decision-support* and analysis data architecture. The data warehouse is the ultimate source of clean, consistent data for the entire organization.

Entity Types and Relationships

An entity is a database object such as a table, view, report, or screen. An entity is a person, a place, or a thing of interest to the data modeler at the highest level of abstraction. Traditional data models describe "entities" and "relationships." Such a strategy focuses on breaking up information into a large number of tables, each of which describes exactly one entity. An entity might be a physical object (e.g., a product or a customer) or it might be a transaction (e.g., a sale or an order's line item). Entities are interrelated through a complex series of joins.

In modeling, data structures are organized to describe "measures" and "dimensions." Measures are the numerical data being tracked. They are stored in central "fact" tables. Dimensions are the natural business parameters that define each transaction. Dimensions are stored in satellite tables that join to the central fact table. For example, the data stored in fact tables includes sales, inventory, magazine subscriptions, expenditures, and gross margins data. Typical tables include time, geography, account, and product data.

The focus in data modeling is to organize information according to the way users intuitively think about their business, and to minimize the number of joins required to retrieve the information into meaningful, integrated reports. Suppose a marketing analyst typically examines sales data as it is requested in the following queries: "Sales by product line manager over the past six months," or, "Sales by account for a given year." In such a case, the data model would consist of a fact table to track sales information. For each sale, there would be a record storing quantity ordered, price, and extended price, among other variables. The satellite tables would include account information, product information, and time information with natural dimensions of the sales information.

Therefore, every sales record would possess a key joining it to each of the dimension tables. Thus, the fact table would store quantity ordered, sales, account code, time code, and product code. Fact tables are generally fully normalized, meaning that there is no duplicate data storage within the table.

Aggregation

Aggregation is the process by which low-level data is summarized in advance and placed into tables that store the summarized or "aggregated" information. These aggregate tables allow applications to anticipate user queries and eliminate the need to repeat resource-intensive calculations that would otherwise be performed each time the summary information is requested.

Attributes

Attribute a property can assume a value for entities or relationships. Entities can be assigned several attributes. Attributes provide the depth of the dimensions beyond identifying codes. Through the attributes, we can find the hierarchies of the dimensions, detailed descriptions of each dimensional element, and extended properties. It is common for dimension tables to have over 100 columns of attributes; properly designed queries or front-end query generators understand these highly denormalized structures to return complex queries quickly.

Assume that our model has a product dimension with an attribute for "type" with "low-fat," "ethnic," "premium," "plain-label," and "special diet" as possible values. This is important and is a key differentiater between relational and multidimensional implementations. Even though there is no defined hierarchy for these attributes, it is possible to generate queries very quickly by using the power of the star schema.

Sparsity

The sparsity are not "entities" or represented as tables. Attributes are the extended descriptions and hierarchies of the dimensions, such as brand, color, and size in the product dimension. Sparsity is handled implicitly. It is likely that facts (dollars, for example) exist for only a small fraction of the market and period. The star schema model handles sparsity by simply not recording records where those combinations are invalid. In a simple star, that translates to thousands of rows at 99 percent sparsity.

Metadata

Metadata includes sources of warehouse data, replication rules, rollup categories and rules, availability of summarizations, security and controls, purge criteria, and logical and physical data mapping. Relational OLAP tools rely on strong metadata dictionaries for helping business users track ongoing changes within the *decision-support* environment. When changes occur, all components—databases, metadata facilities, desktop tools, and reporting applications—automatically reflect the changes. In contrast, the more sophisticated report writers require IS to maintain and monitor metadata, but they do not leverage the labor with system-wide awareness.

In relational/OLAP products, a relationship table depicting the multiple hierarchies is needed in metadata. In relational/OLAP products, a relationship table depicting the multiple hierarchies is needed in metadata. It is mentioned here to help you understand how the tools interpret the relationships. Metadata contains the information to map the warehouse data to the *decision-support* views, the operational sources, and to related data in the warehouse.

The following are examples of metadata. Each requires a data definition and maintenance process:

- Sources of warehouse information, frequency of download, and completeness (Have all monthly feeds been received for January?).
- *Decision-support* mapping of warehouse data: keys, qualifying attributes, security, translations, and so forth.
- Relationships and referential integrity constraints.
- Purge and retention periods.
- Replication and distribution rules.
- Aggregation methods and rules.
- Exception conditions automatically reported.

Relationships and Cardinality

Cardinality is a number of tuples or rows in a relation and is just a lofty way of saying "how many," and "boundedness" simply indicates whether there is an upper limit to the cardinality.

If you build a multidimensional model in a relational database, unbounded cardinality is expected. The opposite is true in the multidimensional databases, where changes in cardinality often require complete reorganization of the database—an extremely time-consuming process. Certain products allow a "reach-through" or "drill-through" process, where analysis can occur at a summary level. Detail at lower levels is not actionable—it is available only in listing format. By defining the boundary for active analysis, you define the limits of your manipulative analytical reach.

When dimensions are large (high cardinality), it often makes sense to split the dimension tables at the level of the attributes, also known as the "snowflake schema." Storing aggregations and derivations yields even more exotic combinations, sometimes referred to as "decomposed stars" or "constellation schema."

The dimensional modeling for relational databases is designed to create fact tables, usually long and thin, and relatively small, short, and wide dimension tables. While the fact tables contain the actual numeric information, all of the interesting information is in the dimension tables. Queries are designed to exploit this by using the dimension tables for counts, control breaks, aggregation paths, and searching for properties of the elements. Many queries can be resolved without even touching the fact table. When "facts" are needed, the method is to gather the key values from the dimension tables and then pull the matching records from the fact table, avoiding costly and time-consuming table scans and complex joins.

Foreign Key

It is a column or combination of columns in one table whose value(s) match(es) the primary key(s) in another table.

Referential Integrity

It is the facility of a DBMS that defines a reliable relationship between two tables and a means of joining those tables. *Decision-support* queries rely heavily on joining the information from one table to the information from another table to find intersections or matching values. For example, some joins might be derived from the primary key and foreign key relationships between the fact and the dimension tables. In other words, referential integrity ties dimensions to facts.

OVERALL STRUCTURE AND THE PLANNING PROCESS

Developing a data warehouse must involve more than simply loading the available data. It must also be more than searching a response to a particular query request. Instead, the approach must be entirely pragmatic.

Two considerations are crucial to keep in mind. First, the typical warehouse service drives off a time base, and, second, the data warehouse system must scrutinize its data and report peculiarities. It thus tracks things over time and observes deviations relative to expectations.

Extraction

Data extraction is a regular, routine process. It needs planning, like any other systems job, although there are some differences in conception and execution. Technical issues abound but can be addressed. The key factor from an executive standpoint is being able to trust the quality of this data.

Monitoring

The data warehouse should consciously be planned to extend with time. Because these systems represent the quintessential "user-driven" environment, management needs to be part of the development process. Management also needs to feel the pride of developing ever-increasing refinement of interrogation processes (both by the machine as well as by themselves). Therefore, while the systems architects may have a fairly clear view of the likely evolution of the system, they should roll out the development in a way which engenders ultimate ownership by the users. This aspect is introspective.

Most companies' business is reflected in large numbers of low-level details. It is difficult for managers to review such volumes. They lose sight of the forest because of all the trees. An effective monitor mechanism allows managers to stipulate boundaries in order that the system can report on trends that exceed such boundaries. This sifting process allows executives to focus on deeper investigation of more relevant data.

Investigation

The data warehouse typically represents a new means of access to information as well as a new approach to the development and the propagation of systems. The investigation utility of the data warehouse is typically a palette made up of icons. The icons, when activated, allow the user to pursue a particular course of inquiry. Output is flexible and may be reports, on screen or on paper, which provide direct visualization of the data at a variety of levels and in graphic form. Icons reflect precreated investigatory processes and allow the user to understand and to explore specific topics. In any given situation the investigation system grows along two distinct avenues:

- The first avenue is intended for use by senior managers and others needing high-level information. The facilities allow non-technical users to explore the financial results of the company, mousing or mousing up and down sets of preformed screens, and to access specific relations (and joins) conditionally to review particular data graphically.
- The second avenue of inquiry in the data warehouse is intended for systems-literate business analysts and usually includes advanced statistical tools such as regression and multivariate analysis.

The investigation module grows by means of a new approach to systems development. In traditional applications development, the user has provided MIS with requirements. Those requirements have been translated into systems which support business operations and which usually cannot be rapidly modified. The traditional approach is not well suited to providing the rapid and flexible access to information which is the hallmark of the data warehouse.

THE MULTIDIMENSIONAL VERSUS RELATIONAL MODEL

The characteristics of the relational model are well understood. Its ability to support operational processes is its *raison d'être*. In contrast, the multidimensional model is designed to support the reporting and analytical needs of knowledge workers, and can best be described by contrasting it with the relational model in the following four fundamental ways:

Transaction View versus Slice of Time

The multidimensional model views information from the perspective of a "slice of time" instead of atomic transactions. The is globally consistent for the enterprise. The relational model is internally consistent. OLTP systems provide for detailed audit trails. Multidimensional models fare better for the big picture. Relationships are modeled explicitly in the relational model and implicitly in the multidimensional model.

OLTP systems record actual events, or transactions. Examples are journal entries, purchase orders, billing items, hamburgers dropped on the floor, or all those collect calls on Father's Day. The multidimensional data model is not concerned with actual events, only the quantitative result of them at some interval in time, such as days, weeks, or months.

Local Consistency versus Global Consistency

A properly designed OLTP system is consistent within its own scope. For example, a general ledger is locally consistent if it properly records all of the relevant transactions, performs allocations, and maintains its account master. But if the data warehouse combines information from several general ledger systems, each with its own chart of accounts, global consistency is not automatic. The multidimensional model starts from a globally consistent view of the enterprise, meaning a single chart of accounts, in this case.

Audit Trail versus Big Picture

When a customer has a question about their credit card bill, they want to see every transaction. When your overnight package is lost, you want to know who the last person was to see it intact. The systems that manage this information ensure the highest level of confidence and security. Is it no wonder that they have shortcomings when dealing with analytical questions? The multidimensional model is designed to answer questions such as, "Will I make money on this deal or not?" or "Who are my best customers and why?" or "What opportunities are we missing?"

Explicit versus Implied Relationships

Entity-relationship modeling is the heart of the relational model. The explicit relationships between customers and sales orders, or between hamburgers and buns are burned into the design of the database. In multidimensional modeling, these relationships are implied by the existence of "facts" at the cross section of dimensions. For example, if there are sales dollars to Customer 987, of Product 1241, then the relationship between customer and product is implied.

BUILDING A DATA MODEL

As you begin to build your model, avoid trying to include everything at once. Instead, concentrate on a specific area, such as customer profitability or sales reporting. This simple statement describes the business process (retail sell-through data), facts (sales dollars, sales units, return units, shipment units, price), dimensions (customer, product, time, and view), and granularity or lowest level of detail (sales, shipments, and returns of individual products.

Operational versus Warehouse Data

This is the operational environment which provides the source data. In order to minimize the impact on the day-to-day OLTP type processing, the only processing required for this layer is "extraction." Because of the varying degree of differences between various operational systems, the data captured must undergo

- Conditioning
- Validating
- Mapping from source to target

The *Decision-Support* System (DSS) enables complex data analysis. Data models designed to support data warehouses require optimization that can handle the challenges of DSS. In *decision-support* systems, there tend to be relatively few concurrent transactions, each accessing very large numbers of records.

Highly normalized data models are designed to provide extremely efficient data access for large numbers of transactions involving very few records. This is what differentiates OLAP systems (On-Line Analytical Processing, or *decision support*) from OLTP systems (On-Line Transaction Processing). This difference has serious implications for the information warehouse designer. Table 7.1 is helpful in understanding the differences between *decision-support* functions and OLTP functions.

Because data processing in OLTP systems is highly structured, complex data models can work well. Transactions generally involve only one or two tables at a time, and often deal with only a single record. This means that complex table rela-

TABLE 7.1 Operational versus Data Warehouse Systems

TOPIC/FUNCTION	OPERATIONAL	DATA WAREHOUSE
Data Content	Current values	Archival data, summarized data, calculated data
Data Organization	Application by application	Subject areas across enterprise
Nature of Data	Dynamic	Static until refreshed
Data Structure, Format	Complex; suitable for operational computation	Simple; suitable for business analysis
Access Probability	High	Moderate to low
Data Update	Updated on a field-by-field basis	Accessed and manipulated; no direct update
Usage	Highly structured repetitive processing	Highly unstructured analytical processing
Response Time	Subsecond to 2–3 seconds	Seconds to minutes

tionships do not interfere a great deal with performance. In contrast, *decision-support* processing can involve accessing hundreds of thousands of rows at a time. In such cases, complex joins can seriously compromise performance.

Plan

A warehouse is only as useful as the data in it. Planning is essential to successfully store and access data. Without a plan, a successful warehouse probably will not happen. It's also important to set realistic expectations. With a plan, achievable expectations can be set. The right sponsor can help assure success, while the wrong one may guarantee failure. Involve your company's data administrators, but don't confuse data administration with database administration. It is better to choose a data warehouse manager who is business- or user-oriented than one who is technically oriented. It's essential to define the data so you don't have overlapping data with a confusing definition or, worse yet, no definition.

The Source Data

It may sound repetitive, but without modeling, a successful warehouse is impossible. Companies who have tried to build a warehouse without modeling have failed—and failed expensively, because they may have spent upwards of a million dollars on the warehouse by the time they discover that it didn't work.

A model is a blueprint of the business. It identifies entities (a person, place, event, or thing) about which the corporation wants to keep information. The attributes of entities form the relationships that are important to the business. From these relationships come the business rules that govern the data. To model data, you must decide which source data you're going to use, that is, which data is important to the business, because you can use only a small portion of your operational data in the warehouse. Don't forget to include such external data as text, images, and possibly voice and video, as well as conventional operational data. The next step is to select the legacy business systems from which you'll obtain the data you want.

Scrub

The existing operational data must be scrubbed. This means clearly defining all data with a single format. (Is the gender format F/M, f/m, Female/Male, 1/0, Woman/Man, or Girl/Boy, for example?) Operational data consists of many systems that were built to add new business to the firm, or to automate some function that had not been needed before, or to resolve a business problem that needed to be automated. With the development of these systems flowed the creative juices of the teams that developed them. Thus, each system developed from a need that resembled no other need except perhaps the platform on which it resided. Extracting data from each system to reside in the warehouse is a significant challenge.

Keep in mind that data residing in the warehouse is not raw production data. Production data normally does not store summary data because it was gathered for use in an operational system to serve precisely that function. Production data is not easily accessed for providing reports. Scrubbing the data puts it in the proper warehouse format, but unless you model the data, your production data simply won't work as data for the warehouse.

These are just a few of the issues that should be considered when building a data warehouse. A "smart" warehouse is one that is specific, measurable, achievable, realistic, and timely. The first step to building a data warehouse model is to pick a business subject area and model it by asking six fundamental questions.

1. What business process is being modeled?
2. What are the measures (or facts)?
3. At what level of detail (granularity) is "active" analysis conducted?
4. What do the measures have in common (the "dimensions")?
5. What are the dimensions' attributes?
6. Are the attributes stable or variable over time and is their "cardinality" bounded or unbounded?

Data Partitioning, Granularity, and Integration

Those enterprises who anticipate building large, complex *decision-support* systems must look for technologies capable of optimizing three, interrelated, *decision-support* database functions:

- Denormalization, a database design that repetitively stores data in tables, minimizing the number of time-consuming joins when executing a query and reducing the number of rows that must be analyzed.
- Summarization, a technique for aggregating information in advance, eliminating the need to do so at runtime.
- Partitioning, the ability to divide a single large fact table into many smaller tables, thereby improving response time for queries as well as for data warehouse backup and reloading.

Aggregating the Data Warehouse

A typical data warehouse begins as a massive store of transactions at the lowest, or "atomic," level. Measures are stored in the main fact table in their most detailed form so that later phases of data analysis and reporting can make use of them.

But extracting data from the most atomic level does not yield optimal performance, even with leading-edge software and hardware. Fact tables tend to be very large, resulting in serious performance challenges. Summing millions of rows takes a long time no matter what software or hardware is used, and no matter how well the data warehouse has been tuned.

A significant percentage of queries against the data warehouse call for summarization, or aggregation, of data elements. A typical user might ask: "Show me total sales for this month." This would be interpreted by the database as, "Add up all the sales for each of the days that this month contains." If there are an average of 2,000 sales transactions per day in each of 200 stores and data is stored at the transactional level, this query would have to process 40,000,000 rows to return the answer. A summary-intensive query like this can take up significant resources.

For commonly accessed data, presummarization is often useful. This enables intermediate results or "aggregates" to be used, significantly reducing resources required to deliver the final query results. To appreciate the value of aggregates, consider a request for July sales. If there is an aggregate table already created to track monthly sales by store, the query has to process only 2,000 rows (the July total for each store). Compared to the 40,000,000 rows the same query would have to process with data stored at the transactional level, the resource savings is several orders of magnitude. In fact, since query response time in a well-tuned warehouse is roughly proportional to the number of rows the query has to process, the improvement in performance with the above summary could be close to a factor of 40,000.

How Much to Aggregate?

Most existing technologies offer database users a drastic choice for every possible combination of queries the user might want, such as,

- no aggregation at all, or
- exhaustive aggregation.

Performing no aggregation is generally out of the question for substantive data warehouses. Aggregating in every possible combination achieves the best possible query performance but at tremendous storage, maintenance, and loading-time cost. First, storing summary information at every possible level consumes enormous amounts of disk space, increasing the storage requirements by a factor of five or more. Second, typical data warehouses have thousands of combinations of dimension elements, and creating a table or tables to hold the aggregates for all those combinations is an overwhelming maintenance task. Finally, building aggregates every time new information is added to the fact table can become so time consuming and resource intensive that the load window required to make the warehouse operational may become unacceptably long.

What is needed is a query engine that uses aggregates intelligently. For example, consider a query that asks for sales summarized by year. Further consider that sales are stored by transaction in the fact table and by month in an aggregate table. The query should be issued against the monthly summary and should add up the 12 records for the 12 months that are stored in the aggregate instead of adding up the thousands of transaction records from the fact table. If the engine can make such a decision, it is unnecessary to create the "sales-by-year" aggregate, since summarizing 12 rows is trivial.

Choosing the Right Aggregates

There are two main considerations when determining which aggregates to create:

- *Usage patterns*—Which aggregates would most improve performance for the specific queries run most often by the enduser?
- *Data density*—Where is the data concentrated, and in which dimension elements do the number of rows steeply increase?

If a given dimension element represents a large number of rows as compared to other elements in the hierarchy, aggregating by that dimension element drastically improves performance. Conversely, if a dimension element contains few rows, or if it contains hardly more rows than the superseding dimension element, aggregating by that dimension element is less efficient.

This analysis becomes more meaningful—and more complicated—as dimensions combine with one another. Defining a data request by multiple dimensions not only decreases the range of data retrieved, but also the density. It is rare, for example, that every product sells in every store, every day. For many products, there may in fact be few sales records for any given day, and the daily product sales data is thus sparse. If, however, all or many products sell in every store, every day, the data is classified as relatively dense. Data density complicates our calculation of how many records a query engine has to process. A sizing simulation based on the facile assumption that every possible record exists, that is, that the data is perfectly dense, skews the performance analysis of each aggregate.

When determining, for example, whether to compile an aggregate summarizing product line sales by region, the number of different products actually sold in each store within the regions is crucial. Consider a simplified database containing four stores in each of two regions (a total of eight stores), selling four products in each of two product lines (a total of eight products).

If only one of the products in a product line sells in each region on a daily basis (sparse data), the number of products in the product line for that day effectively shrinks to one. For the query, "Daily product line sales by region," one product row would be retrieved for each product line (two) in each region (two), for a total of four rows. Similarly, if products were aggregated into a sales-by-product line aggregate, and the same query were posed, the same number of rows would be processed. In this instance, the aggregate offers no performance advantage whatsoever.

If, at the other extreme (dense data), every product in each product line sells in every store, every day, this query would have to process four products for each of two product lines, and for each of the four stores in both regions, for a total of 64 records. But an aggregate summarizing product line sales by region could process this query using only four records, reducing the number of records processed sixteenfold. In a typical database representing thousands of stores and products, the performance advantage would be substantial. An analysis identifying optimal aggregates would favor a product line aggregate in this instance.

The question that must be answered at each step is, "Which aggregate is reduced by the greatest amount the average number of rows a query in this data warehouse has to process?" The algorithm recursively calculates this answer along with the supporting evidence and stores it in the database.

The answer to the second depends on feedback from the user community. The information can be collected on which data is being requested most often, who is requesting it, how long the query took to process, and how many rows were retrieved, and other criteria. This information can then be used to further tune the data warehouse.

Sample Aggregation Sizing

To determine the optimal number of aggregates to create in any given data warehouse, we can conduct a "sizing simulation." The main factors to consider are the total amount of space occupied by the aggregates (cost of disk) and the total number of aggregate tables (cost of load window and maintenance).

Incremental versus Full Aggregation

As mentioned earlier, one disadvantage associated with the aggregation process is the time window required to build the aggregates. For endusers with very large databases and significant aggregation requirements, it can take a tremendous amount of time and computer resources to build all the aggregates needed. Each week, as more information comes into the data warehouse, the aggregates become outdated and thus need to be recalculated. One option is simply to recalculate them from scratch by performing the summary operation on the base fact table. However, in situations where the aggregation time window is a serious problem, this is an impractical solution.

The Star Schema

A physical architecture of the data model is described by the star schema. A defining characteristic of a star schema is that the dimension tables are denormalized. Denormalization is a database design approach in which data is repetitively stored in individual tables for the sake of design simplicity and performance. Thus, dimension attributes may be stored multiple times in a dimension table, depending on which level of the dimension hierarchy the attributes describe.

The simplicity of the star schema in such a model confers the following important advantages:

- It allows a complex, multidimensional data structure to be defined with a very simple data model.
- This makes it easy to define hierarchical relationships within each dimension, and it simplifies the task of creating joins across multiple tables.
- It reduces the number of physical joins the query has to process. This greatly improves performance.

- By simplifying the view of the data model, it reduces the chances of users' inadvertently submitting incorrect, long-running queries which consume significant resources and return inaccurate information.
- It allows your data warehouse to expand and evolve with relatively low maintenance. The star schema's simple and powerful dimensional design provides a flexible foundation for your data warehouse's growth.

Data Normalization

There are situations in which the simplest implementation of modeling, the star schema, is not ideal. There are two possible reasons for this:

- Denormalized schema may require too much disk storage.
- Very large dimension tables can adversely affect performance, partially offsetting benefits gained through aggregation.

Normalizing the Dimensions

Denormalization is a very effective method for simplifying data design and improving performance through the reduction of table joins. However, there are instances where the cost in disk storage may be too high.

For example, consider a product dimension in which there are 100,000 products rolling up to 15 product lines and 5 brands. In a star schema, the corresponding dimension table would have 100,000 rows, and each row would store all of the relevant information for every level of the hierarchy above or equal to its own level (brand manager 100,000 times, product line category 100,000 times, etc.).

In some cases, the number of attributes stored about each element can be substantial. In the above case, every kilobyte of attribute data elements costs 100 megabytes of disk space.

Normalizing the dimension table avoids this additional disk storage. In a normalized model, the primary dimension table would have 100,000 rows but might have only three columns: product_id, product_line_id, and brand_id. In this case, the dimension would contain three additional tables, one for brand attributes, one for product line attributes, and one for product attributes. The brand table would store the brand_id, brand manager, and all other brand attributes. The product line table would store product_line_id, product line category, and all other product line attributes. In a dimension table of 500,000 rows, saving just 2 megabytes per row through normalization of the star saves a full gigabyte of disk.

The "Snowflake Schema"

Normalized dimension tables turn star schemas into "snowflake schemas," named for their added structural complexity.

To understand how snowflake joins can improve performance, consider the above database. Assume that aggregates exist for sales by product line and brand. Assume also that the fact table contains roughly 10 million rows.

Now consider a query looking for sales by product line manager. In the case of either a star or a snowflake, the query would be able to retrieve the sales information from the product line aggregate table. However, in the case of a star, the full 100,000-row product dimension table would need to be joined to the star to retrieve the product line manager information. In the case of a snowflake, the product line attribute table would be separated out from the full 100,000-row product table. The query could thus get the product line manager information it needed from the product line aggregate table and the 15-row product line attribute table—a substantial performance advantage.

To summarize the snowflake architecture, each dimension table stores one key for each level of the dimension's hierarchy (that is, for each dimension element). The lowest-level key joins the dimension table both to the central fact table and to the attribute table that contains the descriptive information about the lowest-level dimension element. The rest of the keys join the dimension table to the corresponding attribute tables.

Disadvantages of Normalization

The main disadvantage of the snowflake versus the star is the relative complexity of the normalized snowflake data structure. If users are generating queries using typical database ad hoc query tools, it will be more difficult for them to navigate through the snowflake. In addition, load programs and overall maintenance become more difficult to manage as the data model becomes more complex.

Partial Normalization

The performance gains and disk storage savings provided by snowflake designs are often worth the price of marginally higher complexity. However, as shown earlier, the value of a snowflake join is greatest for dimensions in which

- There are many rows (in the tens or hundreds of thousands).
- There are many attributes stored at low levels of the dimension hierarchy, and disk space is a significant problem.

Thus, the best solution is often to normalize one or two dimensions and leave the rest of the dimensions in a simple star format. This partial normalization process is referred to as a partial snowflake.

Distribution and Replication Architecture

The simplest architecture consists of two levels: a *decision-support* system front end and a central data warehouse. More and more, warehouses are being built with three- and four-tier architectures: *Decision-Support* front end, desktop database, LAN database, and central database. The increase in power and decrease in cost of platforms allow the data to be placed closer and closer to the enduser. The database architects are attempting to incorporate the definition of local subsets and replication functions into the DBMS.

A data warehouse may incorporate access to desktop, local, and central data. It is often easier to begin with a central-only architecture and then migrate to local and desktop access at a later date.

DATA MODELS FOR WAREHOUSE APPLICATIONS

Realistically, no system can be truly ad hoc. The enterprise must generally understand the *data-access* needs and quite specifically understand the data to be used as a basis for that *access*. A user may have some chance of making up a query on the fly, but he or she has no chance of making up the data from which the query is derived. In many ways, the data model is more important than the data analysis.

It is convenient to think of the historical events (invoices, payments, etc.) as the "warehouse." This is the type of data people want to analyze. While the events form the bulk of the data, they are of little use without supporting data about master entities (customer data, for example), domains (invoice type code), and summarization rules. A data warehouse may contain any or all of the following data types:

- The historical events downloaded from the operational systems.
- Metadata that might include sources of warehouse data, replication rules, rollup categories and rules, security and controls, availability of summarizations, purge criteria, and logical and physical data mapping.
- Summarization of historical events. These are really preemptive queries. The data is aggregated when it is added to the warehouse rather than when it is requested by a specific user.
- Event data sourced from outside services, such as weather or market share data for retailers
- Master entity rollups.
- The master entities referenced by the events.
- Miscellaneous domain data, such as "codes," "flags," validation, translation data, and so forth.

Populating the Data Warehouse

The bulk of data in the warehouse is sourced from operational systems. Closed events and related master data are periodically downloaded to the warehouse platform. Five different categories of data require consideration.

Downloaded Historical Events

This data is the core of the data warehouse. It usually constitutes most of the raw data volume and originates at a distinct and easily attained spot in the operational system. The following are major issues in defining and capturing this data.

Sources of Historical Data

What are the source operational applications? What operational data is needed for the warehouse? What are the performance and application modification effects of creating a data warehouse feed? How are multiple sources consolidated to a single feed? Is the data needed by the warehouse available without major changes to the operational applications or user input? Risk and performance degradation can become dicey issues if data warehouses must muck around in operational programs to create feeds, especially in older legacy applications.

Appropriate Level of Warehouse Event History

Is event data stored at the atomic level (which is more costly but better for ad hoc needs) or at an aggregate level (which is less costly and supports better response time)? Can MIS isolate the frequently used from the seldom used data, vertically (by fields), and/or horizontally (by records)?

Denormalization of Data from Master Entities into the Detail Events

Is the candidate data static? If the data is modified in the related master, is the change propagated to historical events? What is the associated increase in the event record size and Direct Access Storage Device (DASD) capacity? How much performance improvement is achieved by placing common qualifying fields in the event detail and simplifying the query language (for example, moving customer zip code or product group into the invoice detail)?

Frequency of Warehouse Download

How current does the warehouse data have to be? If users need current data, is this a warehouse or an operational system function? What is the most convenient frequency based on the level of warehouse data? What is the most convenient frequency based on the source of data? If downloads are too infrequent, is there a batch window problem with the accumulated volume? (If aggregations are done by week, weekly downloads are probably neat and convenient.) Can the download be scheduled while the warehouse is off-line?

Historical Retention of Events

How long is the data retained? (Users usually want the data to be kept forever and then held for some contingency period after that.) What percentage of the user access is against each historical time period? It is not the developer's function to question the need for ancient history, but the designer should certainly attempt to understand whether a large percentage of the access is against a small percentage of the data.

Validation and Suspense

Is the data coming from the source operational systems reliable or should it be validated on entry to the warehouse? Do rejects require a "suspense" and correction capability?

Master Entities Referenced by Historical Events

The data warehouse is of no use without some supporting data from the master entities referenced by the events. For example, invoices cannot be analyzed without the data from the related customer and product entities. It is from these master entities that most of the query qualification comes. For a query on the dollar sum of all invoices for July that reference a specified product group in a specified territory, the date and the amount are in the invoice, but the product group and sales territory are attributes of the referenced customer and product master entities.

In theory, it would be nice to share the master entities between operational and data warehouse applications. This is generally impractical because of the following:

- Communications costs to link the warehouse platform to the operational data
- Availability (uptime) requirements
- Differing retention needs
- Contention
- Temporal requirements. The warehouse user wants to view the master data as it was when the related history was processed, as it is currently, or both.

The operational masters usually contain a lot of information that is not needed by the warehouse. They are physically designed and tuned for the creation and maintenance of in-process events. Data warehouses generally need this data only for access qualification, summarization, and rollups. Unless the master data is modifiable within the warehouse or will add a large amount of volume, it is probably better to denormalize it into the associated event detail.

The capturing of master changes in the operational systems for transport to the warehouse can be complex. In some cases it may be more expeditious to reload the entire warehouse entity depending on size and versioning issues. Some operational DBMSs have a hook to isolate changes; others do not. Some of the decision making depends on additional factors, such as the following.

Domain Data

Every application has a need for information describing valid contents for coded data or flags. Domain data usually contains a text description for each coded value. Examples include "invoice type" (S=sale, C=credit, R=return) and "month" (01=January). These domains probably exist in the operational system and may be maintained in the warehouse as downloads or updates. They are usually small in volume and can be periodically reloaded to the warehouse. It may be necessary to retain obsolete data still referenced by historical events. Domain data is frequently used by the *decision-support* query system to qualify requests, aggregate data, or simply put descriptions rather than codes on the output screens.

External Data

Many warehouse applications make use of data sourced from outside databases and/or services. Generally they provide some level of market-share information. The common problem is in mapping outside definitions of identifiers (customer, product, provider) to internal nomenclature. A translation mechanism must be designed, which usually involves some loss of data integrity.

In most cases, the market-share data maps to some higher level of rollup than the event data sourced from internal operational applications. For example, sales may be externally reported at the zip code and product group, rather than customer and product, level. If it is at the customer or product level, it is unlikely that internal product or customer keys will be used.

Summary Data

Requests for *decision support* are almost certainly for groupings of data. Summarization, or data aggregation, is the key component of any data warehouse. Each summary must describe the derivation process, the detail entity or entities, qualifying attributes, and amount or quantity of computation. Summary can be accomplished preemptively at the time the data is added to the warehouse, or dynamically at the time the data is replicated to a local warehouse or queried by the enduser.

The warehouse designer must have a good feel for both the potential queries and the data characteristics to evaluate the cost/benefits of candidate summaries. In some cases, it may make sense to reduce cost by summarizing only "interesting" values rather than all records from the derived entity. "Common" values may be the highest volume but the least strategically interesting (ignore ear aches diagnosed in doctors' offices for children during swimming season). In other words, are summarizations based on combinations of attributes or attribute values?

If summarized data is maintained, the response to that one summary category can be improved, but other issues arise.

- What is the performance effect on the warehouse loads?
- What is the probability and effect of resummarizing if the aggregation attributes change? Any changes to the historical events or related master data (change customer territory and reflect it over history) may cause costly re-summarizations (recasting) to any summary table using that data as one of its dimensions.
- What is the probability of summarizing a lot of data that is never analyzed?
- How are summarization decisions altered as the *decision-support* needs change?

DBMS Selection Criteria

Relational DBMS products are used for the bulk of data warehouse applications. These products are well suited to data warehousing's data characteristics (static and long-living), access requirements (aggregated sets of complexly qualified data), and design flexibility (segregation of logical/physical models). But it's difficult to build a generic DBMS product that serves both the warehouse and operational users effectively; features tend to benefit one side while adding to the complexity, cost, or inefficiency for the other.

There are already databases in the warehouse-only niche which stress the obvious advantages of a product that eliminates the features and overhead deemed unnecessary for warehouses. Simpler products should cost less and run faster. The obvious disadvantage is that a company must develop and retain technical skills in different DBMSs. History has proven that effectively managing one DBMS is awfully complicated.

Multidimensional DBMSs have been used effectively for some data warehouse applications. In general, these databases can reduce development cost and speed up response time when the data can be summarized on predictable dimensions. The success of such DBMSs is a function of cost (load time, DASD used and wasted) versus benefit (reduced development cost, faster response). These, in turn, are functions of summary reduction and technical design.

Several multidimensional DBMSs run into excessive performance issues as data volumes increase above 10 gigabytes. Therefore, caution is advised. Some data warehouse solutions have chosen to use multidimensional DBMSs for the summary data and a relational DBMS for the higher-volume detail event history. The following issues should be considered when evaluating these products:

- How much summarization is actually achieved? (Summarizing by customer/product/month doesn't help if a given customer seldom buys the same product in the same month.)
- Does the product allocate space for all possible permutations? (100 customers times 100 products times 24 months = 240,000 possible summary records.)
- How many dimensions can be supported?
- How easy is it to add dimensions or levels?
- Is the multidimensional database populated completely or on a net change basis? (If net change, how are master entity changes recast for history?)
- Does the product support subset qualification within n-dimensions, such as separate dealer and direct totals for customer/product/month, or must dealer/direct be treated as a fourth dimension?
- Does the product support "drill-down" to the source detail in relational or other multidimensional databases?

A data warehouse will probably involve the evaluation and selection of several vendor software products. Obviously, the two major decisions involve the DBMS and the *decision-support* query products. The products are evolving rapidly and tomorrow's solution is sure to be different. For this reason, the designer should be very careful to separate the architecture (data model, population process, query process) from the infrastructure (hardware and software tools).

Decision-Support Applications

Decision-support capabilities are almost certainly a combination of vendor software packages and custom software to enhance capabilities and avoid shortcomings. Performance remains a major issue for any general-purpose query capability going against large volumes of complex data.

The following are some of the functions that must be remembered:

- Ability to recognize which data are presummarized.
- Flexibility to transparently request data that is located in the central, local, or desktop database
- Easy downloading of metadata to control the building of query screens from available and allowable warehouse entities, attributes, and summaries. Most query tools have some sort of QBE (Query By Example) capability to guide selection criteria.
- Security at both the data-type and data-value level.
- Data staging capabilities (temporary data stores for simplification, performance, or conversational access).
- Expert and novice modes of operation.
- Drill-down capability to efficiently access exception data at lower levels.
- Governors or controls to prevent runaway queries. Import capabilities to desktop tool sets.
- Customization capabilities for inefficiently generated data access calls.
- Logging of usage statistics: data access "keys," response times, and so forth.

No one product is likely to provide all the desired features, and some provided features are impractical to use because of performance constraints.

The data warehouse front end should also include some data-triggered capabilities. A strategic reporting engine can generate periodic reports for known data analyses. In addition, there should be some thought to automatic recognition of exceptions. While loading or periodically analyzing the data, the metadata could contain expert systems capabilities to recognize and feed potential trends back to the user. In essence, this function will generate the questions rather than provide any significant answers.

One of the major issues with any *decision-support* tool is the segregation of the client (query) and server (warehouse) responsibilities. Where do the data analysis and manipulation functions occur—at the client or the server? If data is aggregated, filtered, and ordered at the server, it may reduce the volume of data transmitted (bandwidth issues) and allow users to perform data searches more efficiently. It may also be desirable to have excess processing capacity at the desktop and to conversationally evaluate and remanipulate the delivered data.

All *decision-support* tools can look good with the sample databases used to demonstrate the capabilities. Access is flexible and response quick. The trick is to be able to determine whether the flexibility can handle the anticipated data and whether the response is adequate for given volumes and data complexity. If there are shortcomings, and there are, will MIS be able to tune the access, enhance the capabilities, and/or revise user expectations?

DATA MODEL IMPLEMENTATION AND ADMINISTRATION

A comprehensive data warehouse can incorporate, in addition to data downloaded from operational systems, a good deal of information originating in and solely for the purpose of the warehouse. In general, this data is used to control the usage, security, integrity, and cost of the warehouse. Metadata contains the information to map the warehouse data to the *decision-support* views, the operational sources, and to related data in the warehouse.

This data is really where the flexibility and adaptability of the warehouse is determined. Effective vendor tools to handle this metadata, broadly, are not available. A lot of custom-developed code may be necessary to accomplish particular goals.

The following are examples of metadata. Each requires a data definition and maintenance process:

- Sources of warehouse information, frequency of download, and completeness (have all monthly feeds been received for July?).
- Aggregation methods and rules.
- Relationships and referential integrity constraints.
- *Decision-support* mapping of warehouse data: keys, qualifying attributes, security, translations, and so forth.
- Purge and retention periods.
- Replication and distribution rules.
- Exception conditions automatically reported.

The following are some of the steps that can facilitate implementation of a data model within the overall architectural framework. Each requires a process and careful planning.

Step 1—The Operational Data

This step provides the source data for the corporate data warehouse. The source consists of the on-line transaction systems which are deployed by the enterprise. These also include a reasonable level of reporting capability. The only function introduced in this environment is the "extraction and/or propagation" required to capture the data needed in the data warehouse.

It is the objective of the data warehouse implementation to have minimum *impact* on the operation of the system. It is the decisions that are enabled which impact the operational systems rather than the data warehouse.

Because there are usually considerable differences in the quality of data on different operational systems, it is necessary, in some instances, to *condition* the data before it is transported into the data warehouse environment.

It is possible that that the data on the operational systems is completely *valid*, but it must be current and integral to the business processes. If data corruption has occurred for some reason, it must be tackled before proceeding to migrate the data. The corruption of data may have occurred for a number of reasons, such as,

- Data is not critical to the function.
- Some information may be stale because it is not considered reliable.

It is very likely that there is a considerable gap between the data model for the data warehouse and other data models on which the individual operational systems are based. An essential task in building a data warehouse is to properly *map* such data from the operational data to the data warehouse database.

Because of the dangers associated with overengineering the data warehouse, caution should be exercised in data extraction without conditioning and validating *all* the data.

Step 2—Data Migration

The extraction, conversion, migration of data from the source to target, and transformation of the data must be ensured so that the data warehouse database holds only accurate, timely, integrated, valid, and credible data. There are a number of different options for data migration, which offer differing levels of accuracy and complexity.

Refreshing the data on the operational system and onto the data warehouse is probably the most simple option. This option does not involve any data transformation where data is simply refreshed from the operational system directly to the data warehouse database. However, the physical layout may change in terms of hierarchical to flat files or relational, or a combination thereof. The primary advantage is that this can be accomplished quickly and easily. However such data may not build accurate histories since the refreshes occur at intervals and the old data is discarded because it is simply a snapshot of data taken during the year.

The *updating* of data at intervals overcomes the above deficiencies, but it introduces a different set of technical problems. There are a number of alternatives to capture the updates, which have their own advantages and disadvantages. These techniques are

- *Data propagation* is the most sophisticated option to migrate the source data. This propagation could be synchronous or asynchronous. Synchronous propagation works on the principle that the change occurring on the operational system is synchronously transported to the data warehouse. Such migration has a chance to cause significant corruption in the data warehouse database. On the other hand, asynchronous propagation is much safer because the data is propagated to an intermediate stage. If something goes wrong with the process or the data, the data warehouse is not impacted and the propagated data can be corrected before migrating to the data warehouse database.

- In order to optimize the potential of the data warehouse, most likely, it is necessary to *transform* the operational data entities into new merged or derived entities.

- *Data enrichment* is normally the product of data integration. This is usually done by assigning an additional attribute to a data entity if external data is being introduced to the data warehouse.

- The *transport mechanisms* for the migration from operational systems to the data warehouse platform have to support an extremely wide bandwidth. The physical connection depends largely on the proximity of the system. If the systems are physically remote, then the problem of transferring data is amplified.

- Special data migration control programs may be employed to ensure *data integrity*.

- The format of data in a *heterogeneous operational environment* is likely to be diverse and the problem of reformatting must be addressed early.

- *Loading the data* to the target system can be a formidable task, depending upon the volumes. One of the issues which significantly impacts the speed of loading the data to a relational database is the number of indices that must be built on the tables.

Step 3—Database Administration

Administration is an important control activity. It is in this step that the model is actually implemented. Therefore, the compliance with a standard model and quick business benefits has to be precariously maintained. Among the many issues that must be considered, *data granularity* and *metadata* are the most important.

Without *metadata*, it is not possible for the users to interact with the data in the data warehouse since they have no way of knowing how aged the data is, how the tables are structured, what the data definitions or formats are, or where the data originated.

One of the most contentious issues is to determine how *detailed the data* being migrated needs to be. Different levels of *granularity* are required to satisfy different business requirements. For strategic planning purposes, the summary or aggregate data is probably sufficient. However, for marketing analysis, the data required must be fairly detailed.

Step 4—Middleware

The degree to which the data warehouse is accessed by a wide variety of users determines the degree of complexity needed in the middleware. If the access is highly restricted, the access can be provided easily on the existing network. On the other hand, if the access is to be provided to a wide and diverse population of users, the *middleware* must support varied hardware and software options.

The range of system software which is necessary to make the data warehouse accessible in a client/server model is also termed as middleware. It is the middleware that allows an application on a client to execute a request for data on a local (LAN) or remote database server (data warehouse).

Step 5—Decision-Support Applications

The *decision-support* applications are employed to use the data warehouse. Such applications can be classified into a number of categories, based on their design characteristics. Some are for presentation of information in the form of predefined reports and statistical analyses. Some can be interrogative, allowing the users to construct queries and directly interact with the data.

There are other applications employing simulation models for forecasting and planning purposes. The data warehouse provides the infrastructure basis for building such systems. However, the interrogative type of applications are the most popular for data warehouse uses.

Step 6—The User or Presentation Interface

The quality and scope of the interaction between the user and the data warehouse is strongly influenced by the *interface* provided by the model. The *command-line interface* is the most basic interface level and is appropriate for interrogating very complex queries with a SQL program. The *menu-driven interface* provides the user with controlled access to the data.

The query language interface provides the user with powerful interrogative access to the data. These are usually the tools which allow the user to build up SQL statements on a step-by-step basis. This is the most commonly employed interface for *decision-support* and data warehouse analyses.

The Graphical User Interface (GUI) is the most suitable environment for user-friendly interaction with the system. The GUI incorporates windows, pull-down menus, icons, buttons, and pointing devices. This type of interface facilitates exploration of the data by referring via symbols.

A *hypertext interface* is useful in presenting metadata to users. Hypertext uses links between pages allowing the user to join any page to any other page.

Multimedia interfaces, which employ sound, video, and animation, are likely to become a common feature of data warehouse interfaces.

SUMMARY

Historically, access to data has been a technical problem for engineers and a psychological one for the business users. With data modeling, *decision-support* systems offer almost an infinite flexibility to the user. The exploitation of data through the creation and utilization of applications that identify patterns is the mission of the data warehouse. Data modeling is an architected response to the deficiencies in the traditionally evolved information systems.

Traditional entity-relationship data models function effectively in the OLTP world, driving most of today's operational, RDBMS-based applications. Because of the success of these data models, the first graphical *decision-support* systems were implemented using similar designs. As these *decision-support* databases grow larger and more complicated, performance is becoming poorer and systems are becoming more difficult to use and maintain.

Data modeling, the database design approach, improves *decision-support* performance by several orders of magnitude. By presenting information in a format that parallels the multidimensional business environment, the data model makes intuitive sense to users. Moreover, the structural simplicity of data modeling facilitates application maintenance and provides the flexibility to expand the data warehouse.

Although data warehousing holds great potential for dramatic business benefit, the hype clearly outruns proven results. Although data warehouses share some key qualities with traditional development projects—the functional and technical requirements, especially—the demands of dynamic ad hoc queries introduce a distinct series of challenges. MIS organizations contemplating data warehouses should be realistic about the challenges of a system with multiple moving targets, such as user requirements, the software and hardware platforms, and the warehouse data contents.

Data models are very time-consuming to develop because basic analysis, such as the analysis of order, customer, market, channel, and so on, must be performed. It is not unusual for comprehensive modeling projects to cost millions of dollars. Considerable time is required just to get people together because of busy schedules. Rather than use that valuable time for doing baseline work, it is more productive to start with existing template models and edit them as a group.

Organizations need a way to convert their data into actionable OLTP systems based on entities, relationships, functional decomposition, and state transition analysis, but the data model for data warehousing is based on facts, dimensions, hierarchies, and sparsity. A fully normalized OLTP design for an order-entry system could have hundreds of tables, but much simpler data model designs can be tested. A good data warehouse can be implemented in a relational database, a multidimensional database, or an object-oriented database.

8

OLAP IN THE DATA WAREHOUSE ENVIRONMENT

INTRODUCTION

On-Line Analytical Processing (OLAP) applications are rapidly increasing in popularity as organizations attempt to maximize the business value of the data that is available in ever increasing volumes from operational systems, spreadsheets, external databases, and business partners. It is not enough to simply view this data—business value comes from using it to make better informed decisions more quickly and create more realistic business plans.

Throughout modern organizations, decisions are constantly being made about pricing, the deployment of resources, the choice of suppliers, and where and when future investment should be made. In the past, these decisions have often been made based on "gut feeling" and experience rather than solid data, analyses, and tested hypotheses. With the flattening of management structures, reengineered businesses and globalization, the need for better analysis tools is greater than ever.

Data warehouses are being used to bring together data from multiple systems and form a reliable, consistent, and regularly updated set of information that can be used as the "single version of the truth" for decision-making activities. Almost always, these take the form of large relational databases, and conventional relational reporting and query tools can be used directly with these databases. This is a good way of seeing the details and summary of historic performance, but it does not directly support the more integrated, multidimensional view that is often required for informed decision making.

Why OLAP?

Today's dynamic business landscape is marked by the need to adapt quickly to change—whether it is to competitive pressures, shrinking business cycles, or industry and government regulations. At the same time, organizational structures have become flatter, and front-line managers are increasingly required to make quick, intelligent decisions that may significantly impact their business direction or substantially effect their competitiveness. To arrive at these decisions, they need to ask complex questions that reflect the multiple dimensions of their business.

There are many applications on the market today that empower users with comprehensive query and reporting capabilities, typically against Relational Database Management Systems (RDBMSs). However, relational databases, which have a two-dimensional structure (rows and columns), are not designed to provide the multidimensional views of data required for complex analysis. OLAP software, with its sophisticated analytical functions and its ability to represent data in a multidimensional format, is rapidly emerging as the solution of choice for supporting a company's critical business decisions.

What Is OLAP?

OLAP stands for "On-Line Analytical Processing." In contrast to the more familiar OLTP ("On-Line Transaction Processing"), OLAP describes a class of technologies that are designed for live ad hoc data access and analysis. While transaction processing generally relies solely on relational databases, OLAP has become synonymous with multidimensional views of business data. These multidimensional views are supported by multidimensional database technology. These multidimensional views provide the technical basis for the calculations and analyses required by data-warehousing applications.

On-line analytical processing is the next logical step beyond query and reporting, and it is the next evolutionary stage toward creating a total *decision-support* solution. OLAP software tools deliver the technological means for complex business analysis by enabling endusers to analyze data in a multidimensional environment. With OLAP tools, individuals can analyze and navigate through data to discover trends, spot exceptions, and get the underlying details to better understand the ebb and flow of their business activity.

A user's view of the enterprise is multidimensional in nature. Sales, for instance, can be viewed not only by product but also by region, time period, and so on. That's why OLAP models should be multidimensional in nature. This multidimensional user view facilitates model design and analysis, as well as inter- and intradimensional calculations, through a more intuitive analytical model.

On-line analytical processing is a relatively new term and often confused with *decision support*. Most approaches to OLAP center around the idea of reformulating relational or flat file data into a multidimensional data store that is optimized for data analysis. This multidimensional data store, also known as a hypercube (Figure 8.1), stores the data along "dimensions," allowing users to easily analyze the data along the axes of their business. Analysis requirements span a spectrum from statistics to simulation. The two forms of analysis most relevant to mainstream business users are commonly known as "slice and dice" and "drill-down."

At the practical level, OLAP always involves interactive querying of data, following a thread of analysis through multiple passes, such as drill-down into successively lower levels of detail. The information is multidimensional. Users are able to manipulate such multidimensional data models more easily and intuitively than is the

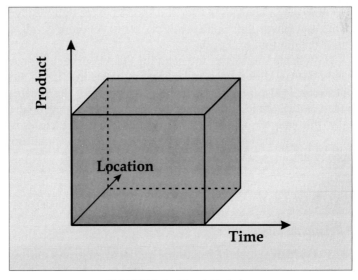

FIGURE 8.1   The 3-D Cube.

case with single-dimensional models. For instance, users can slice and dice, pivot, and rotate consolidation paths within a model. These include the following characteristics.

Slice and Dice

OLAP enables endusers to *slice and dice* consolidated information in order to view data from many different perspectives. Users can "cut" or "rotate" a particular piece of the aggregated data along any dimension. For example, a business analyst at a consumer goods company can view a slice of the data model that shows sales revenue for all soft drinks in the city of Austin over the four quarters of 1996. The analyst can then pivot the model to look at sales revenue for diet cola for all cities in Texas during that same time period. Slice and dice helps users investigate typical business questions such as,

- What product line generated the highest sales revenue in Texas in 1995?
- How do first quarter 1996 certain brand sales compare with first quarter 1995 certain brand sales in the city of Dallas?

Drill-Down

OLAP allows users to "drill" or navigate through information to get more detail. Data navigation helps endusers answer "why" questions, for example, "Why did diet cola sales drop in the Eastern region during the first and second quarters of 1994?" Most OLAP tools enable users to drill down to view finer levels of detail within a data set, but the most complete tools allow users to "drill anywhere." In addition to drilling down, "drill anywhere" includes "drilling up" to look at a coarser view of a data set, or "drilling across" to move laterally from one data set to another on the same level.

During data analysis, a user can spot an exception. Using OLAP data navigation, the user can drill through levels of data to get more detail to help answer "why" questions about that exception.

This chapter addresses the need for OLAP servers. It provides an overview of the fundamental differences and synergies between OLAP and OLTP models and applications. It also provides a technical analysis of the shortcomings of RDBMSs and their associated front-end query tools for multidimensional analysis applications. Finally, this chapter concludes that OLAP and OLTP systems are highly complementary and should coexist within the same enterprise environment to solve different problems.

THE EVOLUTION OF OLAP

The Relational Model

Dr. E. F. Codd developed a relational model to address a multitude of shortcomings that existed in the fields of database management and application development. Prior to his work, the database management systems in the marketplace were homegrown, ad hoc collections of ideas formulated into systems. Such systems were originally designed to solve a particular type of problem and then later were extended to become a more general-purpose solution.

The resulting systems represented a collection of products that were needlessly complex. These also suffered from the concomitant problems of being difficult to understand, install, maintain and use. In addition, no DBMS product supported the maintenance of logical integrity of the data as a DBMS responsibility. Unanticipated enduser access to the data was rarely provided by the DBMS.

Today, existing relational database management systems offer powerful, yet simple solutions for a wide variety of commercial and scientific application problems. In every industry, relational systems are being used for applications that require storing, updating, and/or retrieval of single as well as multiple shared data elements. These are universally applied for every conceivable type of application for operational, transactional, and complex processing as well as *decision-support* systems, including query and reporting.

Need for Analysis

During the last decade, corporate data has grown consistently and rapidly in the megabyte and gigabyte ranges. Enterprises are having to manipulate data in the range of terabytes and petabytes. Concurrently, the *need* for more sophisticated analysis and faster synthesis of better quality information has grown.

Today's markets are much more competitive and dynamic than those in the past. Business enterprises prosper or fail according to the sophistication and speed of their information systems, and their ability to analyze and synthesize information using those systems.

Data in relational systems is also being accessed by a wide variety of unsophisticated users through the use of many different types of tools and interfaces. These include general-purpose query products, spreadsheets, graphics packages, off-the-shelf application packages for human resource management, accounting, banking, and other disciplines. As the emphasis upon interoperability becomes more pronounced, these products are finding their way to users with every conceivable type of hardware architecture.

Figure 8.2 depicts the OLAP server role for various types of databases and files. It illustrates the mediating role that an OLAP server provides with respect to the various types of databases and files in which data may be stored and that the endusers may need. The OLAP server is in the center of the diagram. This mediating role is a very important property that an OLAP server should have.

Of the wide variety of business applications that have been afforded faster, cheaper, and better solutions in the relational DBMS world, perhaps none is more dramatic than query/report processing. Once handled almost exclusively by COBOL application programmers, the combination of the powerful relational DBMS coupled with the easy-to-learn, easy-to-use query/spreadsheet mechanism has enabled endusers to develop and execute these query/report applications themselves.

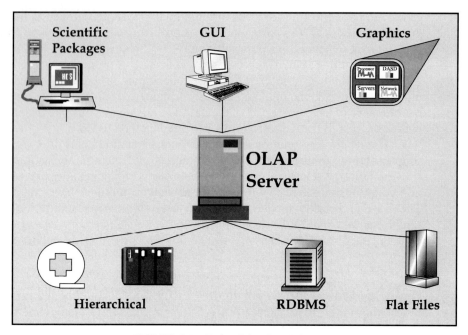

FIGURE 8.2   Role of the OLAP Server.

Thus empowered, the endusers now satisfy their own requirements. Not only are they able to experiment with various data formats and aggregations, they are also able to improve the information content of their reports. In addition, they can do this on demand, while avoiding the long delays waiting for support from database administration and application development. However, there are still significant limitations to their efficacy.

The DBMS products of today rely on front-end products to embellish their support for possible ways in which users might wish to consolidate and view different kinds of data. The existing products provide limited support for dynamic physical representation of the data. Such representations can adjust to provide optimum performance in accordance with the way the data is actually used, but static physical designs often impede certain data analysis activities.

A relational DBMS includes a more powerful means of preserving the logical integrity of the data than any prerelational DBMS. With relational technology, the system complexity of prerelational systems has been replaced by ease of learning, ease of use, and support for ad hoc query and manipulation. This major feature permits enterprises to acquire confidence in the accuracy of the data. At every turn, the relational database management system has become the gateway to enterprise data. Additionally, the relational language of the system has become the interface to that data store for all of the enduser products in many of these environments and architectures.

Until recently, the enduser products that had been developed as front ends to the relational DBMS provided very straightforward simplistic functionality. The query/report writers and spreadsheets have been extremely limited in the ways in which data (having already been retrieved from the DBMS) can be aggregated, summarized, consolidated, summed, viewed, and analyzed.

OLAP CONCEPTS

Today's dynamic business landscape is marked by the need to adapt quickly to change—whether it is due to competitive pressures, shrinking business cycles, or because of industry and government regulations. At the same time, organizational structures have become flatter, and front-line managers have to make quick, intelligent decisions that may significantly impact their business direction or substantially affect their competitiveness. To arrive at these decisions, they need to ask complex questions that reflect the multiple dimensions of their business.

This type of "multidimensional" inquiry requires both access to vast amounts of corporate data and the means to analyze this data from many different perspectives. Figure 8.3. depicts multilevel paths for viewing enterprise information. Companies need to constantly answer complex and multilevel questions that reflect the multidimensional nature of their business.

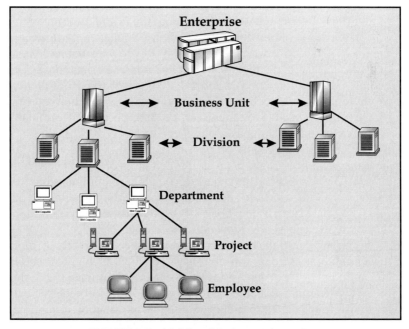

FIGURE 8.3 Multilevel Paths to Information.

A Multidimensional View

The multidimensional view of an organization is much more relevant to decision making than is the list-oriented view that reflects the transaction processing systems. Decision makers at all levels need to see the relevant "big picture": all the applicable revenues, costs, and assets, viewed and analyzed from every perspective. This involves bringing together information from many operational systems, as well as external data and planning assumptions that are not yet in the operational systems (and possibly not in a data warehouse, either).

This requires an ability to compare any part of the business against any other and to define new analyses, without having to design the database with knowledge of every possible analysis in advance. Because an unpredictable number and type of analyses might be needed in a short, intense bout of work, the system response times must be consistently fast.

OLAP application requirements consist of much more than just viewing history with different levels of aggregation. Many new calculations are needed, some quite complex. For example, profitability figures by product, customer, and market may be needed to support investment and pricing decisions throughout an organization.

Users make decisions based on comparisons and trends. Therefore, it must be possible to calculate ratios or percentage differences between any measure of the business and view it from any perspective of the business (e.g., over time, actual versus budget, retail versus wholesale). It must also be possible to build business models for the future which make use of the available detailed historical data and enable iterative changes to the planning assumptions and calculation formulae. The purpose of OLAP is often to make decisions about the future, not simply to review the past.

It is often assumed that data warehouse applications are always read-only from the user's perspective with the users only able to view but not change it. This is certainly true as far as the historical data and approved planning assumptions are concerned, but many *decision-support* activities will consist of analyzing the derived results that accompany changed assumptions or corporate structures. For these activities, users must be able to change certain data, calculation formulae, and structures.

Traditionally, Database Management Systems (DBMSs) have been used to collect, process, and report on operational data, while desktop productivity tools, such as spreadsheets, have been used for enduser-oriented analysis. Even modern relational DBMSs are not intended for flexible, multidimensional enduser analysis, particularly if the users are allowed to change certain parts of the database. And, although they are superb at ad hoc analysis, spreadsheets have neither the capacity nor the ability to easily share information with other users.

This has led to the rapid acceptance of specialized OLAP tools that work with feeder databases or data warehouses to provide reliable, robust data for fast, flexible, multidimensional analysis of large data volumes from the desktop.

It is generally accepted that data warehousing provides an excellent approach for transforming data into useful and reliable information to support the business decision-making process. A data warehouse provides the base for the powerful analytical and decision-making techniques that are so important in today's competitive environment such as data mining and multidimensional data analysis, as well as the more traditional query and reporting. Making use of these analytical techniques along with a data warehouse can result in more informed decision-making capability and lead to a significant business advantage.

The need to access information across the enterprise and present it in a digestible format for the management support process is key to providing competitive advantage. However, management involved in making critical decisions demand information to be topical and accurate if any faith is to be placed in the system. The recent developments in On-Line Analytical Processing (OLAP) have provided a solution that addresses these issues. The advances delivered by OLAP have removed the limitations of early Executive Information System (EIS) systems, which tended to have limited data access and struggled to provide a simple user interface.

OLAP applications have query and response time characteristics which set them apart from traditional On-Line Transaction Processing (OLTP) applications. Specialized OLAP servers are designed to give analysts the response time and functional capabilities of sophisticated PC programs with the multiuser and large database support they require.

A Historical Perspective on Analysis Solutions

There is a great debate in the industry on how to best deliver multidimensional analysis functionality. The evolution of analysis tools has produced two generations of products. EIS software and PC drill tools appeared first, followed more recently by OLAP servers. These products include Executive Information Systems (EISs), designed as stand-alone mainframe solutions, and PC drill tools, designed as stand-alone PC solutions.

The second generation of OLAP products was designed from inception to operate in the client/server environment, with on-line connections between client and server. This generation includes OLAP servers.

First-Generation Analysis Solutions

The first generation of analytical software solutions marked a significant departure from conducting manual searches and analyses toward leveraging corporate data residing on-line. They included mainframe-based EIS solutions and PC-based drill-down tools.

EIS Solutions

The first wave of analysis solutions appeared as executive information systems, in the early 1980s. They were primarily targeted at providing high-level executives with on-line information for making business decisions.

Since most executives at that time had little computer experience, EIS software was designed to provide predefined analysis and had a very simple, dashboard-type screen to encourage user acceptance. EIS solutions empowered business executives to leverage the data in their corporate Information Systems (ISs), but they were very

IS intensive and therefore expensive both in terms of acquisition and maintenance. Contributing factors included:

- *Highly customized* for a particular executive's business requirements. These stand-alone solutions required intensive programming efforts by large expert teams.
- The EIS systems did not include a client portion. Therefore the client part of the solution had to be designed and developed by technical experts.
- Because the user interface was hard coded to the application, every time users wanted to perform a new type of analysis, technical experts would have to reprogram the user interface.

Though EIS solutions were restricted to the elite set of users who could afford them, they helped prove that information technology could contribute to better business decisions. They thus paved the way for other analysis solutions to follow.

PC Drill Tools

The PC drill tool emerged in the late 1980s as an alternative to mainframe-based EIS solutions. Drill tools capitalized on the explosive adoption of personal computers and enabled knowledge workers to analyze the data residing on their local systems. Because they carried the inherent cost efficiencies of PC products, these drill tools were the first analytical software solutions to appeal to a larger set of mainstream users. Figure 8.4 illustrates a schematic diagram for a drill-down process to obtain detail data.

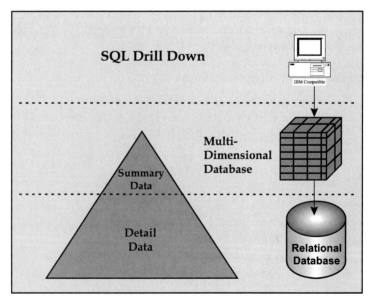

FIGURE 8.4   Drill-Down Process.

PC drill-down processes introduces a significant advance for executing multi-dimensional analysis, the local hypercube. A hypercube is a multidimensional model of data optimized for fast retrieval. By putting a hypercube directly on the user's desktop, PC drills enabled high-performance analysis of data stored locally. However, PC drills carry some limitations, such as,

Demand for Technical Resources. The complexity of PC drill software typically requires an IS expert to build and maintain the hypercubes for endusers, since very few endusers have the technical skill to manage this process.

Relevancy of Data. With the rate that data changes, endusers frequently find that the information in their hypercubes is "stale" or no longer relevant.

Lack of Integration. PC drills are not integrated with query and reporting tools. As a result, a single analytical process requires technical support to physically move data between different tools, applications, or interfaces. This time-consuming process limits the ability of endusers to make decisions "on the fly."

Islands of Information. Because the data set for analysis is static and resides locally, corporations have accumulated many islands of information that are difficult to leverage across the organization.

Second-Generation Analysis Solutions

The combination of multidimensional and client/server technologies has formed the basis of a second generation of analysis software. This generation is represented by OLAP server products. Unlike the stand-alone, first-generation solutions, second-generation OLAP servers adopt a client/server model in which users with intelligent, desktop clients access a multidimensional database server.

The OLAP server provides a high-performance solution to groups of users with well-defined scopes of analysis. This allows these users to benefit from the shared information and distribution of resources provided by a client/server architecture. However, these benefits have not generally been extended to the broad range of mainstream users, who frequently require ad hoc analysis, and who want to leverage the investment in their existing relational databases. The result is an analysis solution that is primarily geared toward "elite" users who can afford the investment required to get the full benefits of an OLAP server.

A branch of second-generation OLAP software addresses user requirements for leveraging relational databases by taking a multidimensional middleware approach. The idea is to have a layer that sits on top of the two-dimensional RDBMS and represents the data in a multidimensional format.

Need for Third-Generation Analysis Solutions

The first and second generations of on-line analytical processing techniques have made significant strides in assisting to make intelligent business decisions based on a wealth of on-line data. The solutions available to date have been adopted by a relatively small segment of the market due to design limitations inherent in the existing technology. Yet, the early successes of these groups has spurred a growing demand among mainstream business users for similar OLAP functionality. Meeting the demands of such users requires a new, third generation of *decision-support* software specifically designed for the requirements of broad enterprise deployment.

A *decision-support* solution must be open, deployable, integrated, and easy to use. In this way, users have the flexibility and ease of use they need, as well as the autonomy they deserve.

- With a flexible solution, companies can leverage the functionality and the investments they have already made in their current computing environment.

- For an OLAP solution to be relevant to a large range of companies, it must be deployable throughout the many layers of an organization and have the ability to scale as the enterprise grows. Wide-scale deployment allows a broad base of users to reap the benefits of OLAP.

- Users need to use one tool for query, reporting, and analysis. In addition, they should be able to perform all of these functions from a single point on their desktops. Tools that fully integrate query, reporting, and analysis offer users autonomy and the most easy, time-efficient way to perform data analysis and reporting.

- Ease of use is one of the most important factors. OLAP tools should present data in a clear and visual way and hide the complexity of multidimensional analysis from users by relying on familiar, intuitive metaphors.

RELATIONAL OLAP

Building a data warehouse has its own special challenges (common data model, common business dictionary, etc.) and is a complex endeavor. However, just having a data warehouse does not provide organizations with the often-heralded business benefits of data warehousing. To complete the supply chain from transactional system to decision maker, enterprises need to deliver systems that allow knowledge workers to make strategic and tactical decisions based on the information stored in these data warehouses.

OLAP systems allow users to intuitively, quickly, and flexibly manipulate operational data using familiar business terms, in order to provide analytical insight. For example, by using an OLAP system, decision makers can "slice and dice" information along a customer dimension and view business metrics by product and through time. Reports can be defined from multiple perspectives that provide a high-level or detailed view of the performance of any aspect of the business.

Decision makers can navigate throughout their database by drilling down on a report to view elements at finer levels of detail or by pivoting to view reports from different perspectives. To enable such full-functioned business analyses, OLAP systems need to (1) devise sophisticated analyses, (2) scale to large numbers of dimensions, and (3) support analyses against large atomic data sets. The following sections explore these three key requirements.

Development of Sophisticated Analyses

The key-performance OLAP systems need to be capable of delivering these metrics in a user-customizable format. These metrics may be obtained from the transactional databases, may be precalculated and stored in the database, or may be generated on demand during the query process.

Need for Scalability

Users analyze data from a number of different perspectives or dimensions. A dimension is any element or hierarchical combination of elements that can be displayed orthogonally to other combinations of elements in the data model. The number of dimensions in OLAP systems range from a few dimensions to hundreds of dimensions. Organizations have large numbers of dimensions in their data models. OLAP applications can typically scale to handle this dimensional richness. A typical OLAP report with four dimensions might contain weekly revenue for promotions by store and by department.

Target marketing and market segmentation applications involve extracting highly qualified result sets from large volumes of data. For example, a direct marketing organization might want to generate a targeted mailing list based on dozens of characteristics, including purchase frequency, purchase recency, size of the last purchase, past buying trends, customer location, age of customer, and sex of customer. Such applications rapidly increase the dimensionality requirements for analysis.

Support Large Atomic Data Sets

Atomic data refers to the lowest level of data granularity required for effective decision making. In the case of a retail merchandising manager, atomic may refer to information by store by day by item. For a banker, it may be information by account by transaction by branch. Most organizations implementing OLAP systems find themselves needing systems that can scale to tens, hundreds, and even thousands of gigabytes of atomic information.

As OLAP systems become more pervasive and are used by the majority of the enterprise, more data over longer time frames will be included in the data store, and the size of the database will increase by at least an order of magnitude. OLAP systems need the horsepower to be able to scale from present to near-future volumes of data.

An Example

A retail business with 200 stores and 350,000 products (of which an average of 100,000 are sold in any given store) that records just revenue information for 13 months at the daily level would have atomic data of approximately 160 gigabytes of information (assuming 20 bytes per row). When inventory, planned sales, promotional, supplier, demographic, and seasonal information are included in the system, this number can rapidly exceed 500 gigabytes.

Customer information is essential for targeting and evaluating the various products. Customer segment, market, zip code, related accounts, interest rate, credit ranking, number of times past 30 days due, and loan status are all examples of useful characteristics that a bank might require. Incorporating these characteristic dimensions into the data model can dramatically increase the size of the system. It is quite common for a banking system to have well over 750 gigabytes of atomic-level information.

MULTIDIMENSIONAL DATABASES

Normally, it is difficult to differentiate one relational database from another, except that they all conform to the same relational model, have roughly the same feature set, and can be accessed by a common language, SQL. The exact opposite situation exists in the realm of MDDs (Multidimensional Databases).

The concept of a multidimensional database is actually rather simple. Rather than storing information as records, and records in tables, MDDs (logically) store data in arrays. Unfortunately, there is not much else that the different flavors of MDDs have in common. Each implementation is substantially different from any other.

- Unlike the relational model, there is no agreed-upon multidimensional model.
- MDDs have no standard access method (such as SQL) or APIs.

The products range from narrow to broad in addressing the aspects of *decision support*. With those facts in mind, one can only evaluate different MDDs in broad categories. At the low end, there are single-user or small-scale LAN-based tools for viewing multidimensional data. The functionality and usability of these tools are actually quite high, but they are limited in scale and lack broad OLAP features. In fact, each of these tools could realistically define a separate category, so diverse are their features and architectures.

There are two multidimensional database capabilities. In the hypercube model, symmetry is the paradigm. This is actually a little misleading, since "cube" implies that each side is of equal length, which is rarely the case in such applications. The term hypercube is meant to describe a similar object of greater than three dimensions, also with flat sides and each dimension at right angles to all of the others.

Designing a hypercube model is a top-down process. First, you decide what aspect, or process of the business you will capture in the model, such as sales activity or claims processing. Next, identify the values that you want to capture, such as sales amounts or elements of costs. This information is almost always numeric. Last, identify the granularity of the data, that is, the lowest level of detail that you will capture. These elements are the dimensions. Common dimensions are measure, time, scenario, geography, product, and customer.

Multidimensional databases (MDDs) are capable of providing stunning query performance, which is mostly a function of anticipating the manner in which data can be accessed. Because information in a MDD is stored in much coarser grain than a Relational Database (RDB), the index is much smaller and is usually resident in memory. Once the in-memory index is scanned, a few pages are drawn from the database. Some tools are even designed to cache these pages in shared memory for performance enhancement.

This means that values in the arrays can be updated without affecting the index. MDDs are well suited for read-write applications. A downside of this "positional" architecture is that even minor changes in the dimensional structure require a complete reorganization of the database. Another major drawback of this model is that every value shares the same dimensionality.

Though implementations vary across products, multicubes dimension each variable separately and deal internally with the consequences. The drawback is that these approaches are less straightforward and require higher learning curves.

Relational OLAP Solutions

Just like the MDDs, this is a rapidly evolving technology. You may consider a relational/OLAP tool if it

- Generates SQL optimized for the target database, including SQL extensions, provides a mechanism to describe the model through metadata, and uses the metadata in real time to construct queries.
- Has a powerful SQL generator, capable of creating multipass selects and/or correlated subqueries.
- Includes a mechanism to at least advise on the construction of summary tables for performance, preferably with the ability to monitor usage.
- Is powerful enough to create non-trivial ranking, comparison and percent-to-class calculations.
- Has the ability to partition the application between clients, servers, and a middle tier for managing threads to the database.

Here are some important relational/OLAP characteristics:

Data warehouse: Data warehouses and relational databases are inseparable. Subsetting the data warehouse into smaller, manageable pieces, or data marts, is better suited for MDDs.

Rapidly changing dimensions: Changes in the dimensional structure require a physical reorganization of the database, which is time-consuming. Certain applications are too fluid for this, and the on-the-fly dimensional view of a relational/OLAP tool is the only appropriate choice.

Data rich applications: The applications with massive amounts of data (10's, 100's or 1000's of gigabytes) and relatively simple relationships are best left to the relational bases.

Development: Some tools require a fairly steep learning curve, particularly those at the high end with the broadest functionality. The 4GL languages of these tools are quite idiosyncratic, and the skills do not transfer well.

Fat client/thin client: Consider products that operate with a "thin client" and place a heavier burden on the server.

Network impact: Closely related, but not identical to the issue immediately above, is the impact placed on the network.

Performance

MDDs have more subtle performance limitations. Queries that cross all arrays, as opposed to reporting from a handful of them, are similar in response time to full-table scans in an RDB. Tuning a RDB with a "pure" star schema design, with pre-calculated and aggregated tables, along with a SQL generator that knows how to take advantage of them, will perform similarly to a MDD.

Advanced relational/OLAP tools provide a middle tier to "multiplex" the clients into a smaller number of active processes on the server. This technique can even serve to maximize the use of caching and shared memory by sharing processes. Also, complex OLAP queries often require multiple SELECT statements. The facility to submit these asynchronously as separate threads through the database server can have a huge impact on performance.

Scalability

Since relational/OLAP tools rely on the RDB for servicing their queries, scalability is usually a function of the underlying database. However, without a middle tier to manage the interaction between client and server, it is possible to overwhelm the database server with the volume of separate processes.

The actual size of the database is critical. Though many OLAP servers can scale up to multigigabyte size, careful analysis of "boundary conditions" (those situations that represent discontinuous reliability or worse, catastrophic failure) is necessary.

RDBs can handle much larger databases and take advantage of more powerful server architectures, but this is a distinct advantage for relational/OLAP. RDBs have no advantage over MDDs architecturally for exploiting SMP and MPP, however.

OLAP COMPONENTS

An OLAP application consists of a number of software and data components, whether it is implemented using a dedicated multidimensional database (Figure 8.5) or using a relational database (RDBMS) plus a relational OLAP tool. It is necessary to understand what role these components play in order to be able to see how the different approaches work, and determine their ability to deliver the desired system benefits.

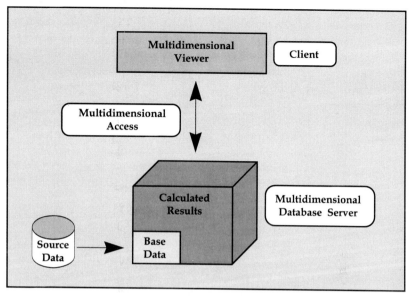

FIGURE 8.5   OLAP Components.

Physical Data Storage

The summarized data is the physical input data and precalculated results at the lowest level. At this level, data is never "open"—it is only accessible through the database management system. Otherwise, security and multiuser access could not be controlled. The data management software has information on what physical data is stored and how it relates to the named data objects that it delivers to the outside world. The physical disk structures are only visible to the data management software.

Figure 8.5 illustrates several components of stored data: the input data, the precalculated results, the indexing structured required to access these quickly, and the metadata to describe and manage the physical data structures in business terms.

Some or all of the potential calculations (e.g., aggregations) are usually performed in advance so that ad hoc user queries can be serviced instantly, without the need to retrieve large amounts of data. The calculated results (or summary tables) are generated from the base data by applying a set of calculation rules. These calculations include analytical formulae as well as data aggregations.

In an MDD, these will always be created by the internal multidimensional processing engine, but in a relational OLAP tool they may be created by a mixture of SQL procedures and an external multidimensional engine. Different relational OLAP tools to provide the summary tables have to be entirely generated without assistance from the OLAP product. Figure 8.6 depicts a simplified architecture of a three-tier relational OLAP model.

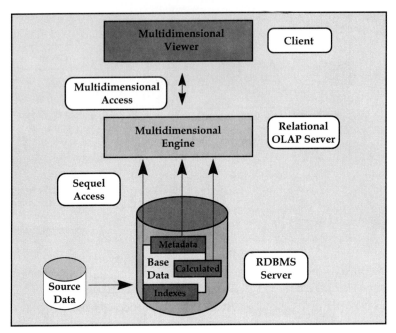

FIGURE 8.6 Three-Tier Relational OLAP Model.

Data Storage in an MDD

In an MDD, the physical data storage will consist of a number of compressed, array-like objects, usually with very compact index and pointer structures. Each array-like object (or block) will consist of groups of cells which can be accessed individually using direct offset calculations as opposed to any form of index.

These blocks are only stored if they contain data and are located using indexing structures. No keys are needed for the individual blocks, because the indexing system directly identifies each block's location on disk. Because the index only needs to identify a relatively small number of blocks rather than many individual rows, MDDs usually have very small indexes. In fact, with MDDs the index is only a tiny fraction of the size of the data space. Because they are so small, it is much easier to keep the whole index in memory, which greatly improves performance.

In most cases, the MDD takes care of all indexing and schema decisions, based on the application metadata, which offers a significant advantage by greatly simplifying the application development process.

Relational OLAP Data Storage

In a relational database, there is no concept of arrays, so multidimensional data has to be mapped into rows in flat tables. This is done using a schema that attempts to balance performance, storage efficiency, and maintainability. Typically, a denormalized "star schema" layout is used, with the base data stored in a single "fact table," and supporting information on dimensions held in other tables.

This denormalized structure is unlikely to be the schema that is used in the operational systems that feed the OLAP application. It may also not be suitable for other query and reporting tools. Thus, the base data will normally have to be duplicated into a set of tables that are designed specifically for multidimensional access rather than transaction processing or even general data-warehouse use.

Precomputed results are usually held in a large number of "summary tables," each with different combinations of aggregation levels. Each will need keys to identify the data, and the tables have to be indexed for efficient access. These keys may sometimes use "human-readable" alpha descriptors, but they commonly use more compact binary integer keys. The latter are more efficient for storage and data retrieval, but a join with a descriptor table will be needed to relate these binary keys to real-world descriptors. This adds an extra process to each retrieval operation and is therefore less efficient.

Storage Efficiency

Deciding on the right balance between storage efficiency and retrieval performance is one of the many design decisions that must be made when using relational OLAP. Part of this process is to allow for maximum required capacity and provide significant flexibility in this area.

The RDBMS itself is likely to have very large capacity, and the relational OLAP application simply uses a schema and indexing approach that are suitable for the expected database size. For all practical purposes, this can be as large as required, but other constraints, particularly performance requirements, will determine the real limits. The key thing to remember is that it is not the RDBMS itself, but the trade-offs in other areas that will determine the storage efficiency, performance, maintainability, calculation functionality, and capacity of the application.

The metadata is usually stored in a number of dimension and other tables. For maximum efficiency, it is often held in specialized formats that are custom-built for the particular relational OLAP. For best performance, the metadata may be compiled into a binary form that maps multidimensional structures to relational tables. There are no agreed upon industry standards yet for metadata storage, so all relational OLAP tools have their own imposed schemas for data tables and metadata.

Data Management

This is the software layer that controls access to and manages the physical data structures on disk. It is this layer that controls multiuser access and manages data locking mechanisms during updates. It also manages access security controls. In an MDD, this layer has intrinsic knowledge of multidimensional structures so data management is based on dimensions and members of dimensions.

Some MDDs provide detailed security and controls right down to the cell level. This is managed directly by the data management layer in the MDD, not by a separate application, so it is efficient and impossible to bypass. Not all MDDs support concurrent updating, but those that do generally lock at a multidimensional block level.

In an RDBMS, security and access controls are based on tables with locking usually based on tables and pages and, possibly, rows. Because these do not relate directly to the multidimensional concepts (e.g., all children of a dimension member) required by the application, the relational OLAP has to manage many of these aspects itself.

For example, the relational OLAP tool must map security by dimension member combination to the intersections of particular rows and columns in particular tables that hold the relevant data. This has the consequence that much of the security and access controls must be implemented by the relational OLAP rather than the relational database itself. The result is that it is possible to bypass the security layer by accessing the database directly from another application.

Multidimensional Manipulation and Calculation

The essence of any OLAP application is the efficient manipulation of large quantities of multidimensional data, and calculating large numbers of derived information from this data. Often, the calculated information will be tens or hundreds of times larger than the input data. On the other hand, MDDs include significant multidimensional calculation capability across all dimensions within the database. They also all have the ability to rapidly serve up appropriate slices of information to the desktop viewing tools.

SQL is not a multidimensional access or processing language. Even though, it is always possible to store multidimensional data in a number of relational tables, SQL does not support multidimensional manipulations or calculations.

Limitations of SQL

A relational OLAP with a smart SQL generator can use the stored metadata to create many multidimensional aggregations and certain other calculations between columns, but the many cross-dimensional calculations (e.g., ratios, allocations) can be done outside the SQL engine.

Relational OLAP must perform such calculations either in the client software (a two-tier architecture) or in an intermediate data transformation engine that operates between the client software and the RDBMS server (a three-tier architecture). This engine may run on the same processor as the SQL database or on a different, networked machine. In either case, a user's query will be formulated by the client software, passed to the mid-tier engine which will, using the metadata, generate the appropriate SQL to retrieve and partially process the relevant base data and precalculated summary data.

Once retrieved, it can perform additional multidimensional processing before finally sending the results to the client. This is a relatively complex process and much of it is performed by the relational OLAP engine, not the SQL database. A three-tier architecture is usually preferred to a two-tier for relational OLAP, but it is not optimum because of the lack of integration between the two server layers.

Relational OLAP applications are confronted with a dilemma when designing their calculation architecture. SQL cannot do full multidimensional calculations, yet it is more efficient to do large-scale calculations within a database engine by taking full advantage of server memory and indexing. It is certainly possible to implement a large-scale separate multidimensional engine outside the database, but this will not be as efficient as processing within the database engine. Therefore, some relational OLAP products are designed to get SQL to do as much of the work as possible, even if this means using a complex database schema and fancy SQL generation.

There is always a set of trade-offs between the higher performance using the RDBMS and the higher functionality that is obtained by using an external multidimensional processing engine. These trade-offs can only be eliminated if the full application processing is done within the server, but this is not possible using only SQL.

Some relational OLAP developers go the opposite way and do almost all the processing and application management in their own engine. This is workable, but reduces the relational database to little more than a file storage mechanism, contributing overhead rather than function.

Because SQL does not facilitate the updating in place of rows in existing summary tables, rows may also be split by time period, so that the arrival of data for a new time period does not force the rebuilding of the historical tables. All in all, a large multidimensional database containing several years of history is likely to have from tens to hundreds or even thousands of summary tables, each created using SQL procedures and/or the external multidimensional engine.

In order to answer any particular query, the engine will have to use the metadata to determine the nearest stored results and tables, query all the relevant base and summary tables, combine the resulting information using temporary tables in the database or in its own memory, perform the remaining multidimensional calculations, and then provide the results to the users. This is not a simple process, either for the application or for the engine that must be used to deliver fast results.

Regardless of the sophistication of the indexing or the performance of efficient SQL on advanced hardware, such queries take longer to service than those performed by a relatively simple MDD, and database maintenance is much more onerous. The addition of an extra consolidation level in a hierarchy causes no change to the database schema in MDD and there may also be no manual changes required to formulae or reports. This is because hierarchies in most MDDs are simply a formula definition and a user navigation aid, not part of the database schema.

By contrast, an additional level in a hierarchy is required for a redesign of a relational database schema if there are stored summary tables for each level of every hierarchy. This is not a change that can be accommodated instantly or easily reduce the flexibility of the OLAP application.

Multidimensional Viewing

This is the most visible and easily assessed portion of any OLAP application. There are many standard features that are needed for manipulating multidimensional data and viewing it in the most convenient format, and it must be possible to change the format instantly. Apart from all the rational criteria that are used to determine viewing requirements, user idiosyncrasies are also important here.

Accountants are most content when they are working in a spreadsheet environment, so they normally prefer their multidimensional OLAP data to be served up directly into their familiar spreadsheets. Executive users, on the other hand, often prefer a simpler, more intuitive EIS style environment. Marketing analysts prefer yet another style of interface, with built-in graphical reporting and standard top-ten reporting. Some users even prefer an interface that is different from all of these, which may require another language, such as Visual Basic.

It is not possible for any single vendor to supply the full range of client tools that are needed. It is also important that the OLAP server be capable of linking to a variety of other relevant clients, including spreadsheets, EIS viewers, Visual Basic, and other more specialized tools. This degree of openness is not satisfied merely through storing the data in any particular format or database.

The viewing tool must be able to take full advantage of all the multidimensional mapping (i.e., records to dimensions) and application data that is held in the metadata. This is not possible if the stored data is viewed directly without going through the relational OLAP application's metadata. In the long run, any OLAP tool must have an open API from the OLAP application server and the links claimed for any particular client tool must be explicitly supported and tested for them to be valid.

Metadata in OLAP

The previous sections have made many mentions of metadata, because this is a key component of any OLAP or data warehouse application. It is used to describe many aspects of the applications, including hierarchical relationships, stored formulae, whether calculations have to be performed before or after consolidation, currency conversion information, time series information, item descriptions and notes for reporting, security and access controls, data update status, formatting information, data sources, availability of precalculated summary tables, and data storage parameters. In the absence of this information, the actual data is not intelligible and it would not be wise to attempt to view or update it.

Because MDDs were intended specifically for OLAP applications, they handle metadata intrinsically (and largely automatically) within the database. RDBMSs are more general-purpose technologies, and such application-specific information is normally built as part of the application development. Thus, relational OLAPs have to implement this themselves. Even though the metadata is usually stored within the RDBMS, only applications which *understand* the metadata can make any business sense of the stored base and summary tables.

This requires that the relational OLAP client software or client API must be used, because direct connections from other applications to the database on the server are unable to take advantage of the multidimensional intelligence. This means the connection is only possible with substantial custom programming, if at all. Conversely, MDDs are able to take advantage of the APIs directly from the database engine, so a variety of other client or server applications can connect directly, without losing the effects of the metadata.

There are no current or proposed standards for OLAP metadata storage, so relational OLAP vendors have no choice but to store it in a proprietary format which (for optimum performance) may even be as a compiled binary object stored outside the RDBMS and hence not managed by it.

OLAP VERSUS OLTP

On-Line Analytical Processing (OLAP) is primarily involved with reading and aggregating large groups of diverse data. Unlike OLTP applications, OLAP involves many data items (frequently many thousands or even millions) which are involved in complex relationships. The objective of OLAP is to analyze these relationships and look for patterns, trends, and exception conditions.

On-Line Analytical Processing

An OLAP database may consist of sales data which has been aggregated by region, product type, and sales channel. A typical OLAP query might access a multigigabyte/multiyear sales database in order to find all product sales in each region for each product type. After reviewing the results, an analyst might further refine the query to find sales volume for each sales channel within region/product classifications. As a last step the analyst might want to perform year-to-year or quarter-to-quarter comparisons for each sales channel. This whole process must be carried out on-line with rapid response time so that the analysis process is undisturbed. OLAP queries can be characterized as on-line transactions which

- Access very large amounts of data, for example, several years of sales data, and analyze the relationships between many types of business elements, for example, sales, products, regions, channels.

- Involve aggregated data, for example, sales volumes, budgeted dollars, and dollars spent.

- Compare aggregated data over hierarchical time periods, for example, monthly, quarterly, yearly.

- Present data in different perspectives, for example, sales by region versus sales by channels by product within each region.

- Involve complex calculations between data elements, for example, expected profit as calculated as a function of sales revenue for each type of sales channel in a particular region.
- Are able to respond quickly to user requests so that users can pursue an analytical thought process without being stymied by the system.

The OLAP server allows convenient access to various data sources from familiar tools. Fast response is a crucial element in OLAP. It bears the same relationship to batch reporting as OLTP bears to batch updates. Information in OLAP applications must be immediately available so that it can be immediately refined for further analysis. In order to facilitate the analytical process, OLAP applications frequently present data in an easily recognizable form such as a spreadsheet.

On-Line Transaction Processing

OLAP applications are quite different from On-line Transaction Processing (OLTP) applications which consist of a large number of relatively simple transactions. The transactions usually retrieve and update a small number of records (usually less than one hundred) that are contained in several distinct tables. The relationships between the tables are generally simple.

A typical customer order entry OLTP transaction might retrieve all of the data relating to a specific customer and then insert a new order for the customer. Information is selected from the customer, customer order, and detail line tables. Each row in each table contains a customer identification number which is used to relate the rows from the different tables. The relationships between the records are simple and only a few records are actually retrieved or updated by a single transaction.

As we can see, both types of database problems—OLAP and OLTP—have specialized requirements. In order to achieve optimal performance and ease of use, it is necessary to design servers which are optimized for each problem domain.

The data warehouse is an RDBMS designed specifically to meet the needs of decision makers rather than the needs of transaction processing systems. Unlike an OLTP system, a data warehouse is specialized for retrieving and analyzing information quickly and easily.

Although these systems share a few similarities, they are quite different. See Table 8.1.

TABLE 8.1 Similarities and Differences

	OLTP	DATA WAREHOUSE
Purpose	Run day-to-day operation	Information retrieval and analysis
Structure	RDBMS	RDBMS
Data Model	Normalized	Multidimensional
Access	SQL	SQL plus data analysis extensions
Type of Data	Data that runs the business	Data to analyze the business
Condition of Data	Changing, incomplete	Historical, descriptive

Data warehousing is the process of extracting and transforming operational data into informational data and loading it into a central data store or "warehouse." Once loaded, it can be easily accessed by decisionmakers using a choice of desktop query and analysis tools.

To move the concept of information databases to the reality of making decisions, the data warehouse software/hardware solution must accommodate this fundamental notion: Users must be able to ask any business question of any data in the enterprise with performance that doesn't inhibit the decision making process.

DATA ANALYSIS TOOLS AND APPLICATIONS

OLAP data analysis tools provide such capabilities as mathematical and statistical functions, multidimensional modeling, and forecasting. They are used to analyze and forecast trends and measure the efficiency of business operations over time. These evaluations provide support for strategic business decision making and insights on how to improve efficiency and reduce costs of business operations.

OLAP allows users to analyze and slice and dice data across multiple dimensions such as time, market, and/or product category. Such tools have existed for many years, but like query and reporting tools, OLAP technologies are now taking advantage of GUIs and client/server computing. Data warehousing for OLAP not only offers the advantage of clean and integrated data, but also historical data essential for forecasting and trend analysis. Warehouses supporting OLAP can be thought of as *Decision-Support* System (DSS) data warehouses.

There is much debate over the use of OLAP tools in Multidimensional Data Analysis (MDA). The debate centers around which type of DBMS is best suited to storing and maintaining multidimensional data. Two kinds of MDA client tools are offered: those accessing data stored in multidimensional database systems (MDBMSs) and those accessing data stored in relational DBMSs.

MDBMSs provide both analytical and data management server capabilities. They supply very good performance for analyzing and drilling down through multiple levels of summarized data, but are less well suited for handling large amounts of detailed data. The current direction of MDBMS is toward providing a pass-through capability to RDBMSs for accessing detailed data in a multitier data warehousing configuration.

When MDA tools are used to access data stored in RDBMSs, the RDBMS provides the data management capability, while the front-end client tool provides the analysis engine. The advantages of this approach are that both summarized and detailed data can be stored in the RDBMS, and data can be shared with other business intelligence tools. To improve performance, many vendors in this category are moving analytical processing into a separate analytical server positioned between the MDA client and RDBMS server.

Data analysis tools typically work with summarized rather than detailed data. Although you can build summaries during analytical processing, it is far more efficient to prebuild them whenever possible. This approach reduces processing overheads and makes work easier for the user. Summaries are often stored in special databases known as data marts, which are tailored to specific sets of users and applications. Data marts are usually built from the detailed historical data stored in a DSS data warehouse, and, in some cases, are constructed directly from operational databases or an operational data warehouse. They may use either RDBMS or MDBMS technology.

Types of Enduser Tools

Business intelligence tools support three main user tasks: querying and reporting of known facts, analysis of known facts, and discovery of unknown facts. Querying and reporting involve displaying data in a visual form, such as a printed report or information displayed on a computer screen. The processing may be done on-line or in batch, using ad hoc or prebuilt queries and reports. Tools supporting this type of task have existed for many years. Many modern tools, however, offer more sophisticated facilities such as Graphical User Interfaces (GUIs), the capability to pass retrieved data to desktop applications using techniques such as Microsoft OLE, and a semantic layer providing a business view of data.

> *Query*, *reporting*, and *data analysis* tools are used to process or look for known facts. In other words, users of these tools know what kind of information they want to access and analyze.

> *Data exploration* involves digging through large amounts of historical detailed data typically kept in a DSS data warehouse. Tools supporting data exploration are sometimes referred to as data mining or data discovery tools. However, some people include them under the heading of OLAP tools, and several even use the term data mining to cover all aspects of business intelligence.

> *Query and reporting* tools are most often used to track day-to-day business operations and support tactical business decisions. In this context, a warehouse offers the advantage of data that has been cleaned and integrated from multiple operational systems. Such a warehouse typically contains detailed data that reflects the current (or near-current) status of data in operational systems and is thus referred to as an operational data store or operational data warehouse.

Data Warehousing Applications

As with all information systems, it is best to view data warehousing's core components against a framework that focuses not on technology, but on the business applications the system is designed to address. In general, the applications served by data warehousing can be placed in one of three main categories.

Personal productivity applications, such as spreadsheets, statistical packages, and graphics tools, are useful for manipulating and presenting data on individual PCs. Developed for a stand-alone environment, these tools address applications requiring only small volumes of warehouse data.

Data query and reporting applications deliver warehouse-wide data access through simple, list-oriented queries and the generation of basic reports. These reports provide a view of historical data but do not address the enterprise need for in-depth analysis and planning.

Planning and analysis applications address such essential business requirements as budgeting, forecasting, product line and customer profitability, sales analysis, financial consolidations, and manufacturing mix analysis—applications that use historical, projected, and derived data.

These planning and analysis requirements, referred to as On-Line Analytical Processing (OLAP) applications, share a set of user requirements that cannot be met by applying query tools against the historical data maintained in the warehouse repository. The planning and analysis function mandates that the organization look not only at past performance but also, more importantly, at the future performance of the business. It is essential to create operational scenarios that are shaped by the past, yet also include planned and potential changes that will impact tomorrow's corporate performance. The combined analysis of historical data with future projections is critical to the success of today's corporation.

Requirements for OLAP Applications

- An application-specific analytical model that integrates robust mathematical functions for computing derived data (ratios, variances, allocations).

- Consolidation of actual, projected, and derived data.

- Read/write environment to support "what-if" analysis and planning.

- Consistently fast response times that allow for an iterative and free flowing analysis session.

- The ability to be deployed and adapted quickly.

- The ability to share and manage large volumes of data.

Several of these requirements are in direct conflict with the operational realities that must be imposed on the storage component of the data warehouse. For example, imposing an application-specific data model on the storage component reduces the flexibility to manage and expand the warehouse. Read/write access generally conflicts with the data integrity controls applied by the IT (Information Technology) organization and business projections, generally created in spreadsheets, are too dynamic to be transformed and stored in the warehouse.

Other requirements are beyond the individual capabilities of the warehouse access tools. For example, the ability to share and manage large data volumes is beyond the capabilities of single-user tools that manipulate small data volumes on the desktop. To address all of these needs, the analytical component of the warehouse, acting as an "analytical data mart," must be implemented.

SUMMARY

Data warehousing is a corporate strategy that addresses a broad range of *decision-support* requirements including personal productivity, query and reporting, and planning and analysis. On-Line Analytical Processing (OLAP) defines a set of user-driven, functional requirements for planning, analysis, and management reporting applications. The inherent organizational requirement for planning and analysis is to help drive improved business performance. Successfully meeting this need requires that the company understand its past performance and prepare for its future.

Users of computer systems have become accustomed to many of the benefits of modern relational database technology. They expect the same level of standards, capacity, performance, openness, and platform portability and are rightly disappointed if other applications fail to deliver these. The obvious answer, it might seem, therefore, is to use an RDBMS for the data storage of multidimensional applications, replacing the MDD that might otherwise have been used.

The promise of OLAP is its ability to help enterprises make intelligent business decisions by providing them with the power to access, combine, and scrutinize company information. With multidimensional analysis, users have the opportunity to understand and forecast their business better. However, many factors muddy the waters. There are numerous applications which provide multidimensional analysis, but they require access to the lowest level of detail each time the query is run. Likewise, we use MDD for applications that would have been impossible in relational OLAP, such as financial modeling. In addition, the relational OLAP tools require RDB.

One thing is certain: Multidimensional databases and relational OLAP are highly creative, capable, and competitive.

First- and second-generation analysis approaches, including EIS solutions, PC drill tools, and OLAP servers, fall short on delivering an OLAP solution with the ease of use, scalability, and cost-effectiveness required to support mainstream business users. EIS and OLAP server products are expensive and appeal only to a small set of users. PC drills are inexpensive, but they lack tool integration and easy on-line access to the central data source. In addition, early-generation analysis solutions require heavy technical assistance, and in some cases, supplemental hardware and software.

In this chapter, we have defined an approach to OLAP that is

- *Open*, allowing companies to leverage their existing computing environments.
- *Deployable*, minimizing the need for IS assistance while maintaining IS control
- *Integrated*, enabling users to efficiently perform a range of business functions, including query, reporting, and analysis.
- *Easy to use*, empowering users with the autonomy to access the business information they need when they need it.

OLAP has begun and will continue to permeate organizations at all levels, empowering users to provide more timely strategic and tactical direction in accordance with the increasing number of internal and external factors impacting contemporary business enterprises. The quality of strategic business decisions made as a result of OLAP may be significantly higher and more timely than those made traditionally.

OLAP applications have unique requirements and multidimensional databases optimized for OLAP provide significant advantages over relational OLAP tools in meeting these needs.

The complexity of performing multidimensional manipulations and calculations on data stored in relational tables means that, for all but the most straightforward data analysis, the expected and much wanted benefits of relational OLAP are actually less likely to be achieved using a relational OLAP tool than using a MDD that is specifically designed to offer high capacity, standards, security, multiuser concurrent data updating with locking, server platform exploitation, and multivendor tool support.

By performing the processing close to the data, with multidimensional structures, indexing, and metadata all integrated with the server's application intelligence, applications can be made easier to implement, functionally richer, faster, more scalable, and more open.

There are indeed many simpler multidimensional analysis applications where the use of a full-blown OLAP tool is not justified, but in many of these cases, a relational report writer with cross tabbing or a spreadsheet with pivot tables may be all that is needed. Again, this is application dependent and so there are certainly applications where a relational OLAP tool can provide an effective solution.

The operative decision guide needs to be simply: What are the requirements of the application at hand and what system best meets the user's functional requirements for that application? By basing tool selection on real application requirements and real tool capabilities, the user's needs will be most effectively fulfilled.

Despite what you may have heard, On-line Analytical Processing (OLAP) doesn't necessarily imply that you must use a multidimensional database as your *decision-support* server. The latest alternative, relational/OLAP tools add *decision-support* capabilities to a relational database engine.

Decision-support architecture is the broader set of requirements necessary to deliver the *decision-support* system, including, but not limited to, data warehouses and OLAP (On-Line Analytical Processing) servers. The focus of this chapter has been to explain the OLAP technology as an application to data warehousing solutions.

9

DATA WAREHOUSING FOR THE PARALLEL ENVIRONMENTS

186

INTRODUCTION

Parallel database technology is the basis for the performance growth necessary to deal with the emerging classes of applications, such as data warehousing, that require processing of enormous amounts of data. The success of a parallel DBMS depends on the efficient operation of many different resources, including processors, memory, disks, and network interconnects. Managing this complex environment presents many challenges, including how to balance processing and storage, identify hot spots and points of contention, analyze and tune the system, or reorganize data and deploy applications flexibly.

The Need for Parallelism

Only a few years ago, symmetric multiprocessing and massively parallel processing systems were considered by many to be niche hardware desperately in search of commercial software that could take advantage of their architectures. Relational database vendors eventually began to build parallelism into their products, but there were still few applications with requirements stringent enough to push users to implement leading-edge systems.

As the trend toward data warehouse computing accelerates, businesses are growing more dependent on relational databases for core applications. These operations are dependent on computing resources that can expand to meet long-term needs and that provide reliable access to data for business-critical applications.

Now, though, as firms flock to build large *decision-support* databases, parallel technology has found its place. Indeed, the companies in the forefront of adopting parallel technology are those building data warehouses: retailers, telecommunications firms, and financial services companies. For each, the business driver is the same—the need to quickly sift through enormous volumes of collected data to create targeted marketing strategies.

The theme is high *scalability*, *operability*, and *availability*. The ability to solve *decision-support* problems by putting multiple nodes to work on the same problem is critical. The issue is to ensure that the database platform is not a one-trick pony. It must be able to make use of all aspects of parallelism.

This means DBMSs must offer more than parallel query—the ability to decompose large complex queries, run the separate components simultaneously, and reassemble them at the end. Parallel load, table scan, backup, and restore are important, as are database partitioning across processor nodes, and "parallel-aware" optimizers that can take advantage of the DBMS's parallel capabilities. Users are also looking for linear scalability, the ability to add more processors without performance degradation. Just in the last few years, we've seen the evolution of database software on parallel platforms. We're starting to see some product maturity.

Single versus Parallel Processors

Databases based on single processor systems can no longer meet the world's growing requirements for cost-effective scalability, reliability, and performance. A powerful and financially attractive alternative to a single-processor driven database is a parallel database driven by multiple processors. Parallel databases link multiple, smaller machines to achieve the same throughput as a single, larger machine, often with greater scalability and reliability than single processor databases.

Parallel database architectures include *shared memory*, *shared nothing*, and *shared disk*. While the shared nothing definition sometimes includes distributed databases (independent databases located on separate systems connected by a network), distributed databases do not provide parallel operation.

Developers know that DBMSs are the heart of most data warehousing applications. A DBMS provides secure access to shared data for client applications and allows client/server developers to split the processing load between the client and the server.

Such an architecture reduces the load on the network and frees the clients to perform more important interface and application processing. DBMSs can even take on some of the application processing load through the use of stored procedures and triggers, bounce back from system crashes using roll-back/roll-forward recovery, and guard data through the use of rules and two-phase commits. DBMSs also provide locking mechanisms and multi-user access controls that protect data from the dangers of concurrent access such as "dead-lock" and "deadly embrace."

Realizing the benefits of a data warehouse requires a great deal of planning and analysis with regard to the data and the computing infrastructure. The technology is not a problem unless and until the data warehouse is very large and a complex query will take considerable time until optimized for the application. While mainstream relational databases are used for warehousing, *parallel databases* are recommended for implementations involving vast amounts of historical data and for multidimensional analysis.

This chapter explains the concept and benefits of parallel technologies and provides an overview of the parallel database architectures available today. It compares those architectures on the basis of scalability, price/performance, reliability, and ease of administration for data warehousing applications.

OVERVIEW OF PARALLEL TECHNOLOGIES

Traditionally the domain of scientific and engineering users, parallel processing is rapidly expanding into commercial applications such as *decision support* and data warehousing. The methods of parallelism allow a system to be expanded by incrementing processors to the required level without the need for a complete system upgrade. Large complex queries can be run against vast quantities of historical data to provide organizations with topical trends and patterns that could not previously have been achieved within a reasonable time frame. Performance-critical data processing applications which provide *decision support* require quick response in order to be effective in a volatile market.

The role of parallel technologies has traditionally been associated with computer-intensive, scientific, and engineering applications, where the provision of multiple processors can allow more individual tasks to run simultaneously and allow large tasks to be broken down into a series of concurrent smaller tasks. In some cases, the use of parallel technology in this way is the only method by which a sensible response time can be reasonably achieved. The use of multiprocessor engines has been with us for a considerable time. Commerce has used them for its OLTP environments, where each machine can support many users.

The use of parallel methods allows a business to expand a system or application-base incrementally as it finds its needs evolve. Many parallel engine sites can be started with a relatively low entry cost that matches the company's existing needs. Then, if the company's needs grow, the system can be expanded by the addition of more disks, or processors and the like, into a more powerful engine. This method of growth has certain advantages when compared to a complete system upgrade which is sometimes the only option in a traditional mainframe environment.

The incremental growth of a parallel system causes little or no user disruption. Increments are often achieved by the insertion of additional boards or drives while the system is still running. This has large business benefits—the loss of a mission-critical system during upgrade would cause a considerable loss of processing time. Parallel technology has an additional benefit in this respect, since by virtue of its design, the loss of any single component would not cause the system to fail but would rather cause the faulty board to be withdrawn from operation and its processing tasks passed onto another component.

Parallel technology can only be fully exploited if the software and complementary hardware support is in place. Parallel enabled software will not provide any added value running on non-parallel hardware. Architectures for parallel processing can exploit the use of multiple processors (low-price CMOS), large amounts of memory, and many disk storage units. The most common architectures are shared nothing, shared disks, and shared memory.

Shared Memory. Often referred to as tightly coupled or Symmetric Multiprocessors (SMP), uses multiple processors that have common memory and share disk storage units (Figure 9.1).

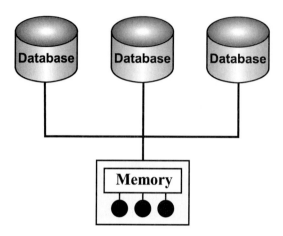

FIGURE 9.1 Shared-Memory Architecture.

Shared Nothing. Often referred to as loosely coupled or Massively Parallel Processing (MPP), uses multiple processors, each with its own memory and disk storage units (Figure 9.2).

Shared Disks. Uses multiple processors, each with its own memory but sharing disk storage units (Figure 9.3).

The shared-nothing architecture is represented by each individual processor having its own private memory and access to its own disks. Message passing is the only method by which the processors can communicate. The IBM Power Parallel System is an example of hardware with this architecture which DB2 Parallel software is designed to complement.

Oracle, Sybase, IBM, and Informix, all produce parallel versions of their complex database engines.

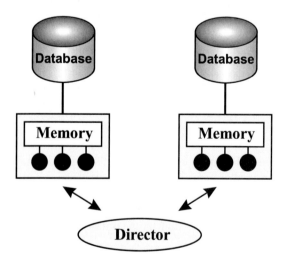

FIGURE 9.2 Shared-Nothing Architecture.

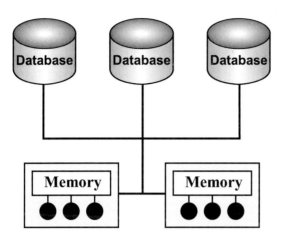

FIGURE 9.3   Shared-Something (Disk) Architecture.

Parallel Technology Issues

Parallel technology is not a solution in itself and is dependent on many other components as stated earlier. The parallel support can only be provided if parallel hardware is also in place. Networking operating systems (e.g., OS/2 SMP, UNIX, MP) and tools play a key role in providing the complete system and should not be compromised if the system is to be effective.

Parallel software systems are designed with specific hardware architectures in mind, with many vendors providing optimized software that will run only on their own proprietary hardware.

Issues to be addressed within the parallel arena include interconnect performance, load balancing, bandwidth, tuning, and performance tools. There are many documented cases that have given competitive edge where the parallel systems have been implemented correctly. If the parallel systems are not implemented with vision, they may prove to be no more than an interesting and expensive experiment. Parallel systems also promise the following technology benefits.

Lower Configuration Cost

Using cheap CMOS technology to add processing power provides a low-cost migration path. The price/performance ratio provided by parallel servers is far superior to that of uniprocessor mainframe counterparts.

Improved Scalability

The number of processors and storage devices can be incremented easily and cheaply as demand increases. The need for complete system upgrade is removed as the support for scalability is integral to the architecture. *Decision-support*/data warehouse databases can rapidly expand beyond the tens of gigabytes into the hundreds of gigabytes. This order of magnitude increases demands for improved scalability of parallel DBMS.

Improved Mid-Range Performance

The performance gains in mid-range systems are now comparable and even superior to mainframe systems.

Parallel Applications

Parallel technology is typically used for data warehousing and data mining. These processes need access to large volumes of data and provide timely responses to problems that previously would not have been cost justifiable. For example, retail systems can now record every transaction from every branch within a chain using bar codes. This information can be used to monitor trends on a daily basis by region, store, or season to assist in more accurately predicting demand and the corresponding supply.

Data Mining

One of the main emerging uses for parallel technology is that of *data mining*. The processing of vast amounts of information, often in an unstructured manner, places high demand on standard server or mainframe technology. This has often provided the impetus for commercial organizations to take another look at parallel technologies, in the hope that they will provide the data processing muscle to crack the data mining nut.

The potential rewards of data mining are vast. The application of these techniques when applied to, say, the retail industry offers several examples where data mining is beneficial. Large retail organizations process phenomenal volumes of data as they track items by store, by department, by season, by region. It is possible that several hundred thousand records could be added to a central data store (or data warehouse) each and every day. Once all this data is collected, it can be made available for data mining. The retailer has the benefit of being able to predict more accurately the requirement for product shipments and can organize "just-in-time" shipments to reduce warehousing and inventory costs.

By applying parallel techniques, it becomes possible to execute highly complex queries which would be unthinkable on almost any other platform. This allows users to refine their train of thought in almost real time to extract the best possible information from the data. Answers to this type of query could be so important that the company could obtain a previously unseen competitive advantage, realize cost reductions, or significantly increase revenues.

Target marketing is another example of the application of data mining. By sifting the masses of historical sales data, it is possible to determine the most likely purchasers of a particular product. For those companies that depend upon either direct mail campaigns or catalog sales, this can become very beneficial. By restricting the mailing to high probability buyers, the business can achieve a higher *hit rate* for a reduced mailing cost. In a wider sense, the idea of target marketing not only applies to catalog or direct mail companies, but to any business that wants to understand its customer preferences and exploit them. This includes insurance companies, banks, building societies, and credit card companies.

PARALLEL DATABASE TECHNOLOGIES

Although parallel database technology is relatively new, it is now past the experimental stage and its benefits are generally well known. On the one hand, the average database user has no need for a parallel database and is inhibited by the cost of the hardware. On the other, increasing volumes of data make a parallel database a cost-effective solution for some organizations.

While a large percentage of the DBMS market will not have any use for parallel database technology, there are several trends in computing which indicate a growing need for this degree of processing power. The most notable is the increasing popularity of data warehousing. When organizations store historical data for *decision-support* purposes, they may require a DBMS which can not only handle the immense volumes of data that are gathered but also continue to cope as the amount increases over time.

Organizations that are not implementing data warehousing but which are running *decision-support* queries on transactional databases are also candidates for parallel databases. Increasing volumes of data and complex *decision-support* queries can threaten the performance of mission-critical transaction processing—parallel database technology can increase processing power so that both types of applications can maintain response times.

In a database management system designed for uniprocessor hardware, database operations are performed in strict sequence: The output of one operation feeds the input of the next and each database task is carried out on a single CPU even if more are available in the system.

The parallel database performs many database operations simultaneously and may even split individual tasks into smaller parts so that the task can be spread across multiple processors. Parallel databases can, therefore, reach very high levels of performance, enabling them to cope with increasing processing demands without losing speed. Multiprocessor platforms allow more CPUs to be added when more power is required. Parallel database technology can even provide performance gains on uniprocessor hardware platforms, as certain operations can be carried out in parallel.

The Impact of Parallel Technology on DBMSs

Parallel technology is having a revolutionary impact on the management of data. It brings together several trends. Parallel technology brings the microprocessor performance curve to large systems and large databases. It will have large economic impact on the use of data, just as desktop systems have become more powerful than the mainframes of just a few years ago. Consequently, large databases can be managed more economically than ever before. Relational databases were really not usable on a very large scale or for very large databases until parallel technology became available.

Multiprocessor Systems

As the demand for more powerful computers has increased at a faster rate than the speed of individual processors, hardware designers have turned to multiprocessor architectures. Multiprocessing systems use more than one processor and share main memory, cache memory, and other resources. The operating system assigns processors to jobs as they arrive or if jobs are waiting, as a processor becomes available.

In a *loosely coupled* system, each processor runs its own copy of the operating system but obtains work from a shared job pool. In a *tightly coupled* system, the entire system runs one copy of the operating system, which allocates processors to tasks. The most common tightly coupled multiprocessor systems are SMP (*Symmetric Multiprocessing*) systems. By processing queries and transactions across multiple CPUs, SMP systems avoid the bottlenecks that can frequently occur in uniprocessor systems and carry out tasks much more quickly. As databases and processing demands grow, SMP systems can be scaled up by adding more processors.

While SMP systems provide an efficient solution to problems of scalability and performance and are currently running effectively with more than 20 processors, they are limited in their support for a larger number of processors. SMP performance does not increase in direct proportion to the number of CPUs added, as the memory bus bandwidth remains the same. More processors mean that data will take longer to pass along the bus. However, DBMSs have been optimized on SMP platforms by increasing the number of database operations that can be performed in parallel and by handling the management of processors more efficiently through dynamic job allocation.

A more scalable solution is offered by *loosely coupled* multiprocessor systems. Initially designed for the heavy computational demands of scientific applications, loosely coupled systems, including *loosely coupled clusters* and *Massively Parallel Processors (MPP)*, allow large numbers of CPUs (in the 10,000 range) to be configured to share a set of disks. Although the systems may also use shared memory, most of their operations occur in memory specifically assigned to individual processors.

In loosely coupled schemes, there are no bottlenecks as additional interprocessor communications channels and system memory are added whenever processors are added. The potential of these architectures for commercial applications, such as multidimensional analysis, for data warehousing is considerable. Some RDBMSs are already taking advantage of such MPP systems.

Vertical Parallelism

Vertical parallelism can be achieved by running different operations concurrently. Spreading the work over many operating system processes allows full use to be made of the available processors and other resources. An example would be when an operation selecting certain database records runs concurrently with a sorting operation. The selected records can be input to the sort routine as they are read, instead of waiting for the reading and selecting operation to finish.

Horizontal Parallelism

Horizontal parallelism is achieved when two or more processing elements work on the same user-visible task at the same time. In this case, the queries are divided into smaller parts which are then processed by different processors concurrently. The database server replicates certain database operations so that multiple copies of each operation can run in parallel. The results of the processing are then combined as if a single thread of execution had performed the operation.

Parallel Disk I/O

Parallel disk I/O allows data to be read from many disks simultaneously, whereas a traditional DBMS reads disks sequentially. When a database table is partitioned across several disks, the parallel system is capable of carrying out the read operation more quickly.

Partitioning

A good partitioning scheme is an essential part of designing a database that will benefit from parallelism. As with non-parallel databases, partitioned data benefits from indexed access. The indexes may also be partitioned. There are five partitioning methods used today:

- Hashing is where data is assigned to disks based on a hash key. A good hashing algorithm will distribute data uniformly across disks, reducing the potential for skewing.
- Round-robin partitioning simply assigns a row to partitions in sequence.
- Allocating rows to nodes based on ranges of values provides flexible placement and works well for ordered values requests. But there is a potential of skewing.
- Schema partitioning allows you to tie a table to a particular partition and is inherently skewed. It provides advantages for small tables that participate in many joins. In such a case, usually all the data is allocated at one node.
- User-defined rules allow allocation of data to a particular partition.

To achieve best results of partitioning, you must assign the allocation scheme to minimize skew and data movement. The choices depend on the queries run against the database.

Parallel Databases

We can now examine how DBMSs take advantage of parallelism. First, let us look at what parallel operations you can perform with a single CPU and disk. The CPU works much faster than the disk I/O, so the CPU must frequently wait for the disk, but, if there is enough memory, you can still perform parallel tasks. For example, the system can buffer data in memory for multiple tasks. It can retrieve data to be scanned and sorted and also retrieve more data for the next transaction. The more disks and controllers the system has, the faster it can feed memory and the CPU. This is an example of parallel I/O.

There are two basic ways to obtain scaleup. First, you can assign small independent transactions to different processors. The more processors, the more transactions the system can execute without reducing throughput. This is known as *transaction scaleup*. This is also useful in executing multiple independent SQL statements. A collection of SQL statements can be broken up, each allocated to a processor. This can be termed as *interquery parallelism*.

A SQL query statement is actually a collection of operations executed on a database. Some of these SQL operations are sequential. A single large SQL query must be broken up into tasks, execute those tasks on separate processors, and recombine them for the answer. This is known as *batch scaleup* or *intraquery parallelism*. The opportunities for scaling or speeding up queries, however, are limited by the number of steps in executing the statement. Steps, such as SORT and GROUP BY, may require all the data from the previous step before they start. This can be termed as *pipelined parallelism*.

If there is more than one data stream, it is possible for some operations to proceed simultaneously. For example, a product table could be spread across multiple disks and a thread could reach each subset of the product data. This is known as *partitioned parallelism*. Because data can be partitioned into many subsets, this technique can increase performance. In practice, there is a combination of simultaneous and sequential SQL operations to be performed. Therefore, partitioned parallelism is typically combined with pipelined parallelism.

All such parallel processing operations can occur in either shared or shred-nothing architectures. The I/O subsystem merely feeds data from the shared disks to the appropriate threads. The algorithms for good SMP performance are, of course, different from those for good shared-nothing (MPP) performance.

It is relatively easy to do transaction and interquery parallelism because you simply assign transactions or SQL statements to processors. Intraquery parallelism is more difficult and requires a good parallel optimizer to decompose the query and find an execution algorithm to take advantage of the parallel architecture.

PARALLEL HARDWARE ARCHITECTURES

To understand what is happening in the parallel database arena, we must understand Symmetric Multiprocessing (SMP) and Massively Parallel Processing (MPP) system hardware. The goal is to provide high performance by adding processor nodes to scale performance linearly. Adding processors to improve performance is not simple. The barriers to scalability stem from three factors:

- The overhead associated with starting processes consumes greater amounts of CPU time as the number of processes increases.

- The processes can interfere with each other by contending for shared resources.

- As tasks are broken down into smaller, more granular processes, it becomes more likely that some indivisible processes will take longer to complete than others. This creates "skewness."

Shared-disk systems can scale to many CPUs, but they become more difficult to administer as the number of CPUs increases. Scalability is also limited because setting locks to manage contention for the shared data can introduce overhead. On the other hand, clusters can tolerate node failures because the remaining nodes can take over the processing.

Shared-Memory Architectures

In addition to disks, systems can also share main memory, which is typically physically centralized. In addition, each processor has local cache memory. These are referred to as *tightly coupled* or SMP because they share a single operating system instance. SMP looks like a single computer with a single operating system. A DBMS can use it with little, if any, reprogramming; however, modifications such as multithreading based on small-grained, light-weight threads can help the DBMS take better advantage of the SMP.

In a shared resource environment, each processor executes a task on the required data, which is shipped to it. Thus, shared resource is often called data shipping. The only problem with data shipping is that it limits the computer's ability for scalability. In an SMP environment, the scaling problems are caused by interprocessor communication, and the time it takes to send code and data to each processor. The number of processors that can work efficiently is limited by the number of accesses to shared memory, the rate at which the local caches are invalidated by work on other processors, and the I/O bandwidth to memory.

Given the power of CPUs today and the speed of memory and buses, the limitations of SMP are not too large in practice. There have been successful implementations of databases in excess of 100 GB on an SMP computer with as few as eight CPUs. However, the table size and types of transactions may be more limiting than the amount of data.

SMP implementations are improving, and the number of processors that can be supported effectively is growing as memory speeds increase, and cache coherency schemes become more sophisticated. Coupled with more powerful processors, SMP hardware may suit all but the largest databases.

Shared-Nothing Architectures

Shared-nothing architectures offer the most scalability. Each processor has its own memory, its own operating system, and its own DBMS instance, and each executes tasks on its private data stored on its own disks. The processors are connected, and messages or functions are passed among them. *Shipping tasks to the data, instead of data to the tasks,* reduces interprocessor communications. For example, one node can request from other nodes particular rows in a table that is partitioned across multiple disks. The other nodes send the rows back to the requester, which merges them into the answer set. Thus, programming, administration, and database design are intrinsically more difficult in this environment than in the SMP environments.

An example is the high-performance switch used in IBM's Scalable Power Parallel Systems 2 (SP2). This switch is a high-bandwidth crossbar, just like the one used in telephone switching, that can connect any node to any other node, eliminating transfers through intermediate nodes.

However, a potential problem in a shared-nothing system stems from the fact that a node failure renders data on that node inaccessible. Therefore, there is a need for replication of data across multiple nodes so that you can still access it even if one node fails, or provide alternate paths to the data in a hybrid shared-nothing architecture. In such cases, the process can "fail-over" to another node that can access the first node's data. In addition, as with shared disk, the interconnected processors can reside in different computers.

Parallel Distinction

The combinations of parallel architectures are common. For example, the nodes in IBM's SP2 can be SMP computers as well as single-CPU machines. MPP simply refers to "lots of CPUs" and not necessarily to a specific architecture. Single SMP computers can manage hundreds of gigabytes of data today. Put them in clusters and the database size can exceed a terabyte.

As data warehousing and data mining applications get more ambitious, larger databases are in the offing. Given the limitations of SMPs for handling multidimensional arrays, shared-nothing architectures (with SMP nodes) are required.

DESIGN OF PARALLEL SYSTEMS

Initially, the market definition of an MPP (Massively Parallel Processor) system centered on the notion of "massive." *MPP* designs offer the promise of unlimited configurations involving hundreds, if not thousands, of microprocessors (CPUs) which could be applied to application problems.

The reality is that while some MPP designs do support hundreds or thousands of CPUs, there are those that do not. Some entry-level "MPP" machines have as few as 8 or 16 CPUs. Indeed, there may be a trend among MPP vendors toward fewer P/Ms (Processor/Memory units, also called "nodes"). For example, IBM's SP2 only scales up to 128+ nodes while Intel®, Teradata®, and Tandem® have already shipped machines with over 200 CPUs.

During the past few years, a newer definition based on the underlying system architectures has emerged. With this new definition, SMP (Symmetric Multiprocessor) and MPP (Massively Parallel Processor) systems can be evaluated side by side. Simply put, SMP architectures are characterized as "shared everything" while MPP architectures are "shared nothing."

In an SMP system, the components—CPUs, physical memory, buses, I/O subsystem (disks and controllers), the operating system, the RDBMS, and the physical database partitions—are shared (refer to Figure 9.5). In an MPP system, none of these components are shared and there is only an interconnect to link the disparate nodes together. This bifurcation better reflects underlying SMP and MPP architectural differences rather than the terms "massive" and "non-massive." Another way of expressing the same point involves the terms "tightly coupled" and "loosely coupled."

SMP and Clustered SMP Systems

SMP systems have proven their scalability and availability in many large enterprises. When implementers consider MPP systems, it is often because they perceive MPP systems to be better able to meet the performance, growth, and capacity demands of today's data-intensive applications. No one can deny the appeal of the theoretical promise of MPP systems to incrementally deliver linear speedup and linear scaleup at low cost, but reality is less neat.

A recent and promising variation involves the notion of "clustered SMP," where multiple "tightly coupled" SMP systems are linked together to form a "loosely coupled" processing complex (Figure 9.4).

Every component of an SMP system is controlled by a single executing copy of an Operating System (OS) managing a shared global memory. Because memory in an SMP system is shared among the CPUs, SMP systems have a single address space and run a single copy of the OS and the application. All processes are fully symmetric in the sense that any process can execute on any processor at any time. As system loads and configurations change, tasks or processes are automatically distributed among the CPUs—providing a benefit known as dynamic load balancing.

An SMP system can support from 2 to 30+ CPUs, producing a near-linear increase in performance as CPUs are added. When additional processing power is needed, more CPUs can be installed in the system, and the OS automatically configures the new hardware. No changes to the OS, application, or data are necessary.

Current SMP machines can address tens of gigabytes (GB) of physical memory and many terabytes (TB) of storage—enough for most commercial OLTP and DSS applications. SMP systems are well suited for OLTP environments where large numbers of users execute a common application accessing a shared RDBMS.

Additionally, DSS systems—which also require high levels of data access and manipulation—benefit from SMP's architectural ability to provide shared memory access to common RDBMS data structures. Eventually, contention for shared-memory resources does place a limit on scaleup in shared-everything systems. However, linear speedup is not only a function of linear scaleup. Speedup is continually being boosted by the emergence of faster CPUs, faster high-capacity memory, and faster disks which, because of cost declines, can be intelligently used in array configurations optimized for performance.

As speedup and scaleup demands of data-intensive applications have outstripped a single SMP system's capabilities, a logical, evolutionary approach has been taken by SMP and RDBMS vendors. Scalable hardware and software technologies

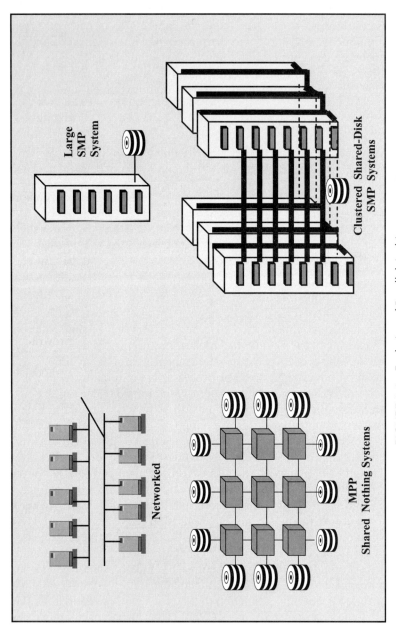

FIGURE 9.4 Evolution of Parallel Architectures.

are allowing shared-everything systems to be clustered (connected) together for greater scaleup, speedup, and availability. Such systems share disk storage, data bus, and multiple, high-bandwidth I/O channels for high throughput levels.

Most RDBMSs allow applications on clustered nodes to share a common database. In addition, modern RDBMSs contain enhancements that allow a single database activity (a query, for example) to execute on multiple CPUs in one or more cluster-connected nodes.

In a clustered SMP configuration, each SMP node has its own copy of the OS but shares the RDBMS by sharing disks. To maintain high availability, specially designed and integrated cluster software constantly monitors the health of system resources and directs system recovery actions in the event of a system fault. Peripherals such as tape drives are pooled together to provide a backup resource to individual system nodes.

A critically important operation in an SMP cluster is the coordination of shared resources. Typically this is accomplished through technology that manages a node's use of a shared resource at a single point in time. Clustering requires shared resource coordination via a lock manager to preserve data integrity across the RDBMS instances, disks, and tape drives. Sequent's Symmetry 5000 SE100 cluster, which supports more than 100 processors, is an example of a clustered system providing this capability.

With clustering, scaleup is a matter of adding more processors, disks, memory, I/O bandwidth, or another node. While clustering SMP systems requires a looser coupling among the nodes, there is no need to replace hardware or rewrite applications.

Clustered SMP systems are more complex than traditional SMP systems but leverage many of their benefits, including an easier programming model, higher availability, automatic fail-over of hardware, system management tools, dynamic on-line backup, dynamic batch load balancing, and so on. A natural benefit of clustered SMP is much greater availability than MPP systems and even more availability than SMP.

Symmetric versus Other MP Designs

SMP designs are not the only solution for designing systems supporting multiple processors. Early multiprocessing systems were designed around an asymmetric paradigm. In an Asymmetric Multiprocessor (AMP) design, one master processor is designated to handle all operating system tasks. The rest of the processors only handle user processes. They are referred to as the slave processors. This design had several disadvantages:

- Adding extra processors actually increases the work requirement for the master processor.
- The master processor becomes the bottleneck.

Fully asymmetric designs represent past technology trends. Most AMP designs are being replaced by fully symmetric systems running operating systems that are capable of supporting SMP paradigms (Windows NT™, SCO UNIX, Solaris, etc.).

The most limiting design feature of SMP systems is memory bus bandwidth. As more and faster processors are added to an SMP design, they spend more time contending with each other for access to main memory. Since all the processors share a common path to memory, there are only a few things that can be done to overcome these problems:

- Make the memory bus wider
- Run the memory bus at higher clock speeds
- Make secondary caches larger

SMP designers are adopting all of these approaches to produce more powerful systems, but the expense of the system increases greatly. The long-term solution is MPP systems where all the processors have a dedicated path to memory, so that contention is eliminated. MPP technology is both exotic and expensive and will remain so for some time.

MPP—Shared-Nothing Systems

Just as AMP designs represent old technology, future technology in this field is represented by massively parallel (MPP) architectures. MPP, or shared-nothing, systems are composed of many loosely coupled Processor/Memory modules (P/M units or nodes) connected to one another by a high-speed communications mechanism optimized for fast message passing. Each node of a shared-nothing system is composed of its own P/M unit, which includes a CPU, associated memory to run programs, disks, one copy of the OS, and one copy of the RDBMS. Independent instances of system and application programs use the common high-speed interconnect to pass messages between cooperating nodes. Application connectivity in MPP systems is provided through message passing (as opposed to shared memory and pointers in SMP systems).

Shared-nothing machines inherently include several barriers that hinder linear speedup and scaleup, including high levels of P/M-to-P/M message passing, specialized data layout, complex custom parallel programming requirements, and unwieldy systems management.

Since each P/M must communicate with others to perform parallel work, parallel operation is inefficient. Generally, the more nodes in an MPP system, the more messages passed between nodes. Increased message passing increases the time it takes for a process to access data (known as latency). Higher latencies mean a slower system.

To reduce latency, MPP vendors have concentrated on *interconnect technologies* and have designed newer MPP architectures that reduce the message passing burden. An example includes IBM's SP2, which uses crossbar switch technology to reduce the number of connections (or hops) between nodes.

As the number of nodes in a shared-nothing machine scale up into the hundreds and perhaps thousands, availability is substantially degraded. Having many more components in an MPP system presents that many more opportunities for failure.

SMP versus Cluster versus MPP

DBMSs have been optimized on SMP platforms by increasing the number of database operations that can be performed in parallel and by handling the management of processors more efficiently, through dynamic job allocation.

The studies described in previous sections lead us to few conclusions. The categorization of SMP, cluster SMP, and MPP are often a little blurry. With enhancements to these technologies, the distinctions are getting even more blurred. But they do refer to architectural design choices regarding how multiple processors will be incorporated into a single computer.

In a typical SMP architecture, the machine has up to a few dozen processors, and each processor shares all hardware resources, including memory, disks, and the system bus. Because each processor can see all of the available memory, communications between processors is straightforward. In other words, one processor can easily view the results generated by another processor simply by looking at the appropriate memory location.

Clusters usually refer to hardware architectures in which a few SMP machines are linked together by an interconnect. This allows a data warehousing application to harness the collective processing power of multiple SMP machines or nodes, rather than being limited to the processing power of a single SMP machine. In a cluster, each node has its own private memory. This makes communication between nodes a little more complex. Instead of looking at another node's primary memory, nodes communicate by explicitly sending messages and data across the interconnect.

MPP machines are, theoretically, similar to clusters in that they support multiple nodes that each have their own private memory and that communicate via passing messages over an interconnect. MPPs usually have uniprocessor nodes rather than SMP nodes. The major advantage of an MPP over SMP cluster is that the interconnects are much more sophisticated. The bandwidth of the interconnect is often designed to increase as more nodes are added and more advanced connection schemes are used. MPP platforms can handle hundreds of nodes, while it can be a challenge to coordinate that many nodes using the message passing communication mechanism.

After a careful study, we can reach the conclusion that no single architecture is universally better than all of the others. But we did discover that SMP is easier to manage and MPP is more scalable. The type of architecture better suited for your data warehouse depends on the size and complexity of your applications.

In general, SMP systems seem to be better suited for either mission-critical or OLTP applications, where the application growth rate is slow and steady and the amount of raw data is relatively smaller in the range of 10 to 100 GB.

On the other hand, MPP systems are best suited for either complex analytical or very large *decision-support* applications, such as data warehousing, where the growth rate of data is unpredictable and the amount of raw data exceeds 200 GB.

EVALUATING SYMMETRIC MULTIPROCESSOR DESIGNS

Many new server and workstation platforms are based on Symmetric Multi-processors (SMPs). This section attempts to describe a symmetric multiprocessor and why it is important. This section will cover

- Multiprocessor architectures
- SMP systems and high availability
- Symmetric multiprocessor applications

Multiprocessor Architectures

Both single and multiprocessor machines share some basic architectural features. Before looking at SMP architectures in more detail, it is useful to examine the basic components of a conventional computer design.

In a single processor system, the CPU is connected to memory via a secondary cache (sometimes referred to as Level 2 cache) and interfaces to peripherals via an I/O bus. In a symmetric multiprocessor design (Figure 9.5), this architecture is expanded to support multiple processors. The main differences are

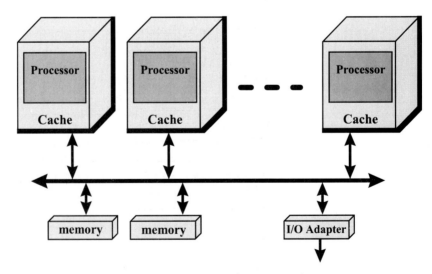

FIGURE 9.5 SMP Architecture Today.

- **High-Speed Memory Bus:** Since several processors need to get access to main memory, a dedicated, high-throughput memory bus is required. Design of the memory bus is critical in producing an efficient SMP architecture.

- **Separate Secondary Cache:** Each processor has its own cache. The provision of separate caches for each processor requires complex logic in the cache controller to make sure that a processor never works on data that has been updated in another processor's cache. As a general rule, the larger the secondary cache, the better an SMP will scale as extra processors are added.

- **I/O to Memory Bus Bridge:** The I/O bus now interfaces with the memory bus rather than directly to a CPU.

In practice, the symmetry of a system is governed by two things:

- **The Hardware Design:** Some companies actually design hardware specifically for the asymmetric architecture. A good example of this is NetFrame, which designs hardware to run Novell NetWare very efficiently while supporting large numbers of users.

- **Operating System:** Some SMP operating systems are really a hybrid of symmetric and asymmetric designs. An example of this approach is how SCO UNIX handles non-SMP-designed device drivers, referred to as non-threaded drivers. Though SCO UNIX MPX is a symmetric operating system, some device drivers have not been written to take advantage of the SMP architecture. A SCO UNIX device driver written for a single processor makes assumptions about the sanctity of kernel data.

  In an SMP environment, these assumptions are no longer true. To overcome this problem, a non-threaded driver is assigned to the first processor. Effectively, this processor becomes a master processor in an asymmetric paradigm. This flexible design allows the third-party market to continue to deliver existing solutions, yet provide time to redesign and develop threaded drivers. In most cases, endusers still see substantial performance benefits in using these non-threaded solutions in an SMP architecture.

SMP Systems and High Availability

Many SMP systems have one or more of the following features to improve the reliability of the system:

ECC Memory: The more memory that is resident in a system, the more likely a parity error will occur (memory failure). ECC memory allows the system to correct for such errors without failing.

RAID Disk Arrays: Disk failure is eliminated by using fault-tolerant RAID subsystems such as RAID 1 or RAID 5. RAID technology also provides superior I/O performance.

Hot Plugable Disk Drives: This feature, used in conjunction with RAID technology, allows a faulty disk drive to be replaced while the server continues to operate. No loss of data occurs, and other than a temporary reduction in I/O performance, this failure is transparent to the users.

Dual Power Supplies: Even if a system is connected to an Uninterruptable Power Supply (UPS), if an internal power supply fails, the system will halt. Load-sharing, dual power supplies eliminate this potential point of failure.

Auto Configuration on Boot: Symmetric multiprocessor servers are generally not fully fault-tolerant. A highly available system will crash, reboot, and, during reboot, the failed processor is removed automatically from the configuration. This allows the system to continue to work with reduced performance until maintenance can be scheduled.

True fault tolerance is the exclusive and expensive domain of vendors such as Tandem. The distinction between fault tolerant and high availability systems is how they react to critical failures such as a processor. A fault-tolerant system can survive any failure without the system being brought down.

Symmetric Multiprocessor Applications

Applications specifically designed for SMP systems can be threaded. A database engine is a good example of an application that can be threaded. Typically, a process like a database engine consists of several logical components, such as,

*   I/O engine
*   Query engine
*   User interface

Since these components or threads can run asynchronously, the database engine can be designed with each thread operating independently, only synchronizing when necessary. Once an application is "threaded," the operating system can schedule the threads simultaneously on different processors.

In the past, fully threaded applications were rare since there was no standard way to provide these features. Any vendor which needed to thread an application had to do a separate port of the application to each SMP architecture. Windows NT gives application developers the chance to thread an application and target it at any system which runs NT. The potentially large usage for NT systems makes the work of threading applications much more attractive.

SMP systems are particularly suited to supporting multiple clients in a client/server architecture. A good example of this is the database server role. Compared to a uniprocessor, SMP systems provide benefits in database performance and availability:

Multiple CPUs

Existing database engines are single threaded. Even a single-threaded engine gains on an SMP system. The performance increase is the result of operating system tasks, such as networking and I/O, being distributed on multiple processors allowing the database to run with few interruptions. In the mid 90s, database vendors introduced multithreaded database engines for Intel SMPs. The threaded versions of some of the major databases are

- ORACLE 7 +
- Sybase System 10 +
- Informix 6 +
- INGRESS 6

High Availability

Hot swappable disk drives and RAID make SMP systems ideal for mission-critical database-related applications. Users have reliable access to the database and protection from disk failure.

Multiple Network Interfaces

A carefully designed network with multiple physical LAN segments offers more network bandwidth. The key to using this bandwidth is a server with multiple network interfaces. Most SMP servers support multiple network interfaces.

The features which make SMP systems ideal as database engines are also important to other server roles such as

- Central file server
- Application server
- Communications gateway

In the graphics world, many applications can be modified to take advantage of multiple processors. Often graphics operations are naturally threadable. Examples include hidden line removal, ray tracing, and screen refresh. Since each thread can be assigned to a different processor, the user will see benefits in overall performance as well as response time.

As SMP becomes mainstream technology, more and more applications will be modified to take full advantage of it. Users will find that applications on workstations and servers will perform more efficiently on multiprocessor hardware.

SELECTING A DBMS

Developers and architects should consider the following step-by-step procedures when selecting a DBMS. First, understand the requirements, including the business problem being solved. List the features that are important and rank them by priority. Consider the applications they will run that connect into the database(s), and what type of middleware layer is in use. Using this information, select operating systems and hardware platforms that best meet these requirements.

There is no foolproof way to select the right DBMS for a data warehouse project. You must consider the power of the platform that hosts the DBMS software, SQL standards, features such as stored procedures and triggers, and database administration and monitoring tools. Let us examine some of the features and functions of DBMSs, as well as the criteria for selecting a DBMS.

Relational and Multidimensional Databases

Although there are many database models being used, relational DBMSs still rule the world of data warehouses. The success of the relational database arises largely from the relational model's simplicity and its ability to successfully map to most problem domains. The use of two-dimensional tables linked by common fields is easier to understand and work with than the traditional network, or hierarchical database systems.

However, the Object Oriented (OO) and multidimensional DBMSs are catching up quickly in some niche application areas. These types of databases work well for systems that store complex data structures or are built for On-Line Analytical Processing (OLAP). Object-Oriented Database Management Systems (OODBMSs) can store data as persistent objects. OO databases are a good fit for tools that use the OO development model in its pure form, and they are also better homes for complex data structures that include the storage of repository information and binary information. *Multidimensional DBMSs* provide a more natural way for endusers to search through data using *data mining tools*.

Relational DBMSs are usually the best fit for client/server systems and expose the data warehouse databases to the least amount of risk. For instance, most popular data warehouse development tools communicate with most relational DBMSs using native database middleware or through ODBC.

Platforms and Processors

In many respects, the platform on which the DBMS runs determines the overall performance of the database server. DBMSs also depend on the operating system's ability to provide disk, caching, and network services efficiently. Therefore, selecting the right platform for your DBMS is as important as selecting the DBMS itself.

Although exceptions exist, x86-, RISC-, and SPARC-based servers dominate the market, with many flavors of UNIX and Windows NT providing host operating system services in both uni- and multiprocessing versions. UNIX is able to provide true preemptive multitasking and multithreading to its native applications, including the DBMS; however, *clustered NT* implementations are becoming more popular.

To exploit the best features of UNIX, DBMS vendors such as Oracle, Informix, and Sybase have mastered UNIX's ability to support numerous simultaneous client connections as stand-alone processes or threads (lightweight processes). They also capitalized on UNIX's excellent I/O performance, memory management, and task management capabilities. All of this comes at the cost of having to manage the complexities of the UNIX operating system.

Although UNIX is still a favored host operating system for DBMSs, Windows NT is rapidly gaining popularity. Windows NT also provides all of the features of UNIX, but it wraps them in a user-friendly, easily manageable package.

SQL Standards

It's important to understand the ANSI/ISO standards before you select a DBMS. Currently there are three SQL standards with which you should concern yourself: SQL-89, SQL-92, and SQL3. SQL-89 is the oldest and most useless of all ANSI SQL standards.

SQL-92 compliance is desirable because it adds many features to your DBMS. SQL3 adds even more features, such as Object SQL capabilities that include encapsulation, methods, user-defined data types, and inheritance.

Working around the OS

Performance is everything in the DBMS arena. To maintain and improve performance, DBMSs bypass the operating system to access system resources directly. For example, most DBMSs (including Informix, Sybase, and Oracle) can bypass an operating system's native file system and go directly to a physical disk partition called a raw disk partition. This way, the DBMS server does not have to absorb the overhead required to go through operating system calls to access the disk. The result is faster disk I/O performance and a faster DBMS.

Parallel Query Processing

The battle cry of scalable DBMSs is parallel processing, or the allocation of the operating system's processing load across several processors. Most hardware and server operating system platforms (including the x86, RISC, and CICS) support multiprocessing. However, they do so in many different ways.

DBMS servers approach multiprocessing by either letting the operating system allocate the database query processing across available processors (*shared memory*), or allowing the DBMS server to allocate the query processing (*shared nothing*). If you select the latter, you must invest in a special version of a DBMS built specifically for parallel query processing.

These servers break up a database query into smaller subqueries that execute concurrently on different processors. A query manager receives the request and allocates its processing among available database engines. Usually, there is one database engine per processor, and it is functionally equivalent to an independent DBMS server. After the query processing is complete, the query manager reassembles the answer sets into a single set that is returned to the client.

Allocating query processing like this was expensive and experimental just a few years ago. Today there are several DBMSs that provide such features, such as, Oracle's Parallel Query Option, Sybase's Sybase MPP, and Informix's Dynamic

Server. Parallel DBMS servers work best in database warehousing systems or other applications in which database *response time* is critical.

Managing Scalability

The ability of a DBMS server to scale is directly related to how well the DBMS can handle client connections. A DBMS server that requires a high memory and processor capacity for each connection can only handle as many users as there are resources available. Sooner or later you hit a wall, and the operating system breaks (usually by running out of physical memory and crashing). DBMS servers handle client connections in three basic ways: processes per client, threading, and/or a combination of approaches.

- The *process-per-client* approach gives each client connection its own process. Connections that operate in their own process address space are protected from other ill-behaved processes. Multiprocessing operating systems make it easy to allocate the connection processes to one or more processors to spread the load. However, it eats up resources, because each client requires a heavyweight process. The DBMSs that use this approach include DB2®, Oracle, and Informix.
- The *threading* approach runs all user connections and the database server in the same address space as threads. Threads are lightweight processes that run faster and require fewer resources than true processes, because there is less context switching. It provides its own internal scheduler, with no dependence on the operating system's process-protection mechanisms and is also more portable from platform to platform, because there are usually few dependencies on native operating system services. Unfortunately, a single ill-behaved process or thread can crash the DBMS. A single thread can saturate a processor and make the other threads wait in line. DBMSs that use this approach include Sybase System 11® and Microsoft SQL Server®.
- Some DBMSs use a *combination of the features of threading and process per client* to create a DBMS server architecture that provides the best of all worlds. Oracle, for instance, uses a multithreaded network listener that makes the initial connections by assigning the client to a component called a dispatcher. The dispatcher in turn places messages from the client on an internal queue. A shared server process takes the message off the queue, executes the request inside the database server engine, and returns the response back to the client again using the internal queue. An advantage to this architecture is that it can maintain a protected processing environment without having to dedicate a process for each user connection. There are, however, some latency issues with the use of the queue.

Security

A DBMS needs to provide security to the database, table, column, and sometimes the row level to assure that only authorized users can view or update data. Although most DBMSs come with basic database and table-level security, they aren't hack-proof by default. There are, however, secure versions of DBMSs that make the DBMS comply with government security standards such as C2 and B1. This means that they will keep a close watch on user activity, age passwords, detect intruders, and perform other "database police" services.

Administration

Database administration tools include any software that can back up and restore a database and perform user administration, security administration, and performance monitoring and tuning.

The database administration tools allow you to watch all aspects of the DBMS, including cache, disk, processor utilization, and so on.

Database Vendors

Several major vendors dominate the parallel database processing scene: Informix Software's Informix On-Line Dynamic Server, Sybase Inc.'s Sybase SQL Server, Computer Associates Inc.'s CA-OpenIngres, IBM's DB/2 family, Oracle's Oracle Server, Microsoft's SQL Server, and Borland's Interbase. Each of these DBMSs can support various platforms, including many UNIX flavors running on x86, RISC, and CICS processors, as well as Windows NT in both single- and multiprocessing incarnations.

IMPLEMENTATIONS IN A PARALLEL ENVIRONMENT

Warehouse Dynamics: Implementations

The parallel versions of products are still pretty new, but they are all starting to show product maturity in terms of the feature set and scalability. Oracle has good scalability on SMP platforms and is improving on MPP. Informix is strong in SMP. *DB2 Parallel Edition* gets a lot of efficiency from parallel joins and optimization, has good scalability, and works well against database partitions.

Although parallel DBMSs can be used for OLTP applications, *decision support* is the area receiving the most attention. DBMS vendors have targeted different segments of the parallel and multiprocessing market, some developing with SMP platforms in mind, others focusing on the MPP segment.

Multiprocessing systems may employ one of the three architectures: *shared memory*, *shared disk* and *shared nothing*. In shared-memory systems, all processors have access to shared memory. SMP platforms are shared-memory systems. Shared-disk systems have their own private memory but must be able to access all data on disks. This architecture is used in system clusters. In shared-nothing systems, each processor has its own memory and its own access to disks. MPP platforms are shared-nothing systems.

Each platform approach has its limitations. Shared-memory systems tend to get bottlenecked around interprocess communications; as a result, their scalability is limited. Shared-disk systems also hit a scalability barrier because of lock contention.

Shared-nothing systems are difficult to administer because each processor has its own disk, as well as its own memory. These systems require very good systems management tools, but they can linearly scale up to hundreds of processors.

The Oracle Parallel Database Solutions

Oracle has implemented a *loosely coupled* database architecture, in addition to SMP, to maximize performance and scalability for centralized applications.

Within the *loosely coupled* architecture framework, Oracle supports two configurations: clustered and massively parallel. Both configurations consist of multiple processors with access to a *shared set of disks*, connected by high-speed communication paths and managed by a Distributed Lock Manager (DLM) that provides data locking services to shared resources across the cluster. The primary difference between the two configurations is scalability at the top end.

The performance needs of most applications today can be supported by clustered configurations of well-established system architectures. Hardware clustered configurations currently supported by Oracle include Digital VAXclusters, IBM HA/6000, NCR 3600, Pyramid MIServer, and Sequent ptx/CLUSTERS.

For applications requiring even more performance and scalability, Oracle supports massively parallel systems. Massively parallel computers contain dozens or even hundreds of processors that operate in parallel, which together can exceed the upper bound of processors, memory nodes, and interconnects that loosely coupled clusters can support.

Oracle offers two parallel products: the Parallel Server and the Parallel Query Option (PQO). The Parallel Server provides access and increased availability to a shared database via multiple Oracle instances. This could be a clustered environment, such as a variety of UNIX clusters or a shared-disk multiprocessor computer such as an nCube. However, it does not parallelize database operations such as SELECT or LOAD. It is primarily aimed at transaction scaleup.

The Oracle Parallel Server

The heart of Oracle clustered and massively parallel database implementations is the Oracle Parallel Server with a dedicated database server that provides database management services to client systems such as personal computers. Both Oracle clustered and massively parallel platform database configurations are based on the Oracle Parallel Server.

The Oracle Parallel Server provides users with access to a single database located on a pool of shared disks on multiple server systems. All users on all clients in the cluster can run transactions concurrently against this database. Remote clients of a distributed database are also accessible through Oracle's distributed database capabilities.

The Oracle Parallel Server offers high throughput capacity, ease of operation, and no potential for transaction loss or other data inconsistencies. All systems in a parallel server environment can be fully utilized for both query and update access at any time.

The marriage between hardware and software (architectures) is very important. *Oracle Parallel Server* is based on a *shared-disk architecture*. For example, when we run it on the SP2 hardware platform, which is shared nothing, we have to build a software lock manager across that architecture. It would be hard to get the same performance or scalability if we didn't do that locking.

Buffered Cache Support

Implementing efficient cache management in a parallel database is both important and complex because it ensures data consistency, and complex because of functionality and performance factors.

The Oracle Parallel Server uses a separate shared buffer cache on each system, because each system has independent memory. Parallel cache management ensures data consistency and integrity by tracking the current location of data blocks as they move in and out of the various systems associated with the database.

Multiple parallel cache managers track a discrete portion of the data blocks in the database. When a system needs a data block that is not already in its local cache, it contacts the appropriate parallel cache management process to determine whether the block is in the cache of another system and to coordinate the transfer of the data block from that node.

The shared-storage architecture of the Oracle Parallel Server provides multiple paths to each disk. Even if one system fails, all the data in the database remains available so processing can continue even through a single node failure. Oracle Parallel Server automatically recovers failed nodes without database administrator intervention.

Parallel Query Option

Parallel Query is comprised of parallel scan, parallel join, and parallel sort technologies that allow multiple processor nodes to automatically share the workload of processing a single query, dramatically improving performance. Parallel Query is compatible with SMP systems, clustered systems, and MPP systems. The Parallel Query Option improves the performance of complex query execution.

The Sybase Enterprise Solutions

Sybase MPP is a parallel relational database that is designed to deliver high performance and scalability. It employs multiple SQL Servers in a *shared-nothing architecture*, in which each SQL Server stores and processes a different portion of the data. No two SQL Servers store the same data or access one another's data; thus they "share" nothing.

Sybase MPP is designed to take advantage of parallelism during every step of database operation processing. All types of requests are performed in parallel, including queries, data manipulation operations (INSERT, UPDATE, DELETE), and utility operations (LOAD, BACKUP, RESTORE). This is achieved by partitioning data among the many SQL Servers that are part of the MPP system and processing the requests concurrently.

Sybase System 11

Sybase System 11 consists of four main database engines: Sybase SQL Server, Sybase IQ, Sybase MPP, and Sybase SQL Anywhere.

SQL Server 11 provides *dynamic load balancing* via a symmetric networking and parallel lock manager, as well as accelerated data access via data partitions and in-place updates. Efficient logging is provided via multiple log caches and expanded group commits.

For the centralized data store approach, which implies preplanned queries and detail reports against very large databases, Sybase provides SQL Server 11 with the Sybase MPP option. Sybase MPP is a subset of SQL Server optimized for MPP environments that utilize a shared-nothing architecture. Sybase MPP provides linear scalability to 128+ processors. It is available on most of the major platforms.

Sybase MPP

Sybase MPP is expressly suited for high-end MPP platforms. In addition to parallel query and load, the Sybase MPP performs parallel inserts, updates, and deletes. Even though much of the data in data warehouses is static in nature, such parallel features are important. People forget that you need to incrementally add and update warehouse data. It's important to add parallelism to these functions, too.

Informix

Informix has implemented the DBMS to support loosely coupled, shared-nothing platforms. This version uses a high-speed interconnect rather than shared-memory messaging. It will also add parallel update, insert, and delete to its existing parallel query and load capabilities. Most of the work is in the management of the database.

The core of the Informix-On-line system is its support of a multithreaded system with small-grained, lightweight threads called virtual processors. These virtual processors are in a pool and the DBMS allocates them dynamically to CPUs, based on requirements such as processing a data partition or pipelined instruction. The number of CPUs can be less than the full complement available to control how much of the machine is dedicated to parallel queries. This is particularly useful in preventing a parallel query in tying up all the processors.

Running on uniprocessor and Symmetric Multiprocessor (SMP) platforms, the server parallelizes all major database activities, including load/unload, index builds, sorts, scans, joins, backups/restores, and aggregation. It also supports loosely coupled parallel environments including clusters and shared-nothing computers. It also supports partitioning of data using hash keys, ranges of values, round-robin assignment, or a formula based on a key value. The WHERE clause in UPDATE, DELETE, and INSERT is also parallelized.

On-Line Dynamic Server

The On-line Dynamic Server is designed for high-volume OLTP environments that require replication, mainframe-level database administration tools. Although this server supports SMP, it does not support MPP, which is the essential differentiating feature between the On-Line Dynamic Server and the On-Line Extended Parallel Server.

The On-Line Workgroup Server is designed for smaller numbers of user connections (up to 32 concurrent) and lower transaction volumes. It is also easier to administer because it offers less complex functionality compared to the higher-end servers.

On the other hand, the On-Line Extended Parallel Server is designed for very high-volume OLTP environments that need to utilize loosely coupled or shared-nothing computing architectures composed of clusters of SMP or MPP systems.

Informix On-Line Dynamic Server is a UNIX-based RDBMS, built on Informix's multithreaded, parallel database server architecture. The On-Line Dynamic Server is designed for high-volume OLTP environments that require replication, mainframe-level database administration tools. It supports SMP with the Informix Parallel Data Query (PDQ) as part of its Dynamic Scalable Architecture (DSA).

PDQ

PDQ enables parallel table scans, sorts, joins, index builds, backups and restores, parallel query aggregation for *decision support*, and parallel data loads.

To make their products parallel, *Informix* reimplemented its database engine for multiprocessing platforms. Informix On-Line Dynamic Server employs shared memory and shared disk and features database partitioning and parallel query capability.

IBM Database Solutions

The DB2 family of relational database products run on a variety of IBM and non-IBM operating system platforms. These include MVS, VM, VSE, OS/400, OS/2, Hewlett Packard's HP-UX, and Sun's Solaris. The DB2 products make use of parallel techniques specific to the platforms they run on where specialized parallel implementations are available.

IBM DB2 AIX/6000 Parallel Edition technology provides multinode parallelism on LAN-connected RISC System/6000, POWER-parallel SP2, and HACMP/6000 complexes.

IBM System/390 Parallel Query Server provides optimized support for the back-end processing of large-scale *decision-support* (DSS) applications. Multiple processors run software based on MVS and DB2.

IBM System/390 Parallel Transaction Server provides a continuously available environment for transaction processing. It is an MVS-based offering, using scalable parallel microprocessors.

In addition to supporting SMP, the DB2 Parallel Edition supports the IBM/SP2 shared-nothing multiprocessor. Data is partitioned across disks via hashing and may be confined to a subset of the available processors as identified in a node group. Parallel query execution is determined by a parallel optimizer. An application connects to a node where a SQL statement is optimized. Then a coordinator process (like Oracle's PQO) acts as an interface between the application and the database. The functions supported include parallel table and index scans, joins, aggregation, and parallel UPDATE, DELETE, and INSERT. Utilities are also parallelized, including LOAD, index, backup, restore, and recovery.

The *Power Parallel SP2* supports up to 64 processing nodes. DB2 Parallel Edition features a modified optimizer that generates a parallel access plan, rather than a serial plan, that is executed in parallel; intraquery parallelism, where a single complex query is split up and executed in parallel; and parallel utilities, including load, index creation, and backup and restore.

AT&T Implementations

Like IBM, AT&T GIS offers both parallel hardware and database software to run on it. AT&T GIS offers the 3500 SMP and the 3600 MPP hardware platforms. The 3600 is designed for *decision-support* applications involving very large databases and complex queries. Its four to eight nodes are all managed from a single point. Up to eight 3500s can be clustered, with each machine separately managed.

In addition to AT&T's own Teradata database and Sybase's MPP Server, the 3600 runs Oracle, and, on a single node, Informix. Oracle also runs in a shared-disk architecture. It requires all units of parallelism to have access to all of the database. This limits the number of nodes you can connect, because every node has to connect to every disk the database resides on. It's a better optimized engine for very simple queries or OLTP.

Recognizing that DBMS technologies are at different stages with different performance characteristics, AT&T also supports a combination approach it calls "cooperative databases" on the 3600. For example, Oracle is good for simple transactions, whereas Teradata excels at large queries. You can configure the 3600 to run both, with one set of nodes running Oracle and another set running Teradata.

Ingress Statistical Query

Computer Associates has implemented *Ingress Statistical Query* Optimizer to handle parallel queries. CA is also adding logical table partitioning, parallel joins, sorts, load, backup, and recovery. CA is targeting low-end hardware platforms for its parallel offerings, especially Windows NT systems.

Tandem Database Solutions

Tandem was one of the first vendors of shared-nothing parallel databases with NonStop SQL, which supports parallel queries and transactions across partitioned data. NonStop parallelizes all SQL, including table scans, joins, aggregation, and database changes. It will partition both indexes and data, with options for hash, round-robin, and range partitioning. Data load, index build, and backup are all parallel operations.

Tandem offers both SMP and MPP hardware platforms. The Integrity line runs Oracle, Sybase, Informix, and Tandem's own NonStop SQL. The Himalaya NonStop line is a massively parallel, shared-nothing architecture that runs Tandem's NonStop SQL/MP.

NonStop SQL/MP support includes database partitioning, parallel data scans, and use of a hashing algorithm that saves time in performing complex joins and compiling aggregates by avoiding lengthy sorts. Four Tandem nodes with 45 CPUs work together as one logical system, and the database is seen as one logical database.

CONCLUSION

Parallel computing machines, as part of an integrated data warehousing strategy, play an important role. Without these beasts of computing power, many of the advantages that companies are looking for could not be realized, at least within reasonable time frames. Through the correct use of massively parallel processing computers in a data warehouse, real, tangible benefits can be realized by responding to market forces on a much shorter time frame than was previously possible.

The technologies provide a cost-effective method of expanding the computing power of the organization in small incremental steps and is available seven days a week, 24 hours a day. Parallel processing machines are not a replacement for a large OLTP-based engine but should be considered as an adjunct to the computing power of the data warehouse, where the analysis of the data moved to the MPP can provide real tangible returns.

It is becoming quite clear that no single database architecture is best for every application. However, a trend is emerging that combines the best of all the architectures into a single machine. One of these is a massively parallel machine that uses small SMP machines as its individual processing nodes.

When these new hybrids reach the market, the notion that SMP, clustered SMP/MPP, and MPP architectures are distinct may disappear entirely. Once these distinct classifications are no longer useful, we will be left referring to all of these architectures by the umbrella terms of parallel architectures or platforms.

Parallel database technology is going in a direction that the gain in capability seems limitless. Tremendous opportunities are buried in the databases of businesses, waiting to be discovered and leveraged. The world is going to change and the database technology is going to be the vehicle to manage this change.

RECOMMENDATIONS

The systems are getting too complex and too dependent on workload variations to rely on simple benchmarks as accurate sources of information. The techniques for data retrieval are wide ranging but increasingly seem to be converging on the Internet and corporate intranets. But there are other technologies that are helping users get the data out. They are the technologies that will drive a sea of change in a way databases are used and maintained. Some of these technologies are

- Extraction and dissection tools, such as data mining, OLAP, and other front-end analysis offerings.
- Next-generation database development, such as multidimensional RDBMSs.
- Increased scalability and robustness, along with other enhancements for data warehouses, data marts, data webs, transaction processing, and other mission-critical applications.
- The development of object-relational database technologies that add more muscle for supporting multimedia data types.
- Web connectivity for electronic commerce based on company databases.
- Universal servers that provide support for multiple data types so databases can be used to manage unwieldy information.
- Better database management tools that enable IS managers to better control databases that will become increasingly multifaceted as user needs change and the demand for data extraction accelerates.

In combination, the use of parallel relational databases and parallel hardware can lead to a system which can possess incredible scalability and power. This allows a small pilot scheme to be scaled with a good degree of confidence in the scalability of both hardware and database. However one word of caution: Do not under any circumstances forget that one of the main points of failure for many data warehousing and client/server environments has historically been attributed to a lack of bandwidth on the network. Future generations of data warehouses will depend more on parallel systems and database architectures to achieve higher performance levels.

Object-oriented data warehouses that support non-traditional data types (audio, video, image, graphics, text) in the same way as traditional data types are getting popular. The object-oriented technology is addressing some of the above mentioned concerns.

Data warehousing has spawned new query optimization, indexing, partitioning, and data compression techniques. This should result in more sophisticated query techniques (dynamic query optimization) to avoid "runaway query" problems. This may give birth to more sophistication and third-generation data warehouses.

SUMMARY

Parallel database technology is still relatively new. It is the basis for the performance growth necessary to deal with emerging classes of applications, such as data warehousing, that require processing enormous amounts of data. It has raised more questions than answers. How well will parallel technology perform and scale for a particular application profile? How hard will it be to use, in terms of writing applications, and designing and managing databases? How will it deal with subsystem failures, including node, disk, processor, and interconnect failures?

The most widely used architecture is the shared memory or Symmetrical Multiprocessor architecture. In this architecture, you have multiple processors with one logical (shared) main memory, one bus, with multiple processors operating at once. The typical SMP architecture is all centered around a shared bus— all processors use the same bus to share the memory and the database I/O. In SMP architecture, you can break a database query into pieces and have more than one piece done on a number of processors operating at the same time, thus saving time.

In an SMP cluster, multiple systems can share peripherals, usually disk. For example, one copy of a database on a shared disk can be operated on by multiple SMP processors. This arrangement provides for increased processing power, increased memory, and increased I/O bandwidth through the multiple nodes. The simple clusters are "shared disk" and all the coordination is achieved through some set of shared records on disk. n-way clusters are in common use today.

The SMP architectures bring high efficiency, some scalability, and some capability for parallel execution. But these are all tightly coupled which creates physical limits.

The shared-nothing systems or the Massively Parallel Processors have dedicated memory and peripherals. Each processor has its own memory and disk and you can combine together as many of these as you want. These processors are combined together via an "interconnect." MPPs are the ultimate in the evolution of parallel systems and scaling is unlimited.

Early versions of the data warehouses are interwoven with operational systems to improve the performance of the enterprise. The next-generation data warehouses will be more elaborate and complex. This will transform data warehouses from useful to critical status. Reliability, security, distribution, scalability, accuracy, and manageability are some of the concerns which the database architecture must continue to address. These concerns get magnified if the implementations involve the Internet or Intranet.

Companies attempting to process high volumes of collected data are building large *decision-support* databases and adopting parallel technology to increase operability and scalability. Parallel technologies such as complex query decomposition, the ability to run components separately and still reintegrate and parallel load, table scan, backup and restore are highly desirable features in DBMSs.

Database partitioning across processor nodes and optimizers is central to the effective application of parallel technology and provides the linear scalability necessary to add processors without performance degradation. Within the parallel and multiprocessing market, vendors are developing SMP and MPP platforms with an emphasis on *decision support*. *Shared memory*, *shared disk*, and *shared nothing* are the architectures possible in multiprocessing systems, each with its limitations.

Parallel relational databases are the future of database management, providing users with a cost-effective means of handling growing databases and changing applications in a high-performance, manageable environment. All vendors discussed deliver a parallel relational database solution that is scalable, providing parallelization and optimization for SMP, MPP, and/or cluster environments.

10

DATA WAREHOUSE TOOLS AND PRODUCTS

INTRODUCTION

You can use a data warehousing system to support a large variety of different business tasks for tactical and strategic decision making. Each of these tasks requires different tools and data. While many current data warehouse schemas are useful for categorizing business-intelligence tools and various types of data warehouses, no universal agreement exists on many of these.

Most enterprises store large amounts of data but make very little use of it when it comes to making strategic decisions. However, there have been significant recent advances in software tools for corporate data analysis. This chapter discusses topics and products that should be of interest to most business planners.

CORPORATE DATA ANALYSIS

There are a wide variety of tools available for analyzing corporate data. These tools are sometimes referred to as *Decision-Support* Systems (DSSs) or Executive Information Systems (EISs). The tools are broken down into a number of different categories, each aimed at a different set of problems.

Process Analysis

Process analysis tools assist in identifying problems with processes such as manufacturing, shipping, or order fulfillment. Process analysis tools highlight areas of poor performance and assist in identifying the causes of problems.

Aggregation Analysis

Aggregation analysis tools examine hierarchical or multidimensional aggregations of data. Such analysis is useful for summarizing information at different levels of detail for reporting budget, sales, or inventory data. Items of interest can usually be broken down into more detail. These tools are generally not suitable for process analysis. Some of the tools that enhance aggregation analysis are

- Acumate ES by Kenan Systems Corp.
- Advance from Lighten, Inc.
- Commander by Comshare.
- Dimension Control by Dimension Data Systems, Inc.
- DSPlus from Kelly Information Systems, Inc.
- Empower and Enterprise Knowledge Server by Metapraxis.
- GENTIUM by Planning Sciences.
- Holos from Holistic Systems.
- Hyperion financial data analysis and reporting tools by Hyperion Software.
- Media by Speedware Corporation Inc.

- PaBLO by Andyne.
- Powerplay and Impromptu by Cognos Inc.
- StarTrieve from SelectStar Inc.

Query

General-purpose query and reporting tools aim to put a user-friendly front end on databases. Simple graphical interfaces simplify the task of formulating queries and present results in graphical formats. These tools are good for ad hoc analysis but do not provide the performance needed to tackle large process analysis and aggregation analysis problems. Some such tools are

- BusinessWEB, a tool for making business information accessible via Web browsers from Management Science Associates, Inc.
- CorVu by CorVu Pty. Ltd.
- Forrest & Trees, InfoReports, and InfoQuery from Platinum Technology, Inc.
- InfoAssistant from Asymetrix Corp.
- IQ/Objects and IQ/Vision from IQ Software Corp.
- Level5 Quest by Level Five Research.
- Voyant by Brossco Systems.

General Purpose

General-purpose tools such as spreadsheets and statistical packages can be configured to solve a wide variety of problems. General-purpose tools are usually versatile, but these tend to be difficult to configure and slow when performing analysis on large corporate data sets. Some examples of general purpose tools are:

- CrossGraphs graphical cross-tabulation tool from Belmont Research Inc.
- Demos, a package for statistical risk and decision analysis from Lumina Decision Systems, Inc.
- Excel spreadsheet from Microsoft Corp.
- Lotus 1-2-3 spreadsheet by Lotus Corp.
- MATLAB numerical analysis and visualization package from The MathWorks, Inc.
- PV-Wave data analysis and visualization package from Visual Numerics, Inc.
- S-Plus statistical analysis and visualization package by Statistical Sciences.
- SAS statistical analysis and visualization package from SAS Institute Inc.
- SPSS from SPSS Inc.

OLAP

On-Line Analytic Processing (OLAP) is a recent term coined by Dr. E. F. Codd. The term has been applied to a wide variety of analysis tools, data warehouse products, and multidimensional databases.

Databases

There are a number of different database types, each tuned to a particular set of problems.

Multidimensional

Multidimensional databases aggregate data into *hypercubes*. For example, this makes them perform well in response to queries requesting summary data, requesting the total sales, broken down by country. Unfortunately, there are no standards yet that define access to multidimensional databases. Some of the commonly used multidimensional database products are

- Acumate ES by Kenan Systems Corp.
- CrossTarget from Dimensional Insight.
- Essbase from Arbor Software Corp.
- Express from Oracle.
- GENTIUM by Planning Sciences Corp.
- HELM by Codework.
- Holos from Holistic Systems.
- Lightship from Pilot Software.
- Media by Speedware Corporation Inc.
- MetaCube from Informix.

Relational

Relational databases store data in tables. They are particularly well suited to processing transaction data. SQL provides a standard way of accessing data from relational databases. Major relational databases are

- Ingres
- Informix
- Oracle
- Sybase

ODBC

Open Database Connectivity (ODBC) is a standard interface for accessing database information. Database vendors each have their own proprietary interface to their database, making it difficult to access data from multiple vendors. ODBC solves this problem by providing a common way to access multiple databases on multiple platforms. Most data access applications support ODBC. ODBC drivers are available from a number of vendors, such as,

- INTERSOLV, supplier of DataDirect ODBC Pack.
- OpenLink Software, ODBC driver supplier.
- Simba Technologies, Inc., supplier of Simba family of products and driver development kits.
- Visigenic Software Inc., supplier of ODBC DriverSet.

Data Warehouses

Data warehouses are used to consolidate data from multiple sources throughout an organization. The data is then available for use in corporate decision making. Some of the more active data warehouse technology providers are

- Apertus Technologies Inc., supplier of Enterprise/Integrator.
- Hewlett-Packard, supplier of Open Warehouse.
- IBM, supplier of Virtual Warehouse.
- MicroStrategy.
- Platinum Technology, Inc., supplier of InfoHub.
- Praxis International, supplier of OmniWarehouse.
- Red Brick.
- Sequent Computer Systems, Inc.
- Software AG.
- Tandem Computers.

Data Indices

The following indices have searching capabilities that can be used to find further related Web pages:

- DejaNews, searchable archive of usenet newgroups.
- EINet Galaxy, hierarchical, searchable index.
- InfoSeek, searchable, automatically created index.
- Lycos, searchable, automatically created index.
- Open Text, searchable, automatically created index.
- WebCrawler, searchable, automatically created index.
- Yahoo!, well-organized, searchable, hierarchical index.
- Alta Vista.

TOOLS

Warehousing systems are instrumental in making tactical decisions about day-to-day business operations and strategic decision making involving longer-term planning and forecasting. These different types of decision making require different business intelligence tools and data, a fact we should take into account when designing and building a data warehousing system.

A well-designed data warehousing system can improve the accuracy and quality of business information, as well as deliver it in an easily understood format to business users. A data warehousing system also supplies users with *business intelligence tools*, allowing them to *query, analyze,* and *report* on known facts as well as discover unknown facts.

Business Intelligence Tools

Business intelligence tools help users determine the kind of information they need to analyze and how to access and analyze that information. *Data mart, operational data store, DSS data warehouse, OLAP,* and *data mining* are just a few of the terms that have become a part of the data warehouse user's vocabulary.

The objective of a data warehousing system is to improve the quality and accuracy of business information and deliver this information to business users in an accessible and understandable form. A data warehouse is simply a place to store data. A data warehousing system, on the other hand, provides a complete end-to-end solution for delivering information to users.

Such tools support three main user tasks: *querying* and *reporting* of known facts, *analysis* of known facts, and *discovery of unknown* facts. Querying and reporting involve displaying data in a visual form—such as a printed report or information displayed on a computer screen. The processing may be done on-line or in batch, using ad hoc or prebuilt queries and reports. Tools supporting this type of task have existed for many years.

Many modern tools, however, offer more sophisticated facilities such as Graphical User Interfaces (GUIs), the capability to pass retrieved data to desktop applications using techniques such as Microsoft OLE and a semantic layer providing a business view of data.

Data Analysis Tools

Data analysis tools are used to perform statistical and mathematical functions, forecasting, and multidimensional modeling. Sometimes referred to as On-Line Analytical Processing (OLAP) tools, data analysis tools enable users to analyze data across several dimensions, including market, time, and product categories.

Such tools are used to analyze and forecast trends and measure the efficiency of business operations over time. These evaluations provide support for strategic business decision making and insights on how to improve efficiency and reduce costs of business operations.

OLAP tools allow users to analyze and slice and dice data across multiple dimensions such as time, market, and/or product category. Such tools have existed for many years, but like query and reporting tools, OLAP products are now taking advantage of GUIs and client/server computing. Data warehousing for OLAP not only offers the advantage of clean and integrated data, but also historical data essential for forecasting and trend analysis. Warehouses supporting OLAP can be thought of as *Decision-Support* System (DSS) data warehouses.

There are two types of OLAP tools for Multidimensional Data Analysis (MDA): those accessing data stored in multidimensional database systems (MDBMSs) and those accessing data stored in relational DBMSs. The debate centers around which type of DBMS is best suited to store and maintain multidimensional data.

MDBMSs provide both analytical and data management server capabilities. They supply good performance for analyzing and drilling down through multiple levels of summarized data, but are less suited for handling large amounts of detailed data. The current direction for the use of MDBMSs is toward providing a pass-through capability to RDBMSs for accessing detailed data in a multitier data warehousing configuration.

When MDA tools are used to access data stored in RDBMSs, the RDBMS provides the data management capability, while the front-end client tool provides the analysis engine. The advantages of this approach are that both summarized and detailed data can be stored in the RDBMS, and data can be shared with other business intelligence tools.

Data analysis tools typically work with summarized rather than detailed data. Although you can build summaries during analytical processing, it is far more efficient to prebuild them whenever possible. This approach reduces processing overhead and makes work easier for the user.

Summaries are often stored in special databases known as *data marts*, which are tailored to specific sets of users and applications. Data marts are usually built from the detailed historical data stored in a DSS data warehouse, and—in some cases—are constructed directly from operational databases or an operational data warehouse. They may use either RDBMS or MDBMS technology.

Discovery and Mining Tools

Query, reporting, and data analysis tools are used to process or look for known facts. In other words, users of these tools know what kind of information they want to access and analyze. However, a new breed of business intelligence tool is becoming quite popular—one used to explore data for unknown facts. This style of processing allows business users to seek out new business opportunities and look for previously unknown data patterns. It may, for example, be used to examine customer buying habits or detect fraud. Such processing (data exploration) involves digging through large amounts of historical detailed data typically kept in a DSS data warehouse.

Tools supporting data exploration are sometimes referred to as *data mining* or data discovery tools. However, some people include them under the heading of OLAP tools, and several even use the term data mining to cover all aspects of business intelligence.

Data Warehouse Query Tools

Query and reporting tools are most often used to track day-to-day business operations and support tactical business decisions. In this context, a warehouse offers the advantage of data that has been cleansed and integrated from multiple operational systems. Such a warehouse typically contains detailed data that reflects the current (or near-current) status of data in operational systems and is thus referred to as an *operational data store* or operational data warehouse.

Evolving to Relational OLAP

One of the true business revolutions is the ability of desktop users to create job-specific queries and submit them against workgroup, departmental, and enterprise data warehouses. But simple report-writer query tools can only answer simplistic operational questions. And sophisticated multidimensional database technology cannot scale with today's terabyte-size warehouses. Therefore, the next-generation query tools for answering difficult ad hoc questions are integrating sophisticated OLAP with state-of-the-industry relational database technology, a powerful union called relational OLAP.

Reporting Tools

Report-writer tools, such as Microsoft Access, are best at retrieving operational data using canned formats and layouts. They adequately answer questions such as, "How many green dresses scheduled to ship this month have not shipped?" Usually the entire application resides on the desktop clients, an example of the *fat-client* design that has plagued many implementers who have tried to move too much data off the data server and onto the desktop for analysis.

Report writers are excellent and cost-effective for mass deployment of applications where a handful of database tables are managed as one database by any of the relational database suppliers' products. But this class of tool technology cannot and should not be forced to stand on its head in order to do more complex, but real-world OLAP applications.

Multidimensional OLAP (Query) Tools

A multidimensional query tool allows multiple data views (e.g., sales by category, brand, season, and store) to be defined and queried.

Multidimensional OLAP tools make ad hoc decision making much more practical than report writers and have been particularly successful in markets such as consumer packaged goods, where market-share analysis is business critical.

Multidimensional tools are based on the notion of arrays, an organizational principle for arranging and storing related data so that it can be viewed and analyzed from multiple perspectives. By summarizing data and arranging it in cross-tabular views, which are by now familiar to spreadsheet users, multidimensional tools offer users a perspective of their data that facilitates comparative analysis. These tools have shown particular strength in forecasting business trends and *what-if* analysis. They empower business users to *roll up* and *drill down* in a discovery search.

There are three basic types of multidimensional OLAP tools:

- *Client-side MDBs*, such as Andyne Computing Ltd.'s Pablo, which maintains precalculated consolidation data in PC memory and are proficient at handling a few megabytes of data.
- *Server-based MDBs* such as Arbor Software's Essbase, Holistic Systems Inc.'s Holos, and Oracle/IRI Software's Express, which optimize gigabytes of data by using any of several performance and storage optimization tricks.
- *Spreadsheets*, such as Microsoft Excel, which allow small data sets to be viewed in the cross-tab format familiar to business users.

Some query tools, such as D&B Software's Pilot and Oracle/IRI Software's Express, are integrated with a Multidimensional Database (MDB) for efficiently storing multiple dimensions using sparse-matrix technology. However, despite the speed and performance obtained from such optimization techniques, MDB technology becomes less practical as database sizes approach between 20 gigabytes and 50 gigabytes.

Size alone is not the only barrier faced by MDB suppliers and their users in complex *decision-support* environments. These systems must continuously and seamlessly interact with other portions of the *decision-support* architectures, with its full compliment of databases, desktop tools, and applications. MDBs have yet to prove that they can deliver the same mandatory features—usage-based privileges and security at several levels, for example—that are expected of any mission-critical system. Furthermore, unless queries have inherent relationships between elements of different records, an MDB cannot efficiently answer them. For example, MDBs—which are highly summarized—cannot themselves drill down to detailed data. An RDBMS is typically used as an adjunct.

While offering scant support for these requirements, current MDBs still lack provisions for

- Connecting multiple databases, including RDBMSs, and allowing them to interact.
- High-availability backup and restore.
- Subsetting multidimensional data for individual analysis and manipulation.
- Updating the database incrementally while users continue to access it.

The enterprise must factor the skills and costs required to implement and use a specialized MDB database. Radically different from core operational systems and

RDBMS-based systems, MDBs not only require a specialized database, but also specialized front-end tools to access information. This means that the likely market evolution for MDBs is as a major but non-mainstream path for high-end *decision support*. MDBs will continue to play an important role in the construction of so-called data marts until relational OLAP tools mature.

Relational OLAP Tools

Relational OLAP is the next logical step in the evolution of complex *decision-support* tools. Relational OLAP combines flexible query capabilities with a scalable multitier architecture while symbiotically depending on and leveraging the capabilities of today's parallel-scalable relational databases.

As relational OLAP and parallel-scalable database technology evolves, a whole new breed of data-mining applications is emerging. These applications empower business users to "drill" for information in virtually any direction, and without the need to preprogram the paths.

An optimized RDBMS can be combined with powerful, flexible query-tool capabilities. By blending these components within a scalable, multilevel architecture, relational OLAP can also be leveraged well beyond 100 gigabytes.

An RDBMS-based data warehouse optimized for *decision support* requires

- A server or client-based SQL query generator that also analyzes multidimensional data and computes aggregates, consolidations, and cross-tabulations.
- An applications-development environment for building and modifying *decision-support* applications that leverages all classes of *decision-support* tools.
- Intelligent agents and alerts that monitor the query environment, run analyses in the background, and notify workers when a predefined business condition or exception is encountered.
- Metadata repositories to identify data warehouse contents and the location of required enterprise data.
- One or more desktop applications that range from simple ad hoc querying to linked query reports and are market driven by being based on human logic and language rather than computer logic and language.

VENDORS

Dozens of vendors offer comprehensive data warehouse programs. This excludes query tools vendors and vendors of niche products, some of whom have established wide-ranging partnerships and strategies for building and implementing data warehouses. In this section, we will discuss some of the major vendors with their product offerings.

PRODUCTS

Arbor's Essbase

Essbase functions as a data consolidation, access, and analysis engine. Maximum data flexibility and access speed are achieved via a "sparse matrix" design, which stores data in arrays instead of tables. It appears as an additional pull-down menu in Excel or Lotus 1-2-3, from which any aspect of its functionality can be accessed. Users can dynamically gain access to corporate financial and operating data residing in legacy data managers and RDBMSs.

IBM

IBM offers a variety of data warehousing solutions to cope with the diversity of requirements found in the marketplace, ranging from a departmental/workgroup solution (often called a data mart) to an enterprise-wide global solution.

Visualizer

Visualizer is IBM's DSS tool. The core module Visualizer Query is supplemented by a number of add-on modules covering charting, statistics, planning, application development and multimedia. Database support by Visualizer extends to the DB2 family, Oracle, and Sybase.

Visualizer helps the user to turn the organization's raw data into usable information and as well as the strong GUI query builder and report writer. Visualizer offers an environment for the rapid development of EIS/DSS systems, a strong set of statistical functions, and the ability to incorporate multimedia information.

Visual Warehouse from IBM

Visual Warehouse can capture data from DB2, VSAM, IMS, Oracle, Sybase, flat files, and Binary Large Objects (BLOBs) and populate the Visual Warehouse data store on either DB2 for OS/2 or DB2 for AIX/6000.

Databases

IBM databases provide client/server support, parallelism, object technology, heterogeneous platform support, multimedia extensions, all of which can enable DB2 as the foundation RDBMS for a data warehouse. Platform support for the DB2 family now includes MVS, VSE, OS/400, AIX/6000 and OS/2 as well as non-IBM platforms like HP-UX and Solaris. The DB2 family provides integrated database support across diverse platforms, enabling improved information flow throughout the business.

Replicators

Replicators are another key element of the IBM data warehousing solution. The ability to replicate parts of the data warehouse to create data marts (data huts) for departmental data mining are a necessary addition for data warehousing, or for the "trickle feed" of data from operational systems to the data warehouse.

Informix Data Warehouse

Informix's parallel relational database management system is the lifeblood of their data warehouse. *On-Line Dynamic Server*™ provides for processing of hundreds of gigabytes of data in data warehouses on Symmetric Multiprocessing (SMP) machines. The INFORMIX-Extended Parallel Server™ supports loosely coupled and Massively Parallel Processing (MPP) machines. On-Line Dynamic Server runs on all major parallel hardware platforms including AT&T GIS, Cray Research Superservers, Hewlett-Packard, IBM Corporation, Pyramid Technology, Sequent Computer Systems, Silicon Graphics, and Sun Microsystems.

The *INFORMIX(R)-NewEra*™ tool set offers both programming and end-user access tools to the data warehouse.

Oracle

Oracle provides a suite of products with the Oracle relational database as the core product. Some of the support for *decision support* and data warehousing include

> *Data Warehouse Engine*—This supports both very large databases and high levels of distribution or the warehouse environment.
>
> *Parallel Load*—This allows loading of large volumes of data required in a data warehouse by Oracle SQL Loader. Loading in parallel provides performance enhancements.
>
> *Replication*—Replicating Oracle-based data sources can be performed by Oracle Advanced Data Replication.
>
> *Data Sources*—Accessing multiple legacy data sources can be performed by Oracle's Open Gateway product set.
>
> *Query/Reporting*—The need to access multiple data sources and report on ad hoc queries is essential to a data warehouse. Oracle Discoverer/2000 provides SQL query and reporting capabilities.
>
> *Metadata*—The link between the data sources and the data warehouse is defined by the metadata. CDE Case aids in the development of metadata.

Software AG's Data Warehouse Solution

The software elements comprising SOFTWARE AG's solution include a database, heterogeneous middleware, and a set of warehouse management and DSS tools. The SOFTWARE AG products supporting the open data warehouse are specifically

ADABAS (data management), ENTIRE (middleware), ESPERANT (query/reporting), and SourcePoint (warehouse automation). For the development stages, SOFTWARE AG offers Natural LightStorm (modeling and design).

ESPERANT

ESPERANT enables users with no knowledge of SQL or physical database structures to generate queries that are both syntactically and semantically correct. Delivered in two main modules, the Administration System and the Query System, ESPERANT provides the enduser with a business-oriented view of the data and enables queries to be created using a simple point-and-click query mechanism. SQL is merely the implementation language; it is generated, not written. *ESPERANT* maps out the endusers' views of data (called DataViews) and automatically extracts information from the RDBMS catalog, or import data from particular CASE tool repositories.

DSS AGENT provides chart types including grid views, 2D and 3D lines, bar, pie, bubble graphs, and geographic map views. *NETMAP* allows you to graphically visualize large quantities of data and interactively analyze important linkages.

The middleware layers within *ENTIRE* provide database independence by providing access to Oracle, Sybase, and Informix. Access is also available to data sources through ENTIRE's ODBC connectivity.

InfoPump

InfoPump allows the periodic bulk copying of data across heterogeneous data sources. InfoPump also provides the capability to integrate a number of different data sources. It can handle differences in data types and naming conventions in each data source.

Sybase OmniSQL gateways

Sybase OmniSQL Server is a gateway that provides transparent access to distributed, heterogeneous enterprise data sources, such as,

ADABAS/CICS	DEC/RMS
DB2/CICS	DB2/2
DB2/DRDA	Informix
DB2/IMS	Ingres
IDMS/CICS	ISAM
SQL/DS	RdB
VSAM/CICS	DB2/400

Sybase System 11

Sybase System 11 consists of four main database engines: Sybase SQL Server, Sybase IQ, Sybase MPP, and Sybase SQL Anywhere.

Sybase SQL Server

Sybase SQL Server features a Logical Memory Manager that provides named caches to reserve space for different types of objects, variable block sizes, and buffer algorithms for faster I/O, a cache-sensitive optimizer to automate the best search-and-replace strategy, and a cache analysis tool. The Logical Memory Manager is specifically designed for mixed workload environments.

SQL Server also provides *dynamic load balancing* via a symmetric networking and parallel lock manager, as well as accelerated data access via data partitions and in-place updates. Logging is provided via multiple log caches and expanded group commits. Included with System 11 is Backup Server, which is a separate server that performs automated backup dynamically.

Sybase MPP

For the centralized data store approach, which implies preplanned queries and detailed reports against very large databases, Sybase provides SQL Server with the Sybase MPP option. Sybase MPP is a subset of SQL Server optimized for Massively Parallel Processing (MPP) environments that utilize a shared-nothing architecture.

The data mart approach implies that users can perform exploratory analysis against lower-cost, departmental servers. For this approach, Sybase provides SQL Server with the Sybase IQ option. Sybase IQ implements the bit-wise indexing technology, which is based on the use of bitmaps to enable all data and data types (including Binary Large Objects, or BLOBs) to be represented as bits within indexes. Column-wise processing is then applied to only the required bits in a specific query.

Sybase IQ

Sybase IQ also supports parallelism. When loading a database, the product distributes the workload across all CPUs. In production environments, Sybase IQ can assign certain tasks, such as sorts and joins, to separate threads, as well as optimize the blocking and caching mechanism for faster response.

Sybase Anywhere

Sybase Anywhere provides replication to and from corporate databases and via SQL remote for mobile databases.

Sybase Enterprise Connect

The Enterprise Connect family of middleware products enable Sybase users to exchange information from platform to platform, database to database, and application to application.

CRITERIA FOR SELECTING SYSTEMS AND VENDORS

The following criteria are designed to help users evaluate vendors that provide data warehousing products and services. These criteria can help users better understand vendors' strategies and the suitability of their products.

What Is the Vendor's Primary Strategic Objective?

Data warehouse vendors can be classified into a number of camps based on the core technology or service they want or need to sell through the data warehouse program. It defines the vendor's computer or software business. Some of these categories are

- *Hardware vendors.* Data warehousing is a channel for their hardware.
- *Database vendors.* Most of their other tools involve establishing connections to the database.
- *Gateway vendors.* Such vendors provide connectivity to heterogeneous relational and nonrelational data sources.
- *Repository vendors.* These are niche providers of data warehousing and systems management functionality for metadata repository. Although creating standards for metadata is a critical industry requirement, it's unclear whether a repository will be the vehicle to achieve universal metadata interoperability.
- *Tools and utility vendors.* Such vendors provide, among other tools, database, CASE, and development tools.

What Is the Vendor's Multidimensional Strategy?

Multidimensional analysis has become a hot commodity lately. This is partially due to the collective efforts of so-called On-Line Analytic Processing (OLAP) vendors, which offer multidimensional databases, applications, and query tools. Every data warehouse vendor has rushed headlong into OLAP to assure real or prospective customers that it has a strategy to enable business users to perform sophisticated analyses of warehouse data.

The attraction of OLAP tools is that they enable users to browse through corporate data, examining the relationships among business entities at varying levels of granularity, with almost instantaneous response time. The reason for the high performance is that OLAP tools precalculate the values at the intersection of all dimensions and hierarchies. In essence, they create large metacubes of data—like multidimensional spreadsheets—which are stored in proprietary formats. In the past two years, a new breed of OLAP tools has emerged that runs against relational databases instead of proprietary OLAP data stores. These tools calculate the summaries and values on the fly instead of precalculating them.

Some data warehouse vendors have chosen to build a multidimensional strategy around OLAP for relational tools. Others have established partnerships with

OLAP vendors to develop technologies to tightly integrate OLAP and relational databases. Still other vendors have decided to build OLAP engines either by embellishing acquired technology or starting from scratch.

Currently, it's too early to tell which of these strategies is the best approach for providing multidimensional analyses. Different approaches may appeal to different types of users.

What Is the Vendor's Metadata Strategy?

Metadata is currently the messiest aspect of data warehousing. Metadata is the information about the content and nature of warehouse data. Metadata consists of data definitions as well as other valuable information, such as where the data originated, when it was last refreshed, who owns it, how it was derived, and so on. Metadata is used by administrators and programmers to manage a data warehouse and by endusers to assist them in querying warehouse data.

Metadata can be generated by CASE tools, application development tools, query tools, extract/transformation software, source and target databases, and data transfer tools. The problem is that each of these sources stores the metadata in different places using different formats and different access methods. Most metadata is proprietary, although there is a growing trend to store metadata in relational format so it can be accessed by SQL. However, this doesn't guarantee a uniform representation of the metadata. Currently, most vendors are working to integrate metadata on a tool-by-tool basis.

What Architecture Does the Vendor Support?

There are six types of data warehouse architectures. Most vendors lead with a single type of architecture but complement that architecture with associated tools.

- *Direct Query*. Direct Query is more a tool-driven architecture than a data warehouse architecture. However, the end result is the same: Endusers gain direct access to corporate data. The problem here is that users must know SQL and arcane database structures, and their queries can impact the performance of operational applications. Spreadsheets, Microsoft Access, and some report writers use a direct query architecture.
- *Event-Driven Systems*. In event-driven systems, applications typically "publish" data to an "information bus" and then "subscribe" to the data they need. One of the subscribing applications can be an archival function that captures all published data and stores and summarizes them into one or more subject-oriented *decision-support* databases. Event-driven systems typically propagate a universal application interface implemented via an Object Request Broker (ORB), message-oriented middleware, or stored procedures that transform all shared data into a common format with common terms and definitions.
- *Mixed Workloads*. The mixed workload architecture provides support for both query and update capabilities. Here, a warehouse is reloaded, causing a change

in data values which, in turn, triggers an update in a remote operational system. An example could be an inventory warehouse triggering a new just-in-time purchasing system. These *decision-support* and operational databases could be on the same machine.

- *Single-Subject Data Warehouses.* The single-subject architecture is considered the classical data warehouse architecture. Here, users directly access subject-oriented data that has been extracted and transformed from one or more operational systems and loaded into a data warehouse. Many companies start with a single-subject warehouse and then either expand the number of subjects in the warehouse or create new single-subject warehouses. The single-subject warehouses are often called data marts, depending on the volume of data and number of users supported. Most data warehouse vendors adhere to this model. This is also true for multidimensional database vendors.

- *Virtual Global Warehouse.* The virtual global warehouse enables companies to create a global view of corporate data. The integration mechanism is a SQL parsing and mapping engine. Virtual global warehouses are usually built from the ground up, knitting together disparate groups that realize they can benefit more by sharing definitions and data than by trying to reinvent a global warehouse on their own.

How Scalable Is the Vendor's Solution?

Vendors should be able to support both startup warehouses and advanced implementations. More importantly, the vendor's solution should be able to scale to expand data volumes, subjects, and users in its warehouse.

Many vendors offer preintegrated products and a guarantee of deliverables. It involves developing automated procedures and utilities to manage the daily flow of data between legacy systems and data warehouses.

To What Extent Has the Vendor Integrated Warehouse Products?

Vendors that have preintegrated products often cut down the time required to select products and get them to interoperate. Products that interoperate are able to communicate across networks and platforms (where necessary) and, more important, to share metadata. The trade-off for offering preintegrated components is sometimes problemetical. Limiting your tools selection to those that are preintegrated eliminates dozens of good tools. Following a best-of-breed strategy means that you will have to do the integration yourself.

How Experienced Is the Vendor?

Perhaps the key criterion in evaluating data warehouse vendors is the quality of technical know-how and methodologies. It takes experienced vendors to help users sort through the business issues involved in deciding to build a data warehouse. It also requires experienced data modelers to ferret out information requirements from endusers.

What Is the Nature of the Vendor's Partnerships?

Partnerships are critical for filling the missing gaps in a vendor's data warehouse portfolio. However, many of the vendors are partnering with the same niche vendors. This is particularly true for vendors of data warehouse management software, query tools, and systems integration services.

How Comprehensive Is the Vendor's Program?

The vendor's program includes tools for modeling data, extracting and transforming data, moving data, and loading data. Warehouses also require a metadata repository. On the front end, data warehouses require query, reporting, and analysis tools, including tools for performing multidimensional analysis, statistical modeling and forecasting, and pattern matching.

CONCLUSION

Data warehousing has revolutionized access to, and the processing of, corporate information. It does this by providing tools that optimize performance for both transactional and *decision-support* RDBMSs. These essentially different uses for data can now be separated but can continue to share the same raw data.

Data warehousing clears the confusion created by data extraction and storage, replacing the traditional environment with a subject-oriented, designed environment. Through the interaction of software and hardware tools that have been customized for *decision support*, the data warehouse provides endusers with fast, corporate-wide information and allows decision makers to analyze market trends ahead of their competition.

The vendors' ability to provide a complete solution to data warehousing largely from within their own product set is perhaps not the issue potential data warehousing implementers should be too concerned about. However, the quality and the technical depth are perhaps the main issues that should be considered. Without adequate expertise in the entire data warehousing process, any potentially successful data warehouse is doomed to fail. Therefore the choice largely depends on finding a vendor who has the quality products and the technical ability to custom tailor a data warehouse to your needs.

In reviewing the criteria for a data warehouse, it is essential to implement powerful, data warehouse management software, an optimally designed parallel database, intuitive data-access tools, and powerful parallel hardware.

11

BUILDING A PRACTICAL DATA WAREHOUSE

INTRODUCTION

A data warehouse is a collection center that offers an organization's decision makers access to "critical" information. But the bigger question is, How does an organization decide which information is critical enough to be collected and stored within the warehouse and which information can remain outside? By analyzing their business strategies and identifying business objectives and critical success factors, organizations can begin to pinpoint the essential and "critical" information.

Building a data warehouse requires complex systems integration work to establish the architecture and tie together the various components. Simplifying this process are a variety of integrated warehouse solutions. As an alternative, putting together best-of-breed products is another option: a database from one vendor, query tools from another, middleware from a third—although some pros say this is more likely to lead to integration problems. In a warehouse product suite, on the other hand, the individual components have already been integrated to iron out performance and connectivity problems. Lots of infrastructural issues are handled behind the scenes, which means better performance and fewer problems with tool compatibility.

In this chapter, we will discuss some of the issues, prerequisites for designing, building, populating, and maintaining a data warehouse.

PREREQUISITE TO SUCCESS

Critical success factors exist within an organization to support the achievement of the organization's goals and objectives. The business plan represents and defines all organizational elements. One of these elements is the definition of strategies that outline the approach for implementing a data warehouse. The data warehouse element should link data to objectives, strategies, and processes. The following criteria must be considered to ensure that the enterprise gets a technically correct solution:

- Identify and analyze key activities that are essential to business mission.

- Look to the business plan for guidance.
- Build access tools that connect the process to the data.
- Begin building data models that support these processes.

In building an enterprise-wide data warehouse, the processes for every business function must be analyzed.

During process analysis, participants identify the specific data entities and attributes that support each process. The enterprise should understand the information source, quantities, trends, and historical data needed to help define the warehouse's scope and infrastructure. Processes are then mapped to legacy data sources and entities before the warehouse project moves forward to defining the technical architecture. This architecture should be built in support of the present and future technical strategies of the organization.

The Technical Architecture

The data warehouse technical architecture must be cost-effective, adaptable, and easily implemented. Proven and reliable technology should be employed—technology that not only supports the current technical infrastructure of the organization but is also flexible for future growth.

As companies spread out into multiple buildings across cities, states, and even countries, their corporate communications infrastructure must be able to adequately support data collection, distribution, replication, and access. By capitalizing on and enhancing existing networks, companies can realize optimal benefits with minimal investment in new technologies or equipment.

Storage Capacity

Storage capacity is another critical component. Large amounts of data are often a requirement for the data warehouse. Relational Database Management Systems (RDBMSs) can be an effective way to store large amounts of data. Use of these databases can offer unsurpassed business analysis and management capabilities. Issues to consider for selecting the right storage media and method include data load times, synchronization, recovery, summarization levels, method of data security implementation, data distribution, data access and query speed, and ease of maintenance.

In large organizations, mainframes and parallel processors can ease the burdens of loading, retrieval, translation, and distribution of large amounts of data. However, some organizations may choose to implement a client/server environment, which can provide convenience and strength at the desktop for accessing, manipulating, and presenting data, and in some instances, can be robust enough to house the entire warehouse.

Data Distribution

Another consideration is the distribution of data throughout the organization. Data must be put into the hands of the people who are responsible for the achievement of business objectives and strategies—the process managers. It does not make sense to build large centralized corporate warehouses when you are in a distributed business environment. The reverse is also true.

Access to Information

Access to the information is the final technical component. For organizations that are drowning in data and dying for information, a well-designed, properly aligned data warehouse can give the right people access to the right information at the right time. Typically graphical user interface tools that enable access to the warehouse should facilitate the retrieval, analysis, and transfer of information.

When properly designed, the data warehouse and its access tools allow users to retrieve information quickly and easily.

PLANNING A DATA WAREHOUSE

When is the proper time to commit to a comprehensive data warehouse? The standard answer is, "it depends"—on expectations of perceived benefit, costs, risks, data volumes, complexity of population and retrieval requirements, hardware and software budgets, and technical support infrastructure.

Data warehouse technology is evolving rapidly and is maturing by the day. When an enterprise embarks on an ambitious warehouse project it should assume that, within a few years, the organization will either change or wish it could change the hardware and software tools initially selected. The more open the architecture, the more likely the enterprise can take advantage of software and hardware evolution. But open architectures often carry initial price premiums in ease and speed of application development, in developer and user training, and in vendor selection and management.

Before embarking on such an ambitious project, some of the following issues must be considered.

Scope and Timing Issues

Modest projects that may seem simple, often are not. Managing user expectations and establishing acceptable compromises must be accomplished before expending a major portion of the budget and time. Even a fairly simple initial project must be carefully planned if it is to serve as a base for a warehouse of expanding scope and capability.

A fast and safe prototype may be a good idea if the user community understands what a prototype proves and, more importantly, doesn't prove. A smaller and simpler data warehouse can speed the implementation and provide a learning experience with reduced risk. Keep in mind, however, that nobody learns the tough stuff until the difficult issues of volume and complexity are introduced. Some advocate a prototype approach that dives into warehousing, expanding as users and technical architects adapt. The difficulty is in recognizing when the base architecture becomes inadequate, functionally or technically, and scrap the prototype.

It is certainly possible to build simple data warehouses that contain reasonable volumes of data from a single source, accessed in few and predictable aggregate categories. One can usually implement this type of warehouse using utility programs to populate the database and package software for retrieval and analysis. But as the volumes grow, with more sources, more data, and more users, the simple warehouse is of little use as a basis for the expanded warehouse. For these reasons, jumping in and attempting ambitious projects may make sense for many businesses, especially given the potentially large Return On Investment (ROI) for strategic business analysis.

Design Considerations for Data Warehouse Applications

Building a comprehensive data warehouse is a full-fledged development project. It is not simply a plug-and-play choice of tools to download and query information. In some ways, it is more difficult than developing an operational system because the requirements are more ambiguous given the necessity of ad hoc analysis.

A systematic project plan must address,

- Designing data models that are easy to understand, map effectively to data sources and queries, and contain the necessary statistics to support physical data design, query optimization, and distribution/replication alternatives.

- Understanding the generic requirements, including current information needs, likely future requirements, history retention, and flexibility to evolve.

- Defining what operational data to capture, the sources of the data, and what additional data is not readily available.

Segregating the Data Warehouse from Operational Systems

Most developers today accept the reality that it is better to keep the operational and warehouse stuff separate. Certainly, separate databases and, perhaps, separate DBMS products and processor platforms, have become more the norm than the exception. Controlled and practical redundancy is actually preferable to out-of-control theoretical data purity. Operational and warehouse data is too different to be the same, as the table below illustrates.

Active, tactical, and current events flow from the operational system to the warehouse to become static, strategic, and historical data. In a perfect world, simply retaining the expired operational data permits strategic reporting from the operational database. This arrangement sounds good in theory but has proven to be impractical. The real-world performance, capacity, and technology limitations cannot be ignored.

OPERATIONAL DATA	WAREHOUSE DATA
Short-lived, rapidly changing	Long-living, static
Requires record-level access	Data is aggregated into sets, similar to relational database
Repetitive standard transactions and access patterns	Ad hoc queries with some specific reporting
Updated in real time	Updated periodically with mass loads
Event driven—process generates data	Data driven—data governs process

Data Volume Considerations

Data volume is often the first issue that comes to mind when evaluating warehouse costs and benefits. In reality, flexibility of use and adaptability to change are more critical feasibility issues. The market is making greater and faster progress in solving the volume problem. Parallel loading and querying and less-expensive and faster storage devices are more palatable than affordable flexibility and ease-of-use of the data model and query tools.

It is useful, however, to put some parameters around the volume issue. When do data volumes move from modest to large, to excessive? *Large* is a relative term and a moving target. It is affected by raw volume, volatility, access requirements, complexity of data relationships, availability requirements, and many other factors. As hardware and software evolve, the tolerance bars are constantly being raised. Below are some general volume guidelines.

- Less than 5 gigabytes of data is *small*. Such a warehouse might run on high-powered PC servers.
- 5 to 100 gigabytes of data is *moderate*. Larger workstations or a mainframe might be needed.
- 100 to 300 gigabytes is *large*. Multiple SMP servers or larger mainframes may be necessary.
- Over 300 gigabytes falls into the *gross range*. A massively parallel processing solution may be needed for this category.

The above issues can, of course, be mitigated by the ability to limit how much data is frequently and comprehensively viewed or summarized so that most queries never look that large. Some additional issues that may affect volumes, may also be considered:

- How does aggregation affect ad hoc needs?
- How much history is sufficient to satisfy most query requirements?
- Can the data be affordably indexed or partitioned so that qualifying data is efficiently isolated?

CORE COMPONENTS OF A DATA WAREHOUSE

There are five key aspects of a data warehousing structure.

- *Policy*. The first step in developing a data warehouse is determining what information will be included, as well as how often that data is updated, backed up, and secured.
- *Transformation*. Before raw data can be stored in a data warehouse, it must be *cleansed* so that it has meaning to users who access it. This transformation may involve restructuring, redefining, recalculating, and summarizing the data fields.
- *Storage*. As data is moved from various operational systems into the warehouse, it must be stored in order to maximize system flexibility, manageability, and overall accessibility. The data stored in the warehouse is historical in nature and represents the key measures of how the enterprise has performed in the past.
- *Analytics*. This is the component of a data warehousing solution which addresses the corporate need for analytical modeling, complex computations, and *what-if* analysis on large data volumes in a multi-user environment.
- *Access*. The ability to select, view, and manipulate data comprises the general category referred to as data access. Desktop tools such as spreadsheets, query tools, and report writers meet this need by presenting a graphical interface for navigating warehouse data.

One of the data warehouse architecture's primary characteristics is a read-only database used for *decision support*. The following are some of the distinguishing characteristics:

- Data is extracted from source systems, databases, and files.
- Data from the source systems is integrated and transformed before being loaded into the data warehouse.
- *Decision-support* data resides in a separate, read-only database.
- Users access the data warehouse via a front-end tool or application.

Some of the major components of a typical data warehousing project that must be considered are the following.

Data Extraction

The data in the data warehouse will come mainly or even completely from production systems. But we need to decide exactly what to extract. The process of extraction may not be simple and we will need specialized software.

We may gather data from other external sources, but most of the useful data is usually held somewhere electronically within the computer systems. There may be a

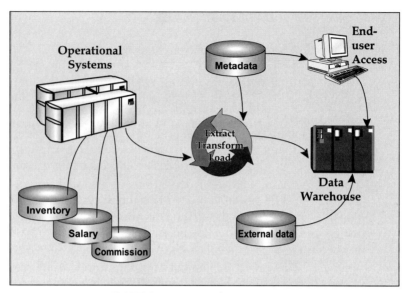

FIGURE 11.1   Metadata Repository.

number of difficulties in extracting this data. The data between different data stores may not be synchronized. There are also fundamental design decisions to be taken as to when and how regularly to extract data to add to the data warehouse.

Repository

The repository holds the metadata (Figure 11.1). This is the map of the data that we hold in the data warehouse. The repository will need to be used by the extraction software that we acquire and by any of the range of middleware and end-user tools that provide access to the data warehouse. As the data changes, so does the repository.

Database

There are different kinds of databases which are used as part of a data warehouse strategy. Only a few products have the capability of running on massively parallel hardware, but such products may be necessary for very large volumes of data. OLAP databases are built for handling multidimensional tables and these may be required for some applications rather than relational databases.

Middleware

Middleware is software which provides general access to data on different databases and on different platforms. Middleware may be provided by other kinds of tools, such as end-user query tools. Data extraction tools are specialized middleware of a kind. There are also general-purpose middleware products, some of which perform better than others.

Query Tools

There are a wide range of query tools that allow the enduser to generate queries easily and to store frequently used query commands. In general query tools need to be able to access repository information and limit users to a subset of the entire data warehouse to avoid the squandering of the available resources.

Decision-Support Tools

The term *decision support* as applied to software products refers to the wide range of tools which can take extracts of data from a database for local querying and graphic modeling of the data. In this grouping of products we can include spreadsheets, graphics software, PC databases, and statistical packages. *Decision-support* tools have a wide range of applications, often embracing sophisticated graphical interfaces, extensive drill-down capabilities, statistical capabilities, and so on.

Analysis and Modeling Tools

There are some specialized tools that provide a wide range of analysis and modeling capability.

Computer Hardware

The computer hardware that may be used covers the whole range of servers. In some instances massively parallel hardware and specially built database engines (with built-in databases) may be appropriate. In others mid-range UNIX servers may be all that is required. Sometimes a single server may be enough. In other instances data may be spread across several servers of different sizes at different locations in the network.

THE ENTERPRISE DATA MODEL

Data warehouses must be built with a broader horizontal view of data around an enterprise data model, integrating data from the legacy applications to consistently and accurately view customer relationships, products, services, and profitability.

Consolidation and integration of information across legacy applications within the model provide the blueprint for the development of the data warehouse. When complete, the data model also provides the criteria to evaluate the completeness and consistency of a design that will allow the migration of legacy information to one common data structure. After the enterprise model is built, the model must be validated by the business users and data mapped from legacy applications to the model, with more validation to follow.

Building the Data Model

The next stage is the implementation of the data model that supports the business requirements. The data model, which includes all entities and required attributes, is transferred from the data modeling stage into the selected repository. The repository or business information directory is used to store the model, all legacy application data dictionaries, data transformation rules, and ultimately business views and rules. The repository, in essence,

- Documents the data model.
- Defines target attributes for mapping all data that should be harvested from legacy applications.
- Provides data for on-line help and data dictionary in the user interface—linking business questions to answers.

Harvesting Legacy Data

Following construction and loading of the entities and attributes into a repository, the next step is to relate the data in the legacy applications or other data sources to the entities and attributes within the repository. The repository serves as the documentation of the origin and destination of all data elements that will be harvested from the legacy applications and mapped to the new repository, as well as the rules that relate to their validation, calculation, transformation, values, and so forth.

Mapping

Mapping is a *bottom-up* process, unlike the repository development process, which is *top-down*. Every data element, or attribute, identified during requirements identification and all data required from legacy systems must be mapped and defined in the new repository. By establishing these relationships within the repository, it can be used to control and drive the collection, loading, and presentation of data-linking business strategies, to business views which in turn link to actual data.

Linking Business Views to the Repository

With a repository built that supports the processes and legacy data collected, the completed model must be linked back to the processes by establishing business views that support the processes. Business views are clusters of data represented by one or more entities and attributes that are linked together to support the measurement of standards and performance objectives defined during the process analysis.

Linking Business Views in the User Interface

By linking business views to business models or processes, this road map can be used to support the access to information. Users are empowered and technical support is minimized. Developed with graphical tools, the interface provides push-button access to predefined reports, as well as ad hoc query tools that enable drill-down and trend analysis capabilities. The data housed in the repository that supports the interface includes processes linked within the repository to the report dictionary, business views, entities, and data elements or attributes, all within the confines of proper security.

The user interface is always the most critical component in aligning the data warehouse with the business strategies. Designed correctly with the incorporation of the repository, the user interface can result in significant productivity gains. Rather than building static screens that require extensive maintenance, users can interface with screens that pull data directly from the repository or metadata. As more data is added to the model, the only change is to the repository resident data. This not only reduces maintenance but also provides greater flexibility to the user, reduces learning curves, hides the complexities of the repository, and minimizes support requirements. This translates into improved productivity.

The user can select the individual elements required for the report or extract. Not only can users drill down the data that resides in the warehouse to make better decisions; they can also drill down to the actual data that defines the success or failure of the process—yielding the final step in linking business strategies to the data warehouse.

Optimizing the Data Repository

The data warehouse is the foundation of any *decision-support* system, and the warehouse repository must address the conflicting goals of system flexibility and data delivery performance. Flexibility is required so that additional attributes, dimensions, and metrics can be added to the warehouse, complementing and leveraging existing data. Quick query response is required in all effective interactive *decision-support* systems, since it not only impacts end-user satisfaction but also directly determines the number of analyses the user can perform.

In designing the data warehouse repository, it is useful to first review the types of tables found in a data warehouse.

Primary Data Tables contain both metrics and attributes and contain the data that endusers are seeking. In large data warehouses, the full-text attribute description is not stored in the primary data table, but rather in a descriptor table, while numeric element ID codes are stored in the primary data table.

Descriptor Tables are often used to replace the ID codes used in queries with common business terms familiar to the user. In smaller warehouses, where load performance and storage concerns are less, text descriptors may appear in the primary data tables to increase data comprehensibility.

Characteristics Tables contain additional information about an attribute and can be used to segment data in an ad hoc manner. The ability to define and join with characteristics tables containing many attributes is a key advantage of RDBMS technology over multidimensional data storage architectures, since multidimensional architectures do not support multitable joins.

Query Performance is strongly correlated to the physical repository. Intelligent data modeling, through the use of techniques such as denormalization, consolidation, and partitioning, can provide orders of magnitude performance gains compared to the use of normalized data structures. There are perhaps as many ways to develop data warehouses as there are organizations. For a successful implementation, the following dimensions need to be considered:

Data Warehouse Scope

The scope of a data warehouse may be as broad as all of the informational data for the entire enterprise from the beginning of time, or it may be as narrow as a personal data warehouse for a single year. There is nothing that makes one of these more of a data warehouse than another. In practice, the broader the scope, the more valuable the data warehouse is to the enterprise and the more expensive and time consuming it is to create and maintain. As a consequence, most organizations seem to start out with functional, departmental, or divisional data warehouses and then expand them as users provide feedback.

Data Redundancy

There are essentially three levels of data redundancy that enterprises should think about when considering their data warehouse options:

- Central data warehouses
- Distributed data warehouses
- Virtual data warehouses

There is no one best approach. Each option fits a specific set of requirements, and a data warehousing strategy may ultimately include all three options.

Central Data Warehouses

Central data warehouses are what most people think of when they are first introduced to the concept of a data warehouse. The central data warehouse is a single physical database that contains all of the data for a specific functional area, department, division, or enterprise. Central data warehouses are often selected where there is a common need for informational data and there are large numbers of endusers already connected to a central computer or network.

A central data warehouse may contain data for any specific period of time. Usually, central data warehouses contain data from multiple operational systems. Central data warehouses are real. The data stored in the data warehouse is accessible from one place and must be loaded and maintained on a regular basis. Normally, data warehouses are built around advanced RDBMs or some form of multidimensional informational database servers.

Distributed Data Warehouses

Distributed data warehouses are just what their name implies. They are data warehouses in which the certain components of the data warehouse are distributed across a number of different physical databases. Increasingly, large organizations are pushing decision making down to lower and lower levels of the organization and in turn pushing the data needed for decision making down (or out) to the LAN or local computer serving the local decision maker.

Distributed data warehouses usually involve the most redundant data and as a consequence the most complex loading and updating processes.

Virtual Data Warehouses

A virtual data warehouse allows endusers to get at operational databases directly, using whatever tools are enabled via the "data-access network." This approach provides the ultimate in flexibility as well as the minimum amount of redundant data that must be loaded and maintained. This approach can also put the largest unplanned query load on operational systems.

Virtual warehousing is often an initial strategy in organizations where there is a broad but largely undefined need to get at operational data from a relatively large class of endusers and where the likely frequency of requests is low. Virtual data warehouses often provide a starting point for organizations to learn what endusers are really looking for.

BUILDING, USING, AND MAINTAINING A DATA WAREHOUSE

Building a data warehouse is a big task. It is not recommended that one undertake the development of an enterprise data warehouse as a single project exercise. Rather, it is recommended that a series of phased requirements be developed and implemented in a serial fashion to allow a more gradual and iterative implementation process. No organization has ever succeeded in developing the data warehouse in a single step. However, many organizations are succeeding in the development of an enterprise data warehouse, step by step or subject by subject.

Data in the data warehouse is non-volatile and is a read-only repository of data (as a rule). However, new elements may be added on a regular basis so that the content tracks the evolution of data in the source database(s) in both content and time.

It is amazing how quickly companies jump on the bandwagon of new technologies and ride off into the wilderness with hopeful dreams of striking gold. It's not the dreams; it is just that few companies take the time to understand the ramifications of chasing each new glittering possibility.

This is true with data warehousing. Like many such fields, data warehousing holds much promise. It allows companies to mine the nuggets of information buried under mountains of corporate data. Data warehousing is different from artificial intelligence in that many companies are really building data warehouses and gaining significant business advantages.

Problems to Avoid

The problem with data warehousing is that people are rushing to build these monsters without regard to how they will impact existing systems architectures or will be integrated with other applications in the enterprise. In that context, data warehousing is no different from many other technologies that have come and gone in the past few decades.

Enterprises are perhaps vulnerable to chasing technologies, especially when the emphasis is often on writing code rather than strategic systems planning. Architecture, methodology, and modeling are dirty words, when it involves the bottom line.

This short-term thinking has several implications for data warehousing.

- Most companies are creating data warehouses in a vacuum—without regard to systems architectures, or other applications and data warehouses. It's obvious that this year's data warehouses will be next year's islands of automation.
- A second problem is that data warehouses ignore process and function. Data warehouses essentially sterilize data, stripping it of application context and isolating it behind one or more relational database engines. Separating data and function is a bad idea. It creates a schizophrenic systems architecture that vacillates between data-centric and application-centric views of the business.

There are three ways to address the problems associated with chasing the data warehouse pot of gold. Selecting the appropriate approach depends on how far along you are in building a data warehouse and whether your company is centralized or decentralized.

- If you're starting from scratch, the best approach is by defining the core business events or messages that get passed between applications.
- If you're already well down the data warehouse path, you can plan to integrate warehouses using a virtual warehouse architecture.

In either case, two barriers must be overcome:

- Making data available, and
- Giving the users a tool to find the right information and then analyze it.

Building a Data Warehouse

Implementing a data warehouse is no easy task. Making data available is difficult enough, but if users cannot retrieve the data, the investment in the warehouse is lost.

Building a data warehouse involves extracting data from various operational databases and populating a specialized database—a data warehouse—which endusers can then access without impacting production systems. This requires an extensive effort to select, map, and transform the data that goes into the warehouse and also a powerful front-end tool that allows users to easily retrieve and analyze the newly available information.

A multitude of additional issues must be explored before undertaking a data warehouse development project. This includes technical issues pertaining to networks, platforms, query tools, data analysis, and distributed data management, as well as business issues pertaining to the informational needs of an organization.

Given the many issues, each organization will move at a different pace in implementing a data warehouse. A data warehouse program can facilitate warehousing at multiple levels, from simple copy management and data replication through full-scale data warehouse development.

Using

Getting data into the warehouse is the first hurdle in empowering endusers. Getting data out is the next. For the most part, data warehouse endusers don't care about the technology behind the warehouse. They care about getting answers quickly. Because of this, making data truly accessible is an important but often misunderstood aspect of warehouse development.

The choice of query tool can significantly affect how well a data warehouse is received and used by an organization's endusers. Front-end tools that are not easy to understand or are not powerful enough to retrieve the data, simply cannot be used. If the users cannot get at data, the warehouse, but not the query tool, will be faulted. Therefore, back-end investments, such as data extracting, scrubbing, transport, and loading, can be negated with the wrong front-end tool.

Maintaining

The most critical phase in a data warehouse life cycle is the phase that lasts the longest: *maintenance*. The greater the use within an organization, the more difficult it is to expand and maintain the data warehouse to satisfy the ever-changing needs of a growing user population.

One of the challenges of maintaining a data warehouse is to devise methods for identifying new or changed data in operational databases. Some ways to identify this data include inserting date/time stamps in database records and then creating copies of updated records and copying information from transaction logs and/or database journals. These new and/or changed data elements are then extracted, integrated/transformed, and added to the data warehouse in scheduled, periodical steps. As the new occurrences of data are added, older data is removed. For example, where particular subject details are held for five years, as the latest week is added, the oldest week is removed.

Given the necessity of ongoing modifications and updates, it's critical that the data warehouse not become a maintenance burden. Continual changes to source data systems as well as target data models can potentially cause enormous strain on the enabling technology or the interface that connects the two.

Before transforming operational data into *decision-support* data, the first step is to properly design and model the warehouse. This structured design process is an important prerequisite for successful data warehouse implementation. Issues such as denormalization of the data must be resolved during this phase to lay a strong foundation for subsequent data access projects.

Once you determine what the warehouse will look like, you can then determine how to build it. Key considerations here include the extracting and scrubbing of operational data. Vendors support existing extraction programs and offer several data extraction methods depending on the complexity of data sources and the complexity of data transformation needed.

The final factor is the warehouse administrator. The administrator programs the warehouse agent that manages critical data warehouse functions such as loading and refreshing the data. It also maps operational data to warehouse data structures and inserts, updates, and loads data into warehouse tables. This is the key that eases maintenance efforts of the data warehouse and allows for a better balance between cost and resource allocation.

Flexible Alternatives for Implementation

Historically, the implementation of a data warehouse has been limited to the resource constraints and priorities of the MIS organization. The task of implementing a data warehouse can be a very big effort, taking a significant amount of time. And, depending on the implementation alternatives chosen, this could dramatically impact the time it takes to see a payback, or return on investment.

There are pros and cons to any implementation technique and it all comes down to a management decision based on the capabilities of the products and resources that are available. But now there are other dimensions to be explored.

There are many approaches to any systems implementation, and data warehousing is no exception. The alternatives are

- *Stand-alone data mart*: This approach enables a department or workgroup to implement a data mart with minimal or no impact on the MIS organization. It may require some technical skills, but those resources could be managed by the department or workgroup. In this case, the data to populate the data mart is primarily provided by sources other than the MIS organization. For example, the department could have its own test or production facility from which it gathers data for input to the data mart. This approach would also apply to those smaller organizations that might not have the support of an MIS organization.

- *Dependent data mart*: This approach is similar to the stand-alone data mart, except that management of the data sources by MIS is required. These data sources could include the operational data and external data, as well the global data warehouse.

  Such implementation should have minimal impact on MIS resources. It could include such things as getting MIS authorizations and some assistance to access the data sources. The workgroup decides what data they want to access and the frequency of access and may even provide the tools and skills necessary to extract the data.

- *Global data warehouse*: The global data warehouse implies that the primary impact and implementation responsibility belong to MIS. They would be responsible for an overall architecture to support the enterprise.

    The requirements and implementation priorities would be based on the needs of the enterprise as a whole. Such a warehouse could physically be centralized or logically centralized and physically distributed over multiple platforms. The design could include support for any number of data marts. Such data marts would not be the same as the stand-alone or dependent data marts previously described. They are data marts designed specifically to be part of the global data warehouse and are populated from it.

All of the standard systems implementation alternatives are still available, except that now there is more flexibility in choosing which to use. Typically, the global data warehouse is planned and designed before any implementation activities are begun. Although this may be the best technical approach, it may not be the most practical since it would significantly impact the payback time for return on investment.

Individual departments or workgroups may feel they need to implement a data mart themselves to satisfy an immediate need. Although it would be beneficial to have an overall plan in place, these types of implementations could happen with or without such an overall plan.

Starting with a small confinable project, they could create a manageable solution and realize a quicker return on investment. Product planners, for example, may need to access history data on product sales, summarized by region. The branch offices may have this data in their operational systems, but the product planners are unable to access it or may find they can access it but it's not in a structure they can work with. In this example, the product planners could create a data mart to satisfy their specific need.

While individual departments or workgroups could implement, manage, and run their stand-alone or dependent data marts, they could also choose to be integrated into the larger global or enterprise data warehouse at a later time. With the data marts originally implemented outside any global data warehouse plan, this would be a more difficult approach. However, it could provide benefits to the overall enterprise with economies of scale and common goals while extending the reach and range available to the departments or workgroups.

With either approach, starting small is advised. Starting small may mean targeting a single subject area or business area. The MIS organization can work with each group to understand their data needs, create an implementation plan, and then deliver the data appropriately summarized for each workgroup's needs—all from a common, consistent source.

The key to delivering a valuable data warehouse is to work from a good business data model. That model reflects the way that people use information, not the way the physical data is stored.

EXPLOITING THE DATA WAREHOUSE ARCHITECTURES

The description thus far has covered the basic, or "generic," elements of a data warehouse. While there is no one "right way" to implement a data warehouse, the generic elements must be part of the architecture for the data warehouse to function correctly.

Part of the task of building a warehouse is to blend the generic elements with your current systems architecture and any other customized conditions that must be incorporated. However, integrating the data warehouse with the current systems architectures may be far less straightforward than you think. At many companies, the current data processing systems architectures are extremely complex and sophisticated. The complexity and sophistication are usually due to a layering of technical, interoperability, strategic, and political considerations.

Building a data warehouse is a process of finding the correct technical solution to *decision-support* needs and creating a solid architecture within the parameters you have to work with. While one architecture may not be better than another, certainly one may be more difficult to implement. In most cases, however, the chosen data warehouse architecture should be the most appropriate technical solution based on the corporation's goals, architecture constraints, and *decision-support* requirements.

Operational databases, designed to support various production applications, are often varied in format. The same data elements, if used by different applications or managed by different DBMS software, may be defined using inconsistent element names, have inconsistent formats, and/or be encoded differently. All of these inconsistencies must be resolved before the data elements are stored in the data warehouse.

By breaking down the warehouse architecture into components, we can gain a better understanding of the role each plays in the overall system and what corresponding infrastructure is required for success. This section provides an overview of how a data warehouse operates. In addition, some of the more complex topics related to data warehousing, data extraction, data transformation, metadata, external data, and databases are also discussed.

Data Extraction

Data is extracted from source systems, database, or files. In most companies, the legacy systems are the dominant source of data. Often, this process may entail extracting specific data fields from many different systems, databases, or files. Sometimes entire files may be extracted, if all the fields are necessary for *decision-support* processing.

Other data may be from external sources. These sources may be in a variety of formats and on different mediums, so selective field extraction from the files may or may not be necessary. In general, it is quite common within a data warehouse architecture for the data sources to be from multiple systems or applications. Source fields may come from different databases, different platforms, and in a variety of data types and formats.

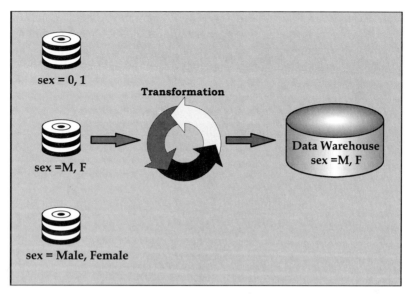

FIGURE 11.2   Data Transformation.

Data Transformation

One of the challenges of any data warehouse implementation is the issue of transforming data. Transformation deals with the inconsistencies in data formats and encoding schemes that may exist even within a single database and that almost certainly exist when multiple databases contribute to the data warehouse (Figure 11.2).

Data management tools are required to extract data from operational database(s) and/or files and then manipulate, or transform, the data as necessary before loading the results into the data warehouse. Taking data from the various operational databases and transforming it into required data for the warehouse is referred to as transformation or the integration of data.

Data transformation also deals with inconsistencies in data content. Once transformation rules are established, definitions can be created and included in the transformation routines. Transformation is a key element in creating the single source of the truth. Careful and detailed planning is required to transform inconsistent data into consistent and reconcilable data sets for loading into the data warehouse.

Data from the source systems is integrated and transformed before being loaded into the data warehouse. If data is coming from multiple systems, databases, and platforms, some form of data integration or transformation becomes necessary.

Metadata

Another aspect of the data warehouse architecture is to create supporting metadata. Metadata is the information about the data that feeds, gets transformed, and exists in the data warehouse. Metadata is a generic concept, but each implementation of metadata uses specific methods and techniques. These methods and techniques are dependent on each organization's requirements, existing capabilities, and user interface requirements. As yet, there are no universally accepted standards for metadata, so metadata must be defined in terms of the data warehousing software selected for a specific implementation.

Typically, metadata includes items such as,

- Data structures that form the view of data known to the data administrator(s).
- Definitions of the system of record from which the data warehouse is built.
- Specifications of data transformations that occur as the source data is replicated to the data warehouse.
- The data model of the data warehouse (i.e., the data elements and their relationships).
- A record of when new data elements were added to the data warehouse, and when old data elements were removed or summarized.
- Levels of summarization, the method of summarization, and their data warehouse tables of record.

Some implementations of metadata also include definitions of the view(s) presented to users of the data warehouse. Typically, multiple views are defined to suit the varied preferences of various groups of users. Schemas and subschemas for operational databases form an excellent source of input when creating metadata.

The metadata serves, in a sense, as the heart of the data warehouse environment. Creating complete and effective metadata definitions can be a time-consuming process, but the better the definitions, the better understanding the user community will have. If you are using integrated software management tools, the efforts pay off in the maintenance of the data warehouse.

External Data

Depending on the application, the scope of the data warehouse may be extended by the ability to access external data. For example, data accessible via on-line computer services and/or via the Internet or Intranet may be made available to users of the data warehouse.

Read-Only Database

Decision-support data resides in a separate, read-only database. Inherent in the data warehouse architecture is the idea that operational and *decision-support* processing are fundamentally different. Operational processing is for running the day-to-day business and are usually on-line transaction processing systems that take in, update, and store the core data created by corporate business systems. The goal of *decision-*

support processing, on the other hand, is to provide easy-to-use analytical information to assist in making tactical and strategic business decisions.

Decision-making processes often require a range of historical data for comparative analysis so users will be able to monitor trends and information patterns over time. The fundamental differences between the functionality of operational and *decision-support* systems also require substantially different styles of database design.

Front-End Tools

Users access the data warehouse by using a front-end tool or application. With most data warehouses, the front line of the system is the data access environment. Although many different variations of data access are possible, in most cases it will be created in a client/server fashion, with the workstation acting as the client and the data warehouse acting as the server.

CREATING THE DATA WAREHOUSE

Based on enduser needs, the first step in creating the data warehouse is to identify and analyze the relevant internal and external data sources.

Data modeling plays a critical role in transforming and integrating internal and external operational data into the warehouse. At this stage, companies have to compile the information, apply the transformation logic from the source to the data models, and decide on what level of data detail or data summarization to keep in the warehouse, as well as how much history to retain.

Building the metadata and cleansing the data are the transitions between production data and data warehouse data. It is a business-oriented guide for the *decision-support* analyst to locate the data and understand its calculation rules. Cleansing and filtering the data consist of converting and consolidating it, solving the problem of data inconsistency in operational databases by applying consistent naming conventions. Companies have the choice to select among the various extraction tools that exist on the market.

Parallel processing and scalability are the key in selecting the right relational database and server. The ability to handle data querying, loading, and indexing in parallel is essential to data warehousing. Parallel processing provides the high performance needed by endusers for *decision support*. Scalability is equally important, as it means companies can add processors and users without affecting existing data, systems, and applications.

Building the physical data warehouse consists of entering the required data from the different data sources. An open relational database and hardware architecture often provide the best physical framework for a data warehouse, offering both lower maintenance costs and higher flexibility.

IMPLEMENTING THE DATA WAREHOUSE

The ultimate goal of data warehousing is the creation of a single logical view of data which may reside in many disparate physical databases. This provides developers and business users with a single working model of the enterprise's data, something which is absent in virtually every organization.

Making data available within the warehouse involves extensive copy management, data replication, data summarization, version control, and utilizing copy and replication technology. Finally the data warehouse must be available to the user. Mechanisms for delivering data to the desktop, mining through different levels of data, and providing connectivity are important.

The most meaningful approach to data warehouse implementation is as a resource with an interface which resides in the middleware layer. The benefits which are to be derived from a well-conceived data warehouse are

- Greater accuracy through elimination of redundancy.
- Improved efficiency through timely access to information.
- More effective decision making.

Prior to any data warehouse implementation, it is important to determine if improved access to information will help achieve corporate goals. Performance benchmarks will have to be put in place to determine if those goals are being met. The data warehouse's main task will be to generate those business opportunities that will help meet corporate goals.

A data warehouse is an answer to business needs, not data requirements. It is not just a copy of the operational data in one single, very large database. Defining enduser needs and deciding on what data will reside in the data warehouse should be based on what is actually needed and not on how much information can be included.

The definition of a function/data cross-reference map will help determine who needs to access what category of data. At the very beginning of a data warehouse implementation, companies will have to identify the enduser vocabulary and define the appropriate business terms to link to categories of data.

Key Layers

A data warehouse architecture consists of different layers that range from the definition of data sources to the implementation of the *decision-support* solution. The architecture has been discussed in detail in previous chapters.

The operational data from legacy systems is the source of information for the data warehouse. Data extraction is the data transformation, transportation, and loading. The database administration includes all of the items related to the design of the database, how much data is going to be managed and used, and the metadata. The middleware layer refers to the client/server architecture and data communications.

Key People

Whether mandated by the top executives or initiated by a single department, a successful data warehouse project requires the involvement and the collaborative efforts of many different parties, including *decision-support* experts, database designers, and endusers.

In the project team, the following groups of people with complementary skills will work together to implement the data warehouse.

- The data capture group is experienced in the management and maintenance of production systems and understands the rules that drive the business. They will determine the relevant data sources and analyze them in depth.

- The database design group specializes in the design and management of different types and sizes of databases. They decide on the necessary data transformation and integration and create the metadata. They are at the core of the data warehouse model. They create it physically and populate it.

The Endusers

Very few business people want to become relational database experts. In order to satisfy endusers' requests for ease of use and autonomy, companies need to implement a front-end tool that will associate common business terms with a combination of data definitions, allowing endusers to use the product rapidly, without extensive training. Endusers also need a powerful and robust solution that will provide unlimited flexibility, even for the most complex queries.

In addition to accessing data, users want to analyze trends, manipulate data, and present it in a meaningful manner. The front-end solution therefore has to provide them with an integrated environment for analysis and reporting.

Implementation for the MIS Department

Architectural fit is an important consideration for the MIS. The data warehouse itself must fit into the existing data processing environment, and the *decision-support* solution must in turn fit into the data warehouse.

Ease of use is an important consideration. The easier it is to implement the front-end tool, the more resources can be allocated to the rest of the data warehousing project. The front-end solution must also allow MIS to implement access controls and limitations in order to avoid runaway queries and other enduser-related problems that could affect the system.

The solution also has to be flexible enough to change with the continuously evolving data warehouse architecture.

FACTORS FOR SUCCESS

For a data warehouse to be truly effective, corporate goals need to be clear, specific, and detailed. The definition of an implementation plan is crucial. Without such a plan, every department will build its own information access environment, resulting in a series of data warehouses that will be unable to communicate with each other.

For most organizations, the challenge is in justifying a data warehouse implementation because it is a long-term approach. As data warehouses require new processes and multidisciplinary skills, corporate management has to be ready to endorse the necessary cultural changes.

A Successful Pilot

Like every other new technology, a data warehouse needs to be well planned and thoroughly set up and cannot be implemented in a few weeks. The required expertise, the potential complexities of working with several new technologies simultaneously, and the amount of data that has to be considered must not be underestimated. In order to be successful, companies have to target a specific area that is best suited for an initial data warehouse pilot and match the project against measurable success factors. They will have to adopt an iterative approach where they will gradually build up the amount of data stored in a data warehouse.

Building for the Future

In order to optimize the data warehouse for the future, it has to be flexible, scalable, and modular enough to be able to grow and evolve.

Data volumes can also vary from one department to another, from tens of megabytes to hundreds of terabytes. Implementing multiprocessing and parallel software and hardware technologies as part of the data warehousing solution allows companies to answer these needs in a cost-effective manner. The front-end solution, as well, needs to be able to integrate into new data processing environments with more users and provide the robustness to access large volumes of data and perform complex queries.

Successful Information Access

The goal of a data warehouse is to provide the largest number of business people with an optimized environment for *decision support*. The front-end solution is the most visible part of the infrastructure and directly affects the acceptance of the data warehouse environment within the user community. If the chosen solution does not provide endusers with timely and independent information access, analysis, and reporting, the data warehouse will not be effectively used.

Thus the front-end tool selection is a very strategic step in setting up the data warehouse environment. Each tool should be carefully analyzed using common data warehouse selection criteria such as the following.

Enduser-Oriented Data Representation

Users access the data warehouse via GUI-based (Graphical User Interface) productivity tools. Many types of tools can be provided to users of the data warehouse. These may include query software, report generators, On-Line Analytical Processing (OLAP), mining tools, and so forth, depending on the types of users and their particular requirements. No one tool can address all requirements.

In order for the data stored in a data warehouse to become useful information, endusers must be able to access the data themselves. A critical part of that access is the data representation, or metadata. Rather than force the endusers to understand complex relational database terminology and technology, the underlying complex data should be represented in simple business terminology. As the data warehouse itself is usually subject oriented, the closer the ties between this data representation and the data warehouse subjects, the easier it will be for endusers to access the information using their own, everyday concepts.

Powerful and Reliable Query Technology

Once endusers have access to the data warehouse information, they will want to create a large variety of queries, ranging in size and complexity. The query technology must not only be robust enough to handle very large and complex queries, but it must also be flexible enough to guarantee that any query will return correct results, regardless of the query elements.

A Scalable Solution

Data warehouses are not static environments; as the organization grows and changes, so does the data warehouse. All components of the data warehouse model must be scalable to respond to this change, including the data access solution. The endusers will not tolerate outdated data representation models or wait weeks or months for new information to become available. Similarly MIS cannot afford to spend hours or days updating the data representation each time the database changes. A true information access solution must be able to respond to database evolution by providing quick and easy ways to update and distribute the data representation model.

The Computing Environment

A key idea behind the enterprise data warehouse is that it does not impose hardware or software restrictions but allows the use of any combination of tools and platforms in a client/server environment. In order for the information access solution to fit in this model, it must be able to operate on and with a wide variety of hardware platforms and databases. The information access solution must also be able to accommodate large organizations and large data warehouses spanning hundreds of users.

By providing endusers with a dedicated *decision-support* environment, corporations can reduce or eliminate report backlogs, enhance decision making, and make significant gains in MIS productivity and data processing costs.

Data Warehouse (Platform)

The platform for the data warehouse is most often a relational database server. When very large volumes of data must be handled, either a cluster configuration of Symmetrical Multiprocessor (SMP) UNIX servers or a specialized Massively Parallel Processor (MPP) server is required.

The integrated/transformed data extracts are loaded into the data warehouse. The choice of platform is critical. The warehouse will grow and one must understand the requirements three to five years down the road. Many organizations pick a platform for various reasons willy-nilly. One of the biggest mistakes organizations make in platform selection is that they assume the system (hardware and/or DBMS) will scale with the data.

The warehouse system fulfills queries passed to the data by the user's data-access software. Although a user visualizes queries in terms of a GUI, queries typically are formulated as SQL requests because SQL is a universal language and the de facto standard for acccss to data.

Administration Tools

Although the data warehouse environment is aimed at allowing endusers to perform their own querying, reporting, and analysis, the MIS staff must be equipped with the proper tools to manage this environment. They must be able to set up and deploy the solution easily from a central point using existing connectivity, maintain strict control over who has access to what data, and ensure that servers, networks, and local machines do not become saturated by runaway queries.

Integrated Reporting and Analysis Tools

While having access to the information in the data warehouse is a prime concern, the enduser will also need to analyze and report on the information. They will most likely need to perform several queries and analyze each data set before arriving at the final information they are looking for. During this iterative process, the enduser should not be forced to use outside tools or resources each time the user wishes to build a new report or analyze a different data set. Therefore, the information-access solution must be fully integrated and interoperable with a complete set of reporting and analysis tools.

SUMMARY

We have discussed the second wave of information technology playing a primary role in the advent of the information age. This has pushed the data warehouse to the forefront of the MIS departments' agenda as the supporting infrastructure for the corporate decision-making process. Reorganizing corporate information for the data warehouse presents an ideal, once-only opportunity to get the database house in order and to dump any unneeded data. All organizations should be glad of this opportunity for increasing the amount of information available to the corporate decision makers while removing unwanted and costly data.

Improved technologies have been the major factor in the current rebirth of the data warehouse. The underlying improvements—parallel databases and their tighter integration with parallel hardware platforms—provide the train of thought processing required. GUI tools enable powerful and intuitive queries to be run against large data sources. Connectivity through middleware enables heterogeneous databases to be connected together to provide a single view. Significantly reduced storage costs enable massive data stores.

The key difference between the operational and the data warehouse environment is that operational data is optimized for transactional processing whereas warehouse data is optimized for query processing. This principle has prompted a database war between relatively new query-optimized databases and the more established relational technologies. Some suggest that the traditional RDBMS is designed for high-volume transaction processing and is not suitable for the data warehouse, which requires a query-optimized and high-performance engine. On the other hand, the proponents of relational technologies are discouraging corporations from buying yet another DBMS, requiring further skills and increased management.

Data warehouse design is based on iterative prototyping, in view of the fact that most organizations require feedback loops with users to provide input for design throughout the initial stages. A successful data warehouse project will depend on the initial design being *scalable* and *flexible*. The evidence from early projects has shown that the only certainty in data warehousing projects is that they will *grow*.

Organizations with the intention of stepping down the data warehousing path will require significant foresight. The *process* is immature and there is a steep learning curve; this is not downsizing or client/server revisited. Data warehousing is the most significant trend to emerge in MIS for a decade, presenting compelling arguments for all corporations to move beyond using MIS purely for automation.

Faster transaction execution means competitive advantage and faster query transaction execution also means competitive advantage. Production systems and query systems are distinct types of systems with different data needs and different resource requirements. Their development needs to be planned separately Production data feeds query systems. There may be many components required to build a comprehensive query environment for an organization. Few, if any, software products provide a complete solution.

Query-based systems need to be developed in an incremental manner because requirements cannot be firmly determined ahead of time.

12

MANAGING THE GROWING DATA WAREHOUSE

INTRODUCTION

A data warehouse is necessary to effectively manage the information base of a large corporation. The design goal of a data warehouse is to consolidate business-analysis data and set it aside in a high-performance relational DBMS with flexible data access from a variety of platforms. Locating the data to put into a warehouse can be a difficult process as older, inadequately documented production systems must be searched and data extracted and relocated as needed.

      Microsoft's ODBC and other standards have simplified connectivity between front-end and back-end tools but do not resolve all compatibility problems. The data warehouse back end is usually a high-performance RDBMS that supports complex queries, analytic processing, and large amounts of data. Front-end tools run on a variety of desktop platforms to give users easy access to information.

The issues surrounding the management of a data warehouse are some of the most challenging subjects facing an organization. The sources of information which reside on the data warehouse cross vertical and horizontal business partitions, such as finance and the sales order processing, each of which probably has their own budget and staff. It can prove to be a major challenge for organizations to obtain the necessary data-access rights to source the data warehouse. The need to utilize the data from many disparate sources means that without adequate high-level management backing, the project is doomed to failure before it has begun.

Keeping a data warehouse in order takes more than a conscientious system administrator. Beyond managing the integrity, flow, validity, and usefulness of the data collected, loaded, and extracted, organizations need to make sure that they are appropriately structured to support the building, management, and maintenance of the warehouse. This takes more than an occasional upgrade or once-a-year spring cleaning. Roles and responsibilities of the warehouse management team must be clearly defined and the ground rules for warehouse use must be explained to and understood by the business users and then supported by warehouse management personnel.

The commitment to *staffing* the warehouse team must match or exceed the original commitment it took to build it. Although most organizations with a data warehouse in place today built it themselves, supplementing their efforts with consulting help, the maintenance and support of the data warehouse inevitably becomes the responsibility of the organization itself.

A warehouse that is easy to maintain and able to mature with the business doesn't just happen—it must be designed that way. During the requirements, architectural design, and construction phases of the warehouse, skills can be developed that enable the support team to move to a level of independence and self-assurance sufficient to support the day-to-day operation and the never-ending evolution of the data warehouse.

A recent client survey indicates that a majority of the enterprises are moving toward full data warehousing strategies compared with only a handful a few years ago. If this is the case, the subject of managing information in a warehouse environment is a critical issue. To some degree the rise of data warehousing is seen by many as the justification to migrate to client/server computing.

Most people can remember the claims made only a few years ago about the effectiveness of client/server as to how it would revolutionize the organizations that took it on board. Well, it certainly caused revolutions in some of those organization where the attempt to downsize mainframe applications failed in spectacular and costly fashion. But the belief is that data warehousing and the advent of more effective middleware, faster databases, high communications bandwidth, and, most significantly, data bridging management software can solve these problems.

IMPLEMENTATION AND MAINTENANCE

The implementation and maintenance of a data warehouse are formed from a series of complex tasks. One of those tasks involves the bridging of data from one location to another, perhaps even correcting and validating the data en route. It is this continual process of updating the warehouse where most of the operational problems are going to occur.

The processes involved in the bridging of data from one location to another into the data warehouse include the following steps:

1. *Data retrieval*—data must be obtained from the operational databases. Generally most involve a heterogeneous set of databases from which the data must be extracted.

2. *Consolidation*—the merging of the various data sets in one master data set. This often involves the standardization of data types and fields.

3. *Scrubbing*—the data is cleaned to remove any inconsistencies or inaccuracies (where possible) in the data. This is perhaps one of the most challenging aspects of a data warehouse.

4. *Summarizing*—elements of the resulting data need to be intelligently summarized in order to obtain a reasonable response time

5. *Forming* a query.

6. *Updating repository*—the repository should be kept up to date with any new data definitions, that is, the metadata should be current and consistent.

7. *Periodic* or *trickle feed update*—the data in the warehouse quickly becomes out of date if new operational data in not added at regular intervals.

ESTABLISHING THE RIGHT ENVIRONMENT

There are three critical technical elements that must be in place within the warehouse's technical architecture: a metadata strategy, the right warehousing tools, and the teams to manage it. Inappropriate architectures, lack of metadata, inefficient, non-integrated tools, or poorly managed environment are guaranteed to create frustrations and inefficiencies.

The Case for Metadata Repository

The heart of a data warehouse architecture is that metadata repository. It is fed from several different sources and provides a window to the warehouse. Where the data resides, who owns the data, what the business rules associated with that data are, what security issues are addressed, and so forth, are some of the characteristics that must always be remembered. The metadata repository makes the whole warehouse environment usable because without it, when the warehouse starts to grow, it becomes ineffective. A well-developed metadata repository integrated with the various tools and an efficient infrastructure definitely contribute to the warehouse's success.

The Importance of Integrated Tools

All data warehousing projects integrate data across the enterprise. The second level of integration comes at the tool level. Warehousing tools today are rarely integrated. Depending on the architecture, warehouse maintenance can be manageable or totally impossible. Maintenance has to be architected from the beginning or the warehouse initiative is guaranteed to fail.

The Technology and the People

Once a technological foundation that is built around metadata and integrated warehousing tools exists, there are numerous cultural and environment issues to address. These *people* issues can just as strongly impact whether the data warehouse becomes the organization's biggest asset or worst nightmare.

The cultural issues center around the shift from structured application development, most often done in a controlled mainframe environment, to a non-structured environment that is client/server, iterative, fast paced, and parallel. In this environment, individuals are empowered and given more creative—though not totally—free rein. Supporting the data warehousing staff with the right training, consulting help, motivation, and definition of roles and responsibilities can help ensure a smooth transition.

The skills sets and job responsibilities necessary to maintain the warehouse are varied and complex. Likewise, they must be coupled with tools and methodologies that are sometimes experimental and are often introduced to an uninitiated team. Supporting the warehouse also requires a fundamental change in mindset and values, moving from a mainframe-centric environment to the world of client/server, from controlled access to free-form access, from limited distribution to broad access, and from structured applications to ad hoc access in an unstructured environment.

Challenges to DBAs

There are different ways of designing databases because of the advent of the warehouse. As we know, usually the database administrators are concerned with designing a database, a technical function. However, now because we have the individual users going against data that comes from a common source, we normalize the data, and then we turn around and denormalize it. So that goes against the grain of traditional DBAs.

Another challenge to DBAs is embracing data redundancy. With the warehouse environment, there is a lot of data redundancy; that is OK because it is read-only and it is for *decision support.*

The Team

To help foster this new mindset quickly, organizations should make a point of selecting the best and the brightest of the organization for the warehouse team. These individuals may come from different disciplines, such as business analysis, data modeling, data administration, applications development, enduser support.

No matter where the resources come from, keeping the group focused and motivated is also important. Most organizations agree that motivating the warehouse team is not a difficult task. The chance to work with emerging technology is often enough to keep the creative energy strong.

The warehouse project is considered one of the most interesting projects. It is leading-edge technology, and even though there's no end, because the warehouse keeps on growing, each population project is different. This is the project with the latest technology, and that is what most *motivated* people want to work with.

Team Roles and Responsibilities

Proper training, mentoring, planning, motivation, organization, and patience can help ensure that the data warehousing team is positioned to provide the highest level of support, thereby returning the highest return on the investment to the organization. Even with this support, if roles, responsibilities, and organizational structure are not clearly defined, disaster can lurk just over the horizon.

The organization and makeup of the data warehousing team can be configured in numerous ways depending upon the organizational processes, management structure, and distribution of resources. Whether the groups number two, three, five, or more also depends upon the size of the organization and the warehouse. Regardless of size and structure, there are a number of key groups that must be included to ensure adequate and broad-based support. These groups include

- Executive sponsors
- Business analysts
- Enduser support
- Technical support
- Management information system

Each one of these groups plays a pivotal role in each phase of the warehouse development, implementation, and maintenance. And because a data warehouse is never finished, these roles do not stop and start. They continue throughout the life of the warehouse.

Executive Sponsors

The most important role in managing the warehouse is truly and simply project leadership. Sponsorship at the executive level is one type of leadership that is necessary to make the warehouse a priority within the organization. Project management of the warehouse team is also needed to ensure the warehouse is aligned with the business needs and to develop project plans to support the warehouse as it matures.

Business Analysts

A critical role, and the team that initiates the warehouse project, are the business analysts. This group is usually responsible for identifying and defining the purpose and target user group for the warehouse and ensuring that the warehouse meets the strategic objectives of the business. Business analysts help gather upfront requirements for the warehouse to save time redefining and redocumenting the effort later.

It is up to the business analysts to ensure that the data warehouse project starts off on the right foot—that the organization is undertaking the effort for the right reasons and that the warehouse can actually fulfill the needs of the business and still be manageable. Analyzing how the warehouse meets the business objectives early on is critical to preventing the warehouse from growing out of control.

Enduser Support

The investment in people, technology, and data can all be wasted if data is not delivered to the people who need it to drive, manage, and measure the organization. It can be further reinforced with

- *Training and Support*: To truly empower users, they must have the tools and the training to realize their potential.
- *User Groups*: Once empowered, users often band together to form user groups and learn from one another. It is a vehicle for the people using the data warehouse to communicate their problem areas, as well as some enhancements that they would like to see. It is a chance for the users to get some education on tools and a chance for MIS staff to hear the concerns about the data warehouse and directions directly from the endusers. Keeping the channels of communication open is important.

Technical Support

Following requirements gathering, the technical and data architectural support requirements must be defined. The skills required to construct these architectures generally come from different skill sets, backgrounds, and disciplines. In addition to the business requirements, detailed data requirements should be fleshed out before the technical details are defined. Data collection rates, volumes, and timing from every point to point in the warehouse dictate the network capacity, transfer rates, storage volumes, and growth rate of the warehouse. The data architectures usually dictate each of these factors.

Data collection, transformation, distribution, and loading must be logically defined by the data architecture team. This group must also possess the skills and experience to define the data models that form the basis of the data warehouse. The initial data model, which supports the business requirements, continues to evolve as legacy application data is mapped to the physical model during the pilot phase of the warehouse and continuously changes with modifications and mapping that occur during the warehouse life cycle.

Management Information Systems

Resources from network services, operations, database administration, and application systems must go beyond defining the initial technical architecture and play an active role in expansion, maintenance, and support of the warehouse. The issues in this realm are large and complex. Multiple vendors are brought together in every facet of information technology to build and support the data warehouse, which is testing the limits of tools on every front.

- *Database Administration*: The size of databases has quickly moved from hundreds of gigabytes to the multiple-terabyte range. The stress on the technology is often transferred to the Database Administration (DBA) staff. The DBA's skills and techniques are being tested along with the tools. Techniques in distribution, security, segmentation, array processing, and other techniques that improve performance at all levels are required to meet demands. If that's not enough, issues of security loom heavy on the minds of data warehousing support teams.

- *Configuration and Network Management*: The level of complexity is not isolated to the databases and the server hardware alone but also spans the desktop environment. The Internet also brings the ability to integrate many diverse systems and media forms. Configuration and network management are essential to consistently control the multitude of platforms.

Foundation for Success

Although an entire foundation must be set in order to construct and manage the warehouse, organizations who have done it successfully say the warehouse can return enormous value to the organization in a relatively short time.

If the data warehouse is properly constructed, with attention paid to metadata and integrated tools, and is then supported by a capable warehouse management team with clearly delineated and documented roles and responsibilities, it becomes the single most important tool within the organization.

KEY ISSUES IN MANAGING A DATA WAREHOUSE

By implementing data warehouses, MIS departments have quickly discovered that their backlog of requests for information, reports, and applications from business units falls dramatically. This saves critical manpower resources and keeps hundreds of other operational applications running.

These benefits, of course, do not underplay the issues involved in managing a data warehouse. It is likely to involve integrating dozens of application systems. But when you consider that an organization is typically sitting on five to ten years of detailed transactional data, rich in its potential for guiding the organization to future success, the business benefits really add up by:

- Giving business units more direct, fast, and convenient access to the data they need.
- Supporting new product developments and innovative marketing strategies.
- Adapting to the constant changes within the business structure.

Manageability Issues

In spite of the many benefits from data warehousing, first-generation data warehouses have exposed many issues and challenges in effectively delivering the significant benefits that they promise. Some of these issues are present in all data warehouses, although many are aggravated as the data warehouse grows in size and complexity. Key among these issues are manageability and operational issues. Following are some key issues:

- How to tune a data warehouse for performance without impacting saved queries and *decision-support* applications.
- How to build the large summary tables necessary for data warehouse performance without impacting the availability of the warehouse.
- How to effectively manage security in a large-scale warehouse environment.
- Ease-of-use issues, such as, how to make warehouses easy to use for non-technical users.
- Flexibility of ad hoc queries while avoiding heavy resource expenditures in application development.
- How do users quickly and easily determine what information is available in one or more data warehouses?
- How do users determine the precise meaning of data?

Factors for Data Warehousing Success

Data warehousing is indispensable for business management since this strategy supports the creativity and individuality of decision makers throughout the enterprise. The following checklist can assist in meeting some of these priorities and objectives.

The Organizational Priorities

- State the corporate goals and vision.
- Understand the business areas, processes, and units within the organization.
- Prioritize these business areas in terms of the desired positive impact and contribution to corporate goals and vision.

- List the key topics/subjects that best represent this business area (product, customer, quality, sales, marketing, manpower, etc.).
- List those competitors, suppliers, or targeted companies that excel in this area.

The Business Priorities

Data warehousing is aimed specifically at business experts and knowledge workers within the organization. The key to success is working closely with the data warehousing project, from management to organization to exploitation. This assists in identifying, planning, and gaining immediate benefit from a data warehouse. To reinforce the process, the following priorities should be taken into account:

- Thoroughly review and document the reasons.
- Investigate similar data warehousing successes at other companies.
- Make sure the sponsor is comfortable with the project.
- Choose members for the project team who have expertise in the area.
- Write a data warehousing mission statement that incorporates the stated goals.
- Have constant review meetings with members of the team.
- Reevaluate the situation and iteratively extend the data warehouse as needed.

The Operational Priorities

Once the operational systems are in place, they will continue to be optimized. This goal is best achieved through data warehouse modeling, since it puts usable decision-making tools in the hands of knowledge workers without affecting the performance of critical operational systems.

MANAGING THE DATA WAREHOUSE

As with DBMSs, the data warehouses need to provide adequate management tools. These include the ability to

- Ensure data warehouse integrity through backup and restore capabilities.
- Establish standards, procedures, and protocols.
- Monitor the heterogeneous network environments.
- Minimize overhead.
- Measure usage.
- Maintain one or more metadata repositories.
- Provide user security at multiple levels.
- Limit resource usage based on user privileges.
- Tune databases for optimum performance.
- And so on.

All major relational engines provide a full suite of data, performance, and security management utilities, which can be extended to the data warehouse.

Establish Standards, Procedures, and Protocols

Since there are numerous local RDBMSs which support the SQL standard for data access, data subsets can easily be downloaded into a variety of engines for local, unattached processing.

Some databases do not support industry-standard SQL interfaces for data access. Rather, they each have their own, proprietary data access APIs. As long as the SQL standard is not supported, proprietary, engine-specific data-access and analysis tools must be utilized.

Performance scalability, the ability to support a multitude of data-access paths, the ability to leverage standard data-access tools, and support for multidimensional data views make relational databases the preferred choice for enterprise-wide *decision-support* implementations.

Maintain Metadata

Metadata is the nerve center of the data warehouse environment. The infrastructure of metadata is complex because it serves several agendas at the same time. In order to successfully manage and maintain metadata, the metadata manager must recognize the need for metadata to be shared across different environments.

The metadata architecture is complex and requires implementation over multiple technologies, especially in heterogeneous environments. However, it is only through metadata that there are uniformity and cohesion between different components of the enterprise data warehouse.

Central Repository

All metadata is collected in a central location and is managed in a (hopefully) single repository and therefore, a high degree of sharability can be achieved. On the other hand, centralized management of a broad and complex metadata infrastructure may prove to be unworkable. While some metadata does need to be collected and managed centrally, many components of metadata may not belong in a centralized repository environment. In addition, the enterprise's distributed environment may not support centralization of such a repository.

Decentralized Repository

Metadata is created and controlled throughout the architected infrastructure in many small and local environments. In such an environment, there is no uniformity, sharability, or exchange of metadata. While each local environment is satisfied with its own needs and goals, there is no cohesion between the environments or the enterprise as a whole.

Shared Environments

Metadata is definitely useful in the operational world. But it is much more practical in the *decision-support* world. Since metadata is the place where the search for new information begins, metadata becomes the nerve center of a *decision-support* system.

The above approaches need to have their best benefits woven into a unified infrastructure for the benefit of the enterprise. The data marts or OLAP environments require their own metadata. All of the metadata at the data mart level, like the metadata at the data warehouse level, can be shared. The data mart level is designed to suit the needs of a given department, whereas the data warehouse metadata is designed to support the needs of the entire enterprise. Once the data passes from the data mart to the workstation, the metadata is passed as well.

Securing the Warehouse

A tremendous amount of effort is spent to build a data warehouse. But, no thought of security is given until after the warehouse has been in operation for a while. However, in some of the implementations, security has become an issue and must be addressed early during the modeling and design phases. There can be a strong case made for security in the database environment, especially in the areas of medical, financial, and personnel records, among others.

It is the responsibility of the design team and the enterprise's security administrator to recognize these needs. It saves the organization many future problems if the security is designed early into the model and the administrators are proactive in securing the sensitive data in the warehouse.

Since the data warehouse may be integrated into the existing operational data infrastructure and the existing DBMSs, the security requirements may vary. One option is to use the existing security functions of the DBMS to grant different privileges to different users. The DBMS security is designed for the operational environment, where the users are allowed to update records in place. Since the data warehouse is a read-only environment, none of the endusers should be granted the right to perform any sort of updates or select table data indiscriminately.

Some installations partition sensitive data into separate sets of tables and only a select group of users can access these tables. This facilitates the use of native DBMS security features to prevent unauthorized access to sensitive data in the warehouse. Even though it is relatively simple to separate the sensitive data, many times some non-sensitive data must be redundantly stored with it.

For a very low level of security, it is necessary to store the encrypted data in the data warehouse. This data can only be accessed by an authorized user who has the decryption key. Various levels of encryption authorizations can be granted to users:

- View only by authorized users.
- View only by the authorized users but there is protection from unauthorized copying. The enduser still needs the decryption routine to view it.

- Protection from unauthorized access during transmission without the decryption key.

From the management point of view, numerous security functions must be built into the data warehouse. Some of these are

- Classification of sensitive data.
- Level of security.
- The selection of endusers and matching them to functions if it is a central data warehouse.
- Selection of the data to be encrypted.
- Selection of the encryption/decryption algorithms.
- Authorization criteria: user name, user ID, and/or workstation ID.
- Audit trails and criteria.
- And so forth.

Security is an important management function and must be carefully designed and not be an afterthought.

Monitor the Network

With most *decision-support* systems, the access to the warehouse will come from a variety of users in a variety of environments. Provisions must be made to manage these network environments and the data warehouse architecture should consciously be planned to extend with time.

Minimize Overhead

Relational DBMS products are used for the bulk of data warehouse applications. These products are well suited to data warehousing's data characteristics (static and long living), access requirements (aggregated sets of complexly qualified data), and design flexibility (segregation of logical/physical models). But it's difficult to build a generic DBMS product that serves both the warehouse and operational users effectively. Features tend to benefit one side while adding to the complexity, cost, or inefficiency for the other.

There already are vendors in the warehouse-only niche who stress the obvious advantages of a product that eliminates the features and overhead deemed unnecessary for warehouses. Simpler products should cost less and run faster. The obvious disadvantage is that a company must develop and retain technical skills in different DBMSs, and history has shown that effectively managing one DBMS is plenty complicated.

Measure Usage

In OLTP systems, this was never an issue. Usage/access paths in an OLTP environment are very well known, and applications can therefore be hard coded to use particular data structures every time. In *decision support*, the usage is very unstructured. The users often decide what data to analyze moments before they request it. If users have to give more thought as to how to get at their data than they give to what data they want to see, then their *decision-support* environment is inadequate.

Performance and Tuning

Under normal circumstances, data warehousing is the process of integrating enterprise-wide corporate data into a single repository from which endusers can run reports and perform ad hoc data analysis. Because of the enormous quantities of information available to companies, data warehouses often grow to be very large. As a result, one of the most significant challenges of implementing a data warehouse model is ensuring high performance.

Traditional entity-relationship data models function effectively in the OLTP world, driving most of today's operational, RDBMS-based applications. Because of the success of these data models, the first graphical DSS systems were implemented using similar designs. As these DSS databases grew larger and more complicated, performance became poorer and systems became difficult to use and maintain.

Because data processing in OLTP systems is highly structured, complex data models can work well. Transactions generally involve only one or two tables at a time, and often deal with only a single record. This means that complex table relationships do not interfere a great deal with performance. In contrast, DSS processing can involve accessing hundreds of thousands of rows at a time. In such cases, complex joins can seriously compromise performance.

Aggregating in every possible combination achieves the best possible query performance but at tremendous storage, maintenance, and loading-time cost. First, storing summary information at every possible level consumes enormous amounts of disk space, increasing the storage requirements. Second, typical data warehouses have thousands of combinations of dimension elements, and creating a table or tables to hold the aggregates for all those combinations is an overwhelming maintenance task. Finally, building aggregates every time new information is added to the fact tables can become so time consuming and resource intensive that the load window required to make the warehouse operational may become unacceptably long.

Denormalization is a very effective method for simplifying data design and improving performance through the reduction of table joins. However, there are instances where the cost in disk storage may be too high. The performance gains and disk storage savings provided by snowflake designs are often worth the price of marginally higher complexity. However, the value of a snowflake join is greatest for dimensions in which

- There are tens or hundreds of thousands rows.
- There are many attributes stored at low levels of the dimension hierarchy, and disk space is a significant problem.

Performance tuning is highly complex and depends upon many factors, including the size of the data warehouse, the complexities of the queries, and overall design of the data warehouse model.

SUMMARY

Data warehousing clears the confusion created by data extraction and storage, replacing the traditional environment with a subject-oriented, designed environment. Through the interaction of software and hardware tools that have been customized for *decision support*, the data warehouse provides endusers with fast, corporate-wide information and allows decision makers to analyze market trends ahead of their competition.

Many data warehouses are far more complex than the examples presented here. A data warehouse project is more difficult to describe than to build. All you really need is an understanding of the business process, the discipline to keep the data model from expanding unnecessarily, and a few basics. A healthy byproduct of every project effort is a deeper and clearer understanding of the elements of your business.

Traditional data models function effectively in the OLTP world, driving most of today's operational, RDBMS-based applications. Because of the success of these data models, the first graphical *decision-support* systems are usually implemented using similar designs. As these *decision-support* databases grow larger and more complicated, performance becomes poorer and systems more difficult to use and maintain.

Although data warehousing clearly holds great potential for dramatic business benefit, the greater success depends on the business processes already in place. Although data warehouses share some key qualities with traditional development projects, the functional and technical requirements, especially, the demands of dynamic ad hoc queries, introduce a distinct series of challenges. Organizations contemplating data warehouses should be realistic about the challenges of a system with multiple moving targets, such as the user requirements, the software and hardware platforms, and the warehouse data contents.

The process of growing and extending a data warehouse is never ending, just as the organization never stops growing and changing. It is an interesting aspect of the data warehouse that it is never complete. Satisfying enduser needs is the key to success of a data warehouse undertaking.

Without adequate management and planning, an entire data warehousing process for any potentially successful project is doomed to fail. Expert guidance from those who have gained experience with a previous installation similar to the one envisaged by the implementers becomes an integral part of this process.

Data warehouses are not magic; they take a great deal of very hard work. In many cases data warehouse projects are viewed as a stopgap measure to get users off our backs or to provide something for nothing. But data warehouses require careful management. A data warehouse is a good investment only if endusers can actually get at vital information faster and cheaper than they can using current technology.

As a consequence, management has to think seriously about how they want their warehouses to perform and how they are going to get the word out to the enduser community. Management has to recognize that the maintenance of the data warehouse structure is as critical as the maintenance of any other mission-critical application. In fact, experience has shown that data warehouses quickly become one of the most used systems in any organization.

Management must also understand that if they embark on a data warehousing program, they are going to create new demands upon their operational systems: demands for better data, demands for consistent data, and demands for different kinds of data.

13

SUMMARY & CONCLUSIONS

The process of building a data warehouse is a long-term undertaking for any company.

INTRODUCTION

Today, business decision makers need answers to a host of questions that directly impact their ability to compete in the marketplace. To manage and use the information competitively, many companies are establishing *decision-support* systems built around a data warehouse. A data warehouse stores a company's operational and historical data in an integrated relational database for *decision-support* applications, business data access, and reporting.

Unlike operational software, which is designed for automating day-to-day operations, *decision-support* systems help management make better decisions by analyzing summarized snapshots of corporate performance. Traditional operational systems are very good at putting data into databases quickly, safely, and efficiently but are not very good at delivering meaningful analysis in return. As a result, the *decision-support* software segment is growing at a much faster rate than transactional operational software. The number of companies implementing data-warehouse-based *decision-support* systems is increasing at an alarming rate.

Data warehousing is not a product, but a strategy, one that recognizes the need to consolidate and separately store data in information systems dedicated to helping business professionals throughout the enterprise make faster and more effective decisions. This strategy should have only one goal: to improve the performance of the corporation.

MANAGING A DATA WAREHOUSE

Data warehousing is a marriage of a number of existing technologies and interests striving toward a new goal. Data warehousing is the complete package of hardware, software, data (and metadata), technologies, and services that enable an organization's decision makers to make better-informed decisions.

Data warehousing should exploit, integrate, and coexist with an organization's existing distributed environment infrastructure. The architecture and integrated tool set should be flexible enough to be customizable. The tools and products depend on the user involved and the sophistication of the analysis required. As data warehouses proliferate within an organization, one can envisage a distributed environment consisting of heterogeneous hardware and software products that are geographically distributed but interlinked to share relevant data.

The complexities of sustaining a distributed, dynamic environment in a cost-effective and robust manner are aggravated by the lack of pertinent standards, lack of skilled personnel, and the unreliability of hardware/software tools. Management disciplines such as security, operations, performance, configuration, change management, and fault/problem management add to this complexity because of the heterogeneity of resources, products, and vendors involved and the geographic distribution of resources to be managed.

Data warehousing factors that exacerbate the already complex issues of managing distributed environments include

- The handling of extremely large data volumes anticipated with data warehouses.
- The synchronization of processes and data between sources and targets on multiple distributed platforms.
- The implementation of security.
- Providing stable service levels and performance management.

Unless this complex environment can be managed in a cost-effective manner, data warehousing will not achieve its full potential within an organization.

DECISION SUPPORT

Many corporations have completed and operationalized their initial executive information and *Decision-Support* (DSS) applications with moderate success. Users have recognized the value of *decision-support* systems and are driving the demand for applications that span additional business functions and are deeper in scope than initial pilot applications. Lacking in many of these initial pilots is an architecture that integrates the relational data warehouse, metadata, and GUI development tools to provide both advanced DSS features and ease of application construction and maintenance requirements.

Without an architectural blueprint, it is nearly impossible to define and develop fundamental DSS objects which, when combined, provide a full complement of *decision-support* capabilities such as a *multidimensional* data views, *drill everywhere*, *data mining*, and *data surfing* for all data in the data warehouse.

The Impact of Decision-Support System Architecture

Decision-support systems have evolved from inflexible mainframe systems, to isolated PC tools, to client/server data dippers, and now, high-performance and extensible enterprise *decision-support* applications.

Today, business decision makers need answers to a host of questions that directly impact their ability to compete in the marketplace. They need clear and meaningful answers to hard, complex questions and they need them quickly. To manage and use the information competitively, many companies are establishing *decision-support* systems built around a data warehouse. A data warehouse stores a company's operational and historical data in an integrated relational database for *decision-support* applications, business data access, and reporting.

Unlike operational software, which is designed for automating day-to-day operations, *decision-support* systems help management make better decisions by analyzing summarized snapshots of corporate performance. Traditional operational systems are very good at putting data into databases quickly, safely, and efficiently but are not very good at delivering meaningful analysis in return.

As *decision-support* systems become more critical to corporate success, the users are beginning to work together as partners on design, deployment, and management. As a result, they can move from simply tapping data and making lists to performing complex analyses producing competitively useful information. The most successful systems have one thing in common—three-tier client/server architecture.

The ideal architecture consists of the components and technologies described in this book, each of which has a distinct purpose in the delivery of data. In order to effectively utilize existing data models and allow reengineering of inefficient models, this architecture should provide seamless access to existing, normalized data models and a variety of performance-optimized data models including consolidated, denormalized, and partitioned structures.

Such an architecture should also leverage metadata to facilitate application construction and minimize application redevelopment as additional data structures are added to the warehouse. It should also contain an engine which interprets analyst data requests and generates SQL queries to retrieve data from the warehouse. The engine should be capable of mathematically processing and cross-tabulating this data to provide the analyst with the exact data views required.

The data warehouse tools are the most visible part of the architecture. These should be constructed using an environment that supports the definition and use of complex criteria sets, the specification of data presentations and rotations, and the seamless integration of desktop personal productivity applications. These tools should also permit creation of agents that automate white-collar work by sifting through and analyzing data and taking actions such as updating transaction processing systems or sending electronic mail, or writing letters.

Decision-Support Applications and Tools

Information system developers have used a variety of tools to create these *decision-support* systems, including third-generation languages, 4GL application development tools, and Executive Information System (EIS) tools. These tools provide valuable application development functionality, but used outside the context of an integrated, *decision-support*-focused architectural framework, often lead to the development of data structure-specific, brittle applications that cut corners on desired functionality.

MIS managers looking to provide DSS applications should strive to revolutionize the delivery of *decision-support* solutions in the same way spreadsheets revolutionized business analysis. Until the release of PC-based spreadsheets such as VisiCalc and Lotus 1-2-3, which contained fundamental analytical objects, the developers were responsible for hand-programming each spreadsheet required by the business user. However, the developers too often must construct these business-oriented applications since corporations have not defined the architecture and the fundamental objects required for *decision support*.

On-Line Analytical Processing (OLAP) applications are an essential component of an enterprise data warehousing *decision-support* solution. OLAP defines a set of user-driven, functional requirements for planning, analysis, and management reporting applications.

In implementing a successful data-access strategy, it is important to recognize that there are appropriate and inappropriate ways to access data, depending on the nature and distribution of that data, as well as types of those applications requiring access to the data. As a result, today's business managers are often forced to spend more time navigating the myriad sources of enterprise data than they spend analyzing the information.

OPERATIONAL DATABASE VERSUS DATA WAREHOUSE

Data warehouses are being developed for the purpose of providing a framework in which to perform data mining, for the purposes of driving *decision-support* systems. The significance of data as a source, not just of operational strategy, has been the key driver in the concept of the data warehouse.

The data warehouse is a subject-oriented corporate database which deals with the problem of having multiple data models implemented on multiple platforms and architectures in the enterprise. What many corporate computer users understand is that the key to identifying corporate threats and opportunities lies locked in the corporate data which is often embedded in legacy systems on obsolescent technologies, and they realize that the businesses need to get at that data today. Many of the same issues that are addressed in distributed databases are also applicable to data warehouses.

The data warehouse is differentiated from an operational database in the following aspects. The data warehouse is

- Accessible to users who have a limited knowledge of computer systems or data structures.
- Subject oriented, most usually on the basis of the *customer*.
- To drive *decision support*.
- Entirely for the task of making data available to be interrogated by the business users.
- Primarily for the purpose of providing data that can be interrogated by business people to gain value from the information derived from daily operations.
- Time-stamped and associated with a defined period of time, that is, calendar periods or fiscal reporting periods.
- Interrogated on the basis of a standard enterprise model.

On the other hand,

- The operational database is used to process information that is needed for the purposes of performing operational tasks.
- The operational database is active for updates during all hours that business activities are executed, whereas the data warehouse is used for read-only querying during active business hours.

FACTORS FOR A SUCCESSFUL DATA WAREHOUSE

There is no magic formula for success, but avoid the classic pitfalls and you may dramatically improve your chances of profitable and long-lasting data warehousing implementations.

You can slap together a schema, build the tables, build the pointers, build a data warehouse, make all the right connections with the middleware, and still fail miserably. That is because the toughest data warehousing problems have nothing to do with the technology. They have to do with delivering value to the users, maintaining the data warehouse, and shifting from a transaction-processing to a *decision-support* mindset.

Through *rightsizing* and *organizational flattening*, more and more organizations are emphasizing data analysis and decision making. Decisions that formerly were the domain of executives and management are now distributed throughout the entire organization. And yet the information systems necessary to deliver the right data to this broader range of endusers has not been able to keep pace. A data warehouse must be designed to meet such requirements. The following factors should be considered prior to any data warehouse implementation:

- Explicitly define the set of business solutions to be achieved by the data warehouse. Provide a sample output desired and a description of possible business actions to be taken.
- Design the data warehouse. Use data-modeling techniques and design a data model that is appropriate for *decision support* by endusers.
- Determine what data is required in the data warehouse. This may include purchasing outside data to augment what is collected by internal operational systems.
- Determine the frequency at which new data will be added to the warehouse and estimate its size. Frequencies may be daily, weekly, monthly, and so on. Set realistic expectations on volumes of data that can be loaded at these times. Otherwise, the warehouse will be obsolete before it is implemented.
- Establish a measurement criteria for a successful implementation, such as performance characteristics, return on investment analysis, or improved management of a key business factors.
- Choose two or three front-end analysis tools.
- Pilot test the data warehouse with a subset of actual data. Make sure the pilot uses the same data as the eventual production system. This helps ensure all the correct data has been collected.
- Have endusers work with the pilot system for a period of time.
- Evaluate a short list of vendors against success criteria.
- Invest in education for client-server technology, networking, and UNIX.

SOME PRACTICAL IMPLEMENTATION ISSUES

Data warehouse updates are frequently quite large and are commonly on the order of tens of gigabytes and can affect millions of tuples in one or many tables. As new applications increase the size and frequency of updates, the servers will need to become adept in responding to quicker methods for updating the data.

Many steps are required to allow for updates of the data in the data warehouse from the data sources, and transforming the source data into a form suitable for storage can be a extremely expensive, especially if the extractor/translator resides on the server with the data warehouse.

All of the responsibilities of the translation of the data require careful load balancing of resources in order to successfully complete the update task. After the data has been translated into a form that the warehouse understands, the records must be filtered to reject invalid data and to ensure that integrity constraints are not violated. These writes must conform to physical storage configuration requirements. All records must be richly indexed to allow for optimized query response, and then, the metadata must be constantly updated to comply with the changing source data landscape.

In order to minimize elapsed time and fit into a short batch window, the (RDBMS) Relational Database Management System must effectively utilize all the system resources including being able to harness and apply the entire processing power of a large parallel processor system.

One of the most difficult areas that needs to be addressed is that of specialized recovery and restart techniques to support data warehouse updates. Efficiently maintaining referential integrity poses a serious challenge for vendors creating data warehouse servers.

Query Optimization

It is possible that a query may have to access millions or even billions of records and may involve computationally complex operations such as joins and/or nested subqueries. In these cases, the system must be able to respond in a manner appropriate to the application for which it was designed.

Many times, the response time is critical to the success or failure of a system based not on failure from a technical standpoint (i.e., the query correctly returned the desired data), but from a business standpoint. Current access methods need to be improved for applications which require computationally expensive operations on a regular basis.

The Importance of User Interfaces

Since one of the requirements of a data warehouse is that they be accessible to users who have a limited knowledge of computer systems or data structures, it is imperative that graphical, self-explaining tools that provide easy access to the warehouse, with little or no training, be available to the users when the system is deployed. It should not be the case that users need to know how to form complex structured queries in order for them to access the desired information.

FINALLY

Data warehouses are of great value to companies seeking to empower their knowledge workers in order to achieve competitive advantage. In spite of their many strengths, first-generation data warehouses may be difficult to use and expensive to maintain—especially as they grow in size and complexity.

Some warehouses provide robust middleware together with administrative and enduser tools to help make data warehouses easy to manage for administrators and easy to use for endusers. Each system is designed to ease the initial and ongoing need to update the warehouse effectively. The correct management of the flow of data into (and out of) the data warehouse will ensure that the best possible benefit can be drawn.

Taken as a whole, the decision-design system architecture should leverage the substantial, growing investments in SQL-compliant relational databases and off-the-shelf GUI development tools and incorporate a DSS-focused engine to provide analysts with a full complement of *decision-support* features.

Many business users see data warehousing as a way to facilitate the business analysis needs of decision makers. A data warehouse empowers decision makers with business information on their desktop, resulting in better decision making.

Through the data warehouse, a company can more easily take advantage of the value of information in order to make key business decisions and continually reshape its products and company to fit the changing dynamics of the global competitive market.

GLOSSARY

Access   The process of reading, seeking, or writing data on a storage unit.

Access Control   The path chosen by a database management system to retrieve the requested data. The process of limiting access to resources of a system only to authorized users, programs, processes, or other systems.

Access Method   A technique used to transfer a physical record from or to a secondary storage device.

Access Pattern   The general sequence in which the data structure is accessed, that is from record to record, from segment to segment, or from tuple to tuple.

Accuracy   A qualitative assessment or a qualitative measure of the error magnitude, expressed as a function of relative error.

Ad Hoc Processing   A casual access and manipulation of data on parameters never used before, usually in an iterative manner.

Ad Hoc Query   Any query that cannot be determined prior to the moment the query is issued. A query that consists of dynamically structured SQL, which is usually constructed by desktop-resident query tools.

Ad Hoc Query Tool   An enduser tool that accepts English-like or point-and-click request for data and constructs an ad hoc query to retrieve the desired results.

Administrative Data   In a data warehouse, the data that helps a warehouse administrator manage the warehouse. Examples of administrative data are user profiles and order history.

Aggregate Data   Data that is the result of applying a process to combine data elements; data that is taken collectively or in summary form.

Alert   A notification from an event that has exceeded a predefined threshold.

Analysis, Multidimensional   The objective of multidimensional analysis is for endusers to gain insight into the meaning contained in databases. The multidimensional approach to analysis aligns the data content with the analyst's mental model, hence reducing confusion and lowering the incidence of erroneous interpretations. It eases navigating the database, screening for a particular subset of data, asking for the data in a particular orientation, and defining analytical calculations. Furthermore, because the data is physically stored in a multidimensional structure, the speed of these operations is many times faster and more consistent than is possible in other database structures. This combination of simplicity and speed is one of the key benefits of multidimensional analysis.

Analytical Processing   Using the computer to produce an analysis for management decisions, usually involving statistical analysis, drill-down analysis, demographic analysis, and profiling.

Applets   An application interface where referencing (perhaps by a mouse click) a remote application as a hyperlink to a server causes it to be downloaded and run on the client.

ANSI   American National Standards Institute.

ANSI Standard   A document published by ANSI that has been approved through the consensus process of public announcement and review. Each of these standards must have been developed by an ANSI committee and must be revisited by that committee within five years for update.

Application   A group of algorithms and data interlinked to support a solution.

Application Advice   A transaction set that documents errors in the content of any transaction set beyond the normal syntax checks.

Application Database   A collection of data organized to support a specific application.

Archival Database   A collection of data containing data of a historical nature.

Array, Multidimensional   A group of data cells arranged by the dimensions of the data. For example, a spreadsheet exemplifies a two-dimensional array with the data cells arranged in rows and columns, each being a dimension. A three-dimensional array can be visualized as a cube with each dimension forming a side of the cube, including any slice parallel with that side. Higher dimensional arrays have no physical metaphor, but they organize the data in the way users think of their enterprise. Typical enterprise dimensions are time, measures, products, geographical regions, sales channels, and so forth. *Synonyms:* Multidimensional structure, cube, hypercube

ASCII   *American Standard Code for Information Interchange.* An 8-bit code for character representation; includes 7 bits plus parity attribute; a field represented by a column within an object (entity); an object may be a table, view or report. An attribute is also associated with an SGML(HTML) tag used to further define the usage.

Asynchronous Transfer Mode (ATM)   ATM is expected to be the primary networking technology to support multimedia communications. ATM has fixed length 53-byte messages (cells) and can run over any media with the cells asynchronously transmitted. Typically, ATM is associated with Synchronous Optical Network (SONET) optical fiber digital networks running at rates of OC-1 (51.84 megabits/sec), OC-3 (155.52 megabits/sec) to OC-48 (2,488.32 megabits/sec).

Atomic   Data stored in a data warehouse or the lowest entity.

Atomic-Level Data   Data elements that represent the lowest level of detail. For example, in a daily sales report, the individual items sold count as atomic data, while rollups such as an invoice or summary totals from invoices are aggregate data.

Atomic Database   A database made up of mostly atomic data; a data warehouse; a *decision-support* system foundation database.

Attribute   A property that can assume a value for entities or relationships. Entities can be assigned several attributes.

Audit Trail   The data that is available to trace activity. A chronological record of system activities that is sufficient to enable the reconstruction, review, and examination of the sequence of environments and activities surrounding or leading to an operation, a procedure, or an event in a transaction from its inception to final results.

Authentication   A mechanism which allows the receiver of an electronic transmission to verify the sender and the integrity of the content of the transmission through the use of an electronic key or algorithm which is shared by the trading partners. This is sometimes referred to as an electronic signature.

Authorization Request   A request initiated by a consumer to access data for which the consumer does not presently have access privileges.

Authorization Rules   Criteria used to determine whether or not an individual, group, or application may access reference data or a process.

Availability   A measure of the amount of time users have access to a working application. The availability of a business-critical function to everyone in the organization who needs it, when they need it, is a key measure of the successful implementation of an application.

Backup   A file serving as a basis for the activity of backing up a database. Usually a snapshot of a database at a specific time.

Backplane   The physical interconnect between the processors and memory. It contains the sockets into which the various boards are inserted. The system bus is carried between computing elements via the backplane.

Bandwidth   Maximum rate at which an interconnect (such as a computer system bus or network), can propagate data once the data enters the interconnect, usually measured in Mb/sec. The bandwidth can be increased by making the interconnect wider or by increasing the frequency of the interconnect so that more data is transferred per second. The communications capacity (measured in bits per second) of a transmission line or of a specific path through the network.

Base Tables   The normalized data structures maintained in the target warehouse database. This is also known as the detail data.

Batch   A computer environment in which programs access data exclusively, and user interaction is not allowed while the activity is occurring.

Batch Environment   A sequentially dominated mode of processing, against one or more databases.

Before Image   A snapshot of a record prior to update, usually recorded on an activity log.

Bidirectional Extracts   The ability to extract, clean, and transfer data in two directions among different types of databases, including hierarchical, networked, and relational.

Bitmap   A specialized form of an index indicating the presence or absence of a condition for a group of records or blocks.

Bitmapped Indexing   A family of advanced indexing algorithms that optimize RDBMS query performance by maximizing the search capability of the index per unit of memory and per CPU instruction. Properly implemented, bitmapped indices eliminate all table scans in query and join processing.

Blocking   Physically locating two or more records so that they can be accessed via a single address.

Braking Mechanism   A software mechanism that prevents users from querying the operational database once transaction loads reach a certain level.

Browser   A software application that is used to allow users to read an HTML document in a user-friendly readable format. Two well-known browsers are Mosaic and Netscape.

Bulk Data Transfer   A software-based mechanism designed to move large data files. It supports blocking and buffering to optimize transfer times.

Business Architecture   A business architecture describes the functions a business performs and the information it uses.

Business Data   Information about people, places, things, business rules, and events, which is used to operate business. It is not metadata.

Business Model   A view of the business at any given point in time. The view can be from a process, data, event, or resource perspective and can be the past, present, or future state of business.

Business Transaction   A unit of work acted upon by a data capture system to create, modify, or delete business data. Each transaction represents a single valued fact describing a single business event.

Cache   A buffer usually built and maintained at the device level. Retrieving data out of a cache is much quicker than retrieving data out of a cylinder. Because the speed with which CPUs access data is so crucial to system performance, adding a small amount of very fast memory close to each CPU yields increased performance. This fast memory holds copies of the most recently accessed data. It is called cache after the French "cacher," to hide. The workings of the caches are hidden from the software in many respects.

Cache Miss   When a processor does not find a needed data item in its cache, a cache miss is said to occur. A request to retrieve the data must then be issued to the next level cache or main memory. In the meantime, the processor stalls waiting for the request to complete. Cache misses are grouped into several categories, the first three of which occur in both single and multiprocessors. They are capacity miss, coherence miss, compulsory miss, and conflict miss.

Calculated Member   A calculated member is a member of a dimension whose value is determined from other members' values (e.g., by application of a mathematical or logical operation). Calculated members may be part of the OLAP server database or may have been specified by the user during an interactive session. A calculated member is any member that is not an input member.

Cardinality   A number of tuples or rows in a relation.

CASE   Computer-Aided Software Engineering.

Catalog   A component of data dictionary that contains a directory of its DBMS objects as well as attributes of each object.

CCITT   The former United Nations standards organization that recommended world-wide communications standards. Its official name was the Consultative Committee on International Telegraphy and Telephony. *See: ITU-TSS.*

Cell   A single datapoint that occurs at the intersection defined by selecting one member from each dimension in a multidimensional array. For example, if the dimensions are measures, time, product and geography, then the dimension members—Sales, January 1994, Potato Chip bags, and United States—specify a precise intersection along all dimensions that uniquely identifies a single data cell, which contains the value of potato chips sales in the United States for the month of January 1994.

Central Warehouse   A database created from operational extracts that adheres to a single, consistent enterprise data model to ensure consistency of *decision-support* data across the corporation. A style of computing where all the information systems are located and managed from a single physical location.

Change Data Capture   The process of capturing changes made to a production data source. It consolidates units of work, ensures that data is synchronized with the original source, and reduces data volume in a data warehouse environment.

Checkpoint   An identified snapshot of the database or a point at which a transaction against the database has been frozen.

Checkpoint/Restart   A means of restarting a program at some point other than the beginning—after a failure or interruption has occurred.

Children   Members of a dimension that are included in a calculation to produce a consolidated total for a parent member. Children may themselves be consolidated levels, which requires that they have children. A member may be a child for more than one parent, and a child's multiple parents may not necessarily be at the same hierarchical level, thereby allowing complex, multiple hierarchical aggregations within any dimension.

Ciphertext   Encrypted output of a cryptograph algorithm. Input to the decryption process.

Classic Data Warehouse Development   The process of building an enterprise business model, creating a system data model, defining and designing a data warehouse architecture, constructing the physical database, and populating the warehouse database(s)

Clear Text   Data in its original form. Input to the encryption process and output of the decryption process.

Client   A software application on your computer, which is used to extract or download some application, data, or service from a host system.

Client/Server   A distributed technology approach where the processing is divided by function. The server performs shared functions—managing communications, providing file, compute, or database services, and so on. The client performs individual user functions—providing customized interfaces, performing screen-to-screen navigation, offering help information, and so on.

Client/Server Architecture   A "networked" environment where a smaller system such as a PC interacts with a larger, faster system. This allows the processing to be performed on the larger system which frees the user's PC. The larger system is able to connect and disconnect from the client's in order to process the data more efficiently.

Cluster   A collection of interrelated whole computers (nodes) that are utilized as a single unified computing resource. The nodes of a cluster run independent copies of the operating system and application(s) but share other computing resources in common, such as a pool of storage.

CMOS   Complimentary Metal Oxide Semiconductor.

COBOL   Common Business Oriented Language.

Column Dimension   *See: Page Display.*

Combinatorial Explosion   The tendency of hypercubes to grow very quickly in size (number of member combinations) as dimensions, (and, to a lesser degree, members) are added to its structure.

Command and Control   This refers to the computer support decision-making environment used by military commanders and intelligence officers.

Commonality of Data   Similar or identical data that occurs in different applications or systems. The recognition and management of commonality data is the basis of physical database design.

Communications Integrity   An operational quality that ensures transmitted data has been accurately retrieved at its destination.

Compaction   A technique for reducing the number of bits required to represent data without losing the content of the data.

Combinatorial Explosion   The tendency of hypercubes to grow very quickly in size (number of member combinations) as dimensions, (and, to a lesser degree, members) are added to its structure.

Condensation   The process of reducing the volume of data managed without reducing the logical consistency of the data.

Consolidate   Multidimensional databases generally have hierarchies or formula-based relationships of data within each dimension. Consolidation involves computing all of these data relationships for one or more dimensions, for example, adding up all Departments to get Total Division data. While such relationships are normally summations, any type of computational relationship or formula might be defined. *Synonyms:* Rollup, Aggregate.

Contention   The condition that occurs when two or more programs try to access the same data at the same time.

Cooperative Processing   A style of computer application processing in which the presentation, business logic, and data management are split among two or more software services that operate on one or more computers.

Corporate Data   All the databases of the company. This includes legacy systems, old and new transaction systems, general business systems, client/server databases, data warehouses and data marts.

CPU   Central processing unit. A processor.

Copy Management   A process that takes all or a snapshot of data from a source environment and copies that data to a new target environment.

Currency Date   The date the data is considered effective.

DASD   Direct Access Storage Device.

Data   A recording of facts, concepts, or instructions on a storage medium for communication, retrieval, and processing.

Data Access Tools   An enduser oriented tool that allows users to build SQL queries by pointing and clicking on a list of tables and fields in the data warehouse.

Database   A collection of interrelated data stored according to a schema. A database can serve single or multiple applications.

Database Administrator (DBA)   The organizational function charged with the day to day monitoring and care of the databases.

Data Dictionary   A database about data and database structures. A catalog of data elements, containing their names, structures, and information about their usage. This can be used for a central location for metadata. A data dictionary concentrates on information relating to the data elements, databases, files, and programs of implemented systems. Many kinds of products in the data warehouse arena use a data dictionary, including database management systems, modeling tools, middleware, and query tools.

Data Mart   A subset of a data warehouse that focuses on one or more specific subject areas. The data is usually extracted from the data warehouse and further denormalized and indexed to support intense usage by targeted customers.

Data Visualization   Techniques for turning data into information by using the high capacity of the human brain to visually recognize patterns and trends. There are many specialized techniques designed to make particular kinds of visualization easy.

Data Directory   A collection of definitions, rules, and advisories of data, designed to be used as a guide or reference with the data warehouse. The directory includes definitions, examples, relations, functions and equivalents in other environments, such as ISIS, IFIS, PPS and DSE.

Database Key   A unique value that exists for each record in a database. The value is often indexed, although it may be random or hashed.

Data Element   The most elementary unit of information that can be identified and described in a dictionary or repository which cannot be subdivided.

Data Element Type   A data element may be one of six types: numeric, decimal, identifier, string, data, or time.

Data Extraction Software   Software that reads one or more sources of data and creates a new image of the data.

Data Flow Diagram   A diagram that shows the normal flow of data between services as well as the flow of data between data stores and services.

Data Fusion   A common command and control approach where the disparate sources of information available to a military or civilian commander or planner are integrated (or fused) together. Often, a GIS is used as the underlying environment.

Data Loading   The process of populating the data warehouse. Data loading is provided by DBMS-specific load processes.

Data Locality and Caching   A key to sequential parallel and distributed computing is data locality. This concept involves minimizing "distance" between processor and data. In sequential computing, this implies "caching" data in fast memory and arranging computation to minimize access to data not in cache. In parallel and distributed computing, one uses migration and replication to minimize time a given node spends accessing data stored on another node.

Data Management   Controlling, protecting, and facilitating access to data in order to provide information with timely access to the data users need.

Data Mapping   The process of assigning a source data element to a target data element.

Data Mining   Data mining is the process of sifting through large amounts of data content relationships. This also known as *data surfing*. A technique using software tools to search for particular patterns and trends.

Data Model   The logical data structure, including operations and constraints, provided by a DBMS for effective database processing. It is a system used for the representation of data. The model shows data elements grouped into records, as well as the association around those records.

Data Modeling   A method used to define and analyze data requirements needed to support the business functions of an enterprise. These data requirements are recorded as a conceptual data model with associated data definitions. Data modeling defines the relationships between data elements and structures.

Data Parallelism   A model of parallel or distributed computing in which a single operation can be applied to cell elements of a data structure simultaneously. Often, these structures are arrays.

Data Partitioning   The process of locally and/or physically partitioning data into segments that are more easily maintained or accessed. Current RDBMS systems provide this kind of distribution functionality. Partitioning of data enhances performance and utility processing.

Data Propagation The distribution of data from one or more source data warehouses to one or more local access databases.

Data Replication The process of copying a portion of a database from one environment to another and keeping the subsequent copies of the data in sync with the original source. Changes made to the original source are propagated and reflected in the copies of data in other environments.

Data Repository A database designed for storage of metadata and access by end-users and administrators.

Data Scrubbing The process of filtering, merging, decoding, and translating source data to create validated data for the data warehouse.

Data Segment A well-defined string of alternating data elements and data element separators. The electronic equivalent of a line item on a business form.

Data Store A place where data is stored: data at rest. A generic term that includes databases and flat files.

Data Structure A logical relationship among data elements that is designed to support specific data manipulation functions (lists, tables, and trees)

Data Surfing *See: Data Mining*.

Data Transfer The process of moving data from one environment to another. An environment may be an application or an operating system.

Data Transformation Creating "information" from data. This includes decoding production data and merging records from multiple DBMS formats. It is also known as data scrubbing or data cleansing.

Data Transport The mechanism that moves data from a source to target environment.

Data Warehouse An implementation of an informational database used to store sharable data sourced from an operational database of record. It is typically a subject database that allows users to tap into a company's vast store of operational data to track and respond to business trends and facilitate forecasting and planning efforts. It is a collection of integrated, subject-oriented databases designed to support the DSS function, where each unit of data is relevant to some moment in time. The data warehouse contains atomic data and lightly summarized data.

Data Warehouse Architecture An integrated set of products that enable the extraction and transformation of operational data to be loaded into a database for enduser analysis and reporting.

Data Warehouse Engine A collective term used for relational databases (RDBMS) and multidimensional databases. A data warehouse engine requires strong query capabilities, fast load mechanisms, and large storage requirements.

Data Warehouse Infrastructure A combination of and interaction of technologies that support a data warehousing environment.

Data Warehouse Management Tools   Software that extracts and transforms data from operational systems and loads it into the data warehouse.

Data Warehouse Network   An integrated network of data warehouses that contain sharable data propagated from a source data warehouse on the basis of user demand.

Database Schema   The logical and physical definition of a database structure.

DBMS   Database Management System.

Decentralized Database   A centralized database that has been partitioned according to a business or enduser defined subject area.

Decentralized Warehouse   A remote data source that users can query/access via a central gateway that provides a logical view of corporate data in terms that users can understand. The gateway parses and distributes queries in real time to remote data sources and returns result sets back to the users.

Decision Support   Data access targeted to provide the information needed by business decision makers. Examples include pricing, purchasing, human resources, management, manufacturing, and so on.

Decision-Support System (DSS)   A system used to support managerial decisions. The software that supports exception reporting, stop light reporting, standard repository, data analysis, and rule-based analysis. A database created for enduser ad hoc query processing.

Decompaction   The opposite of compaction.

Decryption   A process of transforming ciphertext into clear text for security or privacy reasons.

Delimiters   These consist of two levels of separators and a terminator. The delimiters are an integral part of the transferred data stream. Delimiters are specified in the interchange header and may not be used in a data element value elsewhere in the interchange. From highest to lowest level, the separators and terminator are segment terminator, data element separator, and subelement separator.

Denormalization   The technique of placing normalized data in a physical location that optimizes the performance of the system.

Dense   A multidimensional database is dense if a relatively high percentage of the possible combinations of its dimension members contain data values. This is the opposite of sparse.

Derived Data   The result of relating two or more elements of a single transaction or of relating one or more elements of a transaction to an external algorithm. This is also the data that is the result of a computational step applied to reference or event data.

Derived Members   Derived members are members whose associated data is derived data.

Desktop Applications   Query and analysis tools that access the source database or data warehouse across a network using an appropriate database interface. An application that manages the human interface for data producers and information consumers.

Direct Access   Retrieval or storage of data by reference to its location on a volume.

Direct Access Storage Device (DASD)   A data storage unit on which data can be accessed directly without having to traverse through a serial file such as a magnetic tape file. A disk unit is a direct access storage device.

Directory-Based Cache Coherency   A cache coherence mechanism that preserves data coherency by keeping the sharing status and location of each data block in one and only one place for each data block. The place the sharing status is kept is called a directory (or it may be distributed across several directories). The SCI standard implements directory-based cache coherency in a NUMA-Q machine. *Compare with: Snooping Cache Coherence.*

Direct Transmission   The exchange of data from the computer of the sending party directly to the computer of the receiving party. A third-party value-added service is not used in a direct transmission code.

Distributed Computing   The use of networked heterogeneous computers to solve a single problem. The nodes (individual computers) are typically loosely coupled.

Distributed Computing Environment   The OSF Distributed Computing Environment (DCE) is a comprehensive, integrated set of services that supports the development, use, and maintenance of distributed applications. It provides a uniform set of services, anywhere in the network, enabling applications to utilize the power of a heterogeneous network of computers.

Distributed Memory   A computer architecture in which the memory of the nodes is distributed as separate units. Distributed memory hardware can support either a distributed memory programming model, such as message passing, or a shared memory programming model.

Double-Click   A double-click of a mouse button consists of two closely spaced single clicks. A double-click often opens or displays the object selected.

Download   The stripping of data from one database to another based on the content of data found in the first database.

Drag   In describing the functions of a mouse, to drag means to place the mouse pointer over the object desired, click, and hold down the appropriate mouse button to move the object to its new location. When at the new location, the mouse button is released, and the object is dropped . In the text editing context, it is often used to select blocks of text which do not fall on word boundaries, or cover multiple lines.

DRAM   Dynamic Random Access Memory.

DRDA   Distributed Relational Database Architecture. A database access standard defined by IBM.

Drill-Down   The method of exploring detailed data that is used in creating a summary level of data. Drill-down levels depend on the granularity of data in the data warehouse.

DSS (Decision-Support System)   A system of applications that provides the ability to interrogate databases (external and/or internal) on an ad hoc basis, analyze information, and predict the impact of decisions before they are made. Single applications may support decision making; a DSS is a cohesive and integrated set of capabilities that share data and information.

DW   Data Warehouse.

DWA   Data Warehouse Administrator.

Dual Database   The practice of separating high-performance, transaction-oriented data from *decision-support* data.

Dumb Terminal   A device used to interact directly with the enduser where all the processing is done on a host or remote computer.

Dynamic Dictionary   A data dictionary that an application program accesses at run time.

Dynamic Queries   Dynamically constructed SQL that is usually constructed by desktop-resident tools. Queries that are not preprocessed and are prepared and executed at run time.

EEC   Encoded Error Correction.

EIS   Executive Information System.

E-mail   Electronic mail. Text messages sent from one person to another person, on the same or different computer systems. Systems at the same building or site may be connected together with a LAN, while systems at different sites are generally connected by a WAN.

Electronic Envelope   Catch-all term for the electronic address, communications transport protocols, and control information. It is the electronic analogy of a paper envelope, that is, a communications package.

Encoding   A shortening or abbreviation of physical representation of a data value.

Encryption   A process of transforming clear text into ciphertext for security or privacy reasons.

Enterprise   A complete business consisting of functions, divisions, or other components used to accomplish specific objectives and defined goals.

Enterprise Data   Data that is defined for use across a corporate environment.

Enterprise Modeling   The development of a common consistent view and understanding of data elements and their relationships across the enterprise.

Entity   A database object such as a table, view, report, or screen. A person, a place, or a thing of interest to the data modeler at the highest level of abstraction.

Event   A signal that an activity of significance has occurred. An event is noted by the information system.

Event Data   Data about business events that have historic significance or are needed for analysis by other systems. Event data may exist as atomic event data and aggregate data.

Executive Information System   Tools programmed to provide canned reports or briefing books to high-level executives. They offer strong reporting and drill-down capabilities. Such tools also allow ad hoc queries against multidimensional databases, and most offer analytical applications along functional lines such as sales or financial analysis.

Extensibility   The ability to easily add new functionality to existing services without major software rewrites or without redefining the basic architecture.

Extract   The process of selecting data from one environment and transporting it to another environment.

Extract Frequency   The latency of data extracts, such as daily versus weekly, monthly, annually, and so forth. The frequency that data extracts are needed in the data warehouse is determined by the shortest frequency requested through an order, or by the frequency required to maintain consistency of the other associated data types in the source data warehouse.

Failover Cluster   A cluster of computers with specialized software that automatically moves an active application(s) from one machine to the other in the event of an outage involving one node in the cluster.

Fiber Channel   A high-speed switched protocol for interconnecting computers and peripherals.

FIFO   A method of posting a transaction in first-in-first-out order. In other words, transactions are posted in the same order that the data producer entered them.

Filters   Saved sets of chosen criteria that specify a subset of information in a data warehouse.

Flat File   A collection of records containing no data aggregates, nested repeated data items, or groups of data items.

Foreign Key   A column or combination of columns in one table whose value(s) matches the primary key(s) in another table.

Formula   A formula is a database object, which is a calculation, rule, or other expression for manipulating the data within a multidimensional database. Formulae define relationships among members. Formulae are used by OLAP database builders to provide great richness of content to the server database. Formulae are used by endusers to model enterprise relationships and to personalize the data for greater visualization and insight.

Formula, Cross-Dimensional   Formula where all operands within a dimension are common, even in non-OLAP systems; for example, Profit = Sales Revenue − Expense might appear in a simple spreadsheet product. In an OLAP system, such a calculation rule would normally calculate Profit for all combinations of the other dimensions in the cube (e.g., for all Products, for all Regions, for all Time Periods, etc.) using the respective Revenue and Expense data from those same dimensions. Part of the power of an OLAP system is the extensive multidimensional application of such a simply stated rule, which could be specified by the OLAP application builder or created by the enduser in an interactive session. The true analytical power of an OLAP server, however, is evidenced in its ability to evaluate formulae where there are members from more than one dimension. An example is a multidimensional allocation rule used in business unit profitability applications; for example, a company has a Business Unit dimension and one of the business units (XYZ) is funding a special advertising campaign for Product A, and the other business units which also sell Product A are willing to share the advertising costs in proportion to their sales of the product.

Fourth-Generation Language   Language or technology designed to allow the end-user unfettered access to data.

Frequency   The timing characteristics of the data.

Frequently Asked Questions (FAQs)   An acronym that refers to a text file on the Internet that contains answers to frequently asked questions. FAQs are a valuable resource for gaining knowledge on particular subjects of interest. FAQs are compiled by subject matter.

ftp   *File Transfer Protocol* is the most common way to transfer files from one computer to another over the Internet.

Functional Data Warehouse   A warehouse that draws data from nearby operational systems. Each functional warehouse serves a distinct and separate group, functional area, a geographic unit, or a product marketing group.

Functional Decomposition   The division of operations into hierarchical functions (activities) that form the basis for the procedure being executed.

Functional Group   A group of one or more messages or transaction sets bounded by a functional group header segment and a functional group trailer segment. It is a collection of electronic document information for the same business application.

Gateway   A software product that allows SQL-based applications to access relational and non-relational data source.

Geographical Information System (GIS)   A user interface where information is displayed at locations on a digital map. Typically, this involves several possible overlays with different types of information. Functions, such as image processing and planning (such as shortest path), can be invoked.

GIF   GIF (pronounced jiff) stands for *Graphics Interchange Format*. A file compression format used for transferring graphics files over the Internet.

Gigabit   A measure of network performance—one gigabit/sec is a bandwidth of bits per second.

Global Shared Memory   A term frequently used by MPPs to describe the collection of memories from each cell or node in the system. The system has the appearance of one shared memory by using a software layer to fetch data from remote memories on other nodes.

Gopher   A menu-based system for searching Internet resources, the items are arranged hierarchically and each item represents either a file or directory.

gql   *Graphical Query Language* is a graphical query tool used to access information stored in a SQL database. As a user, you may query the data, download data into your own environment, and generate reports.

Granularity The level of detail contained in a unit of data. The more detail there is, the lower the level of granularity. The less detail there is, the higher the level of granularity.

Hash Data allocated in an algorithmically randomized fashion in an attempt to evenly distribute data and smooth access patterns.

Heuristic The mode of analysis in which the next step is determined by the results of the current step of analysis. Used for *decision-support* processing.

Home Page The "page" you specify to be displayed when you start up the WWW interface. Think of it as your home base, or the place you go back to when you get lost! You may create your own home page and store it on your local drive.

Hot List A list of the most frequently accessed World Wide Web pages, also known as "documents." A hot list may also be called "bookmarks."

HTML HTML, or *Hyper Text Markup Language*, a subset of SGML, provides a tag set used to create an HTML document. The tags or elements tell the browser how to display the information. The tags are used to "mark," in a hierarchical format, the different components of the document. If you are going to create your own WWW pages, you will need to gain an understanding of the workings of HTML. A good starting point can be found here.

http The *Hyper Text Transport Protocol* is a fixed set of commands used during a hypertext link between a client and server.

Hyperlink A hyperlink is a logical link between two related pieces of information in the same document or between different documents. It will allow you to quickly jump from one document or location to another transparently. This is the "cool" part of HTML.

Hypertext A hypertext document is a combination of text, links to other documents, sound, graphic images, and film clips.

Hypertext Markup Language (HTML) A syntax for describing documents to be displayed on the World Wide Web.

Hypertext Transport Protocol (http) The protocol used in the communication between Web servers and clients.

Hierarchical Relationships Any dimension's members may be organized based on parent-child relationships, typically where a parent member represents the consolidation of the members which are its children. The result is a hierarchy, and the parent/child relationships are hierarchical relationships.

Hypercube *See: Array, Multidimensional.*

HTML HyperText Markup Language, an SGML document type definition used as an authoring language for the World Wide Web.

Image Copy A procedure in which a database is physically copied to another medium for the purposes of backup.

Increment Data warehouse implementation can be broken down into segments or increments. An increment is a defined data warehouse implementation project that has a specified beginning and end. An increment may also be referred to as a departmental data warehouse within the context of an enterprise.

Index   The portion of the storage structure maintained to provide efficient access to a record when its index key item is known. An index is a link between one table and another. It allows for rapid access to the rows of a table based on the values of one or more columns in another table.

Information   The data that human beings assimilate and evaluate to solve a problem or make a decision. The data that has been processed in such a way that it can increase the knowledge of the person who receives it.

Information Systems Architecture (ISA)   The authoritative definition of the business rules, systems structure, technical framework, and product backbone for business information systems. IS architecture has four layers: business, systems, technical, and product architecture layers.

Information Warehouse   IBM's approach to data warehousing that supports the implementation of either functional, central, or decentralized data warehouses.

Input Members   Input members have values that are loaded directly from either manual entry or by accessing another computer-based data source, as opposed to being calculated from the raw data.

Integrity   The property of a database that ensures that the data contained in the database is as accurate and consistent as possible.

Intelligent Agent   A software object that searches a database on a set schedule, looking for predefined patterns in the values of measures. When patterns that meet these criteria are found, they are automatically brought to the attention of the enduser. For example, an intelligent agent might search a hypercube each time it is updated with new values, looking for cities where sales have dropped by more than 10% from the prior period to the current period and present this information to the sales manager when he logs on to the system.

Integrated Service Data Network (ISDN)   A digital multimedia service standard with a performance of typically 128 kilobits/sec, but with possibility of higher performance. ISDN can be implemented using existing telephone (POTS) wiring but does not have the necessary performance of 1–20 megabits/second needed for full screen TV display at either VHS or High Definition TV (HDTV) resolution. Digital video can be usefully sent with ISDN by using quarter screen resolution and/or lower (than 30 per second) frame rate.

Interactive   A mode of processing that combines some of the characteristics of on-line transaction processing and batch processing. The enduser interacts with data over which the user has exclusive control.

Internet   A world-wide network of networks with millions of users, and growing at the rate of 50% per year. Most value-added networks are connected to the Internet. *See also: World Wide Web.* The Internet is a network of networks linked together through low-level protocols. Every device on the network is assigned an IP address which is used for communicating from device to device.

Internet Protocol (IP)   The network-layer communication protocol used in the DARPA Internet. IP is responsible for host-to-host addressing and routing, packet forwarding, and packet fragmentation and reassembly.

Inverted File Indexes   A more efficient method to access data in an ad hoc or analysis environment. It maintains indexes to all values contained in an indexed field.

ISO   International Organization for Standardization.

Iterative Analysis   The mode of processing in which the next step of processing depends on results obtained by the current step in execution.

ITU–TSS   The United Nations standards organization that recommends worldwide communications standards. Its official name is the International Telecommunications Union–Telecommunications Standardization Sector. Formerly know as CCITT.

Java   A distributed computing language (Web Technology) developed by Sun, which is based on C++ but supports applets.

JIT   Just In Time (inventory).

Journal File   A file that contains update activity for rollback and data recovery purposes. Examples of update activity are commit checkpoints, as well as "before" and "after" operational database images. A journal file may be used to construct snapshot information for the data warehouse.

LAN, MAN, WAN   Local, Metropolitan, and Wide Area Networks can be made from any or many of the different physical network media and run the different protocols. LANs are typically confined to departments (less than a kilometer), MANs to distances of order 10 kilometers, and WANs can extend world-wide.

Latency   The length of time required to retrieve data, starting when the initial request is made and ending when the request is satisfied. It is usually much more difficult and expensive to decrease the latency than it is to increase the bandwidth. The time taken to service a request or deliver a message which is independent of the size or nature of the operation. The latency of a message passing system is the minimum time to deliver a message, even one of zero length that does not have to leave the source processor. The latency of a file system is the time required to decode and execute a null operation.

Local Area Network   LANs are usually restricted to a building. *See also: Router and WAN.*

Local Area Network (LAN)   A grouping of devices, such as PCs, fax machines, and printers, physically connected together by Ethernet wiring, within a fairly limited location.

Loose and Tight Coupling   Here, coupling refers to linking of computers in a network. Tight refers to low latency, high bandwidth; loose to high latency and/or low bandwidths. There is no clear dividing line between loose and tight.

Key, Primary   A unique attribute to identify a class of records in a database.

Key, Secondary   A non-unique attribute to identify a class of records in a database.

Local Directory   A data dictionary propagated from the repository to the desktop containing metadata used for developing desktop applications and for generating transactions. A local directory is also used to bind definitions of local data structures used by desktop applications to the data requested from servers.

Location Transparency   A mechanism that keeps the specific physical address of an object from a user. The physical location is resolved within the system so that operations can be performed without knowledge of the actual physical location.

Log   A journal of activity.

Logging   The automatic recording of data with regard to the access of the data, the updates of the data, and so on.

Logical Data Model   Actual implementation of a conceptual module in a database. It may take multiple logical data models to implement one conceptual data model.

MDD or MDDB   Multidimensional Database Server. An OLAP server that physically stores its data in multidimensional array format. *Synonym*: OLAP Server. *See: RDBMS-Based OLAP Server.*

MDQ   Multidimensional Query tool.

Metadata   Literally, metadata is data about data. Metadata is the description of the structure, content, keys, indexes, and so forth, of data. Metadata includes things like the name, length, valid values, and description of a data element. Metadata is stored in a data dictionary and repository. It insulates the data warehouse from changes in the schema of operational systems.

Mid-Tier Data Warehouse   To be scalable, any particular implementation of the data access environment may incorporate several intermediate distribution tiers in the data warehouse network. These intermediate tiers act as source data warehouses for geographically isolated sharable data that is needed across several business functions.

Migration   The process by which frequently used items of data are moved to more readily accessible areas of storage and infrequently used items of data are moved to less accessible areas of storage.

MIME   Multipurpose Internet Mail Extensions.

Mini Marts   A small subset of a data warehouse used by a small number of users. A mini mart is a very focused slice of a larger data warehouse.

MPP   Massively Parallel Processing. The "shared-nothing" approach to parallel computing.

Massively Parallel Processing (MPP)   The strict definition of MPP is a machine with many interconnected processors, where "many" is dependent on the state of the art. Currently, the majority of high-end machines have fewer than 256 processors. A more practical definition of an MPP is a machine whose architecture is capable of having many processors—that is, it is scalable. In particular, machines with a distributed-memory design (in comparison with shared-memory designs) are usually synonymous with MPPs since they are not limited to a certain number of processors. In this sense, ``many'' is a number larger than the current largest number of processors in a shared-memory machine.

Megabit   A measure of network performance—1 megabit/sec is a bandwidth of bits per second. Note 8 bits represent one character—called a byte.

Message Passing   A style of interprocess communication in which processes send discrete messages to one another. Some computer architectures are called message passing architectures because they support this model in hardware, although message passing has often been used to construct operating systems and network software for sequential processors, shared-memory, and distributed computers.

Methodology   The steps followed to guarantee repeatability of success. A good methodology is built on top of real-world experience.

Middleware   Hardware and software used to connect clients and servers, to move and structure data, and/or to presummarize data for use by queries and reports.

Missing Data, Missing Value   A special data item which indicates that the data in this cell does not exist. This may be because the member combination is not meaningful (e.g., snowmobiles may not be sold in Miami) or has never been entered. Missing data is similar to a null value or N/A, but is not the same as a zero value.

Multidimensional Database (MDD)   A DBMS optimized to support multidimensional data. The best systems support standard RDBMS functionality and add high-bandwith support for multidimensional data and queries. Users that need a lot of slices and dices might appreciate a multidimensional database.

Multimedia Server or Client   Multimedia refers to information (digital data) with different modalities, including text, images, video, and computer-generated simulation. Servers dispense this data, and clients receive it. Some form of browsing, or searching, establishes which data is to be transferred.

Multiple-Instruction/Multiple-Data (MIMD)   A parallel computer architecture where the nodes have separate instruction streams that can address separate memory locations on each clock cycle. All HPDC systems of interest are MIMD when viewed as a metacomputer, although the nodes of this metacomputer could have SIMD architectures.

Multipurpose Internet Mail Extension (MIME)   The format used in sending multimedia messages between Web clients and servers that is borrowed from that defined for electronic mail.

Multicube   A logical hypercube physically composed of several smaller cubes, usually one per measure.

Multidimensional Database (MDBMS, MDBS)   A powerful database that allows users to analyze large amounts of data. An MDBS captures and presents data as arrays that can be arranged in multiple dimensions.

Multidimensional Data Structure   *See: Array, Multidimensional.*

Multidimensional Query Language   A computer language that allows one to specify which data to retrieve out of a cube. The user process for this type of query is usually called slicing and dicing. The result of a multidimensional query is either a cell, a two-dimensional slice, or a multidimensional subcube.

Multiple Simultaneous Hierarchies   The ability of a child to have hierarchical relationships with more than one parent. For example, a child, cola in 12-oz. cans, with two parents: canned drinks and cola drinks. The same detailed data is rolled up through two or more hierarchical aggregation paths. *See: Hierarchical Relationships, Parent, Children.*

Navigation   Navigation is a term used to describe the processes employed by users to explore a cube interactively by drilling, rotating, and screening, usually using a graphical OLAP client connected to an OLAP server.

Nesting (of Multidimensional Columns and Rows)   Nesting is a display technique used to show the results of a multidimensional query that returns a subcube, that is, more than a two-dimensional slice or page. The column/row labels will display the extra dimensionality of the output by nesting the labels describing the members of each dimension.

Network   A physical communication medium. A network may consist of one or more buses, a switch, or the links joining processors in a multicomputer.

Newsgroup   A listing of bulletin boards that you may access. Known for exchanging of ideas through "mailnotes." Newsgroups are designed by subject or interest.

Non-Missing Data   Data which exists and has values, as opposed to null or missing data.

Normalization   The process of reducing a complex data structure into its simplest, most stable structure.

Node   A parallel or distributed system is made of a bunch of nodes or fundamental computing units—typically fully fledged computers in the MIMD architecture.

N(UMA)   UMA—Uniform Memory Access—refers to shared memory in which all locations have the same access characteristics, including the same access time. NUMA (Non-Uniform Memory Access) refers to the opposite scenario.

Null   A null value is a trigger to let you know the value for that row is either missing, unknown, not yet known, or is inapplicable. Placing a zero in the row would not reflect the accurate state of the row, because zero is a value. This way you can search for "missing" data and SQL supports the notion of null values.

Object   A person, thing, place, or concept that has characteristics of interest to an environment. An object is an entity that combines descriptions of data and behavior.

Object Description   All the properties and associations that describe a particular object.

Object-Oriented Analysis (OOA)   A process of abstracting a problem by identifying the kinds of entities in the problem domain, the is-a relationships between the kinds (kinds are known as classes, is-a relationships as subtype/supertype, subclass/superclass, or less commonly, specialization/generalization), and the has-a relationships between the classes. Also identified for each class are its attributes (e.g., class Person has attribute Hair Color) and its conventional relationships to other classes (e.g., class Order has a relationship Customer to class Customer).

Object-Oriented Design (OOD)   A design methodology that uses object-oriented analysis to promote object reusability and interface clarity.

ODBC   A standard for database access. *O*pen *DataB*ase *C*onnectivity is an interface protocol used to access data in a relational database environment. ODBC allows users to access data from several servers using just one application, because ODBC is vendor neutral. ODBC includes the DB-LIB protocol portion of the interface between the client and the server. ODBC is Microsoft's interface layer to various databases. When comparing ODBC with Open Client, ODBC would effectively replace the DB-Lib portion of Sybases' Open Client.

OLAP: On-Line Analytical Processing   On-Line Analytical Processing (OLAP) is a category of software technology that enables analysts, managers, and executives to gain insight into data through fast, consistent, interactive access to a wide variety of possible views of information that has been transformed from raw data to reflect the real dimensionality of the enterprise as understood by the user.

OLAP functionality is characterized by dynamic multidimensional analysis of consolidated enterprise data supporting enduser analytical and navigational activities that include calculations and modeling applied across dimensions, through hierarchies and/or across members trend analysis over sequential time periods slicing subsets for on-screen viewing, drill-down to deeper levels of consolidation, reach-through to underlying detail data rotation to new dimensional comparisons in the viewing area

OLAP is implemented in a multi-user client/server mode and offers consistently rapid response to queries, regardless of database size and complexity. OLAP helps the user synthesize enterprise information through comparative, personalized viewing, as well as through analysis of historical and projected data in various "what-if" data model scenarios. This is achieved through use of an OLAP server.

OLAP Client   Enduser applications that can request slices from OLAP servers and provide two-dimensional or multidimensional displays, user modifications, selections, ranking, calculations, and so forth, for visualization and navigation purposes. OLAP clients may be as simple as a spreadsheet program retrieving a slice for further work by a spreadsheet-literate user or as high-functioned as a financial modeling or sales analysis application.

OLAP Server   An OLAP server is a high-capacity, multi-user data manipulation engine specifically designed to support and operate on multidimensional data structures. A multidimensional structure is arranged so that every data item is located and accessed based on the intersection of the dimension members which define that item.

The design of the server and the structure of the data are optimized for rapid ad hoc information retrieval in any orientation, as well as for fast, flexible calculation and transformation of raw data based on formulaic relationships.

The OLAP server may either physically stage the processed multidimensional information to deliver consistent and rapid response times to endusers, or it may populate its data structures in real time from relational or other databases, or offer a choice of both. Given the current state of technology and the enduser requirement for consistent and rapid response times, staging the multidimensional data in the OLAP Server is often the preferred method.

OLTP On-Line Transaction Processing. OLTP describes the requirements for a system that is used in an operational environment. A type of computing in which the emphasis is on processing transactions as they are received by the application. On-line transaction processing updates master files as soon as transactions are entered at terminals or received as messages over communications lines unlike batch processing which stores transactions and updates the necessary files at a later date.

On-Line Storage Storage devices and storage medium where data can be accessed in a direct fashion.

Open Client Open Client is the connectivity software from Sybase for establishing a connection between various client applications and Sybases' SQL Server "server software." On Intel platforms, Sybase has split Open Client into the combination of Net-Lib and DB-Lib. The Net-Lib portion establishes the connection and the DB-Lib portion is specific to the interface (e.g., character verses graphics).

Operational Data Data used to support the daily company operations.

Operational Database The database of record, consisting of system-specific reference data and event data belonging to a transaction update system. It may also contain system control data such as flags, counters, and indicators. The operational database is the source of data warehouse data. It contains detailed data used to run the day-to-day business operations. The data constantly changes as updates are made and reflects the current value of the last transaction.

Operational Data Store (ODS) An ODS is an integrated database of operational data. Its sources include legacy systems and it contains current or near-term data. An ODS may contain 30 to 60 days of information, while a data warehouse typically contains years of data.

OS Operating System.

Overflow The condition in which a record or a segment cannot be stored in its home address because the address is already occupied. In this situation, the data is stored at another location and is referred to as "overflow."

Owner The object owner is a user or users who have authority over that object, where object is a table, view, or attribute.

Page A basic unit of data on DASD or memory.

Page Dimension   A page dimension is generally used to describe a dimension which is not one of the two dimensions of the page being displayed, but for which a member has been selected to define the specific page requested for display. All page dimensions must have a specific member chosen in order to define the appropriate page for display.

Page Display   The page display is the current orientation for viewing a multidimensional slice. The horizontal dimension(s) run across the display, defining the column dimension(s). The vertical dimension(s) run down the display, defining the contents of the row dimension(s). The page dimension member selections define which page is currently displayed. A page is much like a spreadsheet and may in fact have been delivered to a spreadsheet product where each cell can be further modified by the user.

Parallel Computer   A computer in which several functional units are executing independently. The architecture can vary from SMP to MPP and the nodes (functional units) are tightly coupled.

Parallelism   The ability to perform functions in parallel.

Parameter   An elementary data value used as a criterion for qualification, usually of data searches.

Parent   The member that is one level up in a hierarchy from another member. The parent value is usually a consolidation of all of its children's values. *See: Children.*

Partition   A segmentation technique in which data is divided into physically different units. Partitioning can be done at the application or the system level.

Partitioning   The division of a single, ideal, logical hypercube into several smaller logical cubes in order to address the problem of combinatorial explosion.

PCI   Peripheral Component Interconnect. A standardized bus offering a peak bandwidth of 111 Mb/sec. It is the I/O bus standard used within quads.

Performance   Data, summaries, and analyses need to be delivered in a timely fashion. Performance is often a key issue with data warehouses: The right answer isn't worth much if it shows up after the decisions have been made.

Precalculated/Preconsolidated Data   Precalculated data is data in output member cells that is computed prior to, and in anticipation of, ad hoc requests. Precalculation usually results in faster response to queries at the expense of storage. Data that is not precalculated must be calculated at query time.

Primary Key   A column or combination of columns whose values uniquely identify a row or record in the table. The primary key(s) will have a unique value for each record or row in the table.

Product Architecture   An information architecture that describes standards to be followed in each portion of the technical architecture and vendor-specific tools and services to apply in developing and running applications.

Propagated Data   Data that is transferred from a data source to one or more target environments according to propagation rules. Data propagation is usually based on transaction logic.

Protocol   A set of conventions that govern the communications between process-es. Protocol specifies the format and content of messages to be exchanged. A formal description of message formats and the rules of two or more devices must follow to exchange data.

Quad   The building block of Sequent's NUMA-Q architecture, consisting of four Pentium Pro processors, two PCI buses with seven PCI slots, memory, and a 500MB/sec system bus.

Query   A complex SELECT statement for *decision support*. A specific atomic re-quest for information from a database.

Query Language   A language that enables an enduser to interact directly with a DBMS to retrieve and possibly modify data held under the DBMS.

Query Response Time   The time it takes for the warehouse engine to process a com-plex query across a large volume of data and return the results to the requester.

Query Tools   Software that allows a user to create and direct specific questions to a database. These tools provide the means for pulling the desired information from a database. They are typically SQL-based tools and allow a user to define data in enduser language.

RAID   Redundant Array of Inexpensive Disks.

Rapid Application Development (RAD)   Part of a methodology that specifies in-cremental development with constant feedback from the customers. The point is to keep projects focused on delivering value and to keep clear and open lines of communication. English is not adequate for specification of computer sys-tems, even small ones. RAD overcomes the limitations of language by mini-mizing the time between concept and implementation.

RDBMS   Relational Database Management System.

Reach Through   Reach through is a means of extending the data accessible to the enduser beyond that which is stored in the OLAP server. A reach through is performed when the OLAP server recognizes that it needs additional data and automatically queries and retrieves the data from a data warehouse or OLTP system.

Recovery   The restoration of the database to an original position or condition, of-ten after major damage to the physical medium.

Redundancy   The storage of multiple copies of identical data. In the case where da-ta can be updated, redundancy poses serious problems. In the case where data is not updated, redundancy is often a valuable and necessary design technique.

Referential Integrity   The facility of a DBMS that defines a reliable relationship be-tween two tables and a means of joining those tables. *Decision-support* queries rely heavily on joining the information from one table to the information from another table to find intersections or matching values.

Relationship   Relationships in a relational database are represented by common data values stored in the two tables. This type of relationship allows you to retrieve related data from the database by manipulating the relationships in a simple, easy way.

Relational On-Line Analytic Processing (ROLAP) OLAP based on conventional relational databases rather than specialized multidimensional databases.

Replication A standard technique in data warehousing. For performance and reliability several independent copies are often created of each data warehouse. Even data marts can require replication on multiple servers to meet performance and reliability standards.

Replicator Any of a class of products that support replication. Often these tools use special load and unload database APIs and have scripting languages that support automation.

Report A repeatable, formatted, nonatomic request for information from a database. Usually a report formats and combines several related queries.

Reporting Strategy A top-down collection of methodology, products, plans, and teams that ensure business people can get information reliably, accurately, and understandably. It includes choosing tools matched to the organization's particular needs and existing infrastructure, capturing the business models used by the business people, finding source data, integrating all the above into a data warehouse and/or data marts as needed.

Replicated Data Data that is copied from a data source to one or more target environments based on replication rules. Replicated data can consist of full tables or rectangular extracts.

Repository Environment The repository environment contains the complete set of a business's metadata. It is globally accessible. The repository environment contains expanded sets of metadata and can also be implemented across multiple hardware platforms and database management systems.

Rollup Queries Queries that summarize data at a level higher than the previous level of detail.

Rotate To change the dimensional orientation of a report or page display. For example, rotating may consist of swapping the rows and columns, or moving one of the row dimensions into the column dimension, or swapping an off-spreadsheet dimension with one of the dimensions in the page display (either to become one of the new rows or columns), and so forth. A specific example of the first case would be taking a report that has Time across (the columns) and Products down (the rows) and rotating it into a report that has Product across and Time down. An example of the second case would be to change a report which has Measures and Products down and Time across into a report with Measures down and Time over Products across. An example of the third case would be taking a report that has Time across and Product down and changing it into a report that has Time across and Geography down.

Router The bridge between two or more LANs or a LAN and a WAN.

RDBMS-Based OLAP Server   An OLAP server that physically stores its data in a set of tables in a relational database. *Synonym:* "Virtual" OLAP Server. *See: MDD or MDDB; Multidimensional Database, Star Schema, Snowflake Schema.*

Scalability   The ability to scale to support larger or smaller volumes of data and more or fewer users. The ability to increase or decrease size or capability in cost-effective increments with minimal impact on the unit cost of business and the procurement of additional services.

Scenario   A dimension used in many hypercubes that contains members that describe different versions of measures. For example, budget, actual, forecast, and so forth.

Schema   The logical and physical definition of data elements, physical characteristics, and their relationships.

Scoping   Restricting the view of database objects to a specified subset. Further operations, such as update or retrieve, will affect only the cells in the specified subset. For example, scoping allows users to retrieve or update only the sales data values for the first quarter in the East region, if that is the only data they wish to receive.

Securability   The ability to provide differing access to individuals according to the classification of data and the user's business function, regardless of the variations.

Security   A process of system screening that denies access to unauthorized users and protects data from unauthorized uses. *See also: Encryption.* In many cases security refers to physical security such as keyboard locks or the placing of computers in secure areas behind locked doors. *See also: System Access Control.*

SELECT   A SQL command that specifies data retrieval operations for rows of data in a relational database.

Selection   A selection is a process whereby a criterion is evaluated against the data or members of a dimension in order to restrict the set of data retrieved. Examples of selections include the top ten salespersons by revenue, data from the East region only, and all products with margins greater than 20 percent.

Semantic Mapping   The mapping of the meaning of a piece of data.

Serial File   A sequential file in which the records are physically adjacent, in sequential order.

Server   A service that provides standard functions for clients in response to standard messages from clients. A computer where the server software resides. Such services as filing, mail, communications, and authentication are a few of the services that are available.

Sequential File   A file in which records are ordered according to the values of one or more key fields. The records can be processed in this sequence starting from the first record in the file, continuing to the last record in the file.

SGML   Standard Generalized Markup Language, ISO Standard 8879 for the representation of data structures and relationships. Often associated with text and publishing. *See also: HTML.*

Shared Memory   Memory that appears to the user to be contained in a single address place that can be accessed by any process or any node (functional unit) of the computer. Shared memory may have UMA or NUMA structure. Distributed computers can have a shared-memory model implemented in either hardware or software—this would always be NUMA. Shared-memory parallel computers can be either NUMA or UMA. Virtual or Distributed Shared Memory is (the illusion of) a shared memory built with physically distributed memory.

Shared Memory Cluster   A cluster in which SMP nodes are interconnected together utilizing very high-bandwidth interconnects (1GB+/sec). Each SMP node has its own "local" memory as well as peer-to-peer access to memory on other nodes. Memory is managed coherently and appears to be uniform to the higher-level RDBMS and application layers. NUMA is sometimes offered as an example of a shared-memory cluster, but there is only one copy of the operating system running across all the quads. *See: Reflective Memory Clusters (RMC) for an example of a Shared Memory Cluster.*

Shared Memory Model   A logical architecture for parallel computing in which multiple processors run a single copy of the operating system. The operating system presents the illusion of a single large physical memory ("single address space") and a single very fast processor to all applications running on top of the operating system. In other words, it shields the application developers from the details of the parallel implementation. Most commercial software is written to this model today. NUMA-Q preserves the shared-memory model, even though it is a distributed-memory implementation.

Single-Instruction/Multiple-Data (SIMD)   A parallel computer architecture in which every node runs in lockstep accessing a single global instruction stream, but with different memory locations addressed by each node.

Slice   A slice is a subset of a multidimensional array corresponding to a single value for one or more members of the dimensions not in the subset. For example, if the member Actuals is selected from the scenario dimension, then the subcube of all the remaining dimensions is the slice that is specified. The data omitted from this slice would be any data associated with the nonselected members of the scenario dimension, for example, Budget, Variance, Forecast, and so forth. From an enduser perspective, the term slice most often refers to a two-dimensional page selected from the cube.

Slice and Dice   The user-initiated process of navigating by calling for page displays interactively, through the specification of slices via rotations and drill-down/up.

SMP   Symmetric Multiprocessing. A hardware architecture in which each of several processors have shared and equal access to all resources—the bus, memory, I/O, the network. SMP is the most commercial parallel computing today.

SMTP   Simple Mail Transfer Protocol.

Snapshot   A database dump or the archival of data out of a database as of some moment in time.

Snowflake Schema   A layering of star schema that scales that technique to handle an entire warehouse.

Snowflake Schema Database   A variation of the star schema database in which the dimension tables are normalized. This will improve performance in cases where a star schema dimension table would be so large that unreasonable amounts of disk storage would be required and query performance would be degraded *See: Star Schema Database.*

Solutions Database   The components of a DSS environment where the results of previous decisions are stored.

Source Database   An operational, production database or a centralized warehouse that feeds into a target database.

Sparse   A multidimensional data set is sparse if a relatively high percentage of the possible combinations (intersections) of the members from the data set's dimensions contain missing data. The total possible number of intersections can be computed by multiplying together the number of members in each dimension. Data sets containing one percent, .01 percent, or even smaller percentages of the possible data exist and are quite common.

SQL   Structured Query Language, for accessing relational, ODBC, DRDA, or nonrelational, compliant database systems.

SQL Query Tool   An enduser tool that accepts SQL to be processed against one or more relational databases.

Standard Generalized Markup Language (SGML)   SGML is a metalanguage used for defining document types in a hierarchical form. One important aspect of SGML is that it allows you to code information, in a document type format, and store in a database. The stored file can be treated like any other type of entity that would be found in the database. You may search within an SGML document and easily extract the areas that you need. Traditionally, files would have to be extracted as whole files and you could not dig into the file and search the content. SGML incorporates not only text, but it is also a means of linking images, multimedia, and hypertext into one logical document. SGML is an easy way of exchanging data across dissimilar platforms and software applications. If you wish to learn more about SGML, ISO 8879 is the standard technical document describing in detail precisely what SGML is.

Star Schema   A standard technique for designing the summary tables of a data warehouse. "Fact" tables each join to a larger number of independent "dimension" tables. The tables may be partially denormalized for performance, but most queries will still need to join in one or more of the star tables.

Star Schema Database   A database schema used in some RDBMS-based OLAP servers in which all values of measures are stored in a "fact table" along with simple numeric keys representing the dimension members with which the values are associated. The descriptive member names that are associated with each numeric key in the fact table are stored in denormalized dimension tables, one per dimension of the hypercube. The dimension tables also describe the hierarchical relationships in each dimension. *See: Snowflake Schema Database.*

Static Query   A stored, parametrized procedure, optimized for access to a particular data warehouse.

Storage Hierarchy   Storage units linked to form a storage subsystem, in which some units are fast but small and expensive, and other units are large but slower and less expensive.

Structured Query Language (SQL)   Pronounced "sequel" or SQL. Used with relational databases, it allows users to define the structure and organization of stored data; verify and maintain data integrity; control access to the data; and define relationships among the stored data items. Data retrieval by a user or an application program from the database is also a major function of SQL. The database can be updated (adding, deleting, or modifying data) by a user or an application program. SQL is a fourth-generation language which enables the user to tell the computer what data they want without telling the computer how to get it.

Subject-Oriented Databases   Most companies are building numerous subject-specific warehouses to serve the needs of different divisions, rather than one huge generalized warehouse.

Supercomputer   The most powerful computer that is available at any given time. As performance is roughly proportional to cost, this is not very well defined for a scalable parallel computer. Traditionally, computers costing some $10–$30,000,000 are termed supercomputers.

Symmetric Multiprocessor (SMP)   A symmetric multiprocessor supports a shared memory programming model—typically with a UMA memory system, and a collection of up to 32 nodes connected with a bus.

System Log   An audit trail of relevant system events.

Systems Architecture   One of the four layers of information systems architecture. The systems architecture represents the definitions and interrelationships between applications and the product architecture.

Table   A relation that consists of a set of columns with a heading and a set or rows. This can also be termed as *tuple*.

Tag   A tag is an HTML/SGML element. The element name allows the software to determine the hierarchical position of the data within the HTML document. The element also triggers the software on how to represent the data, whether it is on the screen or printed page.

Target Database   The database in which the data will be loaded or inserted.

TCP/IP   Transmission Control Protocol/Internet Protocol, these protocols are used for transmitting data across the Internet.

Technical Architecture   It defines and describes the interfaces, parameters, and protocols used by the product and systems architectures.

Telnet   Telnet is a protocol that allows you to interact with another device remotely. It allows you to "log in" to a remote device and simulate a direct connect. When you log in to the mainframe and access ISIS, IFIS, PPS, or DSE, you are connecting through Telnet.

TIFF   Tagged Image File Format is a graphic file format used to transfer graphic images across the Internet.

Timestamping   The practice of tagging each record with some moment in time.

Transmission Control Protocol (TCP)   A connection-oriented transport protocol used in the DARPA Internet. TCP provides for the reliable transfer of data, as well as the out-of-band indication of urgent data.

Transaction Set   (USA) The transaction set unambiguously defines, in the standard syntax, information of business or strategic significance. It consists of a transaction set header segment, one or more data segments in a specified order, and a transaction set trailer segment.

Triggering Data   Data that selects and loads data on a scheduled basis.

Tuple   *See: Cell, Table.*

Update   To change, add, delete, or replace values in all or selected entries, groups, or attributes stored in a database.

User   A person or a process issuing commands and messages to the information system.

Web Clients and Servers   A distributed set of clients (requesters and receivers of services) and servers (receiving and satisfying requests from clients) using Web technologies.

WINS   Warehouse Information Network Standard.

World Wide Web (WWW)   A graphical user interface layer that sits on top of Internet. See also HTML. A hypermedia application used for access of data over the Internet. The WWW is based on the HTML standard of marking up *documents.*

World Wide Web and Web Technologies   A very important software model for accessing information on the Internet based on hyperlinks supported by Web technologies, such as HTTP, HTML, MIME, Java, applets, and VRML.

X.25   A synchronous communications protocol defined by the ITU–TSS to establish a virtual connection between two parties (as though it were a dedicated line). This protocol is often referred to as packet switching, after its method of encapsulating portions of the message in small packets for transmission. The protocol was originally defined for data transmission but is now widely employed for voice, video, facsimile, and other applications.

X.75   A communications protocol defined by the ITU–TSS for interconnecting two X.25 networks.

X.400   A communications standard defined by the ISO organization (ITU–TSS) for a store-and-forward messaging system.

BIBLIOGRAPHY

1. Aberdeen Group Research Note. "Data Warehouse Query Tools: Evolving to Relational OLAP." Vol. 8, No. 8, July 7, 1995.
2. Acly, Ed. "Applying Little Client/Server to the Enterprise: Are Customers Being Stonewalled?" Application Development and Reengineering. IDC/Technology Investment Strategies. Framingham, MA, IDC#7096, April 19, 1994.
3. Acly, Ed. "Force-Fitting Little Client/Server: Two Case Studies." Application Development and Reengineering. IDC/Technology Investment Strategies, Framingham, MA. IDC#7111, May 23, 1994.
4. Almasi, G. S., and A. Gottlieb. *Highly Parallel Computing.* Benjamin/Cummings, Redwood City, CA, 1994.
5. Andrews, G. R. *Concurrent Programming: Principles and Practice.* Benjamin/Cummings, Redwood City, CA, 1991.
6. Angus, I. G., G. C. Fox, J. S. Kim, and D. W. Walker. *Solving Problems on Concurrent Processors: Software for Concurrent Processors*, Vol. 2. Prentice Hall, Englewood Cliffs, NJ, 1990.
7. Arbib, J., and J. A. Robinson, eds. *Natural and Artificial Parallel Computation*, chap. 4, pp. 47–90. MIT Press, Cambridge, MA, 1990.
8. Baker, Richard H. *Network Security*. McGraw-Hill, 1995.
9. Barquin, R., and Herb Edelstein. *Planning and Designing the Data Warehouse.* Prentice Hall, Upper Saddle River, NJ, 1996.
10. Benjamin, R., and Herb Edelstein. *Planning and Designing the Data Warehouse.* Prentice Hall, Upper Saddle River, NJ, 1996.
11. Blechar, M. "A Snapshot of the Work-Group-CASE Market." Applications Development & Management Strategies. Gartner Group, Inc., Stamford, CT, Strategic Planning. SPA-260-1044, July 25, 1994.
12. Block, Peter. "Flawless Consulting." Pfeiffer & Company, 1981.
13. Bloom, Paul. "The Soft Underbelly of Powersoft and Gupta Technologies, Part II." Growth Stock Review. Volpe, Welty & Company, San Francisco, CA, September 1994.
14. Bontempo, Charles J., and Cynthia Saracco. *Database Management: Principles and Products.* Prentice Hall, Upper Saddle River, NJ, 1996.
15. Booch, Grady. *Object-Oriented Analysis and Design with Applications.* Benjamin Cummings, Addison-Wesley, Menlo Park, CA, 1994.
16. Brackett, Michael H. *The Data Warehouse Challenge.* John Wiley & Sons, New York, 1996.
17. Brodie, Michael L., and Michael Stonebreaker. *Migrating Legacy Systems: Gateways, Interfaces, and the Incremental Approach.* Morgan Kaufmann, San Francisco, CA, 1995.
18. Brooks, Frederick J. *The Mythical Man-Month: Essays on Software Engineering.* Addison-Wesley Publishing, Reading, MA, 1982.
19. Brown, A.J. "Managing Large Databases With Data Warehousing." Red Brick Systems Sunnyvale, CA, 1996.
20. Cameron, Bobby, and Stuart D. Woodring. "OLTP Meets Client/Server." *The Software Strategy Report.* Cambridge, MA, Forrester Research. Vol. 5, No. 5, August 1994.

21. Cameron, Bobby, and Stuart D. Woodring. "Choosing Client/Server Core Apps." *The Software Strategy Report*. Forrester Research, Cambridge, MA, Vol. 5, No. 9, December 1994.
22. Caudhill, Maureen, and Charles Butler. *Naturally Intelligent Systems*. MIT Press, Cambridge, MA, 1990.
23. Celko, Joe. *Instant SQL Programming*. WROX Publishing, 1995.
24. Chatman, Steve, and Robert Mullen. "Analytical Processing as Executive Decision Support at the University of Missouri System," University of Missouri, Columbia, MO, December 1992.
25. Chawathe, S. S., A. Rajaraman, H. Garcia-Molina, and J. Widom. "Change Detection in Hierarchically Structured Information." *Proceedings of the ACM SIGMOD Conference,* Montreal, Canada, June 1996.
26. Codd, E.F., "Providing OLAP (On-line Analytical Processing) to User-Analysts: An IT Mandate." E.F. Codd and Associates, San Francisco, CA, 1993.
27. Demarco, Tom. *Peopleware: Productive Projects and Teams*. Dorset House Publishing. London, UK, 1987.
28. DePalma, Donald A., and Stuart D. Woodring. "Development On Hold?" *The Software Strategy Report*. Forrester Research, Cambridge, MA, Vol. 5, No. 4, July 1994.
29. Derfler, Frank J. *PC Magazine Guide to Connectivity*. Ziff-Davis Press, Emeryville, CA, 1995.
30. Derfler, Frank J. *PC Magazine Guide to Linking LANs*. Ziff-Davis Press, Emeryville, CA, 1992.
31. Edelstein, Herb, and Janet Millenson. "How To Succeed With End-User Data Access." Euclid Associates, Indianapolis, IN, 1994.
32. Fayyad, Usama M., Gregory Piatetsky-Shapiro, Padhraic Smyth, and Ramasamy Uthurusamy. *Advances in Knowledge Discovery and Data Mining*. MIT Press, Cambridge, MA, 1995.
33. Ferrara, R., and P. A. Naecker. "The Data Warehouse: A Giant Step Forward." *DEC Professional*, 1993, Vol. 12, No. 11, pp. 26–39.
34. Fidel, Raya. *Database Design for Information Retrieval*. John Wiley & Sons, New York, 1987.
35. Finkelstein, Richard. "MDD: Database Reaches the Next Dimension." *Database Programming and Design*, April 1995.
36. Finkelstein, Richard. "Understanding the Need for On-Line Analytical Servers." Performance Computing Inc., Redwood City, CA, 1994.
37. Foster, I. *Designing and Building Parallel Programs*. Addison-Wesley, Reading, MA, 1995.
38. Fox, G. C., M. A. Johnson, G. A. Lyzenga, S. W. Otto, J. K. Salmon, and D.W. Walker. *Solving Problems on Concurrent Processors,* Vol. 1. Prentice Hall, Englewood Cliffs, NJ, 1988.
39. Fox, G. C. "Parallel Computing." Technical Report C3P-830. California Institute of Technology, Pasadena, CA, September 1989.
40. Fox, G. C. "Applications of Parallel Supercomputers: Scientific Results and Computer Science Lessons." In M. A. Arbib and J. A. Robinson, eds. *Natural and Artificial Parallel Computation*, chap. 4, pp. 47–90. MIT Press, Cambridge, MA, 1990.
41. Fox, G. C. "Parallel Supercomputers." In C. H. Chen, ed. *Computer Engineering Handbook*, chap. 17. McGraw-Hill, New York, 1992a. Caltech Report C3P-451d.
42. Fox, G. C. "The Use of Physics Concepts in Computation." In B. A. Huberman, ed. *Computation: The Micro and the Macro View*, chap. 3, pp. 103–154. World Scientific Publishing Co. Ltd., Pasadena, CA 1992b. SCCS-237, CRPC-TR92198. Caltech Report.
43. Fox, G. C., P. C. Messina, and R. D. Williams, eds. *Parallel Computing Works!* Morgan Kaufmann, San Francisco, CA, 1994.
44. Fox, G. C. "Basic Issues and Current Status of Parallel Computing." Technical Report SCCS-736. Syracuse University, NPAC, Syracuse, NY, November 1995a.

45. Fox, G. C. "Software and Hardware Requirements for Some Applications of Parallel Computing to Industrial Problems." Technical Report SCCS-717. Syracuse University, NPAC, Syracuse, NY, June 1995b.

46. Fox, G. C., and W. Furmanski. "The Use of the National Information Infrastructure and High Performance Computers in Industry." *Proceedings of the Second International Conference on Massively Parallel Processing Using Optical Interconnections*, pp. 298–312. Los Alamitos, CA, October 1995c. IEEE Computer Society Press. Syracuse University Technical Report SCCS-732.

47. Frank, Maurice. "A Drill Down Analysis of Multidimensional Databases." *DBMS Magazine*, July 1994.

48. Fritchman, Bruce. "Mainframe to Client/Server—A Progress Report." Lehigh University, Philadelphia, PA, May 1994.

49. Frost, Renee. "Implementing a Data Administration Function and Strategic Data Planning at the University of Michigan," Ann Arbor, MI, 1993.

50. Ganti, Narsim, and William Grayman. *The Transition of Legacy Systems to a Distributed Archictecture.* John Wiley & Sons, New York, 1992.

51. Gartner Group Research Note. "Major Changes Ahead for OLAP: Buyers Beware." Stanford, CT, SPA-OLAP-1331, November 9, 1994.

52. Geiger, Kyle. "Inside ODBC." Microsoft Press, WA, 1995.

53. Geschickter, Chet. "Shop for the Guts, Not for the Makeup." *Client/Server Tool Watch. U.S.A.* Hurwitz Consulting Group, Inc., Boston, MA, Vol. 3, No. 5, July 1994.

54. Gleason, David. "White Paper: Data Warehousing." Platinum Technology, Sunnyvale, CA, 1995.

55. Groff, James, and Paul Weinberg. *LAN Times Guide to SQL.* McGraw-Hill, New York, 1994.

56. Gupta, H. "Selection of Views to Materialize in a Data Warehouse." *Proceedings of the International Conference on Database Theory.* Athens, Greece, January 1997.

57. Gupta, H., V. Harinarayan, A. Rajaraman, and J. Ullman. "Index Selection for OLAP." Technical Note, 1996.

58. Hadden, Cynthia, and Barbara Evans. "The Electronic Factbook: The Foundation for a University-Wide Decision Support System." MIT Press, Cambridge, MA, December 1992.

59. Hammer, J., H. Garcia-Molina, J. Widom, W. Labio, and Y. Zhuge. "The Stanford Data Warehousing Project." *IEEE Data Engineering Bulletin*, June 1995.

60. Harinarayan, V., A. Rajaraman, and J. Ullman. "Implementing Data Cubes Efficiently." *Proceedings of ACM Sigmod Conference*, Montreal, Canada, June 1996.

61. Hariri, S. *High Performance Distributed Computing: Network, Architecture and Programming.* Prentice Hall, Upper Saddle River, NJ, 1996.

62. Hariri, S., and B. Lu. *ATM-based High Performance Distributed Computing,"* Albert Zomaya, ed. McGraw-Hill, New York, 1995.

63. Hendrick, Stephen D., and Anthony C. Picardi. "Scalable Client/Server Computing." Application Development Tools. IDC/Technology Investment Strategies, Framingham, MA, IDC#8528, February 1994.

64. Hendrick, Stephen D., and Anthony C. Picardi. "Departmental Client/Server Computing." Application Development Tools. IDC/Technology Investment Strategies, Framingham, MA, IDC#8617, June 1994.

65. Hillis, W. D. *The Connection Machine.* MIT Press, Cambridge, MA, 1985.

66. Hockney, R. W., and C. R. Jesshope. *Parallel Computers.* Adam Hilger, Ltd., Bristol, UK, 1981.

67. Hoover, Ronald. "Data Administration at Penn State: Problems and Solutions." Penn State University, College, PA, 1990.

68. Hurwitz, Judith. "Beyond a Pretty Face." *Computerworld Client/Server Journal.* November 1994.

69. Huyn, N. "Efficient View Self-Maintenance." *Proceedings of the ACM Workshop on Materialized Views: Techniques and Applications.* Montreal, Canada, June 7, 1996.

70. IBM. "Information Warehouse Architecture I." Document SC26-3244. Poughkeepsie, NY, 1995.

71. IBM. "Information Warehouse: An Introduction." Document GC26-4876. Poughkeepsie, NY, 1995.

72. Inmon, W.H. *Building the Data Warehouse*, John Wiley & Sons, New York, 1992.

73. Inmon, W.H. *Building the Data Warehouse*. QED Publishing Group, Boston, 1992.

74. Inmon, W. H. *Building the Data Warehouse*. John Wiley & Sons, New York 1993.

75. Inmon, W.H. "Guidelines for Selecting Data Warehouse Management Software." Prism Solutions, Inc., 1994.

76. Inmon, W. H., and C. Kelley. *Developing the Data Warehouse*. QED Publishing Group, Boston, 1993.

77. Inmon, W. H., J. D. Welch, and K. L. Gassey. *Managing the Data Warehouse*. John Wiley & Sons, New York, 1997.

78. Inmon, W. H., C. Imhoff, and G. Battas. *Building the Operational Data Store*. John Wiley & Sons, New York 1995.

79. Inmon, W.H., and Richard D. Hackathorn. *Using the Data Warehouse*. John Wiley & Sons, New York, 1994.

80. Inmon, W.H., and Richard Hackathorn. *Using the Data Warehouse*. John Wiley & Sons, New York, 1994.

81. Inmon, W.H., Claudia Imhoff, and Greg Battas. *Building the Operational Data Store*. John Wiley & Sons, New York, 1996.

82. Inmon, W.H., and Chuck Kelley. *Rdb/VMS: Developing the Data Warehouse*. QED Publishing Group, Boston, 1993.

83. Inmon, W.H., and Sur Osterfelt. *Data Pattern Processing*. QED Publishing Group, Boston, 1996.

84. Labio J., and H. Garcia-Molina. "Efficient Snapshot Differential Algorithms for Data Warehousing." To.

85. Kelly, Debra. "Ad-Hoc Query and Reporting Tools for Relational Database Management Systems: Evaluation and Recommendation, University of California, Berkeley." *Advanced Technology Planning, Information Systems and Technology*, July 30, 1994.

86. Kelly, Sean. *Data Warehousing: The Route to Mass Customization*. John Wiley & Sons, New York, 1994.

87. Ken Orr Institute. "Data Warehouses and Client/Server," Santa Clara, CA, 1995.

88. Kimball, Ralph, and Kevin Strehlo. "Why Decision Support Fails and How to Fix It." *Datamation*, June 1994a.

89. Kimball, Ralph, and Kevin Strehlo. "What's Wrong with SQL." *Datamation*, June 1994b.

90. Kimball, Ralph. *Data Warehouse Toolkit*. John Wiley & Sons, New York, 1996.

91. Koch, George. *Oracle: The Complete Reference*. McGraw-Hill, New York, 1995.

92. Koulopolous, Thomas M., and Carl Frappolo. *Electronic Document Management Systems*. McGraw-Hill, New York, 1995.

93. Kung, H. T. "Gigabit Local Area Networks: A Systems Perspective." *IEEE Communications Magazine*, April 1992.

94. Labio, W., D. Quass, and B. Adelberg. "Physical Database Design for Data Warehousing." Technical Note, 1996.

95. Mara, Mark. "Implementing Distributed Computing at Cornell University." Ithaca, NY, 1994.

96. Mattison, Rob. *Data Warehousing: Strategies, Technologies, and Techniques*. McGraw-Hill, New York, 1996.

97. McBryan, O. "An Overview of Message Passing Environments." *Parallel Computing*, Vol. 20, No. 4, pp. 417–444, 1994.

98. Morse, H. S. *Practical Parallel Computing*. Academic Press, Cambridge, MA, 1994.

99. Narayan, S., Y. Hwang, N. Kodkani, S. Park, H. Yu, and S. Hariri. "ISDN: An Efficient Network Technology to Deliver Information Services." International Conference on Computer Application in Industry and Engineering, 1995.

100. Nelson, M. E., W. Furmanski, and J. M. Bower. "Brain Maps and Parallel Computers." *Trends Neurosci.*, Vol. 10, pp. 403–408, 1990.

101. Newton, Judith. "Manual For Data Administration." National Institute of Standards and Technology (NIST) Special Publication 500–208, March 1993.

102. O' Neil, Patrick. *Database: Principles, Programming, Performance.* Morgan Kaufmann, San Francisco, CA, 1994.

103. Parsaye, Kamran, and Mark Chignell. *Intelligent Database Tools and Applications.* John Wiley & Sons, New York, 1993.

104. Pascal, Fabian. *Understanding Relational Databases,* John Wiley & Sons, New York, 1993.

105. Patridge, Craig. *Gigabit Networking.* Addison-Wesley, Reading MA, 1994.

106. Perlman, Radia. *Interconnections: Bridges and Routers.* Addison-Wesley, Reading MA, 1992.

107. Pfister, G. F. *In Search of Clusters: The Coming Battle in Lowly Parallel Computing.* Prentice Hall, Upper Saddle River, NJ, 1995.

108. Poe, Vidette. *Building a Data Warehouse for Decision Support.* Prentice Hall, Upper Saddle River, NJ, 1996.

109. *Proceedings of the 21st VLDB Conference,* Zürich, Switzerland, September 1995.

110. Quass, D. " Maintenance Expressions for Views with Aggregation." *Proceedings of the ACM Workshop on Materialized Views: Techniques and Applications,* Montreal, Canada, June 7, 1996.

111. Quass, D., A. Gupta, I. S. Mumick, and J. Widom "Making Views Self-Maintainable for Data Warehousing." *Proceedings of the Conference on Parallel and Distributed Information Systems,* Miami Beach, FL, December 1996.

112. Quass, D., and J. Widom. "On-Line Warehouse View Maintenance." Technical Note, Menlo Park, 1996.

113. Raden, Neil. "Data, Data Everywhere." *Information Week,* October 30, 1995, p. 60.

114. Rodgers, Ulka. *Oracle—A Database Development Guide.* Prentice Hall, Englewood Cliffs, NJ, 1994.

115. Rymer, J. "Business Intelligence: The Third Tier." *Distributed Computing Monitor,* June 1995.

116. Saylor, Michael J., Manish G. Acharya, and Robert G. Trenkamp. "True Relational OLAP: The Future of Decision Support." *Database Journal,* November/December 1995, p. 38.

117. Simon, Alan R. *Strategic Database Technology: Management for the Year 2000.* Morgan Kaufmann, San Francisco, CA, 1995.

118. Singh, Harry. *Heterogeneous Internetworking.* Prentice Hall, Upper Saddle River, NJ, 1996a.

119. Singh, Harry. *UNIX for MVS Programmers.* Prentice Hall, Upper Saddle River, NJ, 1996b.

120. Slade, Carole, William Giles Campbell, and Stepher Vaughn Ballou. *Form and Style: Research Papers, Reports, Theses.* Houghton Mifflin Company, Boston, MA, 1994.

121. Sprague, Ralph H., and Hugh Watson. *Building Effective Decision Support System.* Prentice Hall, Upper Saddle River, NJ, 1996.

122. Sprague, Ralph H., and Hugh Watson. *Decision Support For Management.* Prentice Hall, Upper Saddle River, NJ, 1996.

123. Stevens, Larry. "Polishing Sales with OLAP." *Open Computing,* December 1995, p. 71.

124. Stone, H. S., and J. Cocke. "Computer Architecture in the 1990s." *IEEE Computer,* pp. 30–38, 1991.

125. Strassmann, Paul. "The Business Value of Computers." *Information Economics,* 1990.

126. Tanenbaum, A. S. *Distributed Operating Systems.* Prentice Hall, Englewood Cliffs, NJ, 1995.

127. Taylor, David A. *Object-Oriented Technology: A Manager's Guide.* Addison-Wesley, Reading, MA, 1990.

128. *The Navigator,* The International Data Warehousing Association Newsletter, Spring 1996.

129. "The OLAP Report: Succeeding with On-Line Analytical Processing." *Business Intelligence,* 1995.

130. Trew, A., and G. Wilson. *Past, Present, Parallel: A Survey of Available Parallel Computing Systems.* Springer-Verlag, Berlin, 1991.
131. Turban, Efraim. *Decision Support Systems and Expert Systems.* Prentice Hall, Englewood Cliffs, NJ, 1995.
132. "Universe of News." *The Business Objects Newsletter*, February 1996.
133. Vaskevitch, David. *Client/Server Strategies.* QED Publishing Group, Boston, 1992.
134. Wiener, J. L., H. Gupta, W. J. Labio, Y. Zhuge, H. Garcia-Molina, and J. Widom. "A System Prototype for Warehouse View Maintenance." *Proceedings of the ACM Workshop on Materialized Views: Techniques and Applications*, Montreal, Canada, June 7, 1996, pp. 26–33.
135. Wirfs-Brock, Rebecca, Brian Wilkerson, and Lauren Wiener. *Designing Object-Oriented Software.*" Prentice Hall, Englewood Cliffs, NJ, 1990.
136. Xenakis, John. "Multidimensional Databases." *Application Development Strategies.* Vol. 6, No. 4, April 1994.
137. Zhuge, Y., H. Garcia-Molina, J. Hammer, and J. Widom. "View Maintenance in a Warehousing Environment." *Proceedings of the ACM SIGMOD Conference*, San Jose, California, May 1995.
138. Zhuge, Y., H. Garcia-Molina, and J. L. Wiener. "The Strobe Algorithms for Multi-Source Warehouse Consistency." To appear in the *Proceedings of the Conference on Parallel and Distributed Information Systems*, Miami Beach, FL, December 1996.
139. Butler, Brian, and Thomas Mace. "SQL Query and Reporting Tools: Straight Answers, Limited Risks." *PC Magazine*, Vol. 14, No. 11, June 13, 1995.
140. Zornes, Aaron. "Next Generation Decision Support (Re-Engineering 'Data Jailhouses' into "Data Warehouses)." META Group, Inc., Boston, MA, 1995.

INDEX